# AN AUSTRO-LIBERTARIAN CRITIQUE OF PUBLIC CHOICE

We do not say that the Public Choice School has not made any positive contribution to political economy. It has. The originators of it, James Buchanan and Gordon Tullock, along with their many followers and collaborators, have done important work on rational voter theory, setting up a meeting agenda, game theory, etc. Nor can we object to the application of economic theory to political issues. Far from it. However, the present book seeks to uncover its many failures. For example, the fact that underneath the veneer of its supposed adherence to value-free positive analysis lies a value-laden support for statism. To wit, its emphasis and reliance on "theoretical unanimity" not the actual unanimity incorporated in every commercial act under free enterprise. We also take issue with its nomenclature "rent seeking" albeit not the concept itself. Why pick on innocuous "rent" to describe crony capitalism?

Thomas J. DiLorenzo,
Professor of Economics
*Loyola University Maryland*
Walter E. Block,
Professor of Economics
*Loyola University New Orleans*

# EDITORIAL ADVISORY BOARD

# AN AUSTRO-LIBERTARIAN CRITIQUE OF PUBLIC CHOICE

Thomas J. DiLorenzo,
Professor of Economics
*Loyola University Maryland*
Walter E. Block,
Professor of Economics
*Loyola University New Orleans*

**ADDLETON ACADEMIC PUBLISHERS • NEW YORK**

*An Austro-Libertarian Critique of Public Choice* by Thomas J. DiLorenzo and Walter E. Block is published with the written permission of both Addleton Academic Publishers and the authors.

Mises Institute
518 West Magnolia Ave.
Auburn, Ala. 36832
mises.org

paperback edition: 978-1-61016-680-5

# CONTENTS

Acknowledgements
Introduction [1]

Part 1: What Is Austrian Economics? [3]
Chapter 1
The Subjectivist Roots of James Buchanan's Economics [4]
Chapter 2
Cultural Dynamics [18]

Part 2: The Austrian Critique of Public Choice [44]
Chapter 3
Competition and Political Entrepreneurship: Austrian Insights
into Public-Choice Theory [45]
Chapter 4
Is Voluntary Government Possible? A Critique of Constitutional Economics [57]
Chapter 5
George Stigler and the Myth of Efficient Government [73]

Part 3: The Austrian Response to *The Calculus of Consent* [88]
Chapter 6
The Calculus of Consent Revisited [89]
Chapter 7
Buchanan and Tullock's "The Calculus of Consent" [102]
Chapter 8
Constitutional Economics and the Calculus of Consent [106]

Part 4: Austrians and Public Choicers on Antitrust [122]
Chapter 9
The Truth about Sherman [123]
Chapter 10
The Myth of Natural Monopoly [132]
Chapter 11
Monopolistic Competition and Macroeconomic Theory by Robert Solow [146]
Chapter 12
The Origins of Antitrust: An Interest-Group Perspective [152]
Chapter 13
Total Repeal of Antitrust Legislation: A Critique of Bork, Brozen, and Posner [160]

Part 5: Rent Seeking [188]
Chapter 14
Property Rights, Information Costs, and the Economics of Rent Seeking [189]
Chapter 15
All Government is Excessive: A Rejoinder to
Dwight Lee's "In Defense of Excessive Government" [204]

Chapter 16
Watch Your Language [241]

Part 6: Taxation [245]
Chapter 17
Utility Profits, Fiscal Illusion, and Local Public Expenditures [246]
Chapter 18
The Expenditure Effects of Restricting Competition in Local Public Service Industries:
The Case of Special Districts [256]
Chapter 19
The Justification for Taxation in the Public Finance Literature:
An Unorthodox View [265]

Part 7: Other Topics in Public Choice [282]
Chapter 20
A Constitutionalist Approach to Social Security Reform [283]
Chapter 21
The Futility of Bureaucracy [298]
Chapter 22
Government and Market: A Critique of Professor James Buchanan's
"What Should Economists" Do? [301]
Chapter 23
Economic Competition and Political Competition: An Empirical Note [314]
Chapter 24
An Empirical Assessment of the Factor-Supplier Pressure Group Hypothesis [321]

**Thomas J. DiLorenzo** is Professor of Economics, Sellinger School of Business, Loyola University Maryland. He earned a BA degree at Westminster College and a PhD at Virginia Polytechnic Institute and State University. He is the author of numerous refereed journal articles and his works are widely discussed on radio and television. His other books include: *The Problem with Socialism* (2016); *Hamilton's Curse: How Jefferson's Arch Enemy Betrayed the American Revolution* (2008); *Lincoln Unmasked: What You're Not Supposed to Know About Dishonest Abe* (2006); *How Capitalism Saved America: The Untold History of Our Country from the Pilgrims to the Present* (2004); *The Real Lincoln: A New Look a Abraham Lincoln, His Agenda, and an Unnecessary War* (2003); *From Pathology to Politics: Public Health in America* (2000); *The Food and Drink Police: America's Nannies, Busybodies, and Petty Tyrants* (1998); *CancerScam: The Diversion of Federal Cancer Funds for Politics* (1997).


**Walter E. Block** is Harold E. Wirth Endowed Chair and Professor of Economics, College of Business, Loyola University New Orleans, and senior fellow at the Mises Institute. He earned his PhD in economics at Columbia University in 1972. He has taught at Rutgers, SUNY Stony Brook, Baruch CUNY, Holy Cross and the University of Central Arkansas. He is the author of almost 500 refereed articles in professional journals, two dozen books, and thousands of op eds. He lectures widely on college campuses, delivers seminars around the world and appears regularly on television and radio shows. He is the Schlarbaum Laureate, Mises Institute, 2011; and has won the Loyola University Research Award (2005, 2008) and the Mises Institute's Rothbard Medal of Freedom, 2005; and the Dux Academicus award, Loyola University, 2007.

# Acknowledgements

The authors of this book thank the journals in which these chapters were first published for permission to reprint.

Part 1: What is Austrian Economics?
Chapter 1: DiLorenzo, Thomas J. (1990), "The Subjectivist Roots of James Buchanan's Economics," *Review of Austrian Economics* 4 (Spring): 180–195.
Chapter 2: Block, Walter (1997), "Compromising the Uncompromisable: The Austrian Golden Mean," *Cultural Dynamics* 9(2): 211–238.

Part 2: The Austrian Critique of Public Choice
Chapter 3: DiLorenzo, Thomas J. (1987), "Competition and Political Entrepreneurship: Austrian Insights into Public Choice Theory," *Review of Austrian Economics* 2(Fall): 59–71.
Chapter 4: Block, Walter, and Tom DiLorenzo (2000), "Is Voluntary Government Possible? A Critique of Constitutional Economics," *Journal of Institutional and Theoretical Economics* 156(4): 567–582.
Chapter 5: DiLorenzo, Thomas J. (2002), "George Stigler and the Myth of Efficient Government," *Journal of Libertarian Studies* 16(4): 55–73.

Part 3: The Austrian Response to The Calculus of Consent
Chapter 6: Block, Walter and Thomas J. DiLorenzo (2001), "The Calculus of Consent Revisited," *Public Finance and Management* 1(3): 305–321.
Chapter 7: Rothbard, Murray (1997), "Buchanan and Tullock's 'The Calculus of Consent,'" *The Logic of Action II*. Glos: Edward Elgar, 269–274.
Chapter 8: DiLorenzo, Tom, and Walter Block (2001), "Constitutional Economics and the Calculus of Consent," *The Journal of Libertarian Studies* 15(3): 37–56.

Part 4: Austrians and Public Choicers on Antitrust
Chapter 9: DiLorenzo, Thomas (1991), "The Truth About Sherman," *Austrian Economics Newsletter*. Auburn, AL: The Mises Institute, 1–6.
Chapter 10: DiLorenzo, Thomas J. (1996), "The Myth of Natural Monopoly," *Review of Austrian Economics* 9(2): 43–58.
Chapter 11: DiLorenzo, Thomas J. (1999), "Monopolistic Competition and Macroeconomic Theory by Robert Solow," *Quarterly Journal of Austrian Economics* 2(4): 83–88.
Chapter 12: DiLorenzo, Thomas J. (1985), "The Origins of Antitrust: An Interest-Group Perspective," *International Review of Law and Economics* 5(1): 73–90.
Chapter 13: Block, Walter (1994), "Total Repeal of Anti-trust Legislation: A Critique of Bork, Brozen and Posner," *Review of Austrian Economics* 8(1): 35–70.

Part 5: Rent seeking
Chapter 14: DiLorenzo, Thomas J. (1988), "Property Rights Information Costs, and the Economics of Rent Seeking," *Journal of Institutional and Theoretical Economics* 144(2): 318–332.

Chapter 15: Block, Walter (2002), "All Government is Excessive: A Rejoinder to 'In Defense of Excessive Government' by Dwight Lee," *Journal of Libertarian Studies* 16(3): 35–82.
Chapter 16: Block, Walter (2000), "Watch Your Language," *Mises Daily*, February 21.

Part 6: Taxation
Chapter 17: DiLorenzo, Thomas J. (1982), "Utility Profits, Fiscal Illusion, and Local Public Expenditures," *Public Choice* 38(3): 243–252.
Chapter 18: DiLorenzo, Thomas J. (1981), "The Expenditure Effects of Restricting Competition in Local Public Service Industries: The Case of Special Districts," *Public Choice* 37(3): 569– 578.
Chapter 19: Block, Walter (1989), "The Justification of Taxation in the Public Finance Literature: An Unorthodox View," *Journal of Public Finance and Public Choice* 3(Fall): 141–158.

Part 7: Other Topics in Public Choice
Chapter 20: DiLorenzo, Thomas J. (1993), "A Constitutionalist Approach to Social Security Reform," *Cato Journal* 3(2): 443–459.
Chapter 21: DiLorenzo, Thomas J. (2002), "The Futility of Bureaucracy," *The Free Market* 20(7).
Chapter 22: Block, Walter (2005), "Government and Market: A Critique of Professor James Buchanan's *What Should Economists Do?*" *Corporate Ownership & Control* 3(1): 81–87.
Chapter 23: DiLorenzo, Thomas J. (1983), "Economic Competition and Political Competition: An Empirical Note," *Public Choice* 40(2): 203–209.
Chapter 24: DiLorenzo, Thomas J. (1981), "An Empirical Assessment of the Factor Supplier-Pressure Group Hypothesis," *Public Choice* 37(3): 559–568.

The coauthors of this book thank William Maye for his tireless administrative and editorial efforts in getting this book off the ground, and into the hands of the publisher.

# Introduction

The first reaction to the title of our book is likely to be "What? An Austro-libertarian *critique* of Public Choice? Surely, there is a typographical error here!"

Many scholars would argue that Austrian economics, the libertarian political philosophy, and public choice are all, well, if not identical, then at least in the same political economic philosophical camp.

To be sure, there is evidence that might support such an interpretation: The Edward Elgar publishing company issues a compendium of their new books. The title of this flyer? "Public Choice and Austrian Economics." It cannot be denied that at least they see an intimate connection between the two. One of James Buchanan's many books *Cost and Choice* is not only entirely compatible with Austrian economics, but makes important contributions to this school of thought. Needless to say, this author, along with Gordon Tullock, is widely acknowledged to be the creator of the entire Public Choice movement.

George Mason University features both the Public Choice and the Austrian schools of thought. There are numerous scholars in the economics department who are practitioners of one or the other of these and more than just a few who consider themselves members of both.

Nevertheless, it is the contention of the present book that while to be sure there are some commonalities between libertarianism, Austrianism and Public Choice, there are also deep dark and wide chasms between all three. We come, in the vernacular, mainly not to praise the latter of this trio, but to underscore many of its flaws.

However, we must also acknowledge that the members of the Public Choice School have also done excellent work in public policy analysis. They have analyzed and popularized the view that men do not sprout angel's wings when they enter government; they are just as profit maximizing, they look after #1 just as much in the civil service as they do anywhere else.

Further, before Public Choice came on the scene, a popular syllogism both within and without the dismal science was as follows:

1. Markets are imperfect
2. We want perfection
3. Therefore, we must have government involvement in the economy to correct market failures.

Thanks to the school of thought started by James Buchanan and Gordon Tullock, this syllogism was turned around on its ear. Because of their skillful popularization, we now have, instead, this greatly improved version of that old saw:

1. Government is imperfect
2. We want perfection.
3. Therefore, we should privatize government services as much as possible; replace bureaucrats with entrepreneurs.

Libertarians can do naught but applaud such a turn-around. Public Choicers have done more than most to de-mystify and de-romanticize the workings of the state apparatus. They have, another welcome initiative, been foremost in applying the basic tools of economic analysis not only to the market, but to government as well, something sorely needed and rarely accomplished (apart from Austrians of course) before their advent.

The obvious difference between the libertarian political philosophy and Austrian economics is that the former is a normative pursuit, while the latter a positive one. Never the twain shall meet, although it must be conceded, they are often confused. How does Public Choice register on the normative-positive scale? It hits both sides. Certainly, its work on such matters as the median voter, the order in which decisions are made, rules, the democratic process, etc., are positive. Its support for governments, the main focus of our criticism, however, is normative.

The essays which follow, the entire remainder of the book, while do acknowledge the contributions of Public Choice to liberty, to our understanding of economics and politics, are also highly critical. But, these thoughts do not emanate from critics of the market. Very much to the contrary, the present authors are strong adherents of the system of natural liberty. Our main complaint is not that Public Choice, too, do not veer in this direction, but that it does not go far enough along that path.

Do not expect much of a critique of the Public Choice School in Part 1. Here, we are but laying the groundwork, mentioning Buchanan's adherence to Austrian economics on subjectivism mostly (but not always) in a very positive manner, and introducing Austro-libertarianism. It is in Part 2 that we begin to fully explore how our Austro-libertarian perspective diverges from that of Buchanan and Tullock and their followers. Part 3 is given over to our negative reaction to what we regard as the single most important book emanating from this school of thought, *The Calculus of Consent.* We then demonstrate how and why we part company from our friends in Public Choice on a range of issues: part 4 on monopoly theory and anti-trust law; part 5 with regard to so-called rent seeking and part 6 which is devoted to taxation. We conclude with part 7, wherein we pursue this school of thought on several miscellaneous fronts.

All of the chapters in this book have been written by either of the two co-authors of the present volume, Tom DiLorenzo or Walter E. Block, and several of them by the two of us, together, as co-authors. The one exception is chapter 7 of part 3, written by our friend, guide and mentor, Murray N. Rothbard. Without expressing any undue modesty, we regard this single chapter as the highlight of the entire book.

# Part 1:
# What Is Austrian Economics?

# Chapter 1
# The Subjectivist Roots of
# James Buchanan's Economics

"I have often argued that the Austrians seem ... to be more successful
in conveying the central principle of economics to students
than alternative schools ... or approaches."
--James M. Buchanan, 197

## 1. Introduction

When James Buchanan was awarded the 1986 Nobel Prize in economics the
Nobel committee cited *The Calculus of Consent*,[1] coauthored in 1962 with Gordon
Tullock, as Buchanan's most important work. But Buchanan himself has stated that
he considers his 1969 book, *Cost and Choice: An Inquiry in Economic Theory*,[2] to
be his most important theoretical contribution.

Even though *Cost and Choice* was published seven years after *The Calculus of
Consent*, it embodies important elements of Buchanan's thinking that are crucial to
his contributions to *The Calculus of Consent* and to much of his other work. Of
particular interest to Austrian economists is the fact that subjective cost theory lies
at the heart of many of Buchanan's contributions to economic theory. Moreover,
other Austrian-school insights, such as methodological individualism and an
emphasis on market (and non-market) *processes,* as opposed to equilibrium
conditions or end states, also figure prominently in Buchanan's work.

Buchanan's Nobel Prize is widely regarded as a salute to public choice
economics. But the award also reflects well on the Austrian school, to the extent
that it has influenced Buchanan's thinking.

## 2. Buchanan's Principles of *Cost and Choice*

Buchanan has clearly stated that subjective cost theory is at the heart of much of
his work in public choice and public policy. This methodological distinction is what
separates much of his work from other economists who have written on public
policy issues. The notion of opportunity cost is usually defined acceptably by most
economists, according to Buchanan, but the problem is that "the logic of the
concept is not normally allowed to enter into and inform the subsequent analytical
applications."[3] Such applications are essential, for a consistent application of the
notion of opportunity cost, writes Buchanan,

> clarifies important areas of disagreement on policy issues. In public
> finance alone, debates over tax incidence, tax capitalization, public

debt burden, and the role of cost-benefit analysis can be partially resolved when protagonists accept common concepts of cost. The unsatisfactory state of welfare economics can at least be understood and appreciated more adequately when the incorporated cost confusions are exposed. The ... debate over the possibility of socialist calculation emerges with perhaps a different glow. Something can be said about such ... topics as the draft and crime.[4]

Buchanan's cost theory "is properly labeled Austrian,"[5] and also owes a debt to developments of the "London School Tradition" during the period of the 1930s to the 1950s.[6]

One of the essential points of *Cost and Choice* is that, to many economists, cost is divorced from the act of choice. To neoclassical economists cost is objective in that it can be estimated *ex post* by external observers, even though market values are set by the subjective evaluations of market participants. Furthermore, in "the predictive science of economics" cost is, according to Buchanan,

> the objectively-identifiable magnitude that is minimized. It is the market value of the alternate product that might be produced by rational reallocation of resource inputs to uses other than that observed. This market value is reflected in the market prices for resource units; hence, cost is measured directly by prospective money outlays.[7]

One consequence of objective cost theory is that the theory "is not a theory of choice at all. Individuals do not choose; they behave predictably in response to objectively-measurable changes in the environment."[8] For according to the objective cost theory:

> Cost ... is faced in the strict sense only by the automaton, the pure economic man, who inhabits the scientist's model. It is the behavior inhibiting element that is plugged into the purely mechanistic market model. The conversion of objective data reflecting prospective money outlays into the subjective evaluations made by real-world decision-makers is of no concern to the predictive theorist.[9]

Buchanan acknowledges an intellectual debt to Philip Wicksteed, who was the first to tie opportunity cost directly to choice. Wicksteed wrote, for instance, that the cost of production, "in the sense of the historical and irrevocable fact that resources have been directed to this or that special purpose, has no influence on the value of the things produced."[10] In this respect cost of production does not affect supply; What does affect supply is *anticipated* cost "in the sense of alternatives still open which must now be relinquished in order to produce this specific article," and which "influences the craftsman in determining whether he shall produce it or not."[11]

Wicksteed's work was refined by Hayek, Mises, and other Austrians, and by some members of the London School. Buchanan summarizes the resultant "choice-bound conception of cost" as follows:

5

(1) Cost must be borne exclusively by the decision-maker; it is not possible for cost to be shifted to or imposed on others.
(2) Cost is subjective; it exists in the mind of the decision-maker and nowhere else.
(3) Cost is based on anticipations; it is necessarily a forward-looking or *ex ante* concept.
(4) Cost can never be realized because of the fact of choice itself; that which is given up cannot be enjoyed.
(5) Cost cannot be measured by someone other than the decision maker because there is no way that subjective experience can be directly observed.
(6) Cost can be dated at the moment of decision or choice.[12]

Buchanan makes an important distinction between choice-influencing and choice-influenced cost. The former is the type of cost discussed by Wicksteed, whereas the latter is the type of (subjective) cost that is the consequence of economic choices. Such costs may be borne by the decision maker, or by others on whom costs may sometimes be shifted. This distinction is critical to much of Buchanan's *work* in public finance and public choice.


## 3. The Importance of Subjective Cost Theory to Public Finance and Public Choice

Buchanan gained an international reputation as a public finance scholar long before the phrase "public choice" was ever coined. Moreover, his subjective cost theory is what distinguishes his work from other prominent public finance theorists such as Paul Samuelson and Richard Musgrave.

Buchanan's work on tax incidence theory is a clear example of how subjectivist insights have shaped his thinking about public finance. Neoclassical public finance theory has focused on the "cost" of taxation in terms of (1) who pays the amounts of money actually sent into the Treasury, and, (2) the "excess burden" or welfare costs of taxation. Both of these costs are assumed to be objective and measurable.

Buchanan takes a very different approach to the issue of tax incidence. Specifically, he was the first modern scholar to examine the relationship between taxes *as costs of public goods* and the importance of those taxes in democratic decision making. Neoclassical tax incidence theory, according to Buchanan, "examines the choice behavior of individuals and firms, but this is not the choice behavior that involves either the financing of public goods or the selection among taxing alternatives."[13] The individual or firm is assumed by the neoclassical theory "to be subjected to an imposed change in the alternatives of *private or market choice*" (emphasis in original).[14]

Neoclassical tax-incidence theory is concerned almost exclusively with the tax-induced changes in the costs of undertaking *private* production, investment, and consumption decisions, but lacks a theory of public choice. The analysis yields no information about the subjective cost of *public* goods.

With the neoclassical approach to tax incidence theory the economist quite naturally views his role as one of adviser to political decision makers. If the economist can identify the effects of a tax on the economy, his role is to advise the presumably benevolent political authorities as to which type of tax would raise the "desired" amount of revenue and at the same time minimize the "excess burden" on society. According to this viewpoint, the economist's role is to construct a social welfare function, even if the members of society, i.e., taxpayers, have no input into the construction of the social welfare function or to the choice of tax instruments.

Buchanan has long recognized that this approach is inherently authoritarian, for in the name of maximizing some idealized notion of "social welfare," it ignores the preferences of those who comprise the society. For example, neoclassical public finance theory holds that individuals would prefer a "lump-sum" tax to an excise tax that raise the same amount of revenue because the former causes no excess burden. But to reach this conclusion, writes Buchanan,

> the economist must assume that the taxpayer is exclusively interested in the post-tax changes in his position and that he is indifferent among tax instruments otherwise. But there are obviously many reasons why the taxpayer may not evaluate alternative tax instruments in the same way that 'the applied welfare economist evaluates them. The taxpayer might, in the first place, prefer to suffer the higher measurable cost imposed by the excise tax because of the wider range of personal options that this form of tax allows' [i.e., to avoid an excise tax on liquor by not purchasing it]. This option feature may well outweigh the excess burden. In the second place, the taxpayer may prefer the excise tax on liquor for consumptuary reasons even though he knows that he, too, bears an excess burden. The tax-induced reduction in liquor purchases by others may be more than enough to modify the relative standing of this tax on his preference scale.[15]

Informed by subjective cost theory, Buchanan suggests an alternative approach by asking the fundamental question: "What are the 'costs' of public goods in the genuine opportunity cost, or *choice-influencing* sense?" (emphasis in original).[16] This question ties costs directly to choice and requires one to identify the choosing agent. The choosing agents are (at least in part) the voters in a democratic decision making structure. Since there are many different types of decision-making structures, democratic and non-democratic, the focus of Buchanan's approach is on how choice-influencing costs affect these decision makers in alternative institutional settings. To Buchanan, it is impossible to evaluate alternative tax systems without a theory of public choice, and that theory must be based on the insights of subjective cost theory.

One of the most important distinctions between Buchanan's and the neo-classical approach to taxation theory was recently described by one of his students,

Richard E. Wagner. Wagner observed that much of the "optimal taxation" literature, which has largely ignored Buchanan's work, is labeled "individualistic," but would appear to be anything but. According to Wagner,

> It is ... a curious piece of vocabulary that affixes the designation 'in-dividualistic' to an analytic construction in which people are manipulated as objects at the disposal of some type of despot, who is presumed to be benevolent by virtue of being named 'Social Welfare Function.' ... [In the optimal taxation literature] policy outcomes are assessed against some transcendent criterion of goodness, independent of any consideration of what the participants might or might not work out among themselves ...[17]

As an aside, it is interesting that Buchanan's suggested approach to the study of tax incidence has been met with intense hostility by some neoclassical theorists. In 1980 he published *The Power to Tax* with Geoffrey Brennan),[18] a book that is, among other things, an exposition of Buchanan's brand of tax-incidence theory. One reviewer for the *Economic Journal* was so offended by the book that he called the authors "fascists" for merely recommending that citizens should be given a greater voice in the choice of tax instruments.

In *The Power to Tax* Buchanan and Brennan disagreed with economic orthodoxy that broad-based taxes are the most "efficient" tax structure. They argued that a system of multiple excise taxes, rather than a few broad-based taxes, would give taxpayers more control over government by permitting them to escape taxation by reducing their purchases of heavily-taxed items. Altering one's consumption patterns in this way would be a way of "protesting" against excessive government spending.

Buchanan's subjectivist cost theory has colored his views of many economic phenomena besides tax incidence. For example, in criticizing benefit/cost studies of governmental programs, Buchanan reminds us that the costs that are discussed in such studies are not choice-influencing costs. Thus, their usefulness is limited at best, and misguided at worst.

In real-world political settings, the costs that influence the choice calculus of an individual voter are his or her own personal share in the costs of government in terms of the alternatives foregone. *The distribution* of taxes certainly makes a difference in the evaluation of governmental programs, but this is ignored by benefit/cost studies.

## 4. Subjective Cost, Public Choice, and Fiscal Institutions

Buchanan's subjectivist roots have also led him to the conclusion that "institutions matter." This may sound simplistic, but to many economists the notion that the means of making choices influence the choices themselves may imply irrational behavior. Buchanan has ignored this criticism, however, and has demonstrated throughout his career how the institutions of fiscal choice *do* matter because they influence public choices.

As Buchanan and Wagner have written, "individual choice behavior is affected by the costs and benefits of choice alternatives as these are perceived by the chooser, and not as they may exist in some objective dimension necessarily measurable by third parties."[19] Furthermore, "different tax institutions will exert differing effects on the individual's perception of his share in the costs of 'public service.' From this; it follows that the form of tax institution, or the tax structure generally, can affect budgetary choices."[20] And, according to Buchanan and Wagner, it is *perceptions* of individuals concerning the differential effects of fiscal institutions that are relevant to public choice.

This type of thinking is at the heart of much of "the new public finance," which Buchanan has had an important role in establishing. One example of this new approach is the literature on "fiscal illusion." According to the so-called fiscal illusion hypothesis, complex and indirect payment structures create a fiscal illusion that will systematically produce higher levels of government spending than those with single-payment structures: In essence, complex and indirect tax structures weaken the cost signals upon which public choices are based.

This notion is similar to the analytical basis of the psychological literature on information processing.[21] In that literature, to the degree to which any message is understood varies directly with the strength of the particular signal to be received and inversely with the noise present when the signal is transmitted. It is easier, for instance, to hear what someone says in a room that is not crowded and filled with background chatter. The fiscal illusion literature espouses a similar interpretation of economic phenomena.

Thus, the size of governmental budgets will be directly related to the complexity and indirectness of tax systems. The *perceived* or choice-influencing costs will be lower under indirect than direct taxation, and will be lower under a multiplicity of tax sources than under a system that relies heavily on a single source. Indirect taxation, therefore, is likely to lead to greater budgetary expansion. Casual evidence supports this hypothesis, as does a body of economic research.[22]

Nevertheless, "orthodox" public finance theorists have largely neglected the theory of fiscal illusion. A reason for this neglect, according to Buchanan and Wagner, is that the orthodox theory "defines rational behavior in terms of objectifiable magnitudes and, furthermore, embodies the hypothesis that ... persons do not systematically err. The subjectively determined perceptions of persons ... have been neglected."[23] Not all economists, however, have ignored objectively determined perceptions, such as those embodied in the fiscal illusion literature. "The ... Austrian School of economists, along with a more specialized tradition in cost theory centering on the London School of Economics in the 1930s, provide notable exceptions."[24]

The theory of fiscal illusion has led to a greater understanding of the effects of alternative tax systems. For example, one reason the inflation tax is so pernicious is because it reduces the *perceived* cost of government. Debt-financed budget deficits are also better understood once one incorporates a subjectivist view of cost. Buchanan's decades-long research on the public debt demonstrates as much as anything the importance of Austrian-school insights to his contributions to economic theory.

## 5. Buchanan and the Public Debt Controversy

Buchanan has been involved in the public debt controversy for over 30 years. He never accepted the dreamy world of Keynesian interventionism, wherein a benevolent government, faithfully obeying the academic economic sages, could "stimulate" the economy through deficit spending. Nor has he accepted the technocratic world of Robert Barro and other believers in the Ricardian "equivalence theorem," which holds that there is no fundamental difference between debt and tax finance. Buchanan has long maintained that federal deficit spending is destructive, for it crowds out private spending and imposes burdens on future generations.

The reason why Buchanan has differed from these schools of thought, on the issue of deficit finance, is his insistence that "institutions matter," which is deduced from his subjectivist cost theory. Deficit spending allows the governmental sector to replace or crowd out private spending because,

> the replacement of current tax financing by government borrowing has the effect of reducing the 'perceived price' of governmental goods and services. This 'relative price' change embodies an income effect of the orthodox Hicksian sort, and this income effect will generate some attempted increase in the rate of private spending. ... To the extent that the costs of governmental goods and services are perceived to be lowered by any degree through the substitution of debt for tax finance, the 'relative' price change will be present.[25]

Furthermore, the reason why deficit spending leads to govern mental expansion is that in response to a reduction in the perceived price of publicly-provided goods and services, taxpayers "increase their demands for such goods and services. Preferred budget level will be higher, and these preferences will be sensed by politicians and translated into political outcomes."[26]

## 6. Money Creation and Subjective Cost Theory

Buchanan's views of the inflation tax are also colored by subjective insights. Much has been written about how inflation effectively constitutes a "tax" on privately-held wealth. But inflation is not really equivalent to a tax, because "no explicit political discussion a decision takes place on either the source or the rate of tax to be imposed."[27] Consequently, "individual citizens are likely to be less informed about the probable costs of an inflation tax than they are about even the most indirect and complex [tax] levy."[28]

Once again, choice-influencing costs are altered by real-world fiscal institutions. But in this instance, the consequences are perhaps even worse than with deficit finance. The problem is that:

> the tax signal under inflation is overwhelmed by the accompanying noise which takes the form of rising prices . ... Psychologically, individuals do not sense inflation to be a tax on their money balances; they do not attribute the diminution of their real wealth to the legalized 'counterfeiting' activities of government. Rather, the sense data take the form of rising prices for goods and services purchased in the private sector. The decline in real wealth is attributed to failings in the market economy, not to governmental money creation... Inflationary finance, then, will generally produce an underestimation of the opportunity cost of public services, in addition to promoting a false attribution in the minds of citizens as to the reason for the decline in their real wealth, a false attribution that nonetheless influences the specific character of public policies.[29]

The so-called inflation tax is pernicious not only because it is a hidden tax on privately-held wealth, but also because it leads to false perceptions of the cause of the inflation. Political demagoguery adds to the confusion, as politicians are naturally inclined to lie to the public and blame the inflation on greedy capitalists, farmers, mortgage bankers, and others in the private sector. The proposed solution typically is to place even more power in the hands of the inflation-generating governmental authorities.

## 7. Methodological Individualism and the Market Process

Rigorous application of methodological individualism is perhaps what most separates the Austrian and Public Choice schools from most others. The idea that the individual should be the unit of analysis has spared public choice and Austrian economists from many of the mistakes of what might be called collectivist economics. The Austrians, for example, have exposed a great deal of macroeconomic nonsense due to the fact that Keynesian theory largely ignored aggregation problems. The Austrian conception of markets, based on the interaction among individuals and on man's inherent "propensity to truck, barter and exchange," is also more useful and informative, in my view, than the perfect competition model.

Buchanan and other public choice theorists have greatly improved our understanding of the political process by scrapping the "organic" view of collective action, which describes government, more or less, as a benevolent despot, making decisions that are assumed to be in "the public interest."

Not so long ago, in 1968, Buchanan remarked:

> Most ... economists take an approach different from my own, and one that I regard as both confused and wrong. In my vision of social order, individual persons are the basic component units, and 'government' is simply that complex of institutions through which individuals make collective decisions, and through which they carry out collective as opposed to private activities. Politics is the activity of persons in the context of such institutions.[30]

Of course, the economics profession has changed significantly since then, particularly in light of the public choice revolution. Methodological individualism has replaced more collectivist views in academic circles.

Nevertheless, it is far from clear that there has been a decisive "victory." Social welfare functions still clutter the economics journals. Moreover, there is no shortage of recommendations for government intervention in the name of the mythical "public interest." Proponents of methodological individualism have made great strides, but the collectivist mindset dies a slow death.

Buchanan has also long been considered a proponent of the Austrian view of the market process. In this regard he is more than just a "fellow traveler"; his work has played an important role in helping to distinguish between the theory of the market as a process and the alternative, neoclassical theory of competitive equilibrium. Thus, in addition to his seminal work on subjective cost theory, Buchanan has helped clarify the Austrian view of the market as a process.

In his 1963 presidential address to the Southern Economic Association, Buchanan explained how the economics profession was apparently being led astray by its focus on the "theory of resource allocation." He forcefully argued that the standard neoclassical definition of economics as the study of the allocation of scarce mean among competing ends "has served to retard, rather than advance scientific progress."[31] The reason for this, according to Buchanan, is that there is very little economic content in much of modern economics. What neoclassical economics, all too often involves is a computation problem, the computation of equilibrium prices, for example which "to the subjectivist, [seems] an absurd exercise."[32]

A good example is the work of Nobel Laureate Tjalling Koopmans, who began his career by working out the optimal allocation of a set of tankers carrying oil across the Atlantic during World War II. Buchanan properly labels such work as engineering, not economics, and claims that he must have been "a confirmed subjectivist long before I realized what I was because I recall thinking in 1946, when Koopmans was lecturing... at the University of Chicago, that there seemed to be absolutely no economic content in what he was doing...."[33]

Buchanan has attempted to persuade the economics profession to abandon its fixation on allocation problems per se, for "if there is really nothing more to economics than this, we had as well turned it all over to the applied mathematicians."[34] This does appear to be the direction the profession has been heading; for "developments of note... during the past two decades consist largely of improvements in ... computing techniques, in the mathematics of social engineering."[35]

Instead of becoming weakly-trained mathematicians (at least by the standards of professional mathematicians), Buchanan suggested replacing the theory of resource allocation with the theory of markets. This would require paying more attention to

> a particular form of human activity, and upon the various institutional arrangements that arise as a result of this form of activity. [Namely,] man's behavior in the market relationship, reflecting the propensity to truck and to barter, and the manifold variations in structure that this relationship can take.[36]

These, Buchanan has written, are the proper subjects of economics.

This approach helps us understand why, in perfect competition, there is no competition (or any trade, for that matter). It also reveals how a market is not competitive by definition, as in the neoclassical model, but that a market *becomes* competitive. "It is this becoming process, brought about by the continuous pressure of human behavior in exchange, that is the central part of our discipline, ... not the dry rot of postulated perfection."[37]

Thus, Buchanan's view of the market system may properly be labeled Austrian. Furthermore, he has urged us to apply this same notion of the economic process to the study of political institutions. This is why public choice theory is largely a study of political *processes,* with policy recommendations usually focusing on altering institutional processes, rather than political outcomes or end states.


## 8. The Importance of Austrian Economics to Public Choice

Buchanan has done seminal work in many areas of economics, but his Nobel Prize was awarded primarily for his role in establishing, with Gordon Tullock, the sub-discipline of public choice. As this paper has shown, many of the essential principles of public choice (and of "the new public finance") have subjectivist or Austrian roots. This fact doesn't seem to have been sufficiently appreciated by the economics profession, however, for a number of reasons.

One possible reason, Buchanan writes in *Cost and Choice,* is that "it is not easy to question long-accepted precepts." He further confessed that he has "found it difficult to prevent the analysis [in *Cost and Choice*] from lapsing into the kind of conventional [neoclassical] methodology that I have often used in other works."[38] Moreover, many economists may balk at seriously considering the impact of subjectivist insights, writes Buchanan, because "in effect, the incorporation of the London [or Austrian] conception of opportunity cost amounts to transforming one of the foundation stones of economic theory. [However,] only when this basic modification is completed can real progress toward changing the superstructure [of economics] be attempted on a large scale."[39]

The public choice revolution provides supportive evidence for this conjecture, since many insights in public choice have subjectivist or Austrian roots. However, there are many instances where the public choice revolution has taken a step backward, in my view, because of insufficient attention paid to these roots. One should not be overly critical of public choice economists, however, for in a recent article Buchanan himself seems to have forgotten his subjectivist roots, thereby walking into a theoretical and public policy mine field.

In a paper entitled "Rent Seeking, Noncompensated Transfers, and Laws of Succession,"[40] Buchanan analyzes the supposed inefficiencies generated whenever potential heirs "compete" for an inheritance. The basic hypothesis is that the "investment of effort, time, and resources in this rent-seeking activity will be socially wasteful."[41] The behavior of children, as potential heirs, is assumed to be analytically identical to the behavior of lobbyists for protectionism, price supports, and all other sorts of government-generated monopoly rents. "To ... potential recipients [of a bequest]," writes Buchanan, "any such value becomes precisely analogous to a rental opportunity that has been artificially created. The frugal rich man whose fortune must be transferred by gifts or bequests stands ... in precisely the same relationship as Queen Elizabeth before her courtiers when she announced the possible assignment of a playing-card monopoly."[42]

This logic led Buchanan to recommend governmentally imposed restrictions on the disposition of inheritances, for "once the probable emergence of wasteful rent seeking is acknowledged ... the efficiency basis for the argument against any and all [government] restrictions on the transfer power [of individuals] vanishes."[43]

Ironically, this argument appears to have much in common with the type of reasoning that Buchanan so effectively criticized in *Cost and Choice*. Specifically, he assumes that benefits and costs are *objective* in order to conclude that "all noncompensated transfers are payments to the recipients."[44]

Gifts and bequests are labeled "noncompensated transfers" in Buchanan's analysis because there is no objectively measurable "payment" for these "transfers." But surely such gifts involve implicit, mutually-advantageous exchanges. In the case at hand, there is an exchange of tangible wealth for psychic income. Altruistic behavior toward the donor is "exchanged" for a more tangible form of wealth. Since such exchanges have persisted for millennia, it is reasonable to assume that there must be "gains from trade" to the participants. This latter interpretation is consistent with the subjectivist principles Buchanan has advocated throughout his career. But in a bizarre repudiation of those principles – at least in this particular paper – Buchanan chooses to ignore them. "To the extent that gifts and bequests are literally payments for equal values received in exchange ... there is no net transfer of value among persons involved and there is no incentive for the emergence of

14

rent-seeking behavior. Hence, for purposes of the analysis in this paper, fully compensated transfers of value can be neglected."[45]

By ignoring this elementary subjectivist insight for the sake of argument, Buchanan renders his case for governmental controls of inheritance untenable. His case is based on neoclassical notions of efficiency, namely, that such "rent seeking" is "socially wasteful." But as he also stated in an earlier work, since individuals base choices on data that are inherently subjective, the economist can identify waste in the actions of other people only by imposing his own standard of value.[46] And this is what Buchanan appears to be doing in this essay. Such work can only impede the public choice "revolution," however, by lending credence to public choice critics who claim that much of public choice is simply a political crusade "masquerading as science."[47]

A second example of how ignoring subjectivist or Austrian insight has impeded research in public choice is a contradiction in the world of Robert Tollison, one of Buchanan's most prolific students. Following Buchanan's advice on viewing the market as a process, rather than as an equilibrium condition, Tollison has written that:

> when competition is viewed as a dynamic, value-creating, evolutionary process, the role of economic rents in stimulating entrepreneurial, decisions and in prompting an efficient allocation of resources is crucial. ... [P]rofit seeking in a competitive market order is a normal feature of economic life. The returns of resource owners will be driven to normal levels ... by competitive profit seeking as some resource owners earn positive rents which promote entry and others earn negative rents which cause exit. Profit seeking and economic rents are inherently related to the efficiency of the competitive market process. Such activities drive the competitive price system and create value (e.g., new products) in the economy.[48]

But a few pages along in the same article Tollison condemns as "wasteful rent seeking'" all forms of non-price competition "in imperfectly competitive markets." The contradiction lies in the fact that if one views competition as a "dynamic, value-creating, evolutionary process," as Tollison initially suggested, then the forms of non-price competition that he labeled wasteful – advertising, R&D spending, product differentiation – are viewed as an essential ingredient of the competitive process, not as wasteful rent-seeking or monopolizing devices.[49]

There is now an emerging literature in public choice that labels almost all forms of private business behavior as "wasteful rent seeking."[50] Oddly, much of this literature recommends government regulation as a means of reducing such waste. But surely, granting even greater powers to government will lead to more, not less, rent seeking. I have written elsewhere[51] how such bizarre reasoning has come about, at least partly, because of the failure of public choice economists to pay sufficient attention to the fundamental Austrian concepts of subjectivism, method-ological individualism, and the concept of the market as a dynamic process. This is why students of public choice, above all, should more fully appreciate the subjectivist roots of James Buchanan's economics.

Finally, it is worth repeating that I have not attempted a comprehensive review of the impact of Austrian economics on the work of James Buchanan. Such an undertaking would require at least a book-length treatment. My only objective has been to point out a relatively neglected aspect of at least some of Buchanan's work, namely, its subjectivist roots. Subjective cost theory is not at the heart of all of Buchanan's work; perhaps not even most of it. At times his writing seems strictly positivist. But a case can be made that many of his most important contributions to economics may be properly labeled "Austrian." Moreover, an equally strong case can be made that the work of Buchanan, and of other public choice scholars, is weakest when it neglects fundamental Austrian-school insights.

## NOTES AND REFERENCES

1. Buchanan, James, and Gordon Tullock (1962), *The Calculus of Consent.* Ann Arbor, MI: University of Michigan Press.

2. Buchanan, James (1969), *Cost and Choice: An Inquiry in Economic Theory.* Chicago, IL: University of Chicago Press.

3. Ibid., ix.

4. Ibid.

5. Ibid.

6. Buchanan, James, and G. F. Thirlby (eds.) (1981), *LSE Essays on Cost.* New York: New York University Press.

7. Buchanan, James, *Cost and Choice,* 112.

8. Ibid.

9. Ibid.

10. Wicksteed, Philip (1910), *The Common Sense of Political Economy.* London: MacMillan.

11. Ibid.

12. Buchanan, *Cost and Choice,* 43.

13. Ibid., 53.

14. Ibid.

15. Ibid., 54.

16. Ibid., 55.

17. Wagner, Richard E. (1985), "Normative and Positive Foundations of Tax Reform," *Cato Journal* Fall: 386 and 388.

18. Buchanan, James, and Geoffrey Brennan (1980), *The Power to Tax.* New York: Cambridge University Press.

19. Buchanan, James, and Richard E. Wagner (1976), *Democracy in Deficit: The· Political Legacy of Lord Keynes.* New York: Academic Press, 126.

20. Ibid.

21. See Wagner, Richard E. (1978), "Revenue Structure, Fiscal Illusion, and Budgetary Choice," *Public Choice* Spring; and DiLorenzo, Thomas J. (1981), "Utility Profits, Fiscal Illusion and Local Public Expenditures," *Public Choice* Fall.

22. Ibid.

23. Buchanan and Wagner, *Democracy in Deficit,* 130.

24. Ibid.

25. Buchanan and Wagner, *Democracy in Deficit,* 138.

26. Ibid., 139.

27. Ibid., 142.

28. Ibid.

29. Ibid., 143.

30. Buchanan, James (1968), "An Economist's Approach to Scientific Politics," in M. Parsons (ed.), *Perspectives in the Study of Politics.* Chicago, IL: Rand McNally, 78.

31. Buchanan, James (1964), "What Should Economists Do?," *Southern Economic Journal* January: 213–222.

32. Buchanan, James (1979), "General Implications of Subjectivism in Economics," in Geoffrey Brennan and Robert D. Tollison (eds.), *What Should Economists Do?* Indianapolis, IN: Liberty Press, 85.

33. Ibid.

34. Buchanan, James, "What Should Economists Do?," 217.

35. Ibid.

36. Ibid.

37. Buchanan, *Cost and Choice,* 83.

38. Ibid.

39. Ibid.

40. Buchanan, James (1983), "Rent Seeking, Noncompensated Transfers, and Laws of Succession," *Journal of Law and Economics* April: 71–85. For another critical look at Buchanan's work from an Austrian perspective see Boettke, Peter J. (1987), "Virginia Political Economy: A View From Vienna," *Market Process* Fall: 7–15, published by the Center for the Study of Market Processes, George Mason University, Fairfax, VA.

41. Ibid., 74.

42. Ibid., 83.

43. Ibid., 76.

44. Ibid., 71.

45. Ibid., 72.

46. James Buchanan, "Is Economics the Science of Choice?," in Brennan and Tollison (eds.), *What Should Economists Do?*, 61.

47. For an elaboration of this point see DiLorenzo, Thomas J. (1988), "Property Rights, Information Costs, and the Economics of Rent Seeking," *Journal of Institutional and Theoretical Economics* Spring.

48. Tollison, Robert D. (1982), "Rent Seeking: A Survey," *Kyklos* 35: 577.

49. See Littlechild, Stephen C. (1981), "Misleading Calculations of the Social Costs of Monopoly Power," *Economic Journal* June: 348–63; and DiLorenzo, Thomas J. (1984), "The Domain of Rent-Seeking Behavior: Private or Public Choice?," *International Review* of *Law and Economics* December: 185–97.

50. Boudreaux, Don, and Thomas J. DiLorenzo, "A Critique of the Economics of Raising Rivals' Costs," unpubl. ms., Department of Economics, George Mason University.

51. DiLorenzo, Thomas J. (1987), "Competition and Political Entrepreneurship: Austrian Insights into Public Choice Theory," *Review of Austrian Economics* 2: 59–72.

# Chapter 2
# Cultural Dynamics

## 1. Introduction

One major purpose of this article is to apply the insights of Murray Rothbard's (1977) unjustly neglected "Toward a Reconstruction of Utility and Welfare Economics" to several issues in economics. Another is to demonstrate the truth of Garrison's (1982) contention that Austrian economics is a moderate philosophy, occupying a mid-point between more extreme views popular within the profession. A third is to show that moderation in the sense of compromise can sometimes constitute a more sensible world view than that occupied by the extremes.

What is the main contribution of Rothbard's "Reconstruction"? It is that demonstrated preference is the linchpin of a proper welfare economics. His point is that people can reveal what enhances their utility only through their free choices.[1] Since I am now writing this article, it proves – as nothing else can do – that I value doing this more than any other alternative, such as sleeping, swimming, or studying. In order to do so, I had to first purchase the means with which to accomplish this task, in this case, a word processor. That being the case, an economist is entitled to deduce from this fact that I valued the computer more than the price I was charged, and, also, that the vendor placed greater value on my money than on his own machine. As it happens, I am employed by the College of the Holy Cross; this means that I prefer the salary they pay me more than the foregone leisure, and that they rank my services higher than their monetary outlay.

As a general rule, it logically follows from the fact that people engage in commercial interaction of this sort that they benefit, at least in the ex ante sense. That is, it cannot be denied that voluntary trade of whatever sort enhances the welfare of all parties to it – otherwise, they would scarcely agree to participate. States Rothbard (1977: 2): "... actual choice reveals, or demonstrates, a man's preferences; i.e., ... his preferences are deducible from what he has chosen in action."

What is the implication of the foregoing for welfare economics? In Rothbard's (1977: 29) view, it is that "... no government interference with exchanges can ever increase social utility." And why, in turn, is this? It is because the unanimity rule, and the impermissibility of interpersonal comparisons of utility, stand as twin barriers against any such conclusion. Yes, forbidding a trade can benefit some people; at the very least, the utility of the prohibitor will have been enhanced, otherwise he would not have taken this step. But if some have been made better off, the utility of others (the would-be trading partners) has been decreased. Unless we may interpersonally compare utility between the winners and losers, or somehow conclude that all "stakeholders" have unanimously agreed to cancel the commercial agreement, we cannot unambiguously conclude that social welfare has been enlarged.[2]

But we can do neither. Given ordinal not cardinal utility, no comparisons across people can ever be made. And it is illogical to think that the would-be traders have agreed not to interact with each other in this manner. Were this true, there would be no need to forbid the trade in the first place.

Trade, in contrast, does pass muster even in the teeth of these twin challenges. States Rothbard (1977):

> ... the very fact that an exchange takes place demonstrates that both parties benefit (or more strictly, expect to benefit) from the exchange. The fact that both parties chose the exchange demonstrates that they both benefit. The free market is the name for the array of all the voluntary exchanges that take place in the world. Since every exchange demonstrates a unanimity of benefit for both parties concerned, we must conclude that the free market benefits all its participants. In other words, welfare economics can make the statement that the free market increases social utility, while still keeping to the framework of the Unanimity Rule. (p. 27)

Notwithstanding the foregoing, there are those who cleave to the notion that statist prohibitions on trade can improve human welfare. These, for obvious reasons, are called "interventionists." But there are others who take the very opposite tack. They claim that trades made compulsory by government can enhance the human situation. Such people, for reasons that are far less apparent, are not usually seen as interventionists.[3] It is the purpose of this paper to show that neither view has incorporated the Rothbardian reconstruction of welfare economics; that both are therefore fallacious.


## 2. Preventing Commercial Interactions

We shall now attempt a rather unusual critique of trade prohibitions such as rent control, minimum wages, tariffs and drug laws. But before we do so, let it be clearly established that enactments of this sort do indeed constitute prevention of trade. Consider first rent controls. It might be objected at the outset that this is a price control, not a trade prohibition. In actual point of fact, however, it is both. Namely, it prevents trades at any price incompatible with the law. For example, if the law requires that a given apartment rent for $500 or less, then it ipso facto prevents trades at $501 or more. Similarly, the minimum wage law is on the face of it an unemployment law, not an employment law. Specifically, it prevents jobs from coming into existence where the pay is below the level stipulated by legislation. Interferences with foreign commerce, further, prevent trades from occurring where the benefits to the contracting parties are less than the tariff which must be paid.

And drug laws prevent all purchases and sales of addictive substances at any price.

The usual criticism of these laws is that they have harmful economic effects. Typically, this is seen as a result of a concatenation of empirical events which renders them deleterious. Our point here, in contrast, is that even if we make the most positive assumptions about these laws possible, the Rothbardian analysis can nevertheless be utilized to show that they cannot improve social welfare. In a sense, this is a more thoroughgoing critique of interventionism than the conventional one. It claims that even if we adopt the best case scenarios for these enactments, they still cannot satisfy the Rothbard criteria.

## 2.1. Rent control

The case against rent control is simple and straightforward.[4] The law retards investment in residential rental units. Property owners, faced with lower profit opportunities, find other, better options for their financial resources. With a lowered supply of housing, prices are inevitably forced upwards, directly contravening the presumed intent of the law. Sometimes this is hidden, as when the monetary rent stays constant, or even decreases, but the actual housing services provided fall more quickly than the declining price. Sometimes it is only slightly hidden, as when rents in new dwellings are higher than otherwise they would have been.

The price ceilings bring in their wake a shortage of rental housing, where demand exceeds supply. The shortfall must be rationed in some manner, and if it is forbidden for prices to do so, then other mechanisms come into play: favoritism, racial discrimination, black markets ("key money"), "first come first served," etc. As well, shortages reduce the vacancy rate below optimal levels, and wasteful queuing for apartments ensues.

The landlord has less of an incentive to maintain and upgrade his property. This leads to an exacerbation of relations with tenants, and to a slide of entire neighborhoods into slum conditions. Often times, lower class housing is "protected" from rent rises even more strongly than are luxury dwellings. As a result, the little money earmarked for investment in this field is shifted from the former to the latter.

The perceived "market failure" to provide housing for the poor then leads to other government programs such as public housing; this further worsens an already bad situation because, typically, tenants who have lost their apartments due to fire are placed at the head of the public housing queue. But landlords who are insured at the higher pre-rent-control housing prices already have little incentive to guard against arson. Given similar motivations on the part of the tenants, it is little wonder that vast areas subject to rent control (e.g. the South Bronx) begin to resemble cities which have been subjected to bombing. Toss in lenient judges who will not evict tenants for non-payment of rent in any month within 90 days of Christmas-

coupled with banks which for good reason insist upon mortgage payments throughout the entire year-and the recipe for urban disaster is complete.

This is the conventional critique of rent control. For our present purposes, however, we wish to paint this law in the most attractive colors possible,[5] and show that a defense cannot be sustained even under these conditions. Accordingly, let us assume a very moderate rent control, which hardly entices resources into other areas; one which allows for generous rent "pass alongs," which barely reduce the incentives which would otherwise obtain to encourage owners to maintain their buildings. We further posit that the overwhelming majority of tenants are poorer than landlords, and that those who receive the greatest rent reductions are the poorest, neither of which is always the case.

In addition, our "ideal" rent control is very much more punitive with regard to luxury than substandard housing. This draws resources away not from the poor, but from the rich. Such a stipulation might hurt the well-to-do, somewhat, but at least insult will not be added to injury for the destitute.

Nor need we apologize for the unreality of our present assumptions. After all, not all cities subject to rent controls come to resemble the South Bronx. All five boroughs of New York City were subject to the same law, and yet their experiences were not at all identical.

The point is, even under a more "rational" rent control regime, we are still not in a position to overcome the objections laid in our path by Rothbard. Without recourse to interpersonal comparisons of utility, the Pareto conditions will not obtain. It is simply not true that at least one person will benefit, and that no one will be harmed. It may well be that less damage will occur under this set of suppositions than others, but it seems farfetched to suppose that no one at all will come to grief. There are, for example, the rich, who will have less housing at their disposal.

We may assume that all of the poor gain more from the lower rents they pay than from the increases they must suffer due to a smaller supply of housing, but this cannot apply to the well off. Further, what about the landlords? They are people too. Their well-being must also be factored into our social welfare equation. Yet it would be the rare interventionist who would be courageous enough to assert that no harm would come to them. If so, there would have been no need for compulsory rent control in the first place. The landlords themselves would have instituted a plan of this sort on a voluntary basis.

## 2.2. Minimum wage legislation

The case against wage minima is equally straightforward. By prohibiting employment contracts which stipulate wages below a given point, any point, there are bound to be some would-be workers with productivity lower than that level who will be rendered unemployable. For example, if there are unskilled laborers with marginal revenue products, of, say, $2 per hour, and the minimum wage level stipulated by law is $5 per hour, then any employer foolish enough to hire such a person would lose $3 per hour. People of this sort, then, are in effect rendered unemployable by this legislation.[6]

Some might object that $2 per hour is an "unconscionable" salary, and laborers would be better off with nothing than with that amount. For with no wage at all, they could avail themselves of unemployment insurance payments, and/or welfare subsidies. Such a package might well amount to more than $80 per week (40 hours X $2 per hour), minus taxes, especially when the disutility of work is taken into account.

The only problem with this objection is that it violates the usual ceteris paribus assumptions. Other things are not being held equal when we compare the welfare of our worker with and without and without me minimum wage law in operation. Specifically, payments from government are being allowed to vary, and this need-lessly complicates the issue. In order to see more clearly the exact effects of this legislation, we must hold everything else constant, particularly side payments of the sort we have been discussing. This can be done in two ways: by assuming either that these "benefits"[7] do not exist at all, or that if they exist, they apply, somehow, whether or not the person is employed.

This is a difficult point to articulate, since the law specifies that unemployment and welfare payments shall not be made when the worker has a job. Legislatures may indeed make such stipulations, and often they do. But we cannot allow them to "repeal" the ceteris paribus requirement. That is, even though it is illegal for employed workers to avail themselves of these government "benefits," we have to act as if it is possible, even if only for the sake of argument, in order to hold other things equal. Otherwise, it is impossible to accurately assess the true effects of minimum wage legislation (see Table 1).

The unsophisticated advocates of wage minima compare the northwest and the southeast quadrants; since $100 is preferable to $80, they conclude that the minimum wage law is beneficial, at least to poor unskilled workers. But this, as we have seen, is to make a comparison where other things are not equal; thus, it does not follow that the law benefits the poor. A more rational comparison is between the northwest and the northeast quadrants, and/or the southwest and southeast. There, no matter how one twists and turns, $180 is an improvement over $100 (in the presence of side payments) just as is $80 over $0 (in their absence).

Table 1.

| | Minimum wage law exists | |
| Welfare, unemployment benefits exist | Yes | No |
|---|---|---|
| Yes | job = $0<br>benefits = $100<br>total = $100 | job = $80<br>benefits = $100<br>total = $180 |
| No | job = $0<br>benefits = $0<br>total = $0 | job = $80<br>benefits = $0<br>total = $80 |

*Note.* Assumptions: hours of work, 40 per week; pay if working, $2 per hour; benefits, whether working or not, $100.

However, there is a more sophisticated objection to the minimum wage law. It is that some empirical studies have shown no unemployment effects of this legislation.[8] It is as if employers have a vertical demand curve for workers: no matter how high the wage, at least within the limits occupied by the typical minima, firms are willing to hire the same number of laborers.[9]

Let us follow the same procedure as before and concede to the critics such as Card and Krueger that the minimum wage law does not have any serious unemployment effects, or even, in the extreme case, none at all. Namely, we stipulate that employers are operating on the basis of a demand curve for this sort of labor of zero elasticity. One could hardly go further in the direction of accommodating the Card-Krueger thesis. Yet, even under these very constrained and unlikely assumptions, the Rothbardian reconstruction of utility and welfare economics cannot be denied. That is, it precludes us from concluding that the minimum wage can enhance social welfare. For even if not a single solitary worker loses his job due to the minimum wage, nor do any laborers who would have been hired in its absence fail to achieve employment status, there will still be at least one person who will lose out as a result of this enactment: the employer who is forced to pay more than he otherwise need have done. We simply cannot say him "nay." The welfare of the owner of the firm (to say nothing of that of his customers) is clearly decreased by this law. Without interpersonal comparisons of utility, it is impossible to conclude that society has benefitted.

## 2.3. Tariffs

If the economic cases against rent control and the minimum wage law are compelling, the same holds true for international[10] trade restrictions.[11]

At the most unsophisticated level, free trade is opposed out of fear that foreigners will take away domestic jobs, either because of sheer efficiency (e.g.

Japan) or willingness to work for very low wages (e.g. Mexico, Bangladesh, etc.). But this argument is easily overcome-at least on an intellectual plane-by resort to the basic proofs concerning comparative advantage, as opposed to absolute advantage.

With very few exceptions indeed, no one, even the most ardent protectionist, really opposes trade of, say, maple syrup for tropical fruit. Even the mercantilists realize it would be foolish for us to grow bananas in hot houses and for the Costa Ricans to house maple trees in gigantic refrigerators. Let us produce enough maple syrup for both countries; let the Costa Ricans produce a likewise amount of bananas; we can each specialize in what we do best, trade with each other, to mutual benefit.[12]

But when it comes to Japan, for instance, a country which is presumed able to outcompete us not just in one or a few industries, but in virtually every one of them, then all bets are off. The free traders may win the debates, but the hearts and minds of the public tend to support protectionism. There are, however, any number of simple numerical examples which show that even though one country may be more efficient at producing all goods than another, it will still be beneficial for them to trade. For while Japan, say, may have an absolute advantage in all goods compared to the US,[13] it will almost of necessity be better in some than in others. Suppose, for example, that Japan can produce 200 stereo sets and 100 bushels of wheat in a given time (a "day"), while America can produce 5 of the former and 75 of the latter. Then, surely, it would enrich both countries if Japan specialized in stereos and America in wheat. We could both have more of each of these commodities in this way (see Table 2).

Japan has an absolute advantage in both commodities and a comparative advantage in stereos. The US has an absolute advantage in neither, but a comparative advantage in wheat. With no trade, the part of the world consisting of these two countries has 175 units of wheat and 205 stereos, for a total of 380; Japanese GDP is 300 and American is 80, also for a total of 380. With free trade, however, total product rises from 380 to 550. The presumption is that this will be shared in such a way so as to improve the welfare of each, otherwise cooperation will not occur.[14]

*Table 2.*

| Commodity | Japan | US | Total |
|---|---|---|---|
| Wheat | 100 | 75 | 175 |
| Stereos | 200 | 5 | 205 |
| GDP, no trade | 300 | 80 | 380 |
| GDP, trade | 400 | 150 | 550 |

*Note.* Assumptions: two countries, two goods, two 'days', commodities are defined in such a way as to have equal value in equilibrium.

So much for the arguments against the unsophisticated opposition to free trade.[15] In sharp contrast, there is a view that is popular with certain elements of the economics profession, based on the so-called "rational tariff models." Here, the contention is that if our import taxes are set carefully enough, they can in effect garner monopoly power for US industry, since with the correct external "pricing mechanism" we are a large enough part of world trade to accomplish this task.

The problems with this view are serious. First is the practical one that our past experience with governmental central planning, in the US and elsewhere (Boettke, 1994), does not encourage the belief that the "optimal tariffs" will be able to be achieved. The Public Choice School (Tullock, 1980a, 1980b) has done yeoman work in showing that tariff or tax rates are not set so as to conform with the theory of economists as to what constitutes the "public good." Rather, they are a result of a political tug of war labeled "rent seeking."[16]

Second is the difficulty that this initiative is incompatible with other elements of the mainstream economist's political program. Central to this is their contention that the only desideratum is the enhancement of economic welfare, or wealth, and that monopoly is anathema to this project. But in the "optimal tariff" movement, they are violating not one but both strictures: here they seek to utilize monopoly "power," in the full realization that while US wealth will be increased, it will come at the cost of a diminution elsewhere. Further, and perhaps even more contrary to their theory, the US gains will be more than matched by the loss to foreigners. This is hardly a perspective one could have expected would garner much support within the profession.

Notwithstanding the foregoing, we shall put the best face on trade prohibitions as possible, as is our wont, lest we be accused of trafficking in straw men. In this case, there are two separate scenarios. First, we assume that the unsophisticated opponents of free trade are correct: foreigners, Japanese, Mexicans, whoever, will "steal" our jobs-by out-producing us, and outcompeting[17] us. Does it follow that tariffs and quotas will improve social welfare? Not a bit of it. For if we interfere with international trade, we make at least two people-those who would otherwise have conducted the trade-worse off. Without recourse to interpersonal comparisons of utility, there is no way to scientifically determine that the gains (to the prohibitors) exceed these losses.

Second, we assume that the welfare of foreigners for some reason does not enter into our calculations, and that the theory of monopoly which underlies optimal tariffs is thus unobjectionable.[18] Under these conditions, it would appear that the proposal will indeed enhance social welfare.

But any such conclusion again reckons in the absence of Rothbard's contribution. Again, his reconstruction of utility and welfare economics stands like a sentry, ready to repel invasions. For, as before, there will be at least two erstwhile traders who will be balked in their goal by interventionism. They will be rendered worse off. And there is nothing in the annals of value free scientific economics which can prove that their misfortune is of lesser moment than the gains the optimal external monopolists can garner.

## 2.4. Drugs

The debate over the legalization of addictive drugs is largely, but not totally, a dispute over the shape of the demand curve. It is uncontroversial (at least in economic quarters) that at present the high price of these materials is due to their very prohibition. Supplies are limited, and hence prices high, because of the danger-from the police and other competing gangs-of bringing to market a controlled substance. Marijuana, for example, is nothing more than a rather hardy weed; ordinarily, cigarettes made out of it would undoubtedly be cheaper than those fashioned from tobacco. Under legalization, supplies would as a result be vastly enhanced.

What then of the demand side? Here, the controversy rages fiercely. Some – mostly those who favor legalization – assert that the lowered prices would scarcely change the amount demanded. For them, decriminalization would be an unrelieved blessing. At the lower legal prices, addicts would not have to rob, kill and prostitute themselves to buy a fix. They could do so for a song. There would be no more violence attendant upon this industry than now prevails with regard to alcohol. Indeed, the parallels between drugs and booze are very strong. Under prohibition, alcohol production was also a very violent undertaking. At present, it is not. Similarly, as with impure "bathtub gin," the impurities, and lack of quality control, would also end as bona fide businesses replaced the fly by nights.[19]

Others-mostly those who oppose legalization-claim that all this might come about, if it does, only at the cost of addicting an exceedingly large percentage of the American public. Their view is that this latter scenario is far too likely, and far too deleterious if it comes about, to risk on behalf of the nebulous benefits, if any, of legalization.

Again, we assume the worst case scenario for economic freedom. We posit, that is, that were these drugs allowed on the market, nothing less than chaos would ensue. And we ask, can value free economics justify prohibition? We answer, it can, but only if the benefits to prohibited buyers and sellers can be ignored. And since they cannot be discounted, given the illegitimacy of interpersonal comparisons of utility, we persist in concluding, with Rothbard, that whatever its merits, our present policy on drugs cannot be defended on the basis of the dismal science.

Let us summarize this section of the paper. We have posited the best case scenario for intervention; maximum rents do not lead to a diminution of housing; increases in the mandated wage do not lead to additional unemployment; tariffs do not disrupt the international division of labor; drug legalization does lead to a vast increase in addiction rates. We have shown that despite this, Rothbard's reconstruction of utility and welfare economics stands as a barrier against the conclusion that social welfare can be increased by enacting such legislation.

Have we demonstrated too much? Have we proven it irrational to support laws such as rent control, minimum wage, tariffs and drug prohibition? Not at all. It is still possible to favor these interventionistic laws, given these heroic assumptions, or even in their absence, for that matter. But this is possible only on normative grounds. As value free economists attempting to sketch out the conditions for welfare maximization, we cannot logically arrive at any such conclusion.

Let us consider one more objection. Can our own logic be turned around against us in our defense of laissez faire? That is, we have defended markets on the ground that no interference with them can be shown in a value free manner to benefit societal welfare. But suppose we start with interventionism as the basis of our analysis. We could then show, utilizing our same Rothbardian methodology, that no forced change from that status quo could unambiguously benefit everyone. This is so because any change is bound to hurt someone. For example, if rent control is rescinded, there will presumably be at least one tenant who can object on the ground that he will be made worse off. Thus, without interpersonal comparisons of utility, we cannot claim an unambiguous increase in the general welfare.

Where, then, is the proper starting point? Strictly speaking, that is not a matter of positive but rather of normative economics. Hence, it must remain outside of our present concerns.

However, the following can still be said, and said once again: "the free market benefits all its participants" (Rothbard, 1977: 27). Consider the tenant who benefits from rent control, and would lose out from its repeal. Whatever he is, he is not a participant in the free market, for rent control is simply incompatible with this system.

## 3. Forcing Commercial Interactions

We have seen that even under the most positive assumptions possible, the cases for rent control, minimum wage, international trade restrictions and drug prohibitions cannot pass muster under the conditions adumbrated by Rothbard.

But these are not the most serious challenges that can be offered up against his reconstruction of welfare economics. For the overwhelming majority of economists reject these four public policies.[20] There is another set of cases, much more popular within the profession, which also cut against the grain of Rothbard's analysis.

Here, the contention concerns not commercial arrangements which are deemed improper by legislative bodies, but rather interactions which fail to take place in the market. That is, instead of maintaining that trades should not take place in order to enhance economic welfare, it is now argued that trades should be forced upon unwilling participants, to this end.

27

Most economists will readily see the error of supposing that the prohibition of trade will improve social welfare. Interestingly enough, the obverse does not hold. That is, there are very few practitioners of the dismal science who acknowledge that if prohibiting trade cannot enhance the welfare of society, neither will forced trade achieve this end. It is to this point that we now turn. Under this rubric we consider three different proposals: monopoly, public goods and externalities, and welfare.

## 3.1. Monopoly

There are two sorts of entities that are conventionally called "monopoly." Somewhat surprisingly, they have nothing at all in common. They are alike as fish and bicycles. The conflation between them, resulting from a sort of definitional laziness, has caused no end of trouble both in public policy analysis and theoretical economics. It has long kept us from thinking clearly about the issues involved.

The first kind of monopoly is an exclusive state grant of privilege to a favored business. Anyone who tries to compete with this type of monopolist goes to jail. In olden times, the king would give a boon of this sort to a preferred duke, or earl, or other nobleman, or warrior. This person would have the monopoly over the sale of salt, or candles, or wine, or sugar, or textiles, in a certain geographical area. It was illegal to compete with this monopolist. Anyone doing so was subject to the full penalties of the law. In the modern era, recipients of such legal protection include the post office, "utilities" such as electric and gas, and, for a time, telephone service, as well as taxicabs, buses, and insurance in certain jurisdictions.

The second kind of "monopoly" really does not deserve that denigration. A "monopolist" of this sort receives no privileged status from the government. Instead, he competes for a market, and succeeds, to a degree greater than allowed for by the theory of perfect competition of neoclassical economics. This view, sometimes called the structuralist view of competition, claims that if a company's sales, or employment, or shipments, or inputs, is too great a proportion of the industry of which it is assigned,[21] then it is guilty of anticompetitive behavior. Kellogg, IBM, Alcoa Aluminum, Microsoft are all very successful companies which have excessively high "concentration ratios," defined on the basis of this theory. Thus, they have all run afoul of our antitrust laws,[22] which are predicated upon these neoclassical notions of competitive behavior.

There is no doubt whatsoever that monopoly of the first sort is incompatible with the Rothbardian insight into the maximization of social welfare. A would-be candle manufacturer in olden times, or a "gypsy" cab driver who wants to compete with the "yellow" or "licensed" taxis, is precluded by law from doing so. Trades between this person and all potential customers are therefore ruled out of court-with a resultant loss in utility. If all market participation enhances welfare, and if antitrust laws ban such commercial interaction, then they lower the level of utility that society would otherwise have obtained.

"Monopoly" of the second sort is a very different matter. So different that we shall cease to speak of it as "monopoly" at all, and instead call it "Large Firms,"[23] shorthand for "firms which have a larger proportion of markets than is compatible with neoclassical competition theory." Why is this very different? For one thing, it is crucial how the Enormity was achieved. If this was done through prohibiting competition, well and good, that is real monopoly. But if accomplished by offering a better product at a lower price, with more service, reliability, quality, superior foresight, ability to attract customers and a work force, then at each point in its rise from a small firm to a gigantic one, it conferred satisfaction on all the people with whom it dealt.

For another, neoclassicists notwithstanding, mere Large Size is irrelevant to market satisfaction. What are their arguments to the contrary? They maintain that when there are numerous firms in an industry, each with a very small market share, then all of them will interpret the market demand (D) they face as absolutely elastic, or flat. This being the case, resources will be allocated at point C (for "competitive") on Figure 1.

However, when a few firms become large enough, or, in the extreme, there is only one remaining, then the dreaded "Monopoly" will occur. Now each of the few firms, or the One Big One, will not interpret the demand curve as infinitely elastic. Rather, it will be seen as it actually is (Figure 2), which will give rise to a marginal revenue curve below it. When marginal revenue and marginal costs are equated, at point Qm, we arrive at the familiar neoclassical conclusion that with "Monopoly" prices will be higher (Pm), quantity less (Qm), and excess profits (APmMB) and dead weight loss (DMC) will arise so as to misallocate resources.

This is neither the time nor the place to go into a full scale critique of this model.[24] We shall content ourselves by mentioning only those fallacies which pertain to Rothbard's "Reconstruction."

First, Figure 2, and the analysis which accompanies it, is no more than an exercise in interpersonal comparisons of utility. Consider the quantity Qc – Qm. According to the mainstream viewpoint, consumers value this quantity of the good to the extent depicted by the area under their demand curve, bounded by Qc and Om.[25] Producers, for their part, can manufacture this amount Qc – Qm of the good at a cost of only the area under the marginal cost curve, between these two points. The difference between the two areas is the Dead Weight Loss (DMC). But cost means opportunities foregone, and only the economic actor himself can ever know what this is. Similarly for demand, which includes, at least potentially, consumers' surplus. Both are notions of subjective utility. To compare them is thus to engage in the forbidden comparison of utility on an interpersonal basis.[26] What the neo-classicals are saying, in effect, is that the amount of good Qc – Qm is worth more to buyers than to sellers. How can they know that, unless they have information about the utility that each places on this amount of good, and the ability to compare them?

Second, there is the little matter of forced exchange. In this regard, the logical positivists who occupy the mainstream of the economics profession go far past the Austrian assertion. In the latter view, there are (ex ante) mutual gains from trade. And that is all. But the former far surpass this affirmation with the claim that forced trades can also benefit both parties. They in effect maintain that if the buyers and the sellers who are now trading for the amount Qm, can somehow be forced to trade for an additional amount, Qc – Qm, further gains to both sides will accrue.[27] Here, they leave the realm of reality and enter one of magic, a world that one would have thought logical positivists would eschew with all their might. How can they know any such thing? If it were true, why wouldn't the two trading partners engage in further trades on their own?

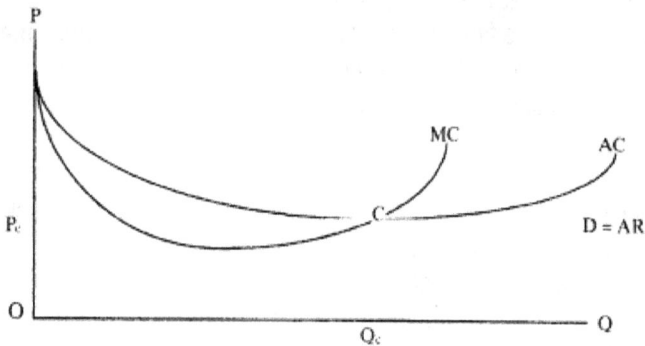

*Figure 1.*

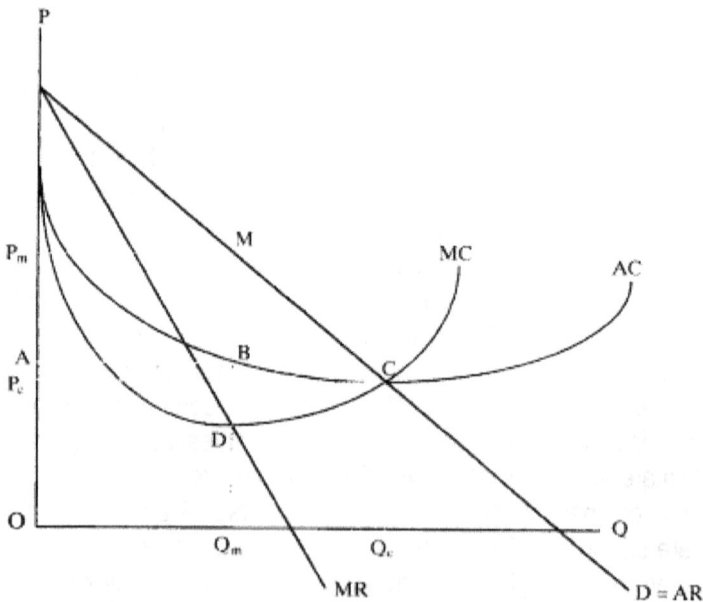

*Figure 2.*

In their reply to this challenge they contrast the flat demand curves facing the perfect competitor with the market demand curve of intermediate elasticity which confronts the Big Firm (e.g. "monopolist"). But this argument must be rejected if only because of its reliance on interpersonal comparisons of utility.

Even apart from this is the fact that their analysis relies on a level of ignorance which is totally incompatible with their assumptions about perfect competition. In the perfectly competitive model, information is supposedly costless. That implies, if it implies anything, that transaction costs are zero. Well, with this state of affairs, why don't the numerous perfect competitors band together and act like a Giant? And if not that, why don't they at least realize that all put together, they face a downward, not an infinitely elastic demand curve?

## 3.2. Public goods

Externalities are another fertile neoclassical ground for the support of forced trades. The argument is that there are some goods which, by their very nature, are not amenable to production through markets. Due to this "market failure," if we want to make these items available, only the government can bring about such a satis-factory state of affairs.

Why has the market "failed"? For two reasons: non-excludability and non-rivalrousness. The former problem is that there are certain products which, when once produced, are impossible (or very expensive) to confine to those who have purchased them. But if the buyers of this service as well as the non-buyers may avail themselves of it, why should anyone make the purchase? Rather, everyone will attempt to "free ride" on the efforts and payments of the others. If each person adopts such a "wait and see" policy, no one will undertake production in the first place. Friedman (1962) gives an illustration of this mindset when he discusses the "neighborhood effect" or "externality" of the poor:

> It can be argued that private charity is insufficient because the benefits from it accrue to people other than those who make the gifts-again, a neighborhood effect. I am distressed by the sight of poverty; I am benefitted by its alleviation; but I am benefitted equally whether I or someone else pays for its alleviation; the benefits of other people's charity therefore partly accrue to me. To put it differently, we might all of us be willing to contribute to the relief of poverty, provided everyone else did. We might not be willing to contribute to the same amount without such assurance. In small communities, public pressures can suffice to realize the proviso even with private charity. In the large impersonal communities that are increasingly coming to dominate our society, it is much more difficult for it to do so (p. 191).

Other examples include defense, parks and lighthouses.[28] In all of these cases, everyone benefits, because of the intrinsically public nature of the good or service; non-payers as well as payers.

The second is non-rivalrousness. Here, the point is that even if we could somehow exclude non-purchasers from enjoying the product, we still should not do so if we want to maximize wealth, or welfare, or utility, or whatever flavor of the month is occupying the thoughts of the neoclassicals. Why not? Because it is costless to allow everyone to utilize items with this characteristic. A typical example of this "market failure" is the radio or television broadcast. If you tune in, this discomforts me not at all; if I tune in, not only does your utility not decrease, you are extremely unlikely to even know that I am also enjoying the program. So why stop anyone from availing himself of an essentially costless service? If you value the broadcast even at the rate of only $.05 per hour, and are charged $.50 per hour for the privilege, then you do without. And society fails to create $.45 worth of wealth per hour, which it could have done at zero marginal cost.

Since there are two criteria used here, excludability and rivalrousness, each of which admits of two states of affairs (presence or absence), this yields a two by two matrix (see Table 3). Let us give examples of each, the better to explicate the doctrines now under consideration. Combination 1 is the most straightforward. Here, neither source of "market failure" is present. It is possible (very cheap, costless) to exclude non-payers from use, and rivalrousness is present. Consider a hot dog. You can be excluded from eating it if you don't pay for it: it is against the law to do so, and you will be thrown in jail if you eat a hot dog you have not purchased.[29] Further, the hot dog is rivalrous: if you eat it, I can't have it, and if I eat it, you are necessarily precluded from doing so. For any entrant into this first category, even the neoclassicals concede that the market can handle production.

However, each of the other three raise problems of "market failure." Take section 2. Here, rivalrousness is not a problem, but excludability is. An instance of this would be parks. It is conceded by the neoclassical advocates of the "market failure" doctrine that a fee can sometimes be charged for admission, as in the case of Disneyland. However, the real estate prices in the surrounding areas typically rise, and the developer has no way of capturing these benefits all for himself. Hence, according to the argument, a lower than optimal number of parks will be built under laissez faire capitalism.

Now consider compartment 3. Here, excludability is not a problem, but rivalrousness is. The broadcast fits this description, because while it is easy to exclude-with jamming devices which can be overridden for a fee-it would be economically inefficient to do so, since the marginal viewer or listener costs no one anything.

Group 4 is very clear cut. Both excludability and rivalrousness present difficulties. No one can be excluded from national defense. If an antiballistic missile or a submarine protects you and your home, it also does so for your neighbor. The incidence of free riding would be so serious, it is maintained, that no firm could collect money to protect people from a foreign invader. Nor is any rivalrousness involved. If your neighbor is already protected under the defense umbrella, it costs not a penny more to include you as well. You can enjoy being defended without reducing his defense, and vice versa. Therefore, even if you could somehow be excluded (which is impossible) this should not be done to you. Doing it would be inefficient, in that you would now not be obtaining a benefit the provision of which harms no one else; it would be in direct contravention of the rule of the Pareto Optimum: it is always efficient to undertake an act if at least one person gains thereby, and no one else loses.

Table 3.

| Rivalrousness | Excludability | |
| --- | --- | --- |
| | Yes | No |
| Yes | 1 | 2 |
| No | 3 | 4 |

Another way to articulate this philosophical vision is through highways and streets. In order to do this we must make two assumptions.

First, an empty highway or street is a non-rival good. You are driving along, and another rider appears about a quarter mile away. You do not impede him; he does not impede you. Neither of you rivals the other for use of the thoroughfare. You can each use it without dis-accommodating the other even in the slightest. In contrast, busy highways and streets are rival goods. Each motorist gets in the way of every other. They all slow each other down, to say nothing of increasing the overall accident rate.

Second, it is possible to exclude people from highway use by setting up toll stations. If they do not pay, they cannot enter. If they try to do so anyway, a severe fine will be imposed upon them with practically a 100 percent chance of being caught. However, it is not possible to exclude people from city streets. Tollways would be impossibly numerous. This would slow traffic down to a standstill. Given these assumptions, it is again possible to illustrate the neoclassical case against the market (see Table 4). Let us consider each of the alternatives in turn. First, according to this schema, the busy highway, somewhat paradoxically, is actually a candidate for privatization,[30] at least insofar as excludability and rivalrousness are concerned. For a road full of vehicles is certainly a rivalrous one. And, by stipulation, it is not only possible but actually feasible to exclude non-payers from access. "Market failure" does not exist in this case, but it does in the other three.

Second, the busy city street. This must inevitably be a public good, but only because of excludability; if non-paying vehicles cannot be precluded, no private enterprise could ever make a go of it. But "market failure" arises due to this factor alone. As far as rivalrousness is concerned, there is no problem. For under crowded conditions, there is no rivalry for the service provided by the streets.

Third, the empty highway. Here we have the reverse of the previous case. Again there is "market failure" and thus the need for public management and control, but now the cause is the very opposite: rivalrousness, not excludability. The latter is not a problem, because we have stipulated that toll booths, even private ones, could work on limited access highways. But now the question arises as to whether or not they should be employed, if efficiency is our goal. And the answer emanating from mainstream economists is that they should not be, since no one gets in anyone else's way on an empty highway. Precluding people from enjoying a benefit which costs no one anything is a violation of the Pareto rule.

*Table 4.*

| Rivalrousness | Excludability | |
| | Yes | No |
| --- | --- | --- |
| Yes | 1. busy highway | 2. busy city street |
| No | 3. empty highway | 4. empty city street |

Fourth, the empty city street. This, too, is a public good, but now for both reasons. No rivalrousness comes into play since the amenity is empty. No one slows down anyone else, nor endangers him. Excludability is also operational, since it would imply that thoroughfares could no longer serve as traffic conduits.

Again, this is neither the time nor place for a full scale attack on all of the logical fallacies committed by this argument.[31] Let us confine ourselves to a broad overview of the critique, with particular attention to Rothbard's contribution.

As far as roads are concerned, the argument is problematic on two grounds. First, it is by no means necessary to stipulate that the market cannot supply city street services. On the contrary, one way this can be done is by supplying them freely; as a "loss leader" in order to sell other goods. This is common practice in all modern shopping malls. Car parking, and road usage all around the complex, are usually gratis, the better to entice the shopper onto the premises. Certainly, use of the pedestrian promenades is supplied at no cost to the shoppers. As well, it is entirely feasible to exclude non-payers by charging prices for both motorists and pedestrians on ordinary city streets. The horror scenario depicted by the road socialists (Block, 1996) depicts a toll booth in front of each and every house, dozens per block. But this is by no means necessary. One alternative is the system used in Singapore, where motorists purchase color coded monthly or yearly permits, which allow them access to various parts of the city, at various times of the day or days of the week. Another is for private enterprise to adopt the universal product code for automobiles, the same system used to keep track of groceries.

Second, there are difficulties with the charge of rivalrousness. This applies both on roads as well as all else. Rivalrousness implies that the costs of providing a good or service are zero. But this proves far too much. For virtually all goods fit this bill, not merely the few nominated by the neoclassicals as public goods. For example, consider any product for which it can be said that there are vacancies: ball parks, theaters, hotels, apartment houses, car rental agencies, steel mills, etc.

When extra capacity is available, by definition the costs of servicing the marginal customer are (virtually) zero. As with the empty road, no one gets in anyone else's way.

In this regard, Rothbard (1977) takes Baumol to task for his assertion,

> that parks are an example of 'collective wants' jointly consumed, since many individuals must consume them. Therefore, the government must supply this service. But going to a theater is even more joint, for all must go at the same time. Must all theaters therefore be nationalized and run by the government? Furthermore, in a broad view, all modern consumption depends on mass production methods for a wide market. There are no grounds by which Baumol can separate certain services and dub them 'examples of interdependence' or 'external economies.' What individuals could buy steel or automobiles or frozen foods, or almost anything else, if enough other individuals did not exist to demand them and make their mass-production methods worthwhile? Baumollian interdependences are all around us, and there is no rational way to isolate a few services and call them 'collective.' (p. 35)

Further, there is a way that a park owner can capture most, if not all, of the increased value of the surrounding real estate. All he need do-before anyone knows the future location of his park-is purchase the contiguous properties at their old, low, pre-park price.

But it is not merely true that numerous reductios can be fashioned to undermine this concept. It is also the case that the doctrine of rivalrousness is false. In order to see this, reflect on the Austrian notion that cost is inherently subjective. It consists of nothing more than opportunities foregone, and these can only be known by the economic actor himself. Take the theater owner. Why should we believe the claim of costlessness, or rivalrousness? The theater owner-as opposed to the outside commentator economist-certainly acts as if there are costs to him of admitting one more patron to the half empty theater. He would react with great outrage were someone to demand to be let in free on the ground that he would not disturb the viewing pleasure of the paying customers. If this cloven hoof were once to be admitted to the tent, it would of course be impossible to organize the theater as a profit making proposition. And if this is true for the theater owner, it applies as well to the proprietor of broadcast airwaves.

There are similar problems for national defense. What of the pacifist? How can we unambiguously conclude that defense is a benefit for him? The answer is, we cannot. If not, the Pareto rules no longer apply; it ceases to be true that at least one person gains and no one loses. By the very logic of the matter, the pacifist loses. Then, too, there is the issue of rivalrousness. The US government, powerful though it may be, is not omnipotent. This means that there will always be realistic scenarios where it can protect either citizen A or citizen B, but not both.[32]

As always, the "Reconstruction" stands as a barrier to government intervention even if all other arguments fail. For taxes are a forced transfer of funds. We cannot deduce mutual benefit, and hence an improvement in economic welfare, unless we eschew the unanimity rule, demonstrated preference, and ignore the illicit nature of interpersonal comparisons of utility.

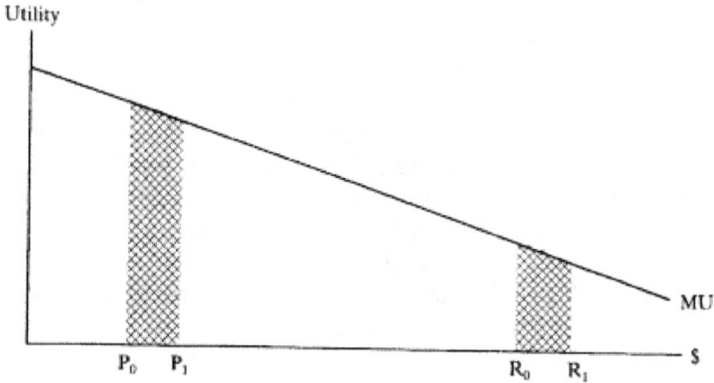

*Figure 3.*

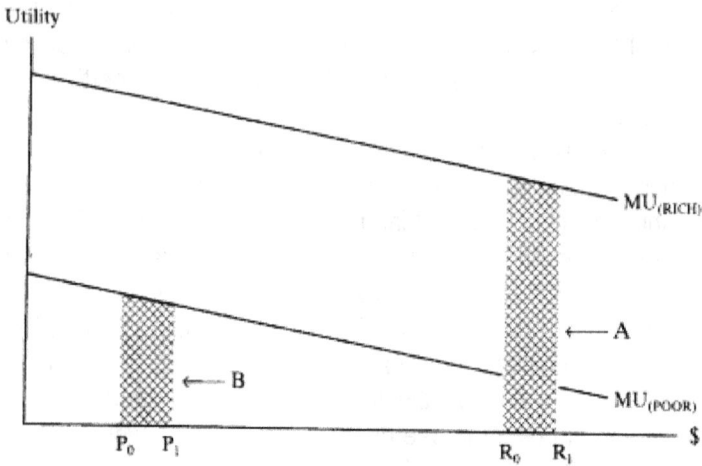

*Figure 4.*

## 3.3. Welfare

The economic case for governmental welfare is straightforward. There is diminishing marginal utility for all goods and services, each separately; this therefore applies to all goods taken together, e.g. money.

In Figure 3, we depict the geometrical relationship between marginal utility and money. It is a declining one, indicating that the richer one is, the less value is any additional dollar. Conversely, the poorer the person, the more valuable to him is his marginal wealth. That being the case, the neoclassical economist goes further and asserts that if we move a rich person from point $R_1$ to $R_0$ (e.g. take away from him

$1,000), and move a poor man from $P_0$ to $P_1$ (e.g. give him this $1,000) we can improve the lot of the latter more than we reduce the welfare of the former. This is because the area under the curve between $R_0$ and $R_1$ is smaller than that between $P_0$ and $P_1$. The difference between the two areas (the difference between how the poor and the rich man benefit from having that $1,000 in their possession) is a measure of the benefit to society from making this forced transfer.

Notwithstanding the 'beauty' and 'elegance' of this presentation, it suffers severely from deep flaws. First, the curve drawn in Figure 3 is based on cardinal, not ordinal utility. But this implies the existence of utils, a measured amount of utility, a manifest piece of nonsense. Second, even assuming the legitimacy of the foregoing, it makes the unsupported assumption that the cardinal utility functions of the rich and the poor are not only alike, but identical. But suppose that the rich had a higher diminishing marginal utility curve, as illustrated in Figure 4. Then, when money is transferred from rich to poor, 'society' loses the difference between area A and B. While it is of course conceivable that the wealthy and the impoverished share the same diminishing marginal utility curves, and even that the one for the latter is higher than the one for the former, there is nothing in all of value free economics incompatible with the relationship as depicted in Figure 4. Third, there are disincentive effects (Murray, 1984). When money is taken from Peter to pay Paul, both have reduced incentives to earn income, compared to the status quo ante. Paul knows his subsidy is predicated upon his poverty; he has less of an incentive to extricate himself from this condition than otherwise. Peter will invest resources in an attempt to evade or avoid the payment; failing that, his leisure-labor allocation will change, in the direction of the former.

And again as before the Rothbardian insights stand as a 'goalie of last resort'. Even if there were no disincentive effects, even if rich and poor share the same utility functions, even if cardinal utility is valid; still, the unanimity assumption-central to Rothbard's analysis-has been breached. If even one rich person objects to the procedure, it cannot be shown as a clear gain in utility or welfare.

## 4. Conclusion

We have analyzed four cases where the majority of economists have advocated prohibiting trades: rent control, minimum wage, tariffs and drugs. Similarly, we have examined three arguments for forcing trades: monopoly, externalities and public goods, and welfare. We have found none of them convincing, and all of them susceptible to Rothbard's "Reconstruction" arguments.

The moderation of the Austrians, it should be clear by now, consists of opposing both sets of interventions into the free market place.

Rothbard (1977) considers the mainstream economists,

... highly inconsistent. On the one hand, action cannot be left up to voluntary individual choice because the wicked free rider might shirk and obtain benefits without payment. On the other hand, individuals are often denounced because people will not do enough to benefit free riders .... Surely the sensible course is neither to penalize the free rider nor to grant him special privilege. This would also be the only solution consistent with the unanimity rule and demonstrated preference. (p. 36)

Thus the Austrian opposition to both interventions amounts to a sort of "golden mean," or intermediate position.


## NOTES

1. For material generally supportive of this view, see Arnold (1982), Benson (1986), Cordato (1992), Gordon (1993), McGee (1993), Machan (1989), Mack (1978).

2. See on this North (1990), Pasour (1996).

3. Perhaps this is because the overwhelming majority of economists take this position, and for some strange reason do not regard themselves as interventionists.

4. For the conventional critique, see Baird (1980), Block (1993b), Friedman and Stigler (1981), Hazlitt (1979), Johnson (1982), Salins (1980), Tucker (1990).

5. For the case in favor of rent control, not on the grounds articulated in the text, see Kristof (1964), Marcuse (1979), Rapkin (1966). These studies were all commissioned by the rent control authorities in New York City, and used to support the continuation of this policy, surely one of the most egregious cases of the prostitution of economics for economic and/or political gain.

6. This can be interpreted as a positive, as well as a normative claim. In the former sense, it amounts to the assertion that this law leads to unemployment. Given the implicit assumption that joblessness is an unwelcome result, the statement in the text is a positive one. For the view that unemployment is the known and welcome result of this legislation, see Higgs (1995).

7. They are at best beneficial only to the recipient. To the taxpayer, forced to finance them, they are anything but. For the view that welfare payments, paradoxically, harm recipients as well, at least in the long run, see Murray (1984), Tucker (1984).

8. Card and Krueger (1994).

9. The Card thesis has not gone unchallenged (Becker, 1995). But this is more than passing curious, in that the critique has emanated from neoclassical economists. According to their own doctrine, economic laws are only tentative, dependent upon the latest empirical evidence. To be sure, economic theory indicates that unemployment will result from minimum wages. But for them this is not apodictic as it is for the Austrians. On the contrary, it is merely a theory which can be falsified or not. True, there have been many empirical 'tests' of this theory which have substantiated it. But on the other hand, there have been a few which have failed to do so. And now, along comes Card with yet another examination of the hypothesis (there being no such thing as an economic "law" in the logical positivist lexicon) offering yet another counter-example to the usual presumption.

The neoclassical logical positivists break up into two groups when faced with this new evidence. Some will accept it without too much demur. Their future research may try to discern why it is that on some occasions the minimum wage leads to unemployment, while on others it does not. These are the true neoclassicals. But others do not accept it at all. They work with great alacrity to uncover flaws in the research purporting to show no connection between wage minima and unemployment. About this second group it can be said "Scratch a neoclassical economist and find an Austrian." For they interpret the relationship between minimum wage legislation and joblessness for the unskilled not merely as a hypothesis, which may or may not be true, or may be true at some times and places but not at others, but rather as a praxeological law which is true based on the very logic of the case. Just like the Austrians.

10. Rothbard (1970) makes the telling point that the division between intra- and international trade is a superficial one. Trade is trade is trade. Crossing national borders, apart from posing additional institutional barriers on commerce, is theoretically uninteresting.

11. According to several surveys (Block and Walker, 1988; Frey et al., 1984), opposition to these three laws commands the greatest consensus in the economics profession out of 27 issues posed.

12. Of course, it is always possible to object that free trade in these two commodities will play havoc with American banana production and with jobs in the Costa Rican maple syrup industry. Somehow, however, these problems are lost sight of in the typical discussion.

13. A rather unrealistic assumption made solely to show the case for free trade even under this 'worst case' scenario.

14. Just for simplicity, we abstract from the possibility that people will not act as nations.

15. The public policy implication of the foregoing is not that the US government negotiate with its counterparts elsewhere for treaties such as those undergirding the North American Free Trade Agreement, or the European Community. (Actually, the former is a misnomer as these arrangements are really customs unions, not free trade compacts.) Rather, the implication is for a unilateral declaration of free trade with all the nations of the world. For if free trade is the desideratum, why limit it to just a few countries?

16. This is an unfortunate terminology, which gratuitously disparages the ancient and honorable profession of seeking rents.

17. There is so much wrong in this scenario it is difficult to take it seriously. First of all, competing is a way of cooperating. The market is the only possible way to organize economic activity amongst billions of people (Mises, 1981). Secondly, it is not true that there are only so many jobs which can be done, and if foreigners (or new technology, etc.) do some of them, there will be fewer remaining for us. On the contrary, as long as there is scarcity, that is, as long as we want more than we have, there will always be employment slots open to allow us to satisfy our unmet needs.

18. We relax this assumption below.

19. On this see Boaz (1990), Friedman (1989), Hamowy (1987), Szasz (1985), Thornton (1991).

20. This holds true at least for the first three of these enactments, if not the fourth.

21. Since the line delimiting one industry from another is an arbitrary one, this decision is also arbitrary.

22. For a view compatible with the total repeal of antitrust law, see Armentano (1972, 1982, 1991), Block (1977, 1982, 1994), High (1985), Mises (1963), Rothbard (1970), Woolridge (1970). For a perspective somewhat critical of antitrust on efficiency grounds, but

which stops far short of calling for total repeal, see Bork (1978), Brozen (1982), Posner (1976), Stigler (1968), Telser (1987).

23. Or Large Size, or Bigness, or Giant or Enormous.

24. See Armentano (1972, 1982, 1991), Block (1977, 1982, 1994), High (1985), Mises (1963), Rothbard (1970), Woolridge (1970).

25. Since we are measuring values, we are now in the realm of cardinal utility, another violation of the Rothbardian "Reconstruction."

26. Ever since the publication of Robbins (1935, 1938) the profession has been placed on notice as to the illegitimacy of this notion. Most economists, unfortunately, have not yet incorporated this into their analysis. They have implicitly violated it, as shown in this article with the three examples, in the present section. But they have also explicitly violated it, even very recently. For example, Kranich states (1994: 178), "Compensation according to effort is based on the moral intuition that two people incurring equal disutility deserve equal rewards. *It thus relies on the presumption that utility is interpersonally comparable*" (emphasis added).

27. Here is an attempt at a reductio ad absurdum of this failure to trade from my personal life. Dick Francis is one of my favorite "escape" novelists. For roughly the last three decades, he has published a novel at the rate of about one per year. I garnered great consumer's surplus from each of these novels. As a result, he has set up an expectation of mine that he would continue to publish a riveting sequel for the foreseeable future. But he has slackened off in the last few years. He is obviously a Monopolistic Withholder. He has written $OQm$ novels, but has failed to carry through with a further $QmQc$, which, in my opinion, amounts to a new episode every 12 months, based on his past practice. Given his failure to maintain his quota, he is clearly taking advantage of me and his other fans. The dead weight loss of his absent novels is enormous. The utility I would derive out of his next few efforts is clearly greater than any disutility he might have in writing them. And surely when we incorporate the unhappiness of Francis' many other fans, the course of public policy is clear: the antitrust division must force him to publish many more stories! If he refuses, he would be in contempt of the law, and they must incarcerate him. (Lest I be confused with a neoclassical economist, I must now clearly state that this public policy analysis is purely tongue in cheek.)

28. For a critique of lighthouses as a good example of a public good, but not, however, unfortunately for a renunciation of the whole idea, see Coase (1974).

29. In the novel *Les Miserables* by Victor Hugo, one of the characters stole a loaf of bread and was severely punished for this crime. The author clearly opposed this, as do all other well meaning "progressives." If the law were ever changed so as to allow people to seize products of this sort from one another without criminal penalty, bread and other such goods would then cease to be "private." They would become "public" goods, since non-payers would no longer be excluded from utilization. Based on what we know of the predilections of socialistic governmental efforts to produce goods and services (Mises, 1981) bread would soon be in very short supply. So, if we want to eat, we should be highly critical of the world view Hugo tried to champion.

30. Road socialists, of course, would object to turning these amenities over to private enterprise on many other grounds. They are too important to be left in the hands of business firms; it is improper to employ the profit motive for so important a service; there would be problems of monopoly, etc. For an alternative view, see Block (1979, 1980, 1983a, 1983b, 1996).

31. See Block (1979, 1980, 1983a, 1983b, 1996) for a critique of road socialism. For an alternative perspective on rivalrousness, excludability and the public goods necessitated by "market failure," see Block (1989, 1993a), Hoppe (1989, 1992), Hummel (1990).

32. Or can protect A only at the cost of less protection for B, and vice versa.

## REFERENCES

Armentano, Dominick T. (1972), *The Myths of Antitrust*. New Rochelle, NY: Arlington House.

Armentano, Dominick T. (1982), *Antitrust and Monopoly: Anatomy of a Policy Failure*. New York: Wiley.

Armentano, Dominick T. (1991), *Antitrust Policy: The Case for Repeal*. Washington, DC: The Cato Institute.

Arnold, Roger A. (1982), "Efficiency vs. Ethics: Which Is the Proper Decision Criterion in Law Cases?," *The Journal of Libertarian Studies* VI(1): 49–58.

Baird, Charles (1980), *Rent Control: The Perennial Folly*. Washington, DC: The Cato Institute.

Becker, Gary (1995), "It's Simple: Hike the Minimum Wage, and You Put People Out of Work," *Business Week Magazine*, 6 March.

Benson, Bruce L. (1986), "The Lost Victim and Other Failures of the Public Law Experiment," *Harvard Journal of Law and Public Policy* 9: 399–427.

Block, Walter (1977), "Austrian Monopoly Theory – A Critique," *The Journal of Libertarian Studies* I(4): 271–9.

Block, Walter (1979), "Free Market Transportation: Denationalizing the Roads," *Journal of Libertarian Studies: An Interdisciplinary Review* III(2): 209–38.

Block, Walter (1980), "Congestion and Road Pricing," *The Journal of Libertarian Studies: An Interdisciplinary Review* IV(3): 299–330.

Block, Walter (1982), *Amending the Combines Investigation Act*. Vancouver, BC: The Fraser Institute.

Block, Walter (1983a), "Public Goods and Externalities: The Case of Roads," *The Journal of Libertarian Studies: An Interdisciplinary Review* VII(1): 1–34.

Block, Walter (1983b), "Theories of Highway Safety," Transportation Research Record No. 912: 7–10.

Block, Walter (1989), "The Justification of Taxation in the Public Finance Literature: A Critique of Atkinson and Stiglitz, Due, Musgrave and Shoup," *Journal of Public Finance and Public Choice* 3: 141–58.

Block, Walter (1993a), "Canadian Public Finance Texts Cannot Justify Government Taxation: A Critique of Auld & Miller; Musgrave, Musgrave & Bird; McCready; and Wolf," *Canadian Public Administration* 36(1): 225–62.

Block, Walter (1993b), "On Rent Control," in David Henderson (ed.), *The Fortune Encyclopedia of Economics*. New York: Warner Books, 421–5.

Block, Walter (1994), "Total Repeal of Anti-trust Legislation: A Critique of Bork, Brozen and Posner," *Review of Austrian Economics* 8(1): 31–64.

Block, Walter (1996), "Road Socialism," *International Journal of Value-Based Management* 9(2): 195–207.

Block, Walter, and Michael Walker (1988), "Entropy in the Canadian Economics Profession: Sampling Consensus on the Major Issues," *Canadian Public Policy* XIV(2): 137–50.

Boaz, David (ed.) (1990), *The Crisis in Drug Prohibition*. Washington, DC: The Cato Institute.

Boettke, Peter (ed.) (1994), *The Collapse of Development Planning*. New York: New York University Press.

Bork, Robert H. (1978), *The Antitrust Paradox: A Policy at War with Itself*. New York: Basic Books.

Brozen, Yale (1982), *Concentration, Mergers, and Public Policy*. New York: Macmillan.

Card, David, and Alan B. Krueger (1994), "Minimum Wages and Employment: A Case Study of the Fast-Food Industry in New Jersey and Pennsylvania," *American Economic Review* 84(4): 772–93.

Coase, Ronald H. (1974), "The Lighthouse in Economics," *Journal of Law and Economics* 17: 357–76.

Cordato, Roy E. (1992), *Welfare Economics and Externalities in an Open-Ended Universe: A Modern Austrian Perspective*. Boston, MA: Kluwer.

Frey, Bruno S., Werner W. Pommerehne, Friedrich Schneider, and Guy Gilbert (1984), "Consensus and Dissension among Economists: An Empirical Inquiry," *American Economic Review* 74(5): 986–94.

Friedman, Milton (1962), *Capitalism and Freedom*. Chicago, IL: University of Chicago Press.

Friedman, Milton (1989), "An Open Letter to Bill Bennett," *Wall Street Journal*, 7 Sept.

Friedman, Milton, and George Stigler (1981), "Roofs or Ceilings?," in Walter Block and Edgar Olsen (eds.), *Rent Control: Myths and Realities*. Vancouver, BC: The Fraser Institute.

Garrison, Roger (1982), "Austrian Economics as the Middle Ground: Comment on Loasby," in Israel M. Kirzner (ed.), *Market Process, and Austrian Economics: Essays in Honor of Ludwig von Mises*. Lexington, MA: Lexington Books, 131–8.

Gordon, David (1993), "Toward a Deconstruction of Utility and Welfare Economics," *The Review of Austrian Economics* 6(2): 99–112.

Hamowy, Ronald (ed.) (1987), *Dealing with Drugs: Consequences of Government Control*. San Francisco, CA: The Pacific Institute.

Hazlitt, Henry (1979), *Economics in One Lesson*. New York: Arlington House Publishers.

Higgs, Robert (1995), "The Myth of 'Failed' Policies," *The Free Market* 13(6): 1, 7, 8.

High, Jack (1984/5), "Bork's Paradox: Static vs. Dynamic Efficiency in Antitrust Analysis," *Contemporary Policy Issues* 3: 21–34.

Hoppe, Hans-Hermann (1989), *A Theory of Socialism and Capitalism*. Boston, MA: Kluwer.

Hoppe, Hans-Hermann (1992), *The Economics and Ethics of Private Property: Studies in Political Economy and Philosophy*. Boston, MA: Dordrecht.

Hummel, Jeffrey (1990), "National Goods vs. Public Goods: Defense, Disarmament and Free Riders," *The Review of Austrian Economics* IV: 88–122.

Johnson, M. Bruce (ed.) (1982), *Resolving the Housing Crisis: Government Policy, Decontrol, and the Public Interest*. San Francisco, CA: The Pacific Institute.

Kranich, Laurence (1994), "Equal Division, Efficiency, and the Sovereign Supply of Labor," *American Economic Review* 84(1): 178–89.

Kristof, Frank S. (1964), *People, Housing and Rent Control in New York City*. New York City: The City Rent and Rehabilitation Administration.

Machan, Tibor (1989), *Individuals and Their Rights*. LaSalle, IL: Open Court.

Mack, Eric (1978), "Voluntarism: the Political Thought of Auberon Herbert," *The Journal of Libertarian Studies* 2(4): 299–309.

McGee, Robert (1993), "If Dwarf Tossing is Outlawed, Only Outlaws Will Toss Dwarfs: Is Dwarf Tossing a Victimless Crime?," *American Journal of Jurisprudence* 38: 335–58.

Marcuse, Peter (1979), *Rental Housing in the City of New York: Supply and Condition 1975–1978*. New York City: The City Rent and Rehabilitation Administration.

Mises, Ludwig von (1963), *Human Action*. Chicago, IL: Regnery.

Mises, Ludwig von (1981 [1969]), *Socialism*. Indianapolis, IN: Liberty Fund.

Murray, Charles (1984), *Losing Ground: American Social Policy from 1950 to 1980*. New York: Basic Books.

North, Gary (1990), *Tools of Dominion: The Case Laws of Exodus*. Tyler, TX: Institute for Christian Economics.

Pasour, E. C., Jr (1996), "Pigou, Coase, Common Law and Environmental Policy: Implications of the Calculation Debate," *Public Choice* 87: 243–58.

Posner, Richard (1976), *Antitrust Law: an Economic Perspective*. Chicago, IL: University of Chicago Press.

Rapkin, Chester (1966), *The Private Rental Housing Market in New York City 1965: A Study of Some Effects of Two Decades of Rent Control*. New York City: The City Rent and Rehabilitation Administration.

Robbins, Lionel (1935), *The Nature and Significance of Economic Science*, 2nd edn. London: Macmillan.

Robbins, Lionel (1938), "Live and Dead Issues in the Methodology of Economics," *Economica* 5: 342–52.

Rothbard, Murray N. (1970 [1962]), *Man, Economy and State*. Los Angeles, CA: Nash.

Rothbard, Murray N. (1977), "Toward a Reconstruction of Utility and Welfare Economics," San Francisco, CA: Center for Libertarian Studies, Occasional Paper No. 3.

Salins, Peter D. (1980), *The Ecology of Housing Destruction: Economic Effects of Public Intervention in the Housing Market*. New York: New York University Press.

Stigler, George (1968), *The Organization of Industry*. Homewood, IL: Richard D. Irwin.

Szasz, Thomas (1985), *Ceremonial Chemistry: The Ritual Persecution of Drugs, Addicts and Pushers*. Holmes Beach, FL: Learning Publications.

Telser, Lester (1987), *A Theory of Efficient Cooperation and Competition*. Cambridge: Cambridge University Press.

Thornton, Mark (1991), *The Economics of Prohibition*. Salt Lake City, UT: University of Utah Press.

Tucker, William (1984), "Black Family Agonistes," *The American Spectator*, 14–17 July.

Tucker, William (1990), *The Excluded Americans: Homelessness and Housing Policy*. Chicago, IL: Regnery-Gateway.

Tullock, Gordon (1967), "The Welfare Cost of Tariffs, Monopolies and Theft," *Western Economic Journal* (now Economic Inquiry) 5: 224–32.

Tullock, Gordon (1980a), "Rent-Seeking as a Negative Sum Game," in James M. Buchanan, Robert D. Tollison and Gordon Tullock (eds.), *Toward a Theory of the Rent-Seeking Society*. College Station, TX: Texas A&M University Press.

Tullock, Gordon (1980b), "Efficient Rent Seeking," in J. M. Buchanan, R. D. Tollison, and G. Tullock (eds.) *Towards a Theory of the Rent Seeking Society*. College Station, TX: Texas A&M University Press, 51–70.

Woolridge, William C. (1970), *Uncle Sam the Monopoly Man*. New Rochelle, NY: Arlington House.

# Part 2:
# The Austrian Critique
# of Public Choice

# Chapter 3
# Competition and Political Entrepreneurship:
# Austrian Insights into Public-Choice Theory

## 1. Introduction

Public choice can be defined as the application of economic theory and methodology to the study of politics and political institutions, broadly defined. Neoclassical price theory has been one of the principal tools of the public-choice theorist, having been applied to address such questions as why people vote, why bureaucrats bungle, the effects of deficit finance on government spending, and myriad other questions regarding the operations and activities of governments. There has indeed been a public-choice "revolution" in economics. But neoclassical price theory has its limitations, many of which have been investigated by Austrian economists. These limitations have implications for the study of public choice. Namely, if neoclassical price theory is itself flawed, then perhaps its applications to the study of political decision making has produced uncertain results.

In this article, I shall explore two strands of Austrian economics – theories of competition and of entrepreneurship – and their implications for public-choice theory. I do not claim to provide an exhaustive examination of public-choice theory from an Austrian perspective, but only to offer a few insights. The first section notes some limitations of applying the neoclassical competitive model to the study of political decision making. The next discusses the implications of placing more emphasis on the role of political entrepreneurship in the study of public choice. The final section contains a summary and conclusions.

## 2. Competition, Entrepreneurship, and Public Choice

One area in which the neoclassical competitive model has been applied by public-choice theorists is the economics of local public finance. There exists a large volume of mostly empirical research purporting that when metropolitan areas are composed of larger numbers of governments, competition among governments for population and, consequently, tax base, induces them to be more cost-conscious, thereby putting downward pressures on government spending (DiLorenzo, 1981a, 1981b, 1982, 1983). Thus, on efficiency grounds, public-choice economists often take the position that more governments within a metropolitan area are preferred to fewer. This is a direct application of the neoclassical competitive model, which holds that more firms in an industry leads to stronger competitive forces. It is also derived from the related structure-conduct-performance (SCP) paradigm of industrial organization theory.

## 3. Industrial Organization and Public Choice

The SCP paradigm asserts that a more concentrated market structure is likely to be more monopolist because, in such a setting, the cost of collusion is lower. But this assumption has been called into question by research that constitutes yet another revolution in economic theory – a revolution in the field of industrial organization (Goldschmidt, Mann, and Weston, 1974; Brozen, 1982). One of the significant features of the "revolution" in the field of industrial organization is that many researchers have taken a more dynamic view of the market as a process. Thus, they have moved closer to the Austrian view of the nature of competition. By taking a more dynamic view of how industries evolve over time, economists have learned (or relearned, according to DiLorenzo and High, 1988) that an important reason why industries become concentrated is the superior efficiency of one or a few firms. "Dominant" firms can only remain that way by continuing to offer competitive products at favorable prices, in the absence of government-imposed entry barriers. Substitutes and potential entry have placed effective limits on monopoly pricing by firms in concentrated industries (Brozen, 1982). Thus, the traditional antitrust prescription of divestiture to avoid monopolization is now widely believed to be sometimes harmful. Focusing attention on the reasons why industries become concentrated has advanced our knowledge over the days when it was simply assumed that market concentration meant monopolization and "market power."

This shift in research emphasis is welcomed by many Austrians, who for decades have criticized the neoclassical competitive model as almost devoid of behavioral content, given its emphasis on static equilibrium conditions rather than the process of competition. "Competition is by its nature a dynamic process whose essential characteristics are assumed away by the assumptions underlying the static analysis. . . . Advertising, [price] undercutting, and improving . . . the goods or services produced are all excluded by definition – 'perfect' competition means indeed the absence of all competitive activities" (Hayek, 1948, p. 96). By viewing competition as a static equilibrium condition rather than as a dynamic, rivalrous process, economists are prone to condemn competitive activities as monopolistic.

These developments in the economics of industrial organization are relevant to the study of public choice. If the neoclassical competitive model – and its derivative, the structure-conduct-performance (SCP) paradigm – are themselves flawed, perhaps the model's applications to the study of the local government "industry" are also subject to question. I contend that by relying on static, market structure models of the local government "industry," public choice economists have often drawn false conclusions. However, by relying on static models, they have not erred in the same direction as the structuralist industrial organization economists. Rather than condemning as monopolist many practices that are inherently competitive, they have done the opposite. By focusing on government structure at a point in time rather than on the dynamic, historical process by which the institutional structure of government evolves, they have sometimes praised as "competitive" government actions that are inherently monopolistic.

Consider, for example, how public-choice economists often interpret U.S. Census Bureau data on local government structure. Among public-choice economists who have studied local government, it is generally agreed that the greater the number of government units in a metropolitan area (the more "fragmented" the governmental structure), the better. Fragmentation creates interjurisdictional competition, which supposedly provides incentives for lowering the costs of service provision. This purportedly lowers expenditures and taxes and also results in higher-quality government services. These conclusions are usually drawn from cross-section data on government expenditure, regressed against several "determinants" of public expenditures, with some sort of proxy for interjurisdictional competition, i.e., number of government units in a metropolitan area. More often than not, the independent variable for government structure reveals that more fragmented metropolitan areas have lower levels of government expenditure, *ceteris paribus.* These empirical studies are similar to the early empirical work in industrial organization that found a positive correlation between market concentration and profitability. More concentrated metropolitan governments are thought to lead to higher levels of *political* "profits" in the form of higher spending than would otherwise occur.

But just as taking a more dynamic or historical view of industrial market structure can yield different interpretations of the causes of market concentration, it can also change one's view of the meaning of a more or less concentrated structure of local government. Consider the example of off-budget government spending at the state and local levels (Bennett and DiLorenzo, 1983).

## 4. Off-budget Spending and the Government Process

Historically, tax revolts and fiscal constraints in the form of statutory or constitutional restrictions on taxing, spending, or borrowing at the state and local levels of government have been met by politicians not by catering to "the will of the people," but, rather, by subverting that will by creating off-budget enterprises (OBEs) that permit them to preach fiscal conservatism by continuing to practice fiscal profligacy. The "solution" politicians have for more than a century applied to the "problem" of taxpayer demands for tax or expenditure restraint is disarmingly simple: separate corporate entities are created by state and local governments, which could issue bonds that are not subject to the legal restrictions on public debt or even to voter approval. These entities are called a variety of names, including districts, boards, authorities, agencies, commissions, corporations, and trusts.

Regardless of their title, an essential feature of all such organizations is that their financial activities do not appear in the budget of the government unit that created them. One distinguishing feature of OBEs is that their operations, at least in theory, are not financed from taxes, but from revenues generated by their activities. Because the taxpayer is not deemed to be liable for the financial obligations of OBEs, voter approval is not required for the debt issued by such organizations and, more importantly, debt restrictions do not apply. However, the idea that off-budget finance should not require voter approval because the projects financed are self-supporting is a myth, for billions of taxpayer dollars are used to subsidize OBE activity (Bennett and DiLorenzo, 1983). The array of activities undertaken by OBEs is quite large and includes the financing of school buildings, airports, parking lots, recreation centers, courthouses, subways, bridges, tunnels, highways, parks, lakes, sewer systems, sports arenas, electric utilities, race tracks, outer space programs (in California), and housing, to name a few examples. In short, any activities that are undertaken on budget by state and local governments (or by private enter-prises, for that matter) are also undertaken by OBEs in every state.

Even if debt restrictions did not exist, politicians would benefit from off-budget activities. The public sector is constrained by numerous regulations designed to protect the public interest. Virtually none of these applies to any OBE. For example, civil service regulations do not apply, so it is easier for politicians to create patronage jobs off-budget; there are no requirements for competitive bidding procedures on contracts, so campaign contributions can be obtained and loyal supporters can be rewarded; the members of the boards of directors of every OBE are political appointees who are not elected or responsible to voters, so that the will of politicians cannot easily be frustrated by a recalcitrant bureaucracy. OBEs are given wide powers by law. They are granted monopoly franchises, may have powers of eminent domain, can override zoning ordinances, are exempt from regulations and paperwork that impose heavy costs on private enterprises, have no legal restrictions on collective bargaining agreements, and are often specifically exempted from antitrust laws regarding price fixing.

Unfortunately, it is impossible to obtain accurate data on the number of OBEs that exist or on their activities. Most states do not keep statistics on their numbers. One thing is known with certainty, however: There are thousands of OBEs throughout the nation, including more than 2,500 in Pennsylvania alone as of 1977 (Schlosser, 1977).

One implication of this research for public choice theory is that the structure of the local government industry at any one point in time does not necessarily reveal how "competitive" government is. Bureau of the Census data on the number of government units in metropolitan areas includes many OBEs, designating them as special districts, public corporations, statutory authorities, and so on. But an increase in the number of such entities often results in a government that is increasingly detached from the consent of the governed, is not subject to direct voter approval at the ballot box, and grants itself extraordinary powers – even by government standards – of eminent domain, zoning authority, and immunity from civil service, collective bargaining, antitrust, and other laws that others in society must comply with. A strong argument can be made that avoiding taxpayer demands for fiscal restraint is the whole purpose of off-budget spending, which renders government more monopolistic. To designate these developments as "competitive" or "efficient" is misleading, at best. But this is precisely the problem public choice economists experience when applying the neoclassical competitive model to the study of local government (see, for example, Blewitt, 1984).

## 5. Efficiency and the Structure of Local Government

Competitive markets are praised by neoclassical economists because, among other reasons, they promote allocative efficiency. Austrian economists, however, have little use for such notions because of their belief that all costs and benefits are subjective. To state that a certain allocation of resources is allocatively efficient and maximizes "social welfare" is to assume that benefits and costs are objective and measurable by some outside observer/social engineer. Moreover, to claim that one allocation of resources is superior to another on neoclassical efficiency grounds requires one to make interpersonal utility comparisons, a sheer impossibility. For instance, if an industry is judged to be producing less than the competitive level, a common policy prescription to promote efficiency is to somehow induce the firm(s) to increase their production (through divestiture, for instance). This may harm the producers since it forces them to do something they did not voluntarily choose to do, but it is said to be efficient because the utility gain to some other group in society – usually called consumers – is said to outweigh the utility loss to the producers.

Policy recommendations based on such efficiency norms often attenuate the rights of political minorities such as "monopolist" producers on the grounds that their utility loss is outweighed by the utility gains of others. This arbitrarily assumes that the property rights of the former group are unimportant. In short, what passes for science is loaded with normative judgments.

There is an alternative (and equally normative) definition of "efficient" institutions that has its roots in Adam Smith's *Wealth of Nations* and embraces the notion of individualist property rights norms: Those institutions are efficient that facilitate mutually advantageous, voluntary exchange (Buchanan, 1964). From this perspective, a "better" allocation of resources can only be determined by people themselves, not by professional maximizers of social welfare functions. The standard of evaluation is ultimately consent among individuals. Also, according to this perspective, the proliferation of the number of local governments cannot be said to be "efficient," since the growth of government embodies a further reallocation of resources from the private to the public sector. The private sector is the exclusive domain of mutually advantageous exchange. Outside of its role of enforcing and protecting private property rights, all government resource allocation is necessarily coercive in the absence of direct democracy and voting rules mandating unanimous consent. The proliferation of local government units, on- or off-budget, represents an expansion of the domain of rent-seeking behavior, which is necessarily coercive, at the expense of a contracted private sector and of the domain of voluntary exchange.

Public-choice economists typically criticize a consolidated local government structure as monopolistic compared to the alternative of a larger number of jurisdictions within a metropolitan area. In many instances, this criticism is probably well grounded. One centralized school district, for instance, is likely to be even more monopolistic than if there were several to choose from by "voting with your feet." As George Orwell might have said, all governments are monopolists, only some are more monopolistic than others.

However, it is not clear that the relevant alternative to a fragmented government structure within a metropolitan area is a more centralized, monopolistic government. Another alternative is a return to private-sector provision of the *private goods* now supplied by local governments: education, libraries, hospitals, airport operation, fire protection, parking lot operation, water supply, police protection, sewerage treatment, parks and recreation, operation of liquor stores, mass transportation, and myriad other activities. One thing all these activities have in common is that no strong case can be made that any of them is a public good. They are all divisible in consumption and exclusion is not costly. Moreover, they are all things that are supplied throughout the country by private businesses as well as by governments, leading one to question the existence of any economic rationale for government provision.

Governments usually grant themselves distinct advantages whenever direct competition with the private sector is permitted (which it often is not) by not having to pay taxes or comply with costly regulations imposed on private enterprises. Thus, these are often money-making operations for local governments that have taken over services that would have alternatively been provided by private businesses. Government imperialism is a more likely explanation than market failure for why these activities are carried out by hundreds of local government jurisdictions. Governments are redirecting resources from the private to the public sector as private firms are either banned by law from competing with government monopolies or are driven out of business because of the special advantages that government service providers have. Viewed in this way, it appears that the public-choice characterization of the "efficient" organization of local government is grossly misleading.

## 6. Public Choice and Political Entrepreneurs

Austrian economists often claim that neoclassical economics ignores many important economic phenomena by not sufficiently emphasizing the role of entrepreneurship in economic organization. Ludwig von Mises broadly defined entrepreneurship to encompass capitalists, workers, consumers, and others: "Economics, in speaking of entrepreneurs, has in view not men, but a definite function" (1966, p. 246). The function of the entrepreneur is to react to (and create) change in the market. The efficiency of markets does not depend upon the equality of price to marginal costs, the familiar equilibrium condition of neoclassical price theory, but, rather, "it depends on the degree of success with which market forces can be relied upon to generate spontaneous corrections ... at times of disequilibrium" (Kirzner, 1974, p. 6). Entrepreneurship is the engine of economic growth and wealth creation in capitalist economies, for according to Robert Tollison:

> When competition is viewed as a dynamic, value-creating, evolutionary process, *the* role of economic rents in stimulating entrepreneurial decisions and in prompting an efficient allocation of resources is crucial. . . . [P]rofit seeking in a competitive market order is a normal feature of economic life. The returns of resource owners will be driven to normal levels . . . by competitive profit seeking as *some* resource owners earn positive rents which promote entry and others earn negative rents which cause exit. Profit seeking and economic rents are inherently related to the efficiency of the competitive market process. Such activities drive the competitive price system and create value (e.g., new products) in the economy. (1982, p. 577)

But neoclassical economics does not view competition as a "dynamic, value-creating, evolutionary process." Rather, it is a static equilibrium condition. And in equilibrium, there is no place for the function of entrepreneurship, since in equilibrium, there are no changes in the given data of endowments, technologies, or preferences. By downplaying or ignoring the role of entrepreneurship and of competition as a dynamic, rivalrous process, neoclassical economics has probably underestimated the wealth-creating and welfare-enhancing capabilities of capitalism.

Similarly, by applying the static, neoclassical model to the study of political "markets," public-choice theorists have probably downplayed or ignored the role of *political* entrepreneurship. But this has not led them to ignore the role of entrepreneurship in *creating* wealth and facilitating exchange, as with the study of private markets. The essence of political entrepreneurship is to *destroy* wealth through negative-sum rent-seeking behavior. Thus, adherence to the static, neoclassical model is likely to lead one to understate the beneficial economic effects of private markets while, when applied to the study of public choice, understating the destructive effects of politics.

In much of public-choice theory, interest groups are viewed as entities that coalesce to express a demand for wealth transfers. In seeking political profit, politicians respond by supplying the transfers through legislation and regulation. Politicians are accordingly labeled "brokers" of legislation (Tollison and McCormick, 1981). Thus, just as a perfectly competitive, profit maximizing firm would cater to consumer demands, politicians passively respond to the wishes of interest groups. But the price theory analogy is not entirely accurate, for in a world of uncertainty, producers are constantly searching for and *creating* profit opportunities by advertising, offering new or different products, and other activities aimed at stimulating the demand for their goods or services. They do not merely respond to changing consumer demands. Similarly, political entrepreneurs do not just passively respond to interest-group pressures; they also try to stimulate the demand for their "services," i.e., the provision of wealth transfers (Mitchell, 1984). Although it has been relatively neglected in the public-choice literature, Richard Wagner (1966) described the importance of political entrepreneurship in a hypothetical example where interest groups are outlawed.

> Consider farm interests after pressure groups are outlawed. It clearly seems contrary to intuition and common sense to claim that farmers would no longer have [political] activities undertaken to increase their real incomes. For a reconciliation we must turn to the political entrepreneur and observe the impact of the outlawing of lobbying upon his profit opportunities. If a political profit existed before the institutional change [i.e., outlawing lobbying], what reason exists for the belief that such profit will not exist after the change? Clearly, for a reduction in the political profit from farm votes, either voting or organizational rules must be changed. Since the outlawing of pressure groups is unrelated to either of these two features, the profit must still exist after pressure groups are outlawed. Therefore, some political entrepreneur would carry their cause to congress. (p. 165)

Wagner further stated that various institutional arrangements often emerge to promote individual interests when free-rider problems prevent the formation of effective interest groups. For instance, one role of government bureaucracies is to serve the wishes of political entrepreneurs with whom they share a common objective: an expansion of the agency's activity (and budget). Bureaucracies have strong incentives to promote and stimulate a perceived need for their activities- every bureaucracy is a vigorous lobbyist. Peter Woll (1977) noted the importance of bureaucratic lobbying in his book, *American Bureaucracy:*

> The ability of administrative agencies to marshal support in favor of particular programs is often severely tested, and as a result the agencies have frequently created public relations departments on a permanent basis to engineer consent for their legislative proposals. It has been estimated that the executive branch spends close to half a billion dollars [in 1971] a year on public relations and public information programs . . . . [A]gencies are expending huge amounts of

funds, time, and effort on indirect and direct lobbying activities. (p. 194)

As recent examples of bureaucratic lobbying expenditures, the U.S. Department of Agriculture in 1984 officially employed 144 full-time public affairs persons with a budget of $6.5 million. The entire department, including subagencies, employs 704 people involved in public affairs (Palmer, 1985). The Department of Education had 21 public affairs professionals and a $1.5 million budget; and the Pentagon listed 1,066 full-time public relations employees. Similar programs are sure to be found in other agencies as well.

The effect of political advertising is likely to be public acquiescence in the continued growth of the government wealth-transfer process. Unlike private advertising, political advertising does not foster competition and lower prices by facilitating comparison shopping, for no comparisons are permitted. Governments usually grant themselves statutory monopolies in the goods and services they provide. Nor are there strong constraints on false advertising by government because of the absence of competitive pressures. Few private businesses, for instance, would risk criticizing false advertising by government enterprises for fear of regulatory retribution by the government authorities. Nor can one expect government regulatory agencies such as the Federal Trade Commission to crack down on fraudulent claims made by government itself. Thus:

> Politicians cannot be held liable for their promises. If a hot dog manufacturer's all-meat product turns out to be 30 percent chicken and bread crumbs, he will most likely encounter difficulty with the government, even if consumers buy the product. But when the government's comparable product turns out to be 60 percent baloney, no regulatory agency will take action. (Wagner, 1976, p. 81)

Moreover, the principal function of political advertising "would seem to be to promote acquiescence about the prevailing public policies. The purpose of public advertising would be to reassure citizens that the fact that their public goods are composed of 60 percent baloney indicates good performance" (Wagner, 1976, p. 97). In this way, political entrepreneurship in the form of public advertising facilitates the process of rent seeking.

Another example of political entrepreneurship is tax-funded politics (Bennett and DiLorenzo, 1985). Hundreds of millions of dollars per year are doled out by the federal government to special interest groups including Ralph Nader-type consumer groups, environmentalists, welfare rights lobbyists, civil rights organizations, labor unions, senior citizens organizations, and various conservative political activists, to name a few examples. The funds are obtained through grants and contracts ostensibly for helping consumers, the unemployed, the elderly, minorities, the environment, and so on, but then are diverted (illegally) for partisan politics. In these instances, Congress is directly stimulating the perceived demand for its "services" by giving taxpayers' money to special interests to lobby, campaign, register voters, publish books (as well as op-eds and political training manuals), hold media events, and conduct other forms of partisan politics. Politicians use tax-funded politics to fabricate demands for legislation and government activity to stimulate the demand for their services. Interest groups that receive government funding can be more blatant in their political activities than government bureau-cracies can since it is illegal for government employees to engage in on-the-job political activity. And, as Gordon Tullock (1983) pointed out, "interest groups normally have an interest in diminishing the information of the average voter. If they can sell him some false tale which supports their particular effort ... it pays. They ... produce misinformation" (p. 71).

In sum, focusing on the role of political entrepreneurship is likely to improve one's understanding of the government process. Demand-side models of the political process (such as the median voter model) can be misleading if they fail to incorporate the fact that political entrepreneurs are experts at fabricating false crises to convince the public to acquiesce in their policy proposals. Voters are rationally ignorant, and much of the information about politics they do receive is propaganda issued by self-serving politicians, interest groups, and bureaucracies. It does not pay to be as well informed about politics as about one's own personal affairs, which permits political entrepreneurs to manufacture a false "will of the people." Joseph Schumpeter (1942) recognized this more than four decades ago: "Human nature in politics being what it is, [politicians] are able to fashion and, within very wide limits, even to create the will of the people. What we are confronted with in the analysis of political processes is largely not a genuine but a manufactured will. ... [T]he will of the people is the product and not the motive power of the political process" (p. 263).

Even though private and political entrepreneurship both serve to transmit information, they produce fundamentally different results. The nature of market activity is to enhance people's propensity to truck, barter, and exchange – generally a positive-sum game – and entrepreneurship facilitates this process. By contrast, the nature of most government activity, including political entrepreneurship, is to promote wealth transfers, which is, at best, a zero-sum game. Mancur Olson (1982) provides evidence that such rent seeking is, in fact, a negative-sum game and a major cause of economic stagnation.

## 7. Conclusions

Austrian economics and public choice are two of the most exciting areas of economic research. With its emphasis on competition as a dynamic, rivalrous process and the role of entrepreneurship, Austrian economics clarifies how markets work. Public-choice theory has been absolutely revolutionary in focusing attention on how the tools of economics can be employed to better understand how govern-ments work. This article is, if anything, a plea to consider the two research programs as complementary. Economic reasoning can and will be applied to advance our understanding of the political process, but one need not adopt the entire neoclassical economic framework to do so. The two strands of Austrian economics discussed here – theories of competition and of entrepreneurship – offer some insights into the government process that neoclassical economics ignores, at best, and possibly even misinterprets. One implication of this is that the type of public-choice research conducted might take on a different focus. Specifically, it would be a wise investment of intellectual resources to conduct more historical studies of the evolution of political institutions from a public-choice perspective. Public choice *is* often a study of comparative institutions, but economic history is one research approach which has, unfortunately, been relatively neglected by public-choice theorists. There is much to learn from economic and political history from a public-choice perspective that just cannot be captured by regression equations of the "determinants" of government spending, taxing, and borrowing.

Not only can a careful consideration of the usefulness of Austrian economics to the study of public choice expand our knowledge of government institutions; it can also prevent us from making mistakes. I have claimed elsewhere (DiLorenzo, 1984) that the economics of rent seeking has become confused. One reason for this is the failure to properly distinguish between rent seeking and profit seeking by not viewing real-world competition as a dynamic, rivalrous process. Consequently, some authors have condemned as "wasteful rent seeking" many activities (e.g., competitive advertising, product innovation, research and development, the market for corporate control) that are an essential part of a dynamic, competitive market. This is a step backward in the public-choice revolution, something that might have been avoided by being aware of some of the limitations of the neoclassical competitive model and its applications to public choice.

## REFERENCES

Bennett, James T., and Thomas DiLorenzo (1983), *Underground Government: The Off-Budget Public Sector*. Washington, D.C.: Cato Institute.
--- (1985), *Destroying Democracy: How Government Funds Partisan Politics*. Washington, D.C.: Cato Institute.
Blewitt, Robert A. (1984), "Off-Budget Activities of Local Government: Comment," *Public Choice* 42(2): 205–12.
Brozen, Yale (1982), *Concentration, Mergers, and Public Policy*. New York: Macmillan.
Buchanan, James M. (1964), "What Should Economists Do?," *Southern Economic Journal* January: 213–22.
DiLorenzo, Thomas (1981a), "The Expenditure Effects of Restricting Competition in Local Public Service Industries: The Case of Special Districts," *Public Choice* 37: 569–78.
-- (1981b), "An Empirical Assessment of the Factor-Supplier Pressure Group Hypothesis," *Public Choice* 37: 559–68.

-- (1983), "Economic Competition and Political Competition: An Empirical Note," *Public Choice* 40: 203–9.

-- (1984), "The Domain of Rent-Seeking Behavior: Private or Public Choice," *International Review of Law and Economics* December: 185–97.

-- and Ralph Robinson (1982), "Managerial Objectives Subject to Political Market Constraints: Electric Utilities in the U.S.," *Quarterly Review of Economics and Business* Summer: 113–25.

-- and Jack C. High (1988), "Antitrust and Competition, Historically Considered," *Economic Inquiry* 26(3): 423–435.

Goldschmidt, Harvey, Michael Mann, and Fred Weston (1974), *Industrial Concentration: The New Learning.* Boston, MA: Little, Brown.

Hayek, Friedrich (1948), "The Meaning of Competition," in his *Individualism and Economic Order.* Chicago, IL: University of Chicago Press.

Kirzner, Israel (1974), *Competition and Entrepreneurship.* Chicago, IL: University of Chicago Press.

Mises, Ludwig (1966), *Human Action.* Chicago, IL: Gateway/Regnery.

Mitchell, William C. (1984), "Schumpeter and Public Choice, Part II: Democracy and the Demise of Capitalism: The Missing Chapter in Schumpeter," *Public Choice* 42(2): 161–74.

Moody's Investors Services (1985), *Moody's Municipal and Government Manual.* New York: Moody's.

Olson, Mancur (1982), *The Rise and Decline of Nations.* New Haven, CT: Yale University Press.

Palmer, Thomas (1985), "Uncle Sam's Ever-Expanding P.R. Machine," *Wall Street Journal* January 10: 26.

Schlosser, P. (1977), *Municipal Authorities in Pennsylvania.* Harrisburg, PA: Department of Community Affairs.

Schumpeter, Joseph (1942), *Capitalism, Socialism, and Democracy.* New York: Harper & Row.

Tollison, Robert D. (1982), "Rent Seeking: A Survey," *Kyklos* 35(4): 575–602.

--- and Robert McCormick (1981), *Politicians, Legislation, and the Economy.* Boston, MA: Martinus Nijhoff).

Tullock, Gordon (1983), *Economics of Income Redistribution.* Boston, MA: Martinus Nijhoff.

Wagner, Richard E. (1966), "Pressure Groups and Political Entrepreneurs: A Review Article," *Papers on Non-Market Decision Making* 1(1): 161–70.

--- (1976), "Advertising and the Public Economy: Some Preliminary Ruminations," in D. Tuerck (ed.), *The Political Economy of Advertising.* Washington, D.C.: American Enterprise Institute, 81–100.

Woll, Peter (1977), *American Bureaucracy.* New York: W.W. Norton.

# Chapter 4
# Is Voluntary Government Possible?
# A Critique of Constitutional Economics

"A 'social contract' theory of government...can be used to place a stamp of approval on all, or most, of the actions of the *existing* government (for example, Rousseau). Thus, the theory of the divine right of kings began as a check on government, as an order to the King to stay within divinely-commanded laws; it was transformed, by the State, into a divine stamp of approval for anything the King might decide to do." (Murray Rothbard)

## 1. Introduction

Public choice theory attempts to model politics as just another market. Political "exchange" is said to be analogous to market exchange, although certain differences are acknowledged. Consequently, the widely-acknowledged benefits of free markets are said to be the result of certain (not all) political "exchanges." "The market and the State are both devices through which co-operation is organized and made possible [where] ... two or more individuals find it mutually advantageous: to join forces to accomplish certain purposes," Buchanan and Tullock (1962, 19) wrote in their landmark study, *The Calculus of Consent.* "The public choice approach to the analysis of political decision making, wrote Buchanan and Tullock (1962, 23f.) incorporates political activity as a particular form of exchange: and as in the market relation. Mutual gains to all parties are ideally expected to result from the collective action . . . the political process . . . maybe interpreted as a positive sum game."

The theme of voluntary government is most prevalent in the sub-discipline of public choice known as constitutional economics, which has its roots in *The Calculus of Consent* and in much of Buchanan's post-1962 research agenda (Tullock's career took a somewhat different path after that early collaboration). We believe that the analogy between politics and markets that is made by constitutional economists is theoretically weak, often factually mistaken, and clouds rather than enhances our understanding of political economy. Government is an inherently coercive institution that has little in common with the non-coercive voluntary exchange of the marketplace.

## 2. State and Market

In *The Calculus of Consent,* the first modern work on constitutional economics, Buchanan and Tullock espouse the so-called public goods theory of the state whereby members of society voluntarily agree to coerce themselves to pay taxes for the provision of public goods. In a Robinson Crusoe economy, they assert, both men (Crusoe and Friday) will recognize the advantages to be secured from constructing a fortress (Buchanan and Tullock [1962: 19]). Yet, one fortress is sufficient for the protection of both. Hence, they will find it mutually advantageous to enter into a political "exchange" and devote resources to the construction of the common good. It is in this sense that politics is said to be "voluntary" and "efficient."

But is it not in human nature to avoid taxing oneself if one can tax someone else instead? And is not this kind of exploitive behavior the very essence of democratic government, since voting rules never require unanimity? All governmental decisions in a democracy are necessarily exploitive of someone.

Political action is typically a means by which one group of people is able to coerce another group to pay for its own free rides. Indeed, in those cases where there is unanimity of agreement within a community on some issue, that issue would not need to be addressed by government at all but would remain in the domain of the private sector. Citizens coalesce every day to voluntarily organize the provision of myriad community benefits - from neighborhood children's sports leagues to multi-million member nonprofit, charitable organizations – without resorting to governmental coercion. If agreement is truly unanimous and the parties to the agreement have the right to secede from it, then there is no need to involve the state at all.[1] Only when there are dissenters is the state invoked to override and crush the dissent as the history of tax revolts proves (Adams, 1993, 1998; Beito, 1989).

Buchanan and Tullock realize that a voting rule of unanimity – which is required for the neoclassical definition of efficiency – is never attainable, so they explore the features of "relative unanimity." But relative unanimity is simply not a substitute for the real thing. It cannot be concluded that coerced minorities (however small in number) benefit from being coerced. By their revealed preferences, the minorities have shown that they would, in fact, be harmed. The only way in which so-called relative unanimity can be labeled as economically efficient is if one presumes that it is possible to make interpersonal utility comparisons, which it is not.

The state is an institution whereby a controlling group uses its powers to exploit non-controlling groups.[2] One cannot realistically expect the controlling group to promote something called the public interest when it can promote the interests of the members of the controlling group instead (Kalt, 1981). Even when governments appear to be altruistic – at least with regard to another group in society – they are practicing such "altruism" by taxing one group and giving that group's wealth away to yet another group (usually in return for the subsidized group's political support).

## 2.1. "Conceptual" Unanimity

Buchanan and Tullock posit in *The Calculus of Consent*, as does Buchanan in numerous subsequent publications, that government can be viewed as "efficient" and "voluntary" in the "constitutional stage of decision making." That is, just as self-interested behavior in the free market can "further the general interests of everyone in the community (the invisible hand theorem)," an "acceptable theory of collective choice can perhaps do something similar in pointing the way toward those rules, for collective choice-making, the constitution, under which the activities of political tradesmen can be similarly reconciled with the interests of all members of the social group" (Buchanan and Tullock, 1962: 23). There may not be unanimous agreement over each individual policy choice, but those individual choices can nevertheless be deemed "voluntary" and not coercive, according to Buchanan and other "contractarians," if one assumes that when the rules of the political game (i.e., the constitution) were chosen there *was* unanimity.

Evidence of actual unanimity is not necessary, only "conceptual unanimity" is. As Buchanan (1977: 127) stated in a more recent publication, "[t]o the contractarian that law is legitimate and just, which might have emerged from a genuine social contract in which he might have participated. That law is illegitimate, and unjust, which finds no such contractual basis." This statement is more or less the keystone of what Viktor Vanberg (1998) has referred to as Buchanan's "enterprise of developing a theoretical approach to the state as a voluntary institution" (i.e., constitutional economics).

According to this viewpoint, the constitution may or may not be a written document. It may merely consist of the existing features of society that theorists can assume everyone (implicitly) agrees to. Politics is admittedly a series of predatory zero-sum games, but in reality such games are really positive-sum because "each and every participant has implicitly accepted the 'contract' embodied in the rules of the game ..." (Buchanan and Tullock, 1962: 254).

Moreover, there need not be any actual political convention at which voting rules are agreed upon by the citizens; their mere existence gives them their legitimacy. And these rules may be in a constant change of flux, even though members of society do not hold any formal constitutional conventions to change the rules. "The 'social contract' is best conceived as subject to contain usual revision and change, and the consent that is given must be thought of as being continuous" (Buchanan and Tullock, 1962: 260). Why it "must" be thought of as such is never explained, only asserted.

In a later publication Buchanan (1975: 96) claims the existence of an "existing and ongoing implicit social contract, embodied and described in the institutions of the *status quo.*" This impossible-to-verify "implicit" contract should cement in place the legitimacy of the *status quo.* According to Buchanan, even "when an original contract may never have been made, when current members of the community sense no moral or ethical obligation to adhere to the terms that are defined in the *status quo,* and... when such a contract... may have been violated many times over... The *status quo* defines that which exists. Hence, regardless of its history, it must be evaluated as if it were legitimate contractually" (Buchanan, 1975: 84f.).

It is worth noting that David Hume (1965: 263) long ago dismissed this notion of tacit "contractual" consent with his example of the conscripted sailor who, by refraining from committing suicide by jumping overboard, does not thereby "consent" to the ship captain's alleged "authority" over him.[3] Hume understood that the greatest of governmental tyrannies could be rationalized by cleverly-crafted theories of "tacit" consent – even if the authors of those theories would themselves he appalled by the governmental actions for which their theories provided intellectual support.

We must also point out that, despite Buchanan's assertions that constitutional political economy has its roots in the political theory of the American founding fathers, the most renowned founding father, George Washington, explicitly rebuked this kind of thinking. In his September 19, 1796 Farewell Address, President Washington warned of the tyranny that would result from any changes in the Constitution that were not the result of a formal convention. "If in the opinion of the People, the distribution or modification of the Constitutional powers be in any particular wrong, let it be corrected by an amendment in the way which the Constitution designates. But let there be no change by usurpation; for though this, in one instance, may be the instrument of good, it is the customary weapon by which free governments are destroyed" (Allen, 1980: 521).

There is also a logical difficulty here. Constitutional economists try to derive a theory of human and property rights from their constitutional framework and they seek to do so on a consensual basis. But how can people give their consent to a contract before it is clear that they have any rights to do so? Where do these rights come from? How can a person agree to be bound by a constitution if it is this very document which can alone establish his rights? If rights are established only by constitutions, then before their advent individuals have no rights. But if they have no rights, what "right" do they have to participate in the construction of a constitution?

## 3. The Myth of the Consensual Origins of the State

Constitutional economics fails to adequately confront the voluminous philosophical, historical, sociological, and economic literature which points to the fact that the origins of the state have always been based on conquest and exploitation, not consent. Buchanan and Tullock and other constitutional economists frequently argue that their theories are normative and, consequently, that their policy prescriptions should be beyond criticism. But in *The Calculus of Consent* and elsewhere the normative theories are used to rationalize actual policy interventions, and in doing so the authors frequently mix normative and positive analyses, including many real-world examples. As such, constitutional economics can become more or less a stamp of approval for virtually any and all government interventions. We reject this line of thought and believe that it is entirely appropriate to criticize such theories from an historical perspective, as we do in the remainder of this section.

Many historians have noted that the origins of the Roman Empire, like other empires in antiquity, were in war and conquest. In the sixteenth century philosophers began investigating this question, and most of them came to agree with Jean Bodin, who wrote in *Six Books of the Commonwealth,* that "[r]eason and common sense alike point to the conclusion that the origin and foundation of common-wealths was in force and violence" (Oppenheimer [1997: 1]). A contemporary of Bodin's, Blaise Pascal (1932: 81), concurred that "[m]ight is the sovereign of the world," and that "[m]en will doubtless fight till the stronger party overcomes the weaker and a dominant party is established."

In *A Treatise on Human Nature* David Hume (1978: 556) argued that "this certain, that if we recount to the first origin of every nation, we shall find, that there scarce is any race of kings, or form of a commonwealth, that is not primarily founded on usurpation and rebellion ...." Hume (1987: 473) reiterated this theme in his essay, "Of the Original Contract," in which he stated that "[a]lmost all the governments, which exist at present, or of which there remains any record in history, have been founded originally, either in usurpation or conquest, or both, without any pretense of a fair consent, or voluntary subjection of the people." Hume further explained that citizens typically were lulled into accepting the state and reconciling themselves to its authority.

Anne-Robert-Jacques Turgot (1973: 69), a precursor of the modern Austrian School of Economics, wrote in 1750 that "[t]he first [governments] were necessarily the product of war, and thus implied government by one man alone. We need not believe that men ever voluntarily gave themselves *one master.*" Another French-man, the historian Augustin Thierry, asserted that every government has been "created by the mixture of several races: the race of the invaders ... and the race of those invaded" (Oppenheimer, 1997: xiii). And Friedrich Nietzsche believed that "the Stale originates in the cruelest way through conquest" (Oppenheimer, 1997: xiii]).

The German sociologist Ludwig Gumplowicz (1963: 199), whom Franz Oppen-heimer called the "pathfinder" of the conquest theory of the state, explained in great detail why he believed that "[e]very political organization ... begins at the moment when one horde permanently subjugates another."

In the late eighteenth century the British philosopher Josiah Tucker pointed out that the Lockean philosophical system, which had inspired the recently-concluded American revolution and which argued that governments derive their just powers only from the consent of the governed, constituted a test that no government could ever pass. The Lockean system, Tucker (1967: 101) argued, was "an universal Demolisher of all Civil Governments, but not the builder of any." Tucker supported his position by pointing out that the newly-created American government, which was supposedly based on Lockean "natural rights," in fact ignored these principles by not allowing any citizens, not even the residents of a single state, the right to live in a "state of nature" without any government at all.

Edmund Burke (1968: 53) wrote in 1756 that "all empires have been cemented in blood" and that "the greatest part of the governments on earth must be concluded tyrannies, impostures, violations of the natural rights of mankind, and worse than the most disorderly anarchies."

Franz Oppenheimer (1997) carried this tradition forward by using the inductive method of history and the deductive method of economic theory (the kind of theory favored by the Austrian School) to show that the origins of the state lie in conquest, subjugation, and exploitation.

Albert Jay Nock's (1983: 40) description of the origins of the state also seems much more accurate than the theories of constitutional economists. According to Nock, "the State invariably had its origin in conquest and confiscation. No primitive State known to history originated in any other manner ... no primitive State could possibly have had any other origin ... the sole invariable characteristic of the State is the economic exploitation of one class by another."

Buchanan and Tullock (1962: 12) simply assume this historical tradition away with the statement that "we ... reject any theory or conception of the collectivity which embodies the exploitation of a ruled by a ruling class ... Any conception of State activity that divides the social group into the ruling class and the oppressed class, and that regards the political process as simply a means through which this class dominance is established and then preserved, must be rejected as irrelevant for the discussion which follows."

No reason is offered for this. It is merely asserted that the phenomenon of one class of citizens using the powers of the state to exploit and plunder another class of citizens using the powers of the state to exploit and plunder another class – a feature of governments throughout human history – "must be rejected." In doing so, Buchanan and Tullock ignore not only Marxist class analysis but all other non-Marxist theories of class domination without offering any explanation for their rejection.

One political theorist who understood and explained virtually every political phenomenon that has been studied by modem public choice scholars is John C. Calhoun, whom many historians consider to have been the last of the American founding fathers in terms of his educational background and political philosophy (Lence, 1992). Calhoun spent four decades (1811–1850) as a US congressman. senator, secretary of war, and vice president. Once democratic government is established, Calhoun wrote in his "Disquisition on Government," the community will inevitably be "divided into two great parties, a major and a mi nor, between which there will be incessant struggles on the one side to retain, and on the other to obtain the majority – and, thereby, the control of the government and the advantages it confers" (Lence, 1992: 16).

This "deeply seated tendency" that is common in all democracies is sure to divide every political community into "two great hostile parties" which are not Marxian class interests but "the payers of the taxes and the recipients of their proceeds" (Lence, 1992: 17). The "necessary result" of democratic government is "to divide the community into two great classes; one consisting of those who, in reality, pay the taxes, and, of course, bear exclusively the burden of supporting the government; and the other, of those who are the recipients of their proceeds," or of "taxpayers and tax-consumers" (Lence, 1992: 19).

While Buchanan and Tullock assert that even an unwritten or "conceptual" constitution is sufficient for what they believe to be voluntary government. Calhoun issued a dire warning against such thinking more than a century earlier. He thought that even a written constitution that ostensibly prohibited the plundering of one class by another is unworkable, and history seems to have proven him correct. Over time, the majority would "endeavor to elude" any constitutional restrictions on its powers and would simply ignore the arguments of the strict constructionists. Appeals to reason, truth, justice, or the obligations imposed by the constitution would be sneered at by the ruling class as "folly" with the result being a "subversion of the constitution" (Lence, 1992: 27).

Calhoun was an intellectual descendant of the early nineteenth-century French "Industrialist" school of political economy, which originated the study of class conflict not in the Marxian sense but in the sense of one group of citizens being exploited by another group via the auspices of the state. Among the members of this school were Augustin Thierry, Charles Comte, Charles Dunoyer, Destutt de Tracy, Benjamin Constant, and Jean-Baptiste Say (Raico, 1998; Euszent and Martin, 1984). The French Industrialists anticipated the modern economic concept of rent (or rather, loot) seeking, for they distinguished between "producers" (businessmen, working people) and "exploiters" who used politics to live off the labor of others.

Buchanan and Tullock (1962: 22) claim to reject all such analyses as "irrelevant" to their discussion, yet at one point they refer to "preventing the undue exploitation of one group by another through the political process."

More recently, Sowell (1998: 5) focused on the cultural effects of governmental conquest down through the ages. But his work also sheds light on the essential nature of the state and its origins. In cataloguing the history of conquests from the Roman Empire through the twentieth century, Sowell observes that "spontaneous atrocities and deliberate systematic terror have long marked the path of the conqueror."

Another contemporary author who has catalogued the exploitive essence of the state is Fred McChesney (1997) who argues persuasively that much of contemporary government is essentially an extortion and protection racket whereby politicians threaten (with proposed laws and regulations) to confiscate the wealth of various individuals or groups unless they receive political payoffs and bribes in the form of campaign contributions and other benefits.

Government, in McChesney's (1997: 2) opinion, seems hardly different from a legalized Mafia. "Payments to politicians often are made, not for particular favors but to avoid ... political disfavor, that is, as a part of a system of political extortion... Because the state, quite legally, can (and does) take money and other forms of wealth from its citizens, politicians can extort from private parties payments not to expropriate private wealth." Among the tools of political extortion are threats to impose price controls, to close off business opportunities, increase a business's costs through regulation or taxation, deny occupational licenses, or even to nationalize an industry.

## 4. A Blank Check for Interventionism

Applying the constitutionalist perspective, Buchanan has even argued that a thief really favors strict law enforcement and the punishment of thieves. The thief does not want his own property to be stolen any more than anyone else does. Thus, it can he said that a thief consents to his own punishment. But, as a rule and as a practical matter, professional criminals do not frequently run to the police for help or lobby for harsher punishment of criminals. Murderers are not enthusiastic sup-porters of the death penalty, nor are thieves supporters of the Middle Eastern custom of cutting off the hands of those who are caught stealing.

Myriad other government interventions have been rationalized and endorsed by contractarians based on the idea that there must be "conceptual" unanimity, even for policies that appear to benefit only a small number of citizens while imposing enormous costs on everyone else. Sometimes elaborate mathematical models are presented to argue that laws that appear to everyone to benefit only narrow special interests really do benefit everyone after all.

One especially clear example is an article by Buchanan and Lee (1992) which addressed a growing body of historical research showing that the original antitrust laws – including the 1890 Sherman Act – were designed to benefit special interests (i.e., uncompetitive businesses that could not compete with the trusts). They argue that the Sherman Act was not necessarily a special-interest law, despite the evidence of special-interest influence in the economic history literature. It is conceivable, they theorize, that the "common interest" of a "coalition of cartels" was served by the antitrust laws.

The essence of their argument is that each private cartel wants protection from competition, but if such protection becomes too widespread then individual cartels may lose out. They do not want to pay monopoly prices for the things they purchase any more than anyone else does. A "coalition of cartels" may voluntarily attempt to police output restrictions, but it is cheaper to let government do it. This is what antitrust laws can do – at least conceptually.

Buchanan and Lee (1992: 223) do not assert that anything like this ever actually happened, but that there just may possibly be a situation whereby "the coalition [of cartels] can be thought of as implicitly supporting [antitrust legislation] by accepting it, and accommodating to it. It is in this sense that we argue that it is useful to conceive of our coalition of cartels, and of its support for antitrust legislation and enforcement."

No cartel actually lobbies for the law; they all just silently accept whatever legislation other politically-active special-interest groups provide for them, in this case the Sherman Antitrust Act. This is essentially a conscripted sailor theory of antitrust. Because businesses did not wantonly violate the antitrust laws (and face criminal penalties) or openly revolt against them too vigorously (and face regulatory retribution, tax audits, or prison), Buchanan and Lee assume that American businesses can be modeled as having "conceptually" supported antitrust laws.

But there is no need to invent such fictions. There is an historical record to study, and research indicates that the Sherman Act benefited smaller, less competitive businesses and gave the Republican Party, which dominated Congress at the time, political cover for the McKinley tariff, which was sponsored by Senator John Sherman himself and passed just three months after the Sherman Act was passed in June of 1890 (DiLorenzo, 1985; DiLorenzo and Boudreaux, 1995; Hazlett, 1992).

In *The Calculus of Consent* Buchanan and Tullock assert that the non-poor can be construed as really being in favor of a welfare state, even if they voice opposition to it publicly. The reason they are for it is that it supposedly provides a form of "income insurance" that is available to them should they become unemployed. Again, as long as everyone is coerced, no one is really being coerced.

Despite their affinity for framing their analysis in constitutional terms, however, Buchanan and Tullock fail to offer an explanation of why government-enforced income transfers for the purpose of establishing a welfare state were outlawed by the US Constitution, at least until the constitutional order was overthrown by the American Civil War. James Madison, the acknowledged "father" of the Constitution, repeatedly denied that such income transfers were constitutional.

The American welfare state did not appear in any significant size until the 1930s, and even then there was fierce opposition to it. Indeed, much of the New Deal was ruled unconstitutional by the US Supreme Court, although later courts, influenced more by politics than by reverence for the Constitution, eventually gave the welfare state their stamp of approval. Still, nothing close to actual unani-mous consent with regard to the welfare state has ever existed. There were tax revolts during the Great Depression (Beito, 1989) and John T. Flynn (1998) catalogued myriad other opponents of the new welfare state during that period.

If one observes the plight of the typical welfare recipient living in squalor in a government housing project in one of America's cities, where law enforcement is weak if not non-existent, the schools are dysfunctional, and job opportunities are scarce. It is just not believable that this is what any rational person would consider to be a desirable system of "income insurance" worth purchasing.

There is much evidence, moreover, that welfarism has encouraged illegitimacy, family breakup, and a weakening of intergenerational linkages (Murray, 1984; 1993; An, Haveman, and Wolfe, 1993; Schultz, 1994). Families used to be the major source of "income insurance" in times of economic trouble or old age, but the welfare state has imposed serious damage on the institution of the family. As an article in the *American Economic Review* concludes, the family has traditionally served as "an informal self-insurance, or 'family-security' setup," but this "setup" has been severely damaged by government old-age insurance, which induces many people to rely on government, rather than families, to provide such security (Ehrlich and Zhong, 1998: 151J).

There is a name for genuine (as opposed to "conceptual") income insurance: savings. But the welfare state and the high level of taxation to finance it deters savings by increasing the rate of time preference.[4] Furthermore, by draining hundreds of billions of dollars annually from the pockets of productive people, the welfare state makes it more likely that more citizens will be in need of charity at some point in their lives.

Contractarian theories provide theoretical cover for what Buchanan has labeled "apparent" coercion and "apparent" redistribution of income from government policy. One may try to interpret away acts of coercion and theft by calling them apparent, but they remain acts of coercion and theft. We agree with Leland Yeager (1985: 271) that the very word "conceptual," as used by contractarian theorists, "indicates that a 'conceptual' agreement is not an actual one, that a 'conceptually' true proposition is not actually true. It is no mere joke to say that 'conceptually' is an adverb stuck into contractarians' sentences to immunize them from challenge on the grounds of their not being true."

## 5. Constitutional Economics versus Constitutional History

Despite its repetition of the word "constitution," *The Calculus of Consent* and much of the literature on constitutional economics frequently ignores the actual history of the ratification of the US Constitution. Granted, Buchanan and Tullock claim that theirs is primarily a normative theory. But their book is full of policy discussions, propositions, and specific proposals for welfare programs, ways of dealing with externality problems, financing government fire departments, etc. (Buchanan and Tullock, 1962). They invoke historical facts to support their theory and claim that their work is in the same philosophical spirit as that of the American founders who, after all, were involved in creating a practical political document when they wrote the Constitution. For these reasons, we believe it is fair and appropriate to discuss the actual history of the US Constitution as a source of criticism of constitutional economics.

The Constitution was anything but unanimously supported: women did not have the right to vote at the time, nor did non-property owners (not to mention millions of slaves). It was adopted with a majority vote of only nine of the thirteen states through statewide political conventions. The Articles of Confederation, which were replaced by the Constitution, did require the support of all thirteen states.

When the Constitution was ratified about three-fourths of the adult males failed to vote in the elections to send delegates to the state ratification elections – either because they were disinterested or because they were disenfranchised by property qualifications. Thus, the delegates to the state ratification conventions were elected by a vote that included only about one sixth of adult males (Beard, 1986: 325). Many of the states that did vote to adopt the Constitution barely did so, and no state voted unanimously in its favor. Virginia, which was the wealthiest and most influential state at the time, passed it by a margin of 89 to 79 votes; New York voted to ratify by a vote of 30 to 27; Rhode Island's margin was a mere two votes, 3 to 32: and North Carolina initially rejected the Constitution by a 184 to 84 margin, voting a year later to ratify once the new constitution was an accomplished fact (McDonald, 1958).

These four states explicitly reserved the right to withdraw from the Union should the new government threaten their liberties. Patrick Henry was so alarmed by the preponderance of military men among the state convention delegates who favored the Constitution that he warned his fellow Virginians of the possibility of "armed hordes [of soldiers] marching under the banner of the new government to subvert Virginia's liberties" (McDonald, 1958: 262). At the Virginia ratifying convention Henry exhibited "stamina, argument, and rhetoric unmatched on either side" of the debate, wrote Herbert J. Storing (1985: 293), the chronicler of the anti-federalist movement.

Henry's main objections were that by centralizing too much power in the central government, the Constitution effectively destroyed genuine federalism; the document represented a quest for "glory and riches" through empire, rather than liberty: there would be no real checks and balances on governmental responsibility, putting citizens at the mercy of "the virtue of the rulers;" the federal power to tax would effectively neutralize the states and impose unspeakable burdens on the people: the Constitution was unduly militaristic, "pretending external dangers and internal turbulence where none exists:" and the absence of a Bill of Rights would inevitably lead to tyranny (Storing, 1985: 294f.).

George Mason, the author of the Virginia Bill of Rights, which was the model for the Constitution's Bill of Rights, was another vigorous opponent of the Constitution who campaigned tirelessly against it.

The so-called anti-federalists were a large and influential group. They feared that the particular form the Constitution had taken would encourage a dangerous arrangement of government powers

The notion that there was anything near unanimous consent over the signing of the constitution is a myth. Albert Jay Nock (1983: 90) even argued quite con-vincingly that the framers of the Constitution "executed a [non-violent] *coup d'Etat,* simply tossing the Articles of Confederation into the waste-basket, and drafting a constitution *de novo,* with the audacious provision that it should go into effect when ratified by nine units [i.e., states] instead of by all thirteen."


## 6. The Failures of Market Failure Theory

In *The Calculus of Consent* Buchanan and Tullock develop their "interdependence cost" model in the context of a discussion of various examples of externality or spillover effects. It is these "market failure" examples that provide their conceptual rationale for the state based on "cost minimization" arguments.

One example is the organization of a "village fire department" which the authors assume to possess public goods characteristics. Conceptually, the fire department can exist through "purely voluntary co-operative action" under the auspices of a "voluntary" government (Buchanan and Tullock, 1962: 491). But, if it were truly voluntary, there would be no need to label it as "government." There are, in fact, myriad volunteer fire departments that are not funded by taxes. Nor is it necessarily true that "individual protection against fire may not be profitable," as Buchanan and Tullock (1962: 44) assert. It seems to us that it would be impossible for a homeowner to purchase homeowners' insurance without fire protection. This would surely provide a. powerful incentive for individuals to voluntarily purchase fire protection – in addition to the incentive provided by not wanting to die in a house fire.

Nor is a Department of Swamp Drainage necessary. Buchanan and Tullock use swamp drainage as another example of a public good because of its mosquito abatement effects. But private land developers have ample incentives to drain swamps before developing their land. And if some swamps remain undrained, so what? Because benefits and costs are subjective, and because interpersonal utility comparisons are impossible, coerced swamp drainage cannot possibly be Pareto-optimal. In a free market some swamps will remain undrained because it is simply not worth it to drain them.

Higher education is another questionable example of the supposed need for state intervention on the grounds of spillover effects. Buchanan and Tullock (1962: 54) argue that because of the inability of students to "mortgage" their future earning power they are unable to borrow the appropriate capital in private financial markets to sufficiently finance higher education. "[C]ollective or state action may be taken which will remove or reduce the private externalities involved here."

But the reason for this supposed market failure is government intervention, not the free market. Promising to work for an employer, or to work to earn money to pay off one's "educational mortgage," is essentially a form of indentured servitude, the method that in essence allowed hordes of immigrants to come to the US. But the 1866 passage of the Thirteenth Amendment to the Constitution outlawed this practice. Thus, the problem is not that such contracts do not arise on the free market; the problem is that they are prohibited by government. The "restrictions on full freedom of contract" that Buchanan and Tullock allude to are not free-market phenomena.

Municipal zoning is also said to be an appropriate intervention where the costs of dealing with spillover effects coercively, through government, are lower than doing so privately through restrictive covenants or corporate ownership. Buchanan and Tullock cite the example of the large bargaining costs involved in the case of a developer seeking to purchase a large number of individual housing units in a city when individual holdouts may have the ability to stop development altogether.

To advocate government zoning laws in this instance is again to embrace the notion of interpersonal utility comparisons. The explicit assumption is that the increased utility of the developer is necessarily higher than the diminished utility of the "holdouts" whom the state forces to sell out. Such comparisons are an impossibility.

A third example of market failure offered by Buchanan and Tullock is the necessity for government-imposed traffic control (lights, etc.). Surely, virtually everyone would agree that this is a proper role for government. But it cannot be denied that in a world of private road ownership there would be no need for *government* traffic lights; the private owners would have a strong incentive to provide them because of the liability costs to them of not doing so. Furthermore, it should also be acknowledged that in many American cities the phrase "traffic control" is an oxymoron, as traffic has become more and more chaotic – and dangerous. Government "controls" traffic about as well as it operates the post office or the department of motor vehicles (Block, 1983).

Buchanan and Tullock chose these examples of externality and public goods problems in the early 1960s and, to be fair, we must acknowledge that it is possible that they would choose different examples today. New forms of contracts with lower transaction costs may well have been invented in the intervening years. Nevertheless, fire departments, swamp drainage, zoning, higher education, and traffic lights are still widely cited throughout the literature on externalities and market failure and are therefore worthy of comment.


## 7. Conclusions

The fatal flaw in the voluntary theory of the state advanced by constitutional economists is that no state ever has been, or ever could be, voluntary. If one really wants to explore the elements and ramifications of a voluntary society, we suggest closer scrutiny of the libertarian philosophy that no person or group of people may legitimately aggress upon the person or property of anyone else; and that every person has a right to private property, including one's own body and the natural resources which they transform by their labor (Rothbard, 1978; 1998). The application of this doctrine is a promising means of understanding what is meant by a voluntary society.

Applied work by Fred Foldvary (1994) on the market provision of social services; Robert Ellickson (1991) on the private, voluntary resolution of disputes over externality problems; Robert Axelrod's (1984) work on the evolution of cooperation; Bruce Benson's (1998) analysis of private criminal justice systems; and free-market environmentalism are just a few among many promising efforts in this regard (Anderson and Leal, 1991). Exploring actual institutions based on voluntarism, as opposed to relabeling the inherently coercive institution of government as conceptually, but not actually, voluntary, is a much more promising avenue of research.

Our disagreement with constitutional economics is more than a definitional one. Buchanan and Tullock label a wide range of seemingly voluntary collective choice institutions as "government" and, admittedly, a reasonable case can be made that, say, a village fire department might make a good example of voluntary government, at least on a relatively small scale. But the distinguishing characteristic is that in a truly voluntary setting the parties to an agreement have a right to secede from the agreement. If they do not wish to be taxed to pay for fire protection, they are free to live outside the agreement and forego the services or seek them elsewhere. This is not the case with tax-financed services. For example, joining a swimming club is a genuinely voluntary act, whereas paying taxes to support a municipal swimming pool necessarily involves some degree of coercion. The phrase "voluntary government" is simply a contradiction in terms.

## NOTES

1. An anonymous referee suggests that it is difficult to conceive that such institutions as mandatory elementary schooling, mandatory old-age insurance, and public street cleaning are a means by which one group of people coerces another group to pay for its free rides. This point is well taken as long as one only (or primarily) considers monetary values. But if we include subjective or psychic benefits, it is not too hard to conceive. After all, there must be some reason why one group (the majority) would coerce another group to pay for something the second group does not wish to pay for. It may be to save themselves money or there may be ideological reasons, such as with the public school movement. All we call deduce is that there is some reason why the first group works to coerce the second group.

2. Some public choice theorists have argued that no real explanation occurs in a democracy since the losers in one contest may become winners in another. This is the view of Dennis C. Mueller (1989), a former president of the Public Choice Society. We find this view that, as long as governmental exploitation is pervasive, it really does not exist – to be bizarre.

3. This was brought to our attention by Leland Yeager (1985: 270).

4. As Hans-Hermann Hoppe (1993: 121) has stated, the introduction of government as "an agency that can effectively claim ownership over resources it has neither homesteaded, produced, nor contractually acquired, also raises the social rate of time preference of homesteaders, producers, and contractors, and hence creates involuntary impoverishment...."

# REFERENCES

Adams, C. (1993), *For Good and Evil: The Impact of Taxes on the Course of Civilization.* New York: Madison Books.

--- (1998), *Those Dirty Rotten Taxes: The Tax Revolts that Built America.* New York: The Free Press.

Allen, W. B. (ed.) (1980), *George Washington: A Collection.* Indianapolis, IN: Liberty Fund.

An, C., R. C. Haveman, and B. Wolfe (1993), "Teen Out-of-Wedlock Births and Welfare Receipt," *Review of Economics and Statistics* 75: 195–208.

Anderson, T., and D. Leal (1991), *Free Market Environmentalism.* San Francisco, CA: Pacific Institute for Public Policy Research.

Axelrod, R. (1984), *The Evolution of Cooperation.* Cambridge, MA: Harvard University Press.

Beard, C. (1986), *An Economic Interpretation of the Constitution of the United States.* New York: Free Press.

Benson, B. (1998), *To Serve and Protect: Privatization and Community in Criminal Justice.* New York: New York University Press.

Beito, D. T. (1989), *Taxpayers in Revolt: Tax Resistance during the Great Depression.* Chapel Hill, NC: University of North Carolina Press.

Block, W. (1983), "Public Goods and Externalities: The Case of Roads," *Journal of Libertarian Studies* 7: 1–34.

Buchanan, J. M. (1975), *The Limits of Liberty.* Chicago, IL: University of Chicago Press.

-- (1977), *Freedom in Constitutional Contract.* College Station, TX: Texas A&M Press.

-- and D. Lee (1992), "Private Interest Support for Efficiency Enhancing Antitrust Policies," *Economic Inquiry* 30: 218–224.

-- and G. Tullock (1962), *The Calculus of Consent: Logical Foundations of Constitutional Democracy.* Ann Arbor, MI: University of Michigan Press.

Burke, E. (1968), "A Vindication of Natural Society," in E. Burke (ed.), *Selected Writings and Speeches.* Gloucester, MA: Peter Smith.

DiLorenzo, T. J. (1985), "The Origins of Antitrust: An Interest-Group Perspective," *International Review of Law and Economics* 5: 73–90.

-- and D. C. Boudreaux (1993), "The Protectionist Roots of Antitrust," *Review of Austrian Economics* 6: 81–96.

Ellickson, R. C. (1991), *Order without Law.* Cambridge, MA: Harvard University Press.

Ehrlich, I., and J.-G. Zhong (1998), "Social Security and the Real Economy," *American Economic Review* 88: 151–157.

Euszent, P. J., and T. L. Martin (1984), "Classical Roots of the Emergent Theory of Rent Seeking: The Contribution of Jean-Baptiste Say," *History of Political Economy* 16: 225–262.

Foldvary, F. (1994), *Public Goods and Private Communities: The Market Provision of Social Services.* Brookfield, VT: Edgar Elgar.

Flynn, J. T. (1998), *The Roosevelt Myth.* San Francisco, CA: Fox and Wilkes.

Gumplowicz, L. (1963), *Outlines of Sociology.* New York: Paine-Whitman.

Hazlett, T. (1992), "The Legislative History of the Sherman Act Revisited," *Economic Inquiry* 30: 263–276.

Hoppe, H.-H. (1993), *The Economics and Ethics of Private Property: Studies in Political Economy and Philosophy.* Boston, MA: Kluwer.

Hume, D. (1965), "Of the Original Contract," in: A. Macintyre and D. Hume (eds.), *Hume: Ethical Writings*. New York: Collier Books.

-- (1978), *A Treatise on Human Nature*. Oxford: Oxford University Press.

-- (1987), *Essays: Moral, Political, and Literary*. Indianapolis, IN: Liberty Fund.

Kalt, J. (1981), "Public Goods and the Theory of Government," *Cato Journal* 1: 565–584.

Lence, R. M. (1992), *Union and Liberty: The Political Philosophy of John C. Calhoun*. Indianapolis, IN: Liberty Fund.

McChesney, F. (1997), *Money for Nothing*. Cambridge, MA: Harvard University Press.

McDonald, F. (1958), *We the People: The Economic Origins of the Constitution*. Chicago, IL: University of Chicago Press.

Mueller, D. (1989), *Public Choice II: A Revised Edition of Public Choice*. New York: Cambridge University Press.

Murray, C. (1984), *Losing Ground*. New York: Basic Books.

-- (1993), "Welfare and Family: The US Experience," *Journal of Labor* Economics 2: 224–262.

Nock, A.J. (1983), *Our Enemy, the State*. Delean, WI: Hallberg Publishing Co.

Oppenheimer, F. (1997), *The State*. San Francisco, CA: Fox & Wilkes.

Pascal, B. (1932), *Pascal's Pensées*. London: J. M. Dent & Sons.

Raico, R. (1998), "Classical Liberal Rots of the Marxist Doctrine of Classes," in Y. Maltsev (ed.), *Requiem for Marx*. Auburn, AL: Ludwig von Mises Institute, 189–220.

Rothbard, M. (1978), *For a New Liberty*. San Francisco, CA: Fox & Wilkes.

-- (1997), *The Logic of Action II*. Edward Elgar: Cheltenham.

-- (1998), *The Ethics of Liberty*. New York: New York University Press.

Schultz, P. (1994), "Marital Status and Fertility in the United States," *Journal of Human Resources* 29: 637–669.

Sowell, T. (1998), *Conquests and Cultures: An International History*. New York: Basic Books.

Storing, H.J. (1985), *The Anti-Federalist: Writings by Opponents of the Constitution*. Chicago, IL: University of Chicago Press.

Tucker, J. (1967), *A Treatise Concerning Civil Government*. New York: Augustus Kelley.

Turgot, A.-R.-J. (1973), "On Universal History," in R.L. Meek (ed.), *Turgot on Progress, Sociology, and Economics*. Cambridge: Cambridge University Press, 41–118.

Vanberg, V. (1998), "The Impossibility of Rational Regulation? Regulation, Free-Market Liberalism. and Constitutional Liberalism," paper presented at the Annual Meeting of the Mont Pelerin Society, Washington, DC, August 31.

Yeager, L. (1985), "Rights, Contract, and Utility in Policy Espousal," *Cato Journal* 5: 269–289.

# Chapter 5
# George Stigler and
# the Myth of Efficient Government

## 1. Introduction

George Stigler took the Chicago School's "perfect markets" model to its logical extreme when, in a 1992 article in the *Journal of Law and Economics*, he declared that

> 1) politics is just another market, complete with 'buyers and sellers of legislation,' and
> 2) all long-lived governmental institutions are therefore 'efficient' by virtue of their having survived for a long time.[1]

Another Chicago School scholar, Donald Wittman, goes even further, calling government failure a "myth" and asserting that democratic government unequivocally promotes the welfare of all citizens.[2] The free market may never meet the perfectly competitive ideal but democratic government, to these two scholars, is Pareto optimal.

This article argues that while there are a few transparent similarities between politics and markets, the fundamental differences between them render the Stigler-Wittman view that politics is "just another market," and therefore always "efficient," dubious at best. Markets are not perfect in any neoclassical sense (nor is anything else on earth, for that matter), and neither is democracy. The Stigler-Wittman view is based on a false view of how both markets and governments operate and also suffers from being ahistorical.

## 2. Efficient Government?

Stigler may have had a reputation as a free-market champion of individualism but, ironically, his argument about "efficient" government was based on methodological collectivism. Rather than examining the behavior of individual actors, even in their roles as members of political interest groups, Stigler posited that "society," not individual decision makers, makes political choices.

> [I]n policy analysis, one may legitimately employ an alternative definition of efficiency that rests on the goals adopted by the society through its government. When a society wishes, for example, to give more income to a group than the market provides, we may surely analyze the efficiency with which this is done. In this . . . view, every durable social institution or practice is efficient, or it would not persist over time.[3]

This means that all common *and statute law* "must be efficient."[4] Stigler's Exhibit A in his catalogue of "efficient" government programs is the sugar price support program, which at the time (1992) was responsible for the transfer of more than $3 billion annually from sugar consumers to a small handful of politically-influential sugar-growing corporations. The program was necessarily efficient, said Stigler, because it had met the test of time: it had been around for 50 years. In keeping with the Chicago tradition of empiricism, this would suggest that Soviet communism, which at the time of Stigler's article was 75 years old, was exactly 50 percent more efficient than the U.S. sugar price support program.[5]

India is the world's largest democracy and has maintained more or less the same socialist institutions for more than 50 years. By Stigler's (and Wittman's) standards, India is arguably the largest purveyor of governmental "efficiency" in the world. Slavery existed for over 80 years under American democracy, which would presumably make it 60 percent more efficient than the sugar program.

Stigler's model explicitly assumes that there is little or no agency problem – no separation of ownership from control – when it comes to the relationship between citizens and government. Goals are adopted by "society" through its government, and as long as those goals are pursued for a long time, they are necessarily "efficient." Moreover, the goals that government sets for us are said to be exceptionally "authoritative," even though no explanation is given by Stigler for the source of this authority.

Chicago School scholars accept competitive equilibrium as their ideal bench-mark and, as such, they also accept the whole framework of welfare or market failure economics, including the supposed necessity of antitrust regulation. But in Stigler's model, there is no corresponding government failure: government is essentially perfectly competitive. Politicians faithfully pursue the goals of "society" in an efficient manner.

Stigler was obviously aware of the voluminous government failure or public choice literature, but his argument ignores it completely.[6]


## 3. Forced Labor and Efficient Government

Government power rests primarily on its use of threats, intimidation, coercion, violence, propaganda, and fraud. If one protests the wastefulness of the sugar price support program, Pentagon fraud, the welfare state, or anything else by refusing to file a tax return, for example, the result will at first be threatening letters, then intimidating demands for payment, and ultimately the use of armed force to confiscate the protester's assets or throw him into prison. The fact that citizens do not revolt and overthrow their governments very often does not mean that they consent to being plundered. As David Hume once pointed out, the fact that a conscripted sailor does not jump overboard and commit suicide does not mean that he consents to being conscripted.[7]

Secession from the corrupt, rent-seeking society that is lorded over by the federal government can also be risky and life threatening, as the Southern Confederates learned more than 135 years ago. Although modern historians usually ignore it, the Confederate Constitution attempted to limit the domain of government much more than the U.S. Constitution did, by outlawing protectionist tariffs and the use of taxpayer funds for corporate subsidies, and by eliminating the General Welfare Clause of the U.S. Constitution, among other things.[8]

But protectionist tariffs, subsidies to railroad corporations, and central banking (which most Southern statesmen also opposed) were the keystones of the 1860 Republican Party platform. Consequently, Abraham Lincoln waged a bloody war in which one out of every four white Southerners between the ages of 20 and 40 was killed by the federal government in order to "save the Union." This phrase was Lincoln's euphemism for creating a centralized state that overthrew the smaller, more decentralized system of government that had been created by the American founding fathers.[9] The right of secession, which many of the founding fathers considered to be *the* principle of the Revolution of 1776, was destroyed, along with the Jeffersonian doctrine of states' rights as a check on the overreaching powers of the central government.

The Jeffersonian dictum enshrined in the Declaration of Independence that governments derive their just powers from the consent of the governed was essentially overturned by Lincoln's war. Southerners no longer consented to be governed by Washington, D.C., and they were forced into an association with that government at gunpoint. From that point on, the American government became more and more the master, rather than servant, of the people.

It is this kind of violence, force, and coercion that lies behind and supports "long-lived government programs." There were no long-lived income transfer programs prior to the War Between the States. By ignoring this history, the Stigler-Wittman theory of governmental efficiency implicitly assumes that forced labor (to pay taxes) is an efficiency-enhancing institution since that is what allows special-interest programs to last for decades despite their inefficiencies and injustices. Indeed, it is fair to say that forced labor is a *prerequisite* for Stigler's brand of governmental "efficiency."

Products or practices that last a long time in private markets can be said to be efficient in that they assist market participants in coordinating their plans better than any alternative arrangements. In government, the income-transfer programs that Stigler and Wittman think are "efficient" can only last if threats, intimidation, fraud, and violence are used to keep them in place. The fact that such tactics must be used is evidence of how grossly *inefficient* such acts of theft really are in the sense that they are *not* the kinds of institutions that assist individuals in plan coordination. If they were truly efficient, people would adopt them voluntarily.

## 4. The Role of Propaganda

Government doesn't always resort to outright violence or threats of violence to maintain its powers; excessive use of such tactics could incite a revolution, as they have on occasion throughout history. Consequently, it also operates a massive fraud operation designed to perpetually pull the wool over the public's eyes.[10] Or, in the polite, euphemistic language of academic discourse, it "manipulates constitutional level transaction costs."[11]

The average citizen is "rationally ignorant" of most governmental policy issues, increasingly so as the size and scope of government increases. The *Federal Register*, for example, contains more than 80,000 pages of fine-print regulations that affect every industry in America, and almost all aspects of our lives. No human could possibly possess knowledge of anything but a minuscule portion of such a monstrous document. Federal tax laws and regulations are just as voluminous. This suggests that it is quite absurd to believe that voters are actually voting for real changes in public policy. How could they be voting for changes in policy if they have no way of understanding what more than a minuscule fraction of government policy consists of?

It is not in the average citizen's financial interest to invest sufficient time to become well informed in any but a few areas of public policy. This gives special-interest groups – including government officials and employees themselves – the latitude to manipulate political outcomes in democracies in ways that benefit themselves *at the expense* of nearly everyone else, which is hardly an "efficient" outcome. More than 50 years ago, Joseph Schumpeter observed that:

> What we are confronted with in the analysis of political processes is largely not a genuine but a manufactured will. . . . So far as this is so, the will of the people is the product and not the motive power of the political process.[12]

The hoary welfare economics dictum that special-interest transfer payments should be considered to be efficient as long as, *in theory,* the winners can compensate the losers (i.e., taxpayers) is a red herring argument. No such compensation has ever occurred, and even if it had, it is not clear that it could ever be efficient by the criteria established by neoclassical economics.

Far from Stigler's (and Wittman's) implicit assumption of near perfect information among voters, real-world voters are, for the most part, grossly uninformed about what government is up to. To make matters worse, much of what they do "know" is self-serving propaganda that is repeatedly broadcast to them by government itself. Government spends billions of dollars attempting to persuade the public that policies that in reality only benefit a small special interest group, including the state itself, are really in "the public interest."

In *Official Lies: How Washington Misleads Us,* James Bennett and I detailed how institutionalized governmental lying pervades all areas of government policy.[13]

In welfare policy, government statistics do not count cash and in-kind subsidies as part of the income of "the poor," nor does government subtract out taxes from the income of the more affluent when publishing its "income distribution" statistics. This allows it to perpetually complain about the "inequity" of capitalism and to advocate egalitarianism.

Farm subsidies go mostly to large corporate farms, although decades of propaganda have convinced millions of Americans that it is the "small family farm" that is the primary beneficiary. From the time oil was discovered in the U.S. in the 1860s, various government agencies have been warning of an impending depletion of the oil supply unless there is a governmental takeover. Government-funded lies about environmental policy are almost too numerous to count. Military policy lies are so pervasive that "Pentagon propaganda" has become a redundancy.

Governmental control of schooling has always been motivated by a desire on the part of politicians to brainwash children in one ideology or another.[14] John Lott has argued that this is so because such brainwashing makes government's income-transfer schemes more palatable to the public, which in turn makes it easier for politicians to maintain power by buying votes with taxpayers' money. In other words, it reduces the transactions costs of wealth transfers.

Although there are countervailing forces, such as certain educational institutions, the internet, talk radio, etc., it is nevertheless true that government still has the ability to drown out most other voices with its vast propaganda resources. And it doesn't need to drown all other voices out; only enough of them so that a majority of the rationally ignorant voting public continues to believe its lies.

These countervailing forces of public opinion have the deck stacked against them in a most lopsided way. When it created the welfare state, the federal government chose to administer its new programs through thousands of ostensibly private, nonprofit organizations. The same is true of many other government programs regarding environmental policy, civil rights policy, old-age policy, labor policy, etc. These nonprofit organizations (including labor unions) receive billions of dollars annually in government grants. Much of this money goes not to assist the poor or the elderly, to improve the environment, etc., but to finance the lobbying for bigger budgets for the governmental agencies that made the grants in the first place.[15]

Here's how it works:

1) Government agencies grant taxpayer dollars to nonprofit groups to ostensibly administer government programs.

2) The groups devote half or more of the money (illegally) to a lobbying and publicity campaign in favor of greater taxpayer funding for the program.

3) Congress is "persuaded" to spend more on the program.

4) This allows the nonprofit groups to receive even bigger grants.

5) The whole cycle starts over again from step 1.

The "will of the majority" is much more of a government-manufactured will than even Joseph Schumpeter imagined. Stigler's basic assumption that governments faithfully respond to the wishes of "society" rests on a very weak foundation indeed.

In addition, nearly every state-funded university in America is a *de facto* "think tank" for the promotion of statism. It should surprise no one that as government funding has so overwhelmingly dominated the financing of higher education, most academics who have anything to say about public policy have become paid mouthpieces of the state. Their claims of academic freedom ring hollow.

Stigler's theory of efficient government is based on a model of perfectly competitive government, but in reality the government has long established a system of barriers to entry into politics that renders national politics monopolistic. This, too, is a fatal flaw in Stigler's model. It has not been at all unusual over the past 50 years for well over 90 percent of all congressional incumbents to be reelected in each election cycle because of the formidable incumbent-protection rules and institutions that have been put into place. Incumbent members of Congress receive over $100 million annually in "free" mailing privileges which they use to send campaign literature to their home districts and states. Challengers must pay their own way.

Each congressional representative has more than two dozen taxpayer-financed "staffers," while senators have about 75 staffers each. These individuals effectively comprise a permanent, taxpayer-funded campaign staff. Challengers must raise money privately to hire their campaign staffs.

Incumbents in Congress have created dozens of committees and subcommittees, the purpose of each is to make sure that each incumbent can be on a committee that specializes in dispensing taxpayer dollars or special favors to the voters of his or her district or state. Farm-state legislators will be on various agricultural committees, for example, whereas those from urban areas will sit on the Banking and Urban Affairs committee. Since it is illegal for challengers to buy votes, this too creates a formidable barrier to entry into politics. Incumbents are free to use taxpayer dollars to buy votes, but challengers can only make vague promises to do so.

In Stigler's perfectly competitive government, any policy that is opposed by enough people will be replaced though the electoral process, just as consumers will replace an inferior product by "voting" with their dollars. But that's only (remotely) possible if there is a reasonable degree of competition in government. In the U.S. federal government, there is not. Even at the state and local levels of government in the U.S., consolidation of local governments and state and federal mandates that tend to homogenize local government policies render state and local government more monopolistic.

Stigler was always a strong proponent of antitrust regulation for the private sector for economic efficiency reasons. Yet, he maintained that monopoly *government* was somehow economically efficient.

## 5. Financial Subterfuge

Another fundamentally fraudulent aspect of democratic governments is their proclivity to hide or disguise the true costs of their operation through various subterfuges, such as off-budget spending, while simultaneously spending billions on propaganda campaigns that wildly exaggerate the supposed benefits of government programs and activities. For well over a century, federal, state, and local governments in the U.S. have responded to citizen demands for tax cuts, expenditure restraints, or debt limitations by paying lip service to these demands while at the same time creating myriad off-budget enterprises that can spend money without the direct approval (via referendum, for example) or even knowledge of the voters.[16] At government's state and local levels, time and time again, when voters reject a spending referenda, politicians routinely respond by establishing off-budget enterprises funded by non-voter approved "revenue bonds." At the federal level, debt finance permits the government to disguise its true cost, as does the "fiscal illusion" created by dozens of well-hidden excise taxes. There is even a "Federal Financing Bank" that was set up in 1974 specifically to place certain kinds of (politically unpopular) spending off the books and to keep it well hidden from the taxpayers.[17]

The essential question that is raised by all these subterfuges is this: If these government programs are genuinely in the "public interest" and efficiency enhancing, why then do politicians consistently go to such great lengths to keep the public from learning about them?

## 6. Government as Extortion Artist

Another characteristic of democratic governments that calls into question the validity of Stigler's government-is-always-efficient claim is Fred McChesney's well-researched thesis that much of modern democratic government is essentially a protection racket.[18] McChesney models and catalogues dozens of examples of politicians threatening (with proposed laws and regulations) to confiscate the wealth of various individuals or groups unless they (the politicians) receive payoffs and bribes in the form of campaign contributions and other payments. "Payments to politicians are often made," writes McChesney, "not for particular favors, but to avoid ... political disfavor, that is, as a part of a system of political extortion."[19] Congressmen and congressional staffers refer to such legislation as "juice bills," designed to "squeeze" money from potential contributors, or "milker bills," designed to "milk" money from corporations that would be harmed by, say, a price control law affecting their industry. The threat of price controls or an excise tax imposed on an industry can result in millions of dollars in campaign contributions from the threatened industries.

Even Stigler's vaunted sugar price support program would fall under McChesney's "extortion" designation. The sugar program, like so many government subsidy programs, must be renewed every couple of years. That way, every couple of years, members of Congress are guaranteed of a new round of bribery as both the sugar farmers and the opponents of the program lobby and make campaign contributions to hopefully shape the "new" bill in their favor. Every five years, this same game is played with a new "farm bill" that goes before Congress. This encourages the maximum amount of rent seeking, and thus the maximum amount of economic inefficiency. Consequently, the longer lived a special-interest transfer program is, the more economic destruction it will have caused in terms of wasteful rent seeking. Stigler and Wittman have it all backward.

## 7. The Myth of Politics as "Just Another Market"

Stigler and Wittman's the-government-is-always-efficient theories assume that there are no significant differences between private property markets and "political markets." "Markets are markets," they would say. Wittman even says that political "markets" are "sufficiently like" private property markets that whatever conclusions hold for private property markets must also hold for politics as well. This is the key assumption of his analysis, and of Stigler's as well, but it is based mostly on faith.

One implication of this assumption is that government pursues its goals every bit as efficiently as does any private business. This is most certainly false because of the stark differences between profit management in private property markets and bureaucratic management in government. As Mises pointed out, because there is no cash value on the market of any governmental agency (they cannot be bought and sold), and there are no profit-and-loss statements in an accounting sense, there is simply no way to know how "efficient" a government enterprise is in pursuing its objectives. Economic calculation is impossible.[20]

In private property markets, entrepreneurs tend to allocate capital in ways that satisfy the most urgent wants of consumers. Resources are allocated and reallocated to their highest-valued uses. No such thing occurs in government, since resources are allocated largely according to the degree of political clout of various special-interest groups, not according to private capital markets. Government budgets only provide information on the amounts of tax dollars spent on particular programs but say nothing (nor can they) about the opportunity costs of those expenditures, i.e., the subjective value of alternative uses of those tax dollars either by taxpayers or by other government agencies.

In profit-seeking businesses, the managers' behavior is guided by considerations of profit and loss; in government, managers' behavior is guided by arcane, voluminous, and often arbitrary bureaucratic rules.[21] It has to be this way if elected officials are to have any control at all over the bureaucracies to which they allocate taxpayers' revenues. In other words, it is impossible to think of government bureaucracies as being "efficient" in the allocation of resources in the same sense as private competitive businesses are, not to mention the widely-discussed incentives for inefficiency that are known to exist in all government bureaucracies. Indeed, there is wide agreement in the public choice literature and elsewhere that government bureaucracies are best viewed as cost or budget *maximizers* rather than as cost minimizers, as is the case with private competitive firms.

## 8. Political Entrepreneurship versus Private Property Entrepreneurship

Private property entrepreneurs succeed by discovering ways to reduce costs and prices, improve product or service quality, or by inventing new products that meet the approval of consumers. They succeed, in other words, by catering to consumers. If they fail to please consumers, they lose money or go bankrupt.

In politics, the opposite is often true: "entrepreneurial" politicians "succeed" by *avoiding* the minor constraints imposed on their behavior by the elections that are held every two or four years. The most "successful" political "entrepreneurs" are the ones who are most adept at convincing a gullible, public-school-educated, rationally ignorant public that they can offer them something for nothing. They are the slickest liars and propagandists. Bill Clinton was arguably the biggest and best liar in American politics over the past half century, and was one of the most successful politicians as well. As discussed above, successful political "entrepreneurs" are good at

• telling official lies about government policy,
• hiding the costs of government with fiscal illusions created by excise taxation and debt finance,
• creating off-budget government enterprises to further hide the true costs of government from the public,
• and allocating large amounts of taxpayer dollars to nonprofit sector special interest groups which grossly exaggerate the benefits and understate the costs of special-interest legislation.[22]

## 9. Dollars versus Votes

In private property markets, consumers "vote" with their dollars, to make a Stigleresque analogy. This means that consumers can decide for themselves just how much of any product or service they want, if they want it at all. And they are perfectly free to change their minds more or less constantly by engaging in market transactions. Moreover, all market exchanges are voluntary; no one is forced into them. Market exchange is always *mutually beneficial* as long as it is voluntary.

In dramatic contrast, political "exchange," takes place very seldom. During any eight-year period, each voter is allowed to vote twice for president, four times for a U.S. representative, and, at most, three times for a U.S. Senator, even though those individuals are among the 535 men and women who allocate more than a third of GDP and enforce literally tens of thousands of regulations that affect nearly all aspects of our lives.[23] Moreover, since citizens have no capability to understand anything but a minuscule percentage of what government does, the act of voting is more analogous to judging a beauty contest or attending a sporting event than to a market transaction.[24]

Voting is an all-or-none choice. No disaggregation of issues is permitted, in the sense that the free market allows consumers to "disaggregate" products (I like Coke, you like Pepsi). Once majority rule has decided the winner, that candidate's administration will prevail, creating "political externalities" to all voters both to the left and to the right of that winning candidate. For example, if we used democracy to determine what kind of shoes to produce, and the majority wanted to produce men's shoes in size 10D, then we would become a nation of sore feet, as everyone with bigger or smaller feet would be inconvenienced and would have to rely on black market shoes. This is analogous to market exchange?


## 10. The Importance of Private Property

On an even more fundamental level, markets rely crucially on private property and the enforcement of contracts. Without private property, there can be no markets; without markets there can be no economically meaningful prices; and without market prices rational economic calculation – and a functioning economy – is impossible. Property rights provide individuals with incentives to work and produce, and to improve one's ability to do so through training and education, for stable property rights allow one to reap the fruits of such labors.

In contrast, for the most part, democratic government involves a process of one group of citizens bribing legislators to *attenuate* the private property rights of others for no other reason than the first group wishes to (legally) steal the others' property.[25] It is the domain of rent-seeking behavior. The business of modern democracy is to attenuate property rights in order to fuel the special-interest, rent-seeking machine. This is very much the *opposite* of voluntary, consensual, private property markets. Merely repeating over and over that "politics is like markets," as Stigler, Wittman, and some other Chicago School scholars have done, does not make it so. The attenuation of property rights that is the defining characteristic of democracy weakens incentives to be productive while increasing the rewards of unproductive rent seeking.

One implication of this analysis is that the people who rise to the top in democratic governments are those who are adept at orchestrating the rent-seeking game. Indeed, years of experience at lower levels of office (city council, state legislature) is the usual prerequisite for higher office. As Hans-Hermann Hoppe puts it, "democracy virtually assures that only dangerous men will rise to the top of government."[26] Dangerous, in the sense that they are adept at destroying property by facilitating the plunder of rent seeking. As rent seeking becomes more pervasive in a democracy, more and more people will decide to try to become adept at it rather than becoming genuinely productive citizens. The proportion of parasites will rise relative to producers, which will cause national wealth to be lower than it would otherwise be. Hoppe has written:

> [A]ny income or wealth redistribution within civil society implies that the recipients are made economically better off without having produced either more or better goods or services, while others are made worse off without their having produced quantitatively or qualitatively less. Not producing, not producing anything worthwhile, or not correctly predicting the future and the future exchange-demand for one's products thus becomes relatively more attractive. . . as compared to producing something of value and predicting the future exchange-demand correctly. Consequently. . . there will be more people producing less and displaying poor foresight, and fewer people producing more and predicting well.[27]

This is not a very "efficient" prospect.

Private property markets induce many people to moderate their time preference rate and be somewhat future oriented. Homeowners, for example, have incentives to preserve the value of their property because any appreciation accrues solely to them upon sale, as do any losses. Democratic government, on the other hand, promotes an increase in the rate of time preference (short-term thinking) – what Hoppe calls the "infantilization of society" – with its constantly expanding taxation and spending, inflation, and unending flood of special-interest legislation designed to satisfy every perceived want of every segment of the electorate.[28] This is another important source of inefficiency to which Stigler and Wittman pay no attention.

## 11. Democracy as Banditry

Modern democracies have evolved into gangs of bandits who rely on the public's worshipful attitude toward democracy (promoted for generations in the government-run schools) to "justify" the game of stealing one person's property in order to buy votes from two or more others with it. But America's founding fathers did not believe in democracy and they did not establish one, and for good reason: they understood that democracy would quickly become the kind of system that we have today. In hindsight, they were naive to believe that the Constitution would be sufficient to block this outcome.

One political theorist who understood this was John C. Calhoun, former American vice president, secretary of war, senator, and congressman. Calhoun understood that under any kind of democracy, the community will inevitably be divided into:

> two great parties, a major and a minor, between which there will be incessant struggles on the one side to retain, and on the other to obtain the majority – and thereby, the control of the government and the advantages it confers.[29]

There would be "two great hostile parties," comprised of "the payers of the taxes and the recipients of their proceeds," with the inevitable result that society will be divided into:

> two great classes; one consisting of those who, in reality, pay the taxes, and, of course, bear exclusively the burden of supporting the government; and the other, of those who are the recipients of their proceeds (the tax-consumers).[30]

Because of the powerful incentives that the tax-consuming class would have to plunder the taxpaying class, Calhoun did not believe that the Constitution was sufficient to keep the government from becoming a permanent instrument of plunder. The tax-consuming majority would perpetually "endeavor to elude" all constitutional restrictions on their plundering ways, and they would wage a relentless propaganda campaign to portray such restrictions as "folly."[31] Calhoun supported the rights of secession and nullification, as did nearly all of the founding generation, and introduced the concept of a concurrent majority – the right of a subgroup of the population, such as a state, to veto unconstitutional legislation. All of these protections against the plunder of democracy were abolished in 1865 when the federal government finally established its supremacy over the states and the citizens, and appointed itself as the final arbiter of constitutionality.[32]

The kind of constitutional republic that existed in the U.S. prior to 1865 had very few income transfer programs. The only contact the average citizen had with the federal government was through mailing a letter. There were no long-lived income transfer programs, and the economy was much more efficient as a result. Yet, it is the post-war democracy, not the constitutional republic of the founding fathers, that Stigler and Wittman theorize as efficient, which again seems altogether backwards. There are many varieties of democracy, but Stigler and Wittman treat all of them equally. In doing so, they ignore centuries of political philosophy, including modern public choice theory, that has much to say about how all the various permutations of democracy have led to very different results over time and space. Economists can arrive at some awfully absurd conclusions if they insist on ignoring the study of history and philosophy while commenting on such momentous issues as the successes and failures of democracy.

# NOTES

1. Stigler, George (1992), "Law or Economics?," *Journal of Law and Economics* 35 October: 455–68.

2. Wittman, Donald (1995), *The Myth of Democratic Failure.* Chicago, IL: University of Chicago Press.

3. Stigler, "Law or Economics?," 459.

4. Stigler, "Law or Economics?," 459. Research in law and economics casts doubt on the notion that even the common law is efficient, however. Paul Rubin and Martin Bailey have shown, for example, how tort lawyers have shaped modern product liability law *to benefit lawyers primarily,* and not even the victims of product liability problems. See Rubin, Paul, and Martin Bailey (1994), "The Role of Lawyers in Changing the Law," *Journal of Legal Studies* 23(2): 807–831. Peter Huber comes to a similar conclusion in his book (1988), *Liability: The Legal Revolution and its Consequences.* New York: Basic Books.

5. Stigler did not explicitly state that he was restricting his comments to democratic governments.

6. Stigler published several articles in *Public Choice,* and included in his references two classics in the field, Buchanan, James, and Gordon Tullock (1962), *The Calculus of Consent: Logical Foundations of Constitutional Democracy.* Ann Arbor, MI: University of Michigan Press, 1962, and Downs, Anthony (1957), *An Economic Theory of Democracy.* New York: Harper, so he can hardly claim ignorance of this literature. Oddly, he does not discuss these works, or public choice in general, in the text of his article. Many of his references, in fact, seem to have no relation to the discussion in the text of his article.

7. Hume, David (1965), "Of the Original Contract," in A. MacIntyre and D. Hume (eds.), *Hume's Ethical Writings.* New York: Collier Books, 263.

8. DiLorenzo, Thomas J. (2002), *The Real Lincoln: A New Look at Abraham Lincoln, His Agenda, and an Unnecessary War.* New York: Forum/Random House.

9. Lincoln's position was always that his "paramount objective" was to "save the Union," even if he could do it without freeing a single slave. His only use of the slavery issue, he repeatedly stated, was as a propaganda tool in the service of his overriding objective, consolidating governmental power in Washington, D.C., by destroying the right of secession.

10. E.g., while hypocritically policing "consumer fraud" through the Federal Trade Commission, government itself is exempt from FTC regulation.

11. Twight, Charlotte (1988), "Government Manipulation of Constitutional-Level Transaction Costs: A General Theory of Transaction-Cost Augmentation and the Growth of Government," *Public Choice* 56: 131–52.

12. Schumpeter, Joseph (1950), *Capitalism, Socialism, and Democracy.* New York: Harper & Row, 263.

13. Bennett, James T., and Thomas J. DiLorenzo (1992), *Official Lies: How Washington Misleads Us.* Alexandria, VA: Groom Books.

14. Sowell, Thomas (1993), *Inside American Education.* New York: Free Press; and West, E.G. (1994), *Education and the State: A Study in Political Economy,* 3rd edn. Indianapolis, IN: Liberty Fund.

15. Bennett, James T., and Thomas J. DiLorenzo (1985), *Destroying Democracy: How Government Funds Partisan Politics.* Washington, D.C.: Cato Institute.

16. Bennett, James T., and Thomas J. DiLorenzo (1983), *Underground Government: The Off-Budget Public Sector.* Washington, D.C.: Cato Institute.

17. Bennet and DiLorenzo, *Underground Government*.

18. McChesney, Fred (1997), *Money for Nothing*. Cambridge, MA: Harvard University Press.

19. McChesney, *Money for Nothing*, 2.

20. Mises, Ludwig von (1998), *Human Action: A Treatise on Economics*. Auburn, AL: Ludwig von Mises Institute, 305.

21. Mises, *Human Action*, 306. See also Downs, Anthony (1966), *Inside Bureaucracy*. Boston, MA: Little, Brown.

22. There is an occasional reformer who genuinely does succeed at making government somewhat more efficient, such as former mayor Brett Schundler of Jersey City, New Jersey, but they seldom last very long in politics, as is the case with Mr. Schundler, who was trounced in New Jersey's November 2001 gubernatorial election.

23. Don Boudreaux makes this point in (1996), "Was Your High-School Civics Teacher Right After All? Donald Wittman's *The Myth of Democratic Failure*," *The Independent Review* 1 Spring: 117.

24. Brennan, Geoffrey, and Loren Lomasky (1993), *Democracy and Decision*. New York: Cambridge University Press.

25. A study prepared for the Joint Economic Committee of Congress in 1998 concluded that only 14 percent of all federal expenditures could conceivably be construed as "economically productive" expenditures that facilitated economic growth, as opposed to pure transfer payments. See Joint Economic Committee (1998), *The Size and Functions of Government and Economic Growth*, report prepared by James Gwartney, Robert Lawson, and Randall Holcombe.

26. Hoppe, Hans-Hermann, "The Democratic Leviathan," www.mises.org. See also his book (2001), *Democracy – The God that Failed*. New Brunswick, NJ: Transaction Publishers.

27. Hoppe, *Democracy – The God that Failed*, 32.

28. Ibid.

29. Calhoun, John C. (1992), *Union and Liberty: The Political Philosophy of John C. Calhoun*, ed. R. M. Lence. Indianapolis, IN: Liberty Fund, 16.

30. Calhoun, *Union and Liberty*, 19.

31. Calhoun, *Union and Liberty*, 27.

32. For more on Calhoun's thought, see the symposium on (2002), "Federalism, War, and Reconstruction: Antecedents and Consequences of the War Between the States," *Journal of Libertarian Studies* 16(2). In particular, see Gutzman, K.R. Constantine, "Paul to Jeremiah: Calhoun's Abandonment of Nationalism," and Cheeck, Jr., H. Lee, "Calhoun, Sectional Conflict, and Modern America."

## REFERENCES

Bennett, James T., and Thomas J. DiLorenzo (1985), *Destroying Democracy: How Government Funds Partisan Politics*. Washington, D.C.: Cato Institute.

———— (1992), *Official Lies: How Government Misleads Us*. Alexandria, VA: Groom Books.

———— (1983), *Underground Government: The Off-Budget Public Sector*. Washington, D.C.: Cato Institute.

Boudreaux, Donald C. (1996), "Was Your High School Civics Teacher Right After All? Donald Wittman's *The Myth of Democratic Failure*," *The Independent Review* 1 Spring: 111–128.

Brennan, Geoffrey, and Loren Lomasky (1993), *Democracy and Decision*. New York: Cambridge University Press.

Buchanan, James, and Gordon Tullock (1962), *The Calculus of Consent: Logical Foundations of Constitutional Democracy*. Ann Arbor, MI: University of Michigan Press.

Calhoun, John C. (1992), *Union and Liberty: The Political Philosophy of John C. Calhoun*. R. M. Lence (ed.). Indianapolis, IN: Liberty Fund.

DiLorenzo, Thomas J. (2002), *The Real Lincoln: A New Look at Abraham Lincoln, His Agenda, and an Unnecessary War*. New York: Forum/Random House.

Downs, Anthony (1957), *An Economic Theory of Democracy*. New York: Harper.

Downs, Anthony (1966), *Inside Bureaucracy*. Boston, MA: Little, Brown.

Joint Economic Committee (1998), *The Size and Functions of Government and Economic Growth*. Report prepared by James Gwartney, Randall Holcombe, and Robert Lawson. Committee print.

Hoppe, Hans-Hermann (2001), *Democracy – The God That Failed*. New Brunswick, NJ: Transaction Publishers.

———, "The Democratic Leviathan," www.mises.org.

Huber, Peter (1988), *Liability: The Legal Revolution and its Consequences*. New York: Basic Books.

Hume, David (1965), "Of the Original Contract," in A. MacIntyre and D. Hume (eds.), *Hume's Ethical Writings*. New York: Collier Books.

McChesney, Fred (1997), *Money for Nothing*. Cambridge, MA: Harvard University Press.

Mises, Ludwig von (1998), *Human Action: A Treatise on Economics*. Auburn, AL: Ludwig von Mises Institute.

Rubin, Paul, and Martin Bailey (1994), "The Role of Lawyers in Changing the Law," *Journal of Legal Studies* 23(June): 807–831.

Schumpeter, Joseph (1950), *Capitalism, Socialism, and Democracy*. New York: Harper and Row.

Sowell, Thomas (1993), *Inside American Education*. New York: Free Press.

Stigler, George (1992), "Law or Economics?," *Journal of Law and Economics* 35(2): 12.

Twight, Charlotte (1988), "Government Manipulation of Constitutional-Level Transaction Costs: A General Theory of Transaction-Cost Augmentation and the Growth of Government." *Public Choice* 56(2): 131–152.

West, E.G. (1994), *Education and the State: A Study in Political Economy*, 3rd edn. Indianapolis, IN: Liberty Fund.

Wittman, Donald (1995), *The Myth of Democratic Failure*. Chicago, IL: University of Chicago Press.

# Part 3:
# The Austrian Response to
# *The Calculus of Consent*

# Chapter 6
## The Calculus of Consent Revisited

## 1. Introduction

Buchanan and Tullock (1962, hence BT) have a reputation as radical defenders of private property, markets, free enterprise, limited government and libertarianism. While this account is to some degree correct,[1] the present paper shall argue that it is exaggerated. It will show that their supposed adherence to these doctrines and philosophies is at best a moderate, not a radical, one, because of numerous errors with respect to their theories of democracy, ruling class, constitutionalism, contract, voting, methodological individualism, and the relation between government and private enterprise.

## 2. Linguistics

Let us consider BT's[2] unfortunate misuse of language. The most basic distinction in all of political economy is surely the one between actions that are coerced upon unwilling victims, and those that are undertaken on a voluntary basis. The latter BT categorize as "private," reasonably enough. But the former they characterize as "collective," surely a misnomer. For the word "collective" implies that a group of people join together, on a voluntary basis, and do something en masse. Clearly, a better choice of words to highlight this differentiation would have been "private" for voluntary contracts between two consenting parties, and "coercive" for those arrangements where some people act under the duress imposed by others.

As for "collective," this, too, is a legitimate word in the English language, and must therefore have some use or other. The most meaningful referent would be to the actions of three or more people that cannot be analyzed into several two-way pairings; e.g., a golf party or dinner and a movie arrangement. The distinction between collective and private would refer merely to the number of people involved in a decision. This is not a world shaking difference; rather it is one barely worth making. In any case, the two distinctions yield a two by two matrix:

|           | Private | Collective |
|-----------|---------|------------|
| Voluntary | A       | B          |
| Coercive  | C       | D          |

Here, A stands for private voluntary actions, such as the purchase of a newspaper for $.50. There are only two participants, hence the private characterization, and since there is no force or the threat of force, it is categorized as voluntary. B is also voluntary, but here there are three or more participants who are not based on numerous pair wise agreements. An example would be where a large group of people starts up a golf club, or decide where to go for dinner and a movie. The case of the ordinary firm would be an example of A; even though there are large numbers of people involved, each of them, the employees, has a contract with only one person, the owner of the business.

In C, the interaction is coercive and private. An example would be Crusoe enslaving Friday, or one holdup man robbing a single victim. D is equally coercive, but here there are three or more people who participate. Examples include tyranny of the majority, where a larger group forces its will on a smaller group.

The important comparison is between the two rows. Whether an act takes place on a voluntary basis, or where one party, no matter its size, physically threatens another, no matter its size, is a matter of supreme importance. In contrast, the separation between the two columns, however important for some purposes, is of far less account, at least philosophically speaking. Whether force is threatened is crucial; how many people are involved, is not.

According to BT,

> Collective action is viewed as the action of individuals when they choose to accomplish purposes collectively rather than individually, and the government is seen as nothing more than the set of processes, the machine, which allows such collective action to take place (13).

But this is disingenuous. It glosses over the vital distinctions made above between force and agreement. Collective action, when accomplished through the intermediation of the state, is no longer merely collective. Due to the police power of the government, it becomes turned into coercive collective action.

States Hoppe (1993: 18, 19):

> What has commonly been overlooked, though, -- especially by those who try to make a virtue of the fact that a democracy gives equal voting power to everyone, whereas consumer sovereignty allows for unequal 'votes' -- is the most important deficiency of all: Under a system of consumer sovereignty people might cast unequal votes but, in any case, they exercise control exclusively over things that they acquired through original appropriation or contract and hence are forced to act morally. Under a democracy of production everyone is assumed to have something to say regarding things one did not so acquire, and hence one is permanently invited thereby not only to create legal instability with all its negative effects on the process of capital formation, but, moreover, to act immorally.

## 3. Democracy

BT ask, "How shall the dividing line between collective action and private action be drawn?" (5). This would seem to indicate either that they do not take cognizance of the more complex two by two matrix discussed above, or that their concern is with what we have called the unimportant issue.

The proof of this is their continual interpretation of collective decision making in terms of political or democratic elections. The point is, this belongs in the coercive, not the voluntary sector. Why? How can it be claimed that democratic voting is coercive? The obvious answer is that the minority is compelled to accept the wishes of the majority.

But the other side of this debate is not without its reply. It claims that all participants in the democratic process have *agreed* to be bound by its decision.[3] Therefore, there is no coercion involved. Indeed, there cannot be. It is just as if a person purchased a newspaper for $.50, and then, after being given the paper, refused to pay the agreed upon amount of money. To force him to disgorge the coins would *not* violate his rights. On the contrary, to allow him to keep these funds would be a theft from the vendor. In like manner, if a person agrees to be bound by majority vote, and then balks when he loses the election, to compel him to honor his agreement is not to violate his rights. On the contrary, to allow him to do so would be coercive to the majority.

Now let us consider the critique. On the one hand, Spooner (1966) is definitive in his claim that, as a matter of *fact*, the minority did not agree to be bound by majority decision making. All evidence seeming to the contrary (willingness to vote, to pay taxes, etc.) can be interpreted not as agreement, but as a defensive measure attempting to make the best of a bad (coercive) situation.

Second is Schumpeter (1942), who remarks on the type of democratic views espoused by BT as follows:

> The theory which construes taxes on the analogy of club dues or the purchase of the service, of, say, a doctor only proves how far removed this part of the social sciences is from scientific habits of mind (p. 198).

In the view of Hoppe (1993: 13):

> The most prominent modern champions of Orwellian double talk are J. Buchanan and G. Tullock. They claim that government is founded by a 'constitutional contract' in which everyone 'conceptually agrees' to submit to the coercive powers of government with the understanding that everyone else is subject to it too. Hence government is only *seemingly* coercive but *really* voluntary. There are several evident objections to this curious argument. First, there is no empirical evidence whatsoever for the contention that any constitution has ever been voluntarily accepted by everyone concerned. Worse, the very idea of all people voluntarily coercing themselves is simply inconceivable, much in the same way as it is inconceivable to deny the law of

contradiction. For if the voluntarily accepted coercion is voluntary, then it would have to be possible to revoke one's subjection to the constitution, and the state would be no more than a voluntarily joined club. If, however, one does not have the 'right to ignore the state' – and that one does not have this right is, of course, the characteristic mark of a state as compared to a club – then it would be logically inadmissible to claim that one's acceptance of state coercion is voluntary. Furthermore, even if all this were possible, the constitutional contract could still not claim to bind anyone except the original signers of the constitution.

How can Buchanan and Tullock come up with such absurd ideas? By a semantic trick. What was 'inconceivable' and 'no agreement' in pre-Orwellian talk is for them 'conceptually possible' and a 'conceptual agreement.' For a most instructive short exercise in this sort of reasoning in leaps and bounds, see Buchanan (1977). Here we learn (17) that even the acceptance of the 55 mph speed limit is possibly voluntary (Buchanan is not quite sure) since it ultimately rests on all of us conceptually agreeing on the constitution, and that Buchanan is not really a statist, but in truth an anarchist (11).

It is even possible to go further in this criticism (McGee, 1992). For suppose that BT were correct and Spooner, Schumpeter and Hoppe are mistaken concerning their views of the original contract. That is, people *did* at one time unanimously get together and sign a constitution, obligating all of them to be bound, thereafter, by majority rule (or whatever other voting requirements were stipulated); and that this was not done, defensively, as it were under duress, a la Spooner. It still does not follow that this "contract" is binding upon anyone, even the signatories, let alone their descendants. In order for this constitution to pass muster, it would have to overcome one further hurdle, that set by Rothbard (1973, 1982) for contracts. In his view, *consideration* is absolutely imperative if an erstwhile "agreement" is to qualify for the honorific of "contract." Without at least some sort of consideration passing hands from one party to another, what we have is merely a "promise," not a contract.[4] And, while it would be moral for a man who promises a woman he will marry her to carry through on his promise, this is not legally binding. Nor would the establishment of a government be legally binding, based on mere promises, even if it were at one time unanimous.

## 4. Ruling Class

State BT in this regard:

> We shall also reject any theory or conception of the collectivity which embodies the exploitation of a ruled by a ruling class. This includes the Marxist vision, which incorporates the polity as one means through which the economically dominant group imposes its will on the down-

92

trodden. Other theories of class domination are equally foreign to our purposes. Any conception of State activity that divides the social group into the ruling class and the oppressed class, and that regards the political process as simply a means through which this class dominance is established and then preserved, must be rejected as irrelevant for the discussion which follows (12).

Now this is more than just passing curious. Had BT given *reasons* for their rejection of class analysis, commentators could have agreed or disagreed with them, and, in so doing, made a rational choice as to whether to support this theory or not. But nowhere in BT are such considerations to be found. Instead, they content themselves with the mere announcement that they have ruled such theories out of court. Is this due to a "revelation" (see BT, 4) of some sort, not vouchsafed to the rest of us?

Just because BT will not consider this sort of analytic framework is no reason for us to refrain from it. On the contrary, we do well in this context to consider the class analysis of John J. Calhoun, no Marxist, he, who bases his analytic framework on the tax-subsidy system. In his view, society can be divided into those who, on net balance, pay more to the state than they receive from it, and those who pay less to the state than they receive from it. The former are net tax payers, or the exploited; the latter are net tax receivers, or the exploiters (Lence, 1992). It would be one thing if BT were to criticize this perspective; it is quite another to reject it out of hand, without being able to point to any counter evidence, or lapse from logic in the case.

The puzzle is that BT have also expressed themselves as if they were themselves Marxists, or at the very least libertarian Calhounians, when they refer to "preventing the undue exploitation of one group by another through the political process" (22). But if there are no classes, how can one group organize with the purpose of exploiting another?

## 5. State and Market

In the view of many commentators, the government is the only entity in society with a legal monopoly of force. The Mafia, the Blood, the Crips, and the Hell's Angels may all use coercion as part and parcel of their everyday activities, but the law does not legitimize such occurrences. The state, too, uses force, but it alone has the legitimacy that only the law can provide.

In sharp contradistinction, it is illegal for ordinary business firms to "take the law into their own hands." If faced with a customer who cannot pay his bills, it is impermissible for a corporation to send out "enforcers" or "leg breakers" to ensure that this does not occur too often. Instead, the aggrieved business must petition the state for redress, given the latter's monopoly over the use of coercion.

But this is not at all the perspective of BT. Instead, they are firm believers in the view of the state as part of the market. They maintain that:

> The market and the State are both devices through which co-operation is organized and made possible... The individual enters into an exchange relationship in which he furthers his own interest by providing some product or service that is of direct benefit to the individual on the other side of the transaction. At base, political or collective action under the individualistic view of the State is much the same. Two or more individuals find it mutually advantageous to join forces to accomplish certain common purposes. In a very real sense, they 'exchange' inputs in the securing of the commonly shared output (19).

Say if you will that government is just another business firm. But realize that it is rather a special type of business firm, one that enjoys the police power. Under these assumptions, there are two kinds of firms: one that features the legitimate power to initiate violence against non-aggressors, and the others, which do not. But this is rather awkward. Much simpler is the ordinary English language usage, eschewed by BT, according to which entities with the police power are called governments, and those without it are called corporations.


## 6. Public Service

BT are on record with the quite reasonable view that when people enter government, they do not suddenly sprout angel's wings; that on the contrary, they maintain the same self-interestedness they display as participants in the market sector. For example, they state: "... the average individual acts on the basis of the same overall value scale when he participates in market activity and political activity." And they specifically criticize political theorists whose views "have been grounded on the implicit assumption that the representative individual seeks not to maximize his own utility, but to find the 'public interest' or 'common good'" (20).

All well and good. However, then, how can this sentiment be reconciled with the following:

> ... both men (Robinson Crusoe, Friday) will recognize the advantages to be secured from constructing a fortress. Yet one fortress is sufficient for the protection of both. Hence they will find it mutually advantageous to enter into a political 'exchange' and devote resources to the construction of the common good (19).

Will neither Crusoe nor Friday engage in "opportunistic" behavior? Will neither attempt to get the other to contribute the lion's share to the common good, while he contributes as little as possible, and instead benefits as a free rider? BT's depiction, as quoted above, sounds as if both men did sprout angel's wings.

## 7. Political Markets

BT are very serious about the analogy between markets and politics. They go so far as to talk of the latter in terms of "political markets." But they go even further than this, likening Adam Smith's invisible hand to coercive collectivism:

> Adam Smith and those associated with the movement he represented were partially successful in convincing the public at large that, within the limits of certain general rules of action, the self-seeking activities of the merchant and the moneylender tend to further the general interests of everyone in the community. An acceptable theory of collective choice can perhaps do something similar in pointing the way toward those rules for collective choice-making, the constitution, under which the activities of political tradesmen can be similarly reconciled with the interests of all members of the social group (23).

Another analogy between political and economic market is that both are forms of exchange, and in each case the presumption is that these exchanges are mutually beneficial. Here is the BT claim:

> The economic approach, which assumes man to be a utility-maximizer in both his market and his political activity, does not require that one individual increase his own utility at the expense of other individuals. This approach (the Public Choice perspective of BT, that is) incorporates political activity as a particular form of *exchange*; and, as in the market relation, mutual gains to all parties are ideally expected to result from the collective relation (23; material in brackets supplied by present authors).

This is why BT claim that "the political process ... may be interpreted as a positive sum game" (24). This is perhaps their most basic core fallacy. The very idea that politics, like economics, would be a mutually beneficial endeavor! A brief look at what goes on in Washington, D.C.[5] should disabuse even the most superficial scholar of politics of that particular notion. To be sure, there are beneficiaries. As it happens, most of the richest counties in the U.S. are located within a few mile radius of the nation's capital. But a large part of the "business" of the denizens of this city consists of transferring vast amount of funds from some (the exploited) to others (the exploiters), with a significant percentage of the proceeds finding its way into the pockets of the "transferors" (Hill and Anderson, 1980; Osterfeld, 1988).

There is little doubt that what goes on in markets is indeed mutually beneficial. Trade is *always* beneficial in the ex ante sense, and usually so even in the ex post sense. That is because the commercial arrangements are at all times agreed upon by both parties to the exchange. The political "market," in sharp contrast, cannot boast of such mutuality. On the contrary, it is earmarked with predation, where one party (the net tax beneficiary) gains at the expense of the other (the net tax payer).

## 8. Charles Beard

Happily, BT do not rest content with mere assertion. They instead consider a theory contrary to their own, that of Charles Beard. In their criticism, they charge him with "the failure to distinguish two quite different approaches to political activity, both of which may be called, in some sense, economic" (25). The first is their own.

> The second approach assumes that the individual is motivated by his position or class status in the production process. The social class in which the individual finds himself is prior to, and determines, the interest of the individual in political activity. In one sense, the second approach is the opposite of the first since it requires that, on many occasions, the individual must act contrary to his own economic interest in order to further the interest of the social class or group to which he belongs.
>
> Beard attempted to base his interpretation of the formation of the American Constitution on the second, essentially the Marxist, approach, and to explain the activities of the Founding Fathers in terms of class interest. As Brown has shown, Beard's argument has little factual support, in spite of its widespread acceptance by American social scientists (26).

But this critique is not without flaws of its own. First of all, an economic critique of U.S. Constitutionalism need not rely on the view that social class, rather than self-interest, would be the primary motivating force. One can borrow a leaf from the Calhounian notebook, and interpret self-centered activity in the political realm not in support of group interests, but in terms of individual ones. Second, social class can be seen as a proxy for self-interest. That is, one may support one's own group not out of love for it per se, but out of the belief that this is the most efficient means toward self-aggrandizement. Third, there is an internal contradiction in this analysis. The BT view of men not sprouting angel's wings when they enter public service is compatible with what BT have to say about Beard. So why are they criticizing him, given that he does no more than BT do themselves? According to the logic of BT's critique of Beard, their own theory, too, is "Marxist."

Let us put this into other words: BT claim that their theory utilizes "the individualist-economic, or the utility-maximizing assumption about behavior in the political process" (27). Well, so, too, does Beard's, if we interpret him sympathetically. If we do not, we may still rely on the Calhounian class analysis to make essentially the Beardian point, that the "fix" was in, with regard to the creation of the U.S. constitution; e.g., that this process was a product of utility maximization applied to the political process. This is what BT's theory is all about. Why do they so strenuously object to the very same theorizing when it appears in the work of Beard, or of Calhoun?

## 9. Methodological Individualism

BT announce themselves as methodological individualists. By this they mean to reject the "organic conception of the collective unit." They see methodological pluralism as "essentially opposed to the Western philosophical tradition in which the human individual is the primary philosophical entity." Moreover,

> since we propose to construct a theory of collective choice that has relevance to modern Western democracy, we shall reject at the outset any organic interpretation of collective activity (11).

This is all well and good, not only because it is consonant with Western traditions. There is also the obvious point that there is no such thing as a "group will" or a "group mind." If the social sciences are to study group behavior, they will perforce have to do it by analyzing individuals, as they interact with one another.[6]

What, then, are we to make of BT when they refer to "the objectives of the group as a whole." They do so in the following context:

> Insofar as possible, institutions and legal constraints should be developed which will order the pursuit of private gain in such a way as to make it consistent with, rather than contrary to, the attainment of the objectives of the group as a whole (27).

The obvious rejoinder is to cite the BT of p. 11 against the BT of p. 27. The point is, there are no objectives of the "group as a whole." Only individuals can have objectives. The group as such cannot. Or, to put this in another way, any objectives that the group as a whole is supposed to have can either be reduced to the objectives in the minds of the individuals that comprise it, or are nonexistent and nonsensical.

The reference of BT to "the objectives of the group as a whole" is rendered even the more puzzling by a passage that occurs a few pages later. Here, they state,

> Are we to consider the collectivity as the decision-making unit, and therefore, are we to scale or order collective choices against some postulated social goal or set of goals? Or, by contrast, are we to consider the individual participant in collective choice as the only real decision-maker and, as a result, discuss rational behavior only in terms of the individual's own goal achievement? It is evident from what has been said before that we shall adopt the second of these approaches (31).

How, then, to explain BT's "the objectives of the group as a whole?"

## 10. Rationality

BT defend the neoclassical position on this issue:

> To judge whether or not individual behavior is 'rational' or 'irrational,' the economist must try first of all to place some general minimal restrictions on the shapes of utility functions. If he is successful in this effort, he may then test the implications of his hypotheses against observed behavior.
>
> Specifically, the modern economist assumes as working hypotheses that the average individual is able to rank or to order all alternative combinations of goods and services that may be placed before him and that this ranking is transitive. Behavior of the individual is said to be 'rational' when the individual chooses 'more' rather than 'less' and when he is consistent in his choices (33).

This may well be the traditional stance in this regard, but it is highly problematic. First of all, how will the economist know if he is successful in his effort to "place some general minimal restrictions on the shapes of utility functions?" Is there an independent criterion, over and above "testing the implications of his hypotheses against observed behavior"? (33). Secondly, why the transitivity requirement? Why can't a person prefer a}b, b}c, and then c}a? If these are truly independent events there is no logical reason to suppose that this cannot occur. It takes place, continually, in everyday life: on day one a person prefers apples to oranges; on day two he chooses oranges over bananas; and on day three he picks bananas instead of apples.

Thirdly, "consistency in choices" implies a denial of the fact that these pair-wise comparisons are truly independent. The implication, here, is that there are not three separate events: choosing between a and b, b and c, and then c and a. Transitivity implies that they all occur at the same point. But it is impossible to make more than one choice at any given time. Fourth, BT must implicitly assume that the individual who does the ranking cannot change his mind. And why not? Solely, it would appear, so that we can "test" the theory. But this is only a logical positivist fetish (Rothbard, 1962; Mises, 1963; Hoppe, 1988, 1991, 1992; Blanschard, 1964). Why should be allow the strictures of this philosophy to deny that which we full well know is true, namely that people do indeed change their minds?

## 11. Trade, Economies of Scale

According to Buchanan and Tullock (1971):

> ...when individual interests are assumed to be identical, the main body of economic theory vanishes. If all men were equal in interest and endowment, natural or artificial, there would be no organized economic activity to explain. Each man would be a Crusoe. Economic theory

thus explains why men co-operate through trade: they do so because
they are different (4).

This appears as if it should be true, but it is not. Even under the conditions posited by BT, exchange would still occur. This is because of economies of scale, and the benefits of specialization. Two people might have the same potential to be a concert pianist or a brain surgeon. If they each do both, they will achieve an indifferent level of success. In contrast, if the first spends all of his time on the one, and the second on the other, they will each become far more skilled. But if they specialize in this manner, they will have to trade, even though they also have the same tastes, provided only that they wish to consume both services.

## 12. Political Truth

In like manner, their analysis of "political theorists" (4) sounds like a truism, but is no such thing. In the view of BT:

> Political theorists, by contrast, do not seem to have considered fully the implications of individual differences for a theory of political decisions. Normally, the choice-making process has been conceived of as the means of arriving at some version of 'truth,' some rationalist absolute which remains to be discovered through reason or revelation, and which, once discovered, will attract all men to its support.

There are several problems here. First, it is unclear what an explanation for trade has to do with "truth" in politics. Certainly the one does not logically imply the other. That is, one may take BT's mistaken explanation of trade in terms of differences, and combine it with their view of "truth," or the very opposite. In neither case would there be a self-contradiction. Second, revelation on the one hand, and either rationalism or reason on the other, do seem to be at least somewhat incompatible. One wonders at the juxtaposition of these two very different epistemological categories, unless of course revelation is merely being wielded to cast doubt and aspersions on the possibility of achieving "truth" in the political realm. Third, we hereby confess to having a soft spot for this very doctrine. It is our belief, perhaps naive, that one day all those calling themselves rational will subscribe to the free enterprise philosophy. If BT dismiss this as blind faith, so be it.

## 13. Conclusion

BT fail utterly to distinguish between collectivism and coercion, one of the most important distinctions in all of political economy. They think, in effect, that when we wish to do something collectively, that is, with many participants, we must of necessity initiate aggression against non-aggressors. This leads them into a series of errors concerning anarchism, ruling class, the analogy between economics and politics, democracy, contracts, public service, methodological individualism and rationality.[7]

## NOTES

1. Compared to many writers, of course, they are this, and more.
2. All otherwise unidentified page citations refer to this book.
3. According to BT, "Our theory of constitutional choice has normative implications only insofar as the underlying basis of individual consent is accepted" (7).
4. We are grateful to Stephen Kinsella for pointing out the necessity of combining the Rothbardian contractual analysis with the theory of the origin of the state.
5. Or in any of the state capitols, or, indeed, in the councils of most cities, towns and villages (Bolick, 1993).
6. For a criticism of Nozick (1977) on this point, see Block (1980).
7. See also DiLorenzo and Block, forthcoming; Block(a), forthcoming; Block(b), forthcoming; Rothbard, 1997.

## REFERENCES

Blanshard, Brand (1964), *Reason and Analysis*. La Salle, IL: Open Court.
Block, Walter(a), "Another Look at the Calculus of Consent." *Forthcoming*
Block, Walter(b), "Constitutional Economics and the Calculus of Consent." *Forthcoming*
Block, Walter (1980), "On Robert Nozick's "On Austrian Methodology,'" *Inquiry* 23(4): 397–444.
Bolick, Clint (1993), *Grassroots Tyranny: The Limits of Federalism*. Washington D.C.: Cato Institute.
Buchanan, James M., and Gordon Tullock (1962/1971), *The Calculus of Consent: Logical Foundations of Constitutional Democracy*. Ann Arbor, MI: University of Michigan.
Buchanan, James M. (1977), "A Contractarian Perspective on Anarchy," in his *Freedom in Constitutional Contract*. College Station, TX: Texas A & M University Press.
DiLorenzo, Thomas J., and Block, Walter (2000), "Is Voluntary Government Possible? A Critique of Constitutional Economics," *Journal of Institutional and Theoretical Economics* 156(4): 567–582.
Hoppe, Hans-Hermann (1988), *Praxeology and Economic Science*. Auburn, AL: Mises Institute, Auburn University.
Hoppe, Hans-Hermann (1991), "Austrian Rationalism in the Age of the Decline of Positivism," *Journal de Economistes et des Etudes Humaines* 2(2/3): 243–268
Hoppe, Hans-Hermann (1992), "On Praxeology and the Praxeological Foundation of Epistemology and Ethics," in J. Herbener (ed.), *The Meaning of Ludwig von Mises*. Boston, MA: Kluwer.
Hoppe, Hans-Hermann (1993), *The Economics and Ethics of Private Property: Studies in Political Economy and Philosophy*. Boston, MA: Kluwer.
Lence, Ross M. (ed.) (1992), *Union and Liberty: The Political Philosophy of John C. Calhoun*. Indianapolis, IN: Liberty Fund.

McGee, Robert W. (1992), "The Theory of Secession and Emerging Democracies: A Constitutional Solution," *Stanford Journal of International Law* 28(2): 451–476.

Mises, Ludwig von (1963), *Human Action*. Chicago, IL: Regnery.

Nozick, Robert (1977), "On Austrian Methodology," *Synthese* 36: 353–392.

Osterfeld, David (1988), "'Social Utility' and Government Transfers of Wealth: An Austrian Perspective," *Review of Austrian Economics* 2: 79–95.

Rothbard, Murray N. (1962), *Man, Economy and State*. Los Angeles, CA: Nash Publishing.

Rothbard, Murray N. (1973), *For a New Liberty*. New York: Macmillan.

Rothbard, Murray N. (1982), *The Ethics of Liberty*. Atlantic Highlands, NJ: Humanities Press.

Rothbard, Murray N. (1997), "Buchanan and Tullock's The Calculus of Consent," in *Logic of Action II*. Cheltenham: Edward Elgar, 269–274.

Schumpeter, Joseph A. (1942), *Capitalism, Socialism and Democracy*. New York: Harper.

Spooner, Lysander (1870/1966), *No Treason: The Constitution of No Authority*. Larkspur, CO: Ralph Myles.

# Chapter 7
# Buchanan and Tullock's "The Calculus of Consent"

## 1. Introduction

I am so out of sympathy with James M. Buchanan and Gordon Tullock's "The Calculus of Consent" that I don't think a particularly detailed critique to send to them would be worthwhile. I recognize that there are some merits to the piece: a searching for methodological individualism in political science, an emphasis upon unanimity rather than majority rule, and a harking back to the constitutional system of 1900 as better than the situation today. But these merits are, I believe, more ad hoc than integral to the main body of work. In considering the work as a whole, they are far overshadowed by the numerous flaws and fallacies.

In the first place, their repeated references to "unanimity" are, at first, appealing, but they are highly misleading. A "social contract" theory of government, as you know, can be used in two different ways, and this difference is extremely important: it can be used to set up an ideal toward which the government should be transformed (essentially the view of John Locke), or it can be used to place a stamp of approval on all, or most, of the actions of the existing government (for example, Rousseau). Thus, the theory of the divine right of kings began as a check on government, as an order to the King to stay within divinely commanded laws; it was transformed, by the State, into a divine stamp of approval for anything the King might decide to do. While there are elements of both in Buchanan and Tullock, the major emphasis of the "unanimity rule" is not so much to set up a unanimity ideal, as to put a stamp of approval on existing government actions as being "really" backed by unanimous consent. I have noted this before in Buchanan's writings.

How is this done? In many ways, some of which are so involved in their transparent rationalizations as to be almost absurd. The basic way is to set up a dichotomy between "constitutional decisions" and concrete decisions of government policy. Buchanan and Tullock admit that concrete decisions might represent conflict: A and B winning out over, and even at the expense of, C. But "constitutionally," which is a term that they use quite vaguely but which apparently means the rules for government decision-making, they assume that these rules are somehow "unanimously" agreed to, and therefore that, in a sense, the concrete political decisions are also unanimous. Thus, the unanimity rule, seemingly libertarian, actually turns out to be more of a fallacious support for the status quo – whatever the status quo happens to be – than a plea for libertarian principle.

Why all of us are supposed to be behind the constitutional decisions, Buchanan and Tullock do not really support. They say that a thief is really for a law against stealing so as to keep his own property, so that it can be said that even a thief in a way approves of his own punishment. I think this is absurd; a professional thief is clearly opposed to laws against stealing (it is a rule of honor among professional criminals not to run to the police for help – and also a wise precaution for them). How did Buchanan and Tullock manage to get into this trap? By blithely assuming that when the "constitution" is being considered, no one knows whether or not he will be able to benefit by the various rules in specific situations, so it is to everyone's self-interest to have rules, as it were, in the general interest. Now this appears to me to be completely insupportable; people do have certain interests, and they will be able to gauge to what extent a rule will benefit or not benefit them. (This is especially true because Buchanan and Tullock think of the "constitution" as continuing, rather than as the original writing.) The professional thief knows he is a professional thief, and therefore that the weakening of laws against stealing, or constitutional provisions against stealing, will benefit him, and so on.

Further, by unanimity Buchanan and Tullock by no means always refer to real unanimity; instead, they speak of "relative unanimity" or "80 percent unanimity," and so on. In short, when the chips are down, they are willing to waive unanimity in order that the "costs of decision" for the group or society be minimized. "Relative unanimity" is obviously a misleading use of semantics.

In short, despite a lot of talk about unanimity being called for, the upshot of the discussion is that (a) unanimity is weakened by numerous qualifications and circumlocutions – and that (b) much of the existing structure of government is endorsed as being "really" unanimity! This, of course, is worse than simply adhering to majority rule, and comes perilously close to the "we owe it to ourselves," "we are the government" position of the Left.

The worst example of this, including the definite tendency to rationalize the existing situation as reflecting unanimity, is the concept of "income insurance" to justify actions of government that "redistribute" income. Now it is obvious that when government takes from A and deliberately gives to B, this can hardly be called a gesture of unanimity, or people voluntarily banding together to purchase a service from government. But Buchanan and Tullock try to say this, by asserting that the wealthy really favor being taxed more than the poor, because they are taking out "income insurance," knowing that when they will be poor, the government, like an insurance company, will help them. And, in another place, they say that people really want to be coerced so long as they are all coerced, so that, everybody is really not being coerced. Not only do I consider all this nonsense, but it is dangerous nonsense as well, because it provides new support for the idea that anything that the State does, no matter how blatantly coercive, is "really" backed by everyone.

The placing of the stamp of approval on the State as being really unanimous, furthermore, permeates the entire analysis of this book. For the whole point of the book, the "new contribution," is that Buchanan and Tullock treat the State as just another service agency, basically voluntary, supplying "collective goods" to everyone, minimizing "external costs" when it can do so, and so on. The State is assimilated into the rubric of just another voluntary agency (albeit with complications), and each individual therefore decides on his value scale how much to allocate to private agencies and how much to government. This, I say, is the nub of the entire analysis of the book, and I think it is utterly and absolutely wrong. A significant quote from Buchanan and Tullock will point this up:

> We view collective decision making, collective action, as a form of human activity through which mutual gains are made possible. Thus, in our conception, collective activity, like market activity, is a genuinely cooperative gain. By contrast, much of orthodox political thought seems to be based on the view that the collective choice process reflects a partisan struggle in which the beneficiaries secure gains solely at the expense of the losers.

I think it quite evident that "orthodox political theory" is infinitely superior to the construction of Buchanan and Tullock, and that even though on concrete questions, Buchanan and Tullock will want to reduce to some extent the current level of government operations, the impact of their analysis – of the book itself – will be much more to place a stamp of approval on State action which even "orthodox theory" hadn't placed upon it.

The nub of the distinction between State and market is that, on the market, all parties gain and benefit from market actions, whereas, in State action, the gains of one group can only be at the expense of others. Buchanan and Tullock's concept would obliterate the most vital distinction between State and market activity.

Furthermore, Buchanan and Tullock are considerably inferior to the "orthodox" New Welfare Economists, who at least formally recognize, even though they try to get around it, that there has to be unanimity for them to make "scientific" statements of whether society is better off, without introducing their own ethical judgments. (The New Welfare Economists, following Pareto, have in this sense always paid formal obeisance to the unanimity principle.) But Buchanan and Tullock, believing that State action is, on the whole, "really unanimous," believe that they can go much further in making "scientific" pronouncements without bringing in their own value judgments, and thus they sin more than the usual "welfare economists" in smuggling in their own ethical judgments as scientific statements. This is particularly true in their grandiose conception of how "social costs," where they proclaim that individuals all decide on the exact proportion of government activity in regard to which they can minimize "social costs"; but how can "social costs" be even discussed when some people are gaining at the expense of others? To say, for example, that it will lower "social costs" (and therefore, for some reason, it will be good) if the few holdouts in a community who don't want to build a road be forced to pay in taxes for the road, is a fallacious conception – although this is involved in the whole analytic structure of Buchanan and Tullock. For it will undoubtedly minimize the costs of the impatient people who want to get on with the job without "obstruction"; on the other hand, it will greatly raise the "costs" of those who staunchly oppose the road and do not wish to be forced to pay for it. Why is the former, and not the latter, "society"? The upshot is that despite much talk by Buchanan and Tullock of their staunch individualism, especially methodological individualism, they are not consistent individualists at all. They smuggle in, through the back door, societarian and organicist conceptions, namely, in their discussions of social costs.

There are also certain grave epistemological flaws in the book. For one thing, Buchanan and Tullock are, methodologically, confirmed positivists – which is one reason why their theoretical structure is so slipshod. It is bound to be slipshod when their methodological doctrine is that assumptions don't have to be true in order to work, that theory is arrived at by "testing hypotheses" against empirical fact, and all the rest of the positivist trappings which apply the methodology of physics to the sciences of human action.

And second – what is really a corollary – is their misapprehension of what political theory is all about. In modern times, political theory has abandoned political philosophy: that discipline that deals with the problem of the nature of the State, what the State should and should not do, and so on. (It has abandoned political philosophy because it has given up the idea that there is a rational discipline of ethics, of which political philosophy is, in a sense, a subdivision.)

Hence, they want to construct a value-free political theory. But while such a theory is important and meaningful in economics, where the theory is based on the fact that people use means to achieve ends – it is empty and sterile in political theory. For, after all, politics is a matter of concrete decisions, which in contrast to everyday decisions of consumers and business firms should be based on general principles. Give up the idea that there are such principles – that is, give up political philosophy – and you are left adrift with no rudder, and no genuine political theory. This is what has happened; and we have been left with "political science," with all the positivist trappings, the value-free "models," the quasi-mathematics, the jargon, and so on. Buchanan and Tullock are in this sterile "political science" tradition. But in a sense they carry this unfortunate modern tendency much further. For by blithely assuming that there is no real difference between the State and private institutions and actions, by assimilating government to private actions, they have really become "political philosophers" – and very bad ones. And from this stems their treatment of political action as if it were just another good or service like beans and apples, and which is simply valued, like beans and apples, on our value-scales. This "economic" approach to politics, far from the great new advance they think it is, as far as I am concerned, is the death knell of all genuine political philosophy.

# Chapter 8
# Constitutional Economics
# and the Calculus of Consent

## 1. Introduction

James Buchanan and Gordon Tullock are widely credited with creating the Public Choice School.[1] Its main elements include constitutional political economy, an analysis of different voting-rights regimes, and the insight that human beings do not suddenly sprout angel's wings when they become government bureaucrats (hence, there is *government failure* as well as *market failure*). The latter is devoted to an investigation of the premises upon which a legitimate government is predicated, and to an understanding of human and property rights in a constitutional democratic order. In this paper, public choice constitutional economics shall be subjected to critique.

## 2. Defining Human and Property Rights

From their constitutional framework, Buchanan and Tullock attempt to define human and property rights. In their view, a constitution is a voluntary agreement, much like a contract, to which all citizens give their consent. Thus, they claim that "constitutional decisions themselves . . . are necessarily collective."[2]

What does this mean, though? How could this sentiment be translated? It appears that Buchanan and Tullock mean to assert that there are no rules "engraved upon stone tablets," no "God-given" rules, in effect, which tell us how to live. Rather, individuals must come together to hammer out a collective agreement addressing the rules under which we must get along. At first glance, this sounds eminently sensible. After all, it is very much in keeping with Buchanan and Tullock's gratuitous attack on "revelation."[3]

However, there is a grave logical difficulty in this way of proceeding. On one hand, Buchanan and Tullock want to derive human and property rights from their constitutional framework. On the other, they want to assert that this is done on a consensual basis. But how can people give their consent to a contract before it is clear that they have rights in the first place?[4]

Buchanan and Tullock find it "useful to 'jump over' the minimal collectivization of activity involved in the initial definition of human and property rights,"[5] but this is the essence of their problem. They cannot just "jump over" it and hope to retain any semblance of rationality for their public choice theory. To their credit, Buchanan and Tullock recognize that there is a problem here. They concede that it is difficult even to discuss the problems of individual constitutional choice until the range of individual power of disposition over human and nonhuman resources is defined. Unless this preliminary step is taken, we do not really know what individuals we are discussing.[6]

Also, reasonably, they maintain that an analysis of this preliminary step "would carry us too far afield."[7] After all, there is a division of labor in all pursuits, scholarly ones included. However, in this case, such an argument simply will not do. If public choice is truly to be a constitutional theory, they must show how this initial step is consonant with the constitution. However, they make no such attempt. Instead, they content themselves with noting that "for our purposes, *any* delineation of property embodying separable or group shares provides a suitable basis."[8] By taking this stance, they preclude themselves from even trying to incorporate constitutionalism into the basic premises of their doctrine.


## 3. Voluntary Government: A Logical Contradiction

We come now to a truly puzzling bit of writing on the part of our authors. In their view,

Voluntary action may emerge which will include all members of the social group. Here the action may be institutionally indistinguishable from political action. Governmental institutions may be employed to effect purely voluntary cooperative action. The characteristic feature would be the absence of any of the coercive or compulsive power of the government. An example might be the organization of a village fire department.[9]

Below, we shall refer to this as statement *A.*

It would be difficult to imagine a more confused statement than this. Consider the following: even if the group is small and relatively homogeneous, it is just barely conceivable that "voluntary action may emerge which will include all members of the social group." But given the difficulty of even a dozen friends coming to an agreement as to which movie to attend, and which restaurant to patronize afterward (or should it be beforehand?), it is *extremely* unlikely that a "social group" of a size to warrant such a description would garner unanimous assent for *anything.*

But suppose it did. It would *still* not be the case that "the action may be institutionally indistinguishable from political action." On the contrary, it would be entirely distinguishable. For voluntary action is that which is agreed to by *all* participants; political action is that which is *not.*

If a government institution were employed, by its very nature it would not be to effect purely voluntary cooperative action. On the contrary, it would be the embodiment of a contract that did not include at least one member of the society. If it included them all, why call this governmental? On the contrary, it would be purely private.

Consider now the fire department which each and every soul in the village agreed to support. This would indeed be characterized by "the absence of any of the coercive or compulsive power of the government." In that case, why, for the love of logic, call it "government"? Suppose that the entire town had agreed to play bingo, or to go on a picnic? Would this make such an activity a statist one? Hardly. Why, then, consider a voluntary fire brigade, organized on identical principles, an element of the government?

Now consider the Buchanan and Tullock statement that we shall label *B*:

> The choice between voluntary action, individual or cooperative, and political action, which must be collective, rests on the relative costs of organizing decisions, on the relative *costs of social interdependence*.[10]

Consider the following two-by-two matrix:

|  | Voluntary-Market | Coercive-Political |
|---|---|---|
| Private | (1) | (2) |
| Collective | (3) | (4) |

From statement *B*, we learn that there are three possible states of affairs: (1) depicts the case where two individuals trade; this is the market; (3) indicates voluntary cooperative effort on the part of a large number of people; examples include private charity, the kibbutz, and the commune; and (4) is the government which, at the very least, must raise taxes from some people who are willing to pay only because of physical sanctions; if all were willing to pay, then (4) would collapse into (3). We are also given to understand that one of the boxes is empty, namely, (2), because Buchanan and Tullock tell us that "political action . . . must be collective." The key to this matrix is that institutions can be distinguished both on the basis of how many people take part (one or two on the one hand, many on the other) and the issue of whether there is full agreement among all participants.

But statement *A*, in contrast, directly contradicts the distinction between the two columns. Here, Buchanan and Tullock seem to think that there is no difference between (3) and (4), at least in the case of the voluntary village fire company. Alas, they cannot have it both ways. Either *A* or *B* is correct, but not both together. As our previous remarks have indicated, *A* is problematic on numerous grounds.

There are numerous private institutions like the volunteer fire brigade.[11] Among them are such collective, but private and voluntary, organizations as the church, the golf club, the family circle, the Boy Scouts, and the bowling league. They are all cooperative ventures, run collectively, not through for-profit markets, that no one is forced to join. They are not funded through taxes.[12] Why call them political, or part of the public sector, as do Buchanan and Tullock? On this ground, logical consistency would imply that the Boy Scouts are actually a governmental organization, surely a *reductio ad absurdum* of the whole scheme.

## 4. A Conceptual Classification

In this section, the authors present the nub of their public choice justification for the state. How will it be rationally determined if a given task should be assigned to the public or private sector? The same way in which decisions are made in the market: cost minimization. If it costs more to do a job collectively, it is reasonable to assign it to free enterprise. If it costs more to do the work individually, through markets, it is reasonable to assign it to socialism.[13] In this analysis, they are squarely back in the land of $B$.

There are, again, only three possible categories: voluntary individual action, voluntary cooperative action, and collective political action. The fourth possibility, voluntary political action, once more becomes the null set. So much for having "government institutions employed to effect purely voluntary co-operative action."[14]

How do we know this? Because, in their scheme, there are only three cost considerations. The first is described as follows: "For any activity, the expected minimum present value of total costs expected to be imposed by collective decision-making shall be designated by the letter $g$."[15] As for the second, "We designate by the letter $a$ the expected costs resulting from the purely individualistic behavior of private persons." With regard to the third, "The expected costs of an activity embodying private contractual arrangements designed to reduce [to internalize] externalities will be designated by the letter $b$."[16]

For our purposes, $a$ stands for purely individualistic behavior, e.g., markets, where cooperation is only implicit. Explicitly, people are not cooperating; they are competing through markets. In contrast, $b$ denotes cooperative or collective voluntary action: the mediating institutions we have encountered before. And $g$, of course, indicates government operation, organized through democratic elections,[17] where the unwilling minority is coerced into going along with the decision arrived at in this manner.

These three categories yield six different cases, depending upon the relative costs of each. They are as follows:

1. $a < b < g$
2. $a < g < b$
3. $b < a < g$
4. $b < g < a$
5. $g < a < b$
6. $g < b < a$

Edifying as a discussion of each case would be, there is no need to analyze them all. For our purposes, it matters not a whit whether $a < b$ or $b < a$. Both $a$ and $b$ are part of free enterprise, and are equally legitimate elements of capitalism. It does not matter whether several working women with small children form a baby-sitting cooperative ($b$), or whether one of them goes into business for herself and charges a price for this service to the others ($a$). Which of these is less expensive in the relevant sense, and thus which will be used, is outside the concerns of this paper. Our sole interest is in the cases where Buchanan and Tullock claim that $g$ is cheaper – that is, more efficient – than either $a$ or $b$, and that government intervention into the marketplace is, therefore, justified. This being the case, Buchanan and Tullock's six-part discussion can easily be abbreviated. Categories 1 and 3 drop out because, in these cases, Buchanan and Tullock allow that $g$ is "more expensive" than either $a$ or $b$. Moreover, parts of 2 and 4 fall by the wayside since they depict situations where $g$ is inferior to one or the other of $a$ and $b$. As a result of these considerations, we derive the following:

2. $g < b$
4. $g < a$
5,6. $g < c$

where $c$ denotes capitalism – that is, either $a$ or $b$. With this condensation, we can discuss the specifics of their argument.


## 5. Discussion

Buchanan and Tullock reach their first jarring note in their treatment of the contention that $a > 0$.[18] In their view,

> The color of the automobile that your colleague drives certainly influences your own utility to some extent. Spillover effects are clearly present, but you will probably prefer to allow your colleague free individual choice as regards this class of decisions.[19]

The problem here is not so much with the specific notion that $a > 0$; after all, as long as $a < g$, even though $a > 0$, even Buchanan and Tullock do not argue for the intervention of $g$. Rather, the difficulty is with their entire manner of proceeding. They argue that they[20] can determine the costs of things which do not emanate from market transactions. However, we cannot determine the strength of $g$ and $c$ in the absence of markets, and neither can they. Indeed, no one can; it is an utter impossibility, given that costs are opportunities foregone, and that only the economic actors themselves are in a position to appraise the costs of what they had to give up in order to attain any value.

Car color is perhaps the easiest case that Buchanan and Tullock can manufacture for themselves. But even here, their seemingly innocuous remarks are by no means as unassailable as they seem to believe. Suppose a band of hippies move into a high-class neighborhood, and bring with them an automobile colored in the style of a Jackson Pollock painting, that is, with a mishmash of different hues, pigments, shades, and tints. Is it credible to think that none of their stiff-upper-lip neighbors will take umbrage? Hardly. But we need not resort to fanciful examples of car color. We know for a fact that this is precisely how people feel about exterior house paint, as illustrated by the fact that numerous condominium development and restrictive covenant contracts stipulate that all parties to the agreement shall use a certain hue.

This is the case of the red underwear all over again.[21] People care about all such things – and probably many more than we can even imagine. If Buchanan and Tullock cannot come up with even one example of a pure private good with no spillovers or externalities, to that extent their entire theory is undermined.

Of course, much of the reason why there are uninternalized externalities in automobile color is due to a lack of private property rights in roads, highways, streets, and sidewalks.[22] Were these transportation arteries privatized, people would be able to express their likes and dislikes through markets, and the problem would not even arise. That is, if the Jackson Pollock car appalled enough people, many road owners would forbid it from their property. Presumably, it would be used on thoroughfares where people did not mind it so much or even liked it.

Would this work perfectly? Not a bit of it. No institution known to man and tailored to his use can accurately be described in such a manner. But at least it would function voluntarily. No one would be forced, as in the $g$ alternative, to act against his will with his own property. If Buchanan and Tullock want to utilize their method, it is incumbent upon them to discern a non-arbitrary measure of the "cost" of coercion. Not only has this never been done, it has never even been attempted.

A hint of this can be seen in how the private enterprise system deals with the challenge of the home painted in a manner that is offensive to neighbors. In order to protect themselves from this type of negative externality, individuals can engage in restrictive covenants with one another or buy into condominium developments that govern not only how the exterior walls can be painted, but even, in some cases, the curtains, fences, or backyard furniture which may be used.

As for the challenge of the red underwear owner, an entirely different analysis is in order. The problem here is to demonstrate that this is not only harmful, but that it constitutes a rights violation. For there is an alternative theory to the one put forth by Buchanan and Tullock. It is libertarianism, the notion that all acts are allowed, provided only that they are undertaken with a person's legitimately owned property, and are engaged in a manner which does not violate the rights of other people.[23] Since no one can demonstrate that the person with red underwear[24] violates another person's rights, no legal action is legitimate.

## 6. Higher Education

What is the main exhibit in Buchanan and Tullock's case for the government being more cost effective than the market ($a < g$)? Amazingly enough, it is higher education. They argue:

> The organization of higher education, especially professional training, may provide a helpful example. Due to the institutional restrictions on the full freedom of contract in capital values of human beings, the arrangements that might arise to insure the removal or reduction of certain externalities in higher education may be quite difficult to secure. Although students may recognize that they will be the primary beneficiaries of further professional training and that investment in such be financially sound, their inability to 'mortgage' their own earning power may prevent them from having ready access to loan markets. Of course, collective or state action may be taken which will remove or reduce the private externalities involved here.[25]

But this is no "market failure." Rather, the government has failed to do its self-proclaimed job as guarantor of contracts. That is, the state has announced itself as unwilling to enforce student loan contracts where human capital is used as collateral. To be more specific, fears of slavery and the hysteria surrounding the Fourteenth Amendment to the Constitution – on the part of the government – have caused this so-called "market" failure.

Let us squarely face reality. The moral problem with nineteenth-century slavery was that it was coercive. Totally innocent persons were dragged from home and hearth, kicking and screaming, and sent thousands of miles away to do forced labor. Replace this coercive element with voluntary agreement, and, although the shell would remain the same, this "curious institution" would be radically altered. Our society, thanks to analysis of the sort offered by Buchanan and Tullock, has failed to realize that there is all the difference in the world between slavery, which arises from coercion, and voluntary servitude, which emanates from consensual adult agreement. It is as if opposition to Nazi death camps requires opposition to hotels as well.

Moreover, Buchanan and Tullock's argument also surprises us in retrospect because of Milton Friedman's opposition to it. After all, broadly speaking, we would not expect Friedman to be different from Buchanan and Tullock on any significant issue of economics or politics. Yet, in Friedman's view, if there is a case for state action in education based on the externalities argument, it is precisely in the opposite direction from the one staked out by Buchanan and Tullock. That is, he argues that elementary education, not graduate school, is the arena in which this problem arises. Says Friedman:

> The social gain presumably is greatest for the lowest levels of school-ing, where there is the nearest approach to unanimity about content, and declines continuously as the level of schooling arises. . . . For higher schooling, the case for nationalization on grounds either of neighborhood effects or technical monopoly is even weaker.[26]

When highly intelligent people start with roughly the same premises, reason in much the same manner, and yet arrive at diametrically opposite conclusions, something very basic must be wrong. The difficulty, we suggest, is with the failure to adhere to the tenets of subjectivism: to realize that "one man's meat is another's poison." By definition, there is no market in external effects. This means that anyone can say anything about the direction of causation in this regard, and not find oneself refuted by the evidence. Buchanan and Tullock see externalities particularly in higher education, not in elementary education. Friedman makes the diametrically opposite case. We suggest that this is less than fully surprising because there are no independent criteria upon which such judgments can be based.

A similar situation has occurred in an analogous area. Because of the supposed "wage gap" between females and males, feminists argue in favor of imposing wages on the market on the basis of "objective" considerations (skill, effort, responsibility, and working conditions).[27] One of the many problems with this notion is that diverse rating agencies, equally devoted to this feminist cause, have derived incompatible results from similar data.[28]

Buchanan and Tullock's analysis of higher education externalities is just as arbitrary. There are no objective criteria – such as could be supplied by markets – so world-renowned scholars who start from the same basic premises reach different conclusions.[29]

## 7. Zoning Legislation

Buchanan and Tullock sharply distinguish between, on the one hand, assembling the land parcels needed to create a large new enterprise, such as a suburban shopping center, and, on the other hand, the operation of an "already developed residential area."[30] In the former case, they aver, the market works just fine.[31] But in the latter, our old friend "market imperfections" again rides to the fore. Specifically, the problems involve "neighborhood atmosphere, view, absence of noise, etc."[32]

The typical conclusion at this point would be a call for municipal zoning in order to overcome the externalities. But Buchanan and Tullock are much too sophisticated to be taken in by such a simplistic ploy. Instead, they wax eloquent about "covenants, corporate ownership," and the "interest of a large realtor to purchase many single land units in the area" as a way of internalizing these externalities.[33]

Although they do not fall into this elementary trap, neither do they entirely escape it. In their view, it is all an empirical question. On the one hand,

> the voluntary action will always be more desirable in the sense that it cannot place any unwanted restrictions on use of property. [But] if collective [read: coercive!] action is expected to be considerably more efficient . . . this advantage of voluntary action [will] be overcome.[34]

The basic problem with this line of reasoning is that it depends, ultimately, on interpersonal comparisons of utility. Buchanan and Tullock can defend zoning in instances where the value of "unwanted restrictions on use of property" is lower than the difference between private and public action where the latter is "considerably more efficient," so much so that it is sufficient to "overcome" the presumptive advantage of markets. Yet, what is this but mongering in interpersonal utility comparisons?[35]

In this specific case, moreover, Buchanan and Tullock's analytic framework is marred by a failure to realize that there is a reason why city property is spread about among so many people: prior government failure. Take New York City as an example. When it was settled, municipal authorities laid out the present street grid. Parcels were sold off in tiny bits. Now imagine a scenario in which the market is responsible for such a task. There is little doubt that the configuration of ownership would have much more nearly approached the situation implicitly called for by Buchanan and Tullock in their analysis of the proposed suburban shopping center now in the process of being assembled. That is, there likely would never have arisen a situation where literally tens of thousands of separate people would have become owners. Instead, the situation would more likely have resembled the Rockefeller Center area, where one entity controls several square blocks.

Consider their remarks in this regard:

> It may prove quite difficult to reorganize the developed residential area. The large realtor who desires to purchase multiple units in an area from single-unit owners may encounter prohibitive bargaining costs. The single owner-occupier who desires to may try to exploit his individual bargaining position to the maximum and may, in the extreme case, secure for himself the full amount of the 'surplus.' Faced with single owners of this persuasion, the entrepreneur will have little incentive to undertake the organizing costs that will be necessary. In such cases, collective action through zoning may be indicated.[36]

This quotation encapsulates Buchanan and Tullock's faulty analysis. Interpersonal comparisons of utility run rampant: Evidently, the utility of the large entrepreneur is to be weighted more heavily than that of the small "exploiting" holdouts. Never do Buchanan and Tullock recognize that such parties may have psychic income goals unrelated to "robbing" the large capitalist, much less that this very goal is as legitimate as any other in the market. They simply do not appreciate the fact that prior government failure is responsible for the "plight" of the land developer; the state has created the problem in the first place, and it is problematic to call for further such action as a solution.[37] If anything is clear, it is that further intervention will only bring a whole new host of problems.[38] It is far better to call for privatization of roads, thereby addressing the initial cause of the problem, than to call for additional governmental "fixes."

## 8. The Fifth and Sixth Categories

In these two cases, Buchanan and Tullock claim that $g < a < b$ or $g < b < a$. In addition to the traditional fire and police protection arguments, dealt with above, they mention traffic lights. Here they erect a huge straw man, and then begin to pummel it:

> The expected costs of organizing decisions voluntarily on the location of traffic lights, for example, may be minimized by no traffic control at all. However, this value may be much in excess of the costs that the individual expects to incur as a result of organizing traffic control collectively. The cost reduction that may be accomplished by collectivization becomes more significant when it is noted that such regulatory activities will normally be delegated to single decision-makers who will be empowered to choose rules for the whole group. Activities in this set involve high external costs if organized privately, but the external costs resulting from adverse collective decisions are not significant.[39]

Are the only alternatives either state control of traffic lights or no control at all? These are the stark options offered to us by Buchanan and Tullock. Were these our only choices, the decision would be a difficult one indeed, not the easy one imagined by our authors. Yes, no control at all seems a daunting prospect. Imagining no traffic lights at all, or only those agreed upon by, say, all citizens of a town at a large public meeting, boggles the imagination. One can see traffic grinding to a halt, replete with astronomical levels of road fatalities. On the other hand, however, this scenario does not seem too different from what we now enjoy! Highway deaths and traffic congestion are, seemingly, part and parcel of our modern existence. At times, one might almost be ready to risk traffic "anarchy." How could it be worse than what we now suffer from?

Of course, there is a third alternative, one that never seems to occur to road socialists such as Buchanan and Tullock: the free market. Private ownership of roads leads to private, voluntary agreements between drivers and road owners; such agreements would surely include speed limits, safety features, stop lights, and so on. While it would take us too far afield to discuss the detailed workings of such a system, it should be clear that this constitutes a third option to either government traffic lights or nothing at all. Nor are Buchanan and Tullock in any position to claim that its costs would be higher than $g$, since their failure to discuss it at all implies that they are completely unaware of it as a viable alternative.

## 9. Implications

Buchanan and Tullock make a claim that is somewhat outside of the mainstream of neoclassical economic thought:

> [T]he existence of external effects from private behavior is not even a necessary condition for an activity to be collectivized on rational grounds. The activities described by the sixth ordering [$g < b < a$; e.g., police, fire], which are perhaps the most important ones performed by governments, may be characterized by the absence of externalities in the final equilibrium resulting from free individual choice. Contractual arrangements will tend to be worked out on a voluntary basis, which will effectively reduce and may completely remove the externalities. The advantage of collective organization for activities in this group lies wholly in its *greater efficiency*.[40]

Now, it is one thing to assert that state coercion is justified by externalities. Although there are flaws in this argument, as we have seen, at least it has the advantage of a certain amount of precedent within the economics profession. But Buchanan and Tullock go much further than that, claiming that this is not needed, and will not even suffice. Instead, sheer efficiency is what vindicates statist coercion. We pass lightly over the interpersonal comparison of utility objection, although this cries out as a rebuke of their position. We address ourselves to the issue of what it is about government that makes it more efficient than the market. Its only distinctive characteristic, *vis-à-vis* the market, is its monopoly of legal force. But how can this make it more efficient? And even if it were more efficient in the provision of these services, why would the natural advantages of government carry through to endeavors other than police protection?

## 10. Conclusion

More important than any specific deviation from the principles of private property and free enterprise are the underlying philosophical errors which lead Buchanan and Tullock in this direction in the first place. These are, as we have seen, part and parcel of their "constitutional economics." One need not reject the Public Choice School in its entirety to extirpate these mistakes; there are too many salutary elements of it for that. But one might well conclude that "constitutional economics" itself needs reconsideration.

### NOTES

1. Buchanan, James M., and Gordon Tullock (1962), *The Calculus of Consent: Logical Foundations of Constitutional Democracy.* Ann Arbor, MI: University of Michigan Press.
2. Ibid., 6
3. Ibid., 4.
4. For an elaboration of this point, see DiLorenzo, Thomas J., and Walter Block (2000), "Is Voluntary Government Possible? A Critique of Constitutional Economics," *Journal of Institutional and Theoretical Economics* 156(4): 567–582.

Libertarian philosophy, which is the foundation for our critique, starts with an explication of rights and builds a structure from there. For a libertarian discussion of rights based on the "argumentation ethic," see Hoppe, Hans (1993), *The Economics and Ethics of Private Property: Studies in Political Economy and Philosophy*. Boston, MA: Kluwer Academic Publishers. For the more general case of the libertarian philosophy, see Rothbard, Murray N. (1978), *For a New Liberty*. New York: MacMillan; Rothbard, Murray N. (1982), *The Ethics of Liberty*. Atlantic Highlands, NJ: Humanities Press; Hoppe, Hans (1989), *A Theory of Socialism and Capitalism*. Boston, MA: Kluwer; Benson, Bruce L. (1989), "Enforcement of Private Property Rights in Primitive Societies: Law without Government," *Journal of Libertarian Studies* 9(1): 1–26; Benson, Bruce L. (1989), "The Spontaneous Evolution of Commercial Law," *Southern Economic Journal* 55: 644–661; Benson, Bruce L. (1990), *The Enterprise of Law: Justice Without the State*. San Francisco, CA: Pacific Research Institute for Public Policy; Friedman, David (1989), *The Machinery of Freedom: Guide to a Radical Capitalism*, 2nd ed. LaSalle, IL: Open Court; Machan, Tibor (1975), "Law, Justice, and Natural Rights," *Western Ontario Law Review* 14: 119–130; Machan, Tibor (1989), *Individuals and their Rights*. LaSalle, IL: Open Court; Nozick, Robert (1974), *Anarchy, State, and Utopia*. New York: Basic Books; and Block, Walter (1994), "Libertarianism vs. Libertinism," *Journal of Libertarian Studies* 11(1): 117–128.

5. Buchanan and Tullock, *Calculus of Consent*, 46.

6. Ibid., 46–47.

7. Ibid., 345 n. 3.

8. Ibid., 345 n. 3, emphasis added.

9. Ibid., 49.

10. Ibid., 48, emphasis in original.

11. Michael Novak, in *The Spirit of Democratic Capitalism* (New York: Simon and Schuster, 1978), calls them "mediating institutions."

12. They may be given tax *exemptions*, but this is not to be interpreted as a tax subsidy or benefit given to them by the government. The only way to rationalize such an interpretation would be to posit that the government really owns the entire GDP, and whatever is untaxed — that is, whatever wealth it leaves to us, the creators, is really a "gift" from government to us.

13. Of course, Buchanan and Tullock never use the "S" word, but this should not be allowed to obfuscate the essence of their theory.

14. Buchanan and Tullock, *Calculus of Consent*, 49.

15. Ibid., 49–50.

16. Ibid., 50.

17. What of the case where there is but one dictator, not a dictatorship of the majority? This, too, fits our *g* model. Buchanan and Tullock, however, give it short shrift, first because they are concerned with voting, and second because they think that this implies consent (hence, the title of the canonical book for public choice).

18. This statement in and of itself is entirely unobjectionable. It is their discussion of it that is problematic.

19. Buchanan and Tullock, *Calculus of Consent*, 52.

20. Or someone else, e.g., a disinterested bureaucrat, it does not matter.

21. "If an individual chooses to wear red underwear, presumably no other member of the social group suffers a cost. To any given individual, therefore, the organization of this activity

privately involves no external costs." Buchanan and Tullock, *Calculus of Consent*, 45. For more on this, see Walter Block, "Another look at *The Calculus of Consent*," forthcoming.

22. For defenses of the notion that institutional arrangements along these lines are feasible no matter how counter-intuitive they sound at the outset, see Block, Walter (1979), "Free Market Transportation: Denationalizing the Roads," *Journal of Libertarian Studies* 3, no. 2: 209–238; Block, Walter (1980), "Congestion and Road Pricing," *Journal of Libertarian Studies* 4(3): 299–330; Block, Walter (1983), "Public Goods and Externalities: The Case of Roads," *Journal of Libertarian Studies* 7(1): 1–34; Block, Walter (1983), "Theories of Highway Safety," *Transportation Research Record* 912: 7–10; Block, Walter (1996), "Road Socialism," *International Journal of Value-Based Management* 9(2): 195–207; Block, Matthew, and Walter Block (1996), "Roads, Bridges, Sunlight, and Private Property Rights: Reply to Gordon Tullock," *Journal des Economistes et des Etudes Humaines* 7(2/3): 315–326; Cadin, Michelle, and Walter Block (1997), "Privatize the Public Highway System," *The Freeman* 47(2): 96–97; Gunderson, Gerald (1989), "Privatization and the 19th Century Turnpike," *Cato Journal* 9(1): 191–200; Klein, Dan (1990), "The Voluntary Provision of Public Goods? The Turnpike Companies of Early America," *Economic Inquiry* 28(4): 788–812; Klein, Daniel B., and John Majewski (1992), "Economy, Community, and the Law: The Turnpike Movement in New York, 1797–1845," *Journal of Economic History* 26(3): 469–512; Klein, D. J. Majewski, and C. Baer, "From Trunk to Branch: Toll Roads in New York, 1800–1860," *Essays in Economic and Business History* (Conference Proceedings), 191–209; Klein, D., and G. J. Fielding (1992), "Private Toll Roads: Learning from the Nineteenth Century," *Transportation Quarterly* July: 321–341; Klein, D., and G.J. Fielding (1993), "How to Franchise Highways," *Journal of Transport Economics and Policy* May: 113–130; Klein, D., and G. J. Fielding (1993), "High Occupancy/Toll Lanes: Phasing in Congestion Pricing a Lane at a Time," *Reason Foundation Policy Study* 170 November: 1–16; Roth, Gabriel (1966), *A Self-Financing Road System*. London: Institute of Economic Affairs; Roth, Gabriel (1967), *Paving for Roads: The Economics of Traffic Congestion*. Middlesex: Penguin; Roth, Gabriel (1987), *The Private Provision of Public Services in Developing Countries*. Oxford: Oxford University Press; Rothbard, Murray N. (1978), *For a New Liberty*. New York: Collier; and Woodridge, William C. (1970), *Uncle Sam the Monopoly Man*. New Rochelle, NY: Arlington House.

23. See, in this regard, Rothbard, *The Ethics of Liberty*; Nozick, *Anarchy, State, and Utopia*; Epstein, Richard (1985), *Takings: Private Property and the Power of Eminent Domain*. Cambridge, MA: Harvard University Press; Hoppe, *A Theory of Socialism and Capitalism*; and Hoppe, Hans (1993), *The Economics and Ethics of Private Property: Studies in Political Economy and Philosophy*. Boston, MA: Kluwer Academic Publishers.

24. Except for the person who has contractually obligated him to wear non-red underwear, which he refuses to do.

25. Buchanan and Tullock, *Calculus of Consent*, 54.

26. Friedman, Milton (1962), *Capitalism and Freedom*. Chicago, IL: University of Chicago Press, 88, 98.

27. For this argument, see Gornick, Vivian (1978), *Essays in Feminism*. New York: Harper and Row; Bernard, Jesse (1962), *Academic Women*. University Park, PA: Pennsylvania State University Press; Gunderson, Morley (1982), *The Female-Male Earnings Gap*. Toronto: Ontario Ministry of Labor; and Robb, Roberta E. (1978), "Earnings Differentials between Males and Females," *Canadian Journal of Economics* 11(2): 350– 359.

For a critique of this argument, see Levin, Michael (1984), "Comparable Worth: The Feminist Road to Socialism," *Commentary* September; Levin, Michael (1987), *Feminism and Freedom*. New York: Transaction Books; Block, Walter, and Walter Williams (1981), "Male-Female Earnings Differentials: A Critical Reappraisal," *Journal of Labor Research* 2(2): 385–388; and Sowell, Thomas (1982), "Weber and Bakke and the Presuppositions of Affirmative Action," in *Discrimination, Affirmative Action, and Equal Opportunity*, eds. Walter Block and Michael Walker. Vancouver: Fraser Institute.

28. Burr, Richard E. (1986), "Rank Injustice: The Arbitrary Record of Comparable Worth," *Policy Review* Fall: 73–74.

29. Hoppe, in *The Economics and Ethics of Private Property*, p. 5, makes the same point in a different, but related, context. He states, "The examples given by different authors of alleged public goods vary widely. Authors often classify the same good or service differently, leaving almost no classification of a particular good undisputed, which clearly foreshadows the illusory character of the whole distinction."

30. Buchanan and Tullock, *Calculus of Consent*, 55.

31. However, as further evidence of the arbitrariness of this analysis, there are numerous other supposed advocates of the free market—that is, followers of the schools of Public Choice or the University of Chicago Law-and-Economics tradition—who have reached the exact opposite conclusion. See, for example, Hirsch, Werner Z. (1979), *Law and Economics: An Introductory Analysis*. New York: Academic Press, 127: "exclusionary zoning is found to have positive implications for the efficient allocation of resources in the presence of local property taxation, particularly if it takes the form of construction permit fees."

32. Buchanan and Tullock, *Calculus of Consent*, 55.

33. Ibid., 56.

34. Ibid., 56, material in brackets supplied by present authors.

35. Interpersonal comparisons of utility are rife within the profession. One can hardly read mainstream economics without being confronted with such fallacies. However, it is more than passingly curious that Buchanan should indulge in this line of argument, considering the fact that he, at least in another context, explicitly disavows them. See Buchanan, James M. (1969), *Cost and Choice: An Inquiry into Economic Theory*. Chicago, IL: Markham; Buchanan, James M., and G. F. Thirlby (1981), *L.S.E. Essays on Cost*. New York: New York University Press; and Barnett II, William (1989), "Subjective Cost Revisited," *Review of Austrian Economics* 3: 137–138.

36. Buchanan and Tullock, *Calculus of Consent*, 56–57.

37. This is just like saying that although government minimum-wage laws have caused teenage unemployment, instead of getting rid of such laws, the state should institute new programs, such as unemployment insurance, to "solve" the very problem it created in the first place.

38. See, e.g., Siegan, Bernard (1970), "Non-Zoning in Houston," *Journal of Law and Economics* 13(1): 71–147; also Siegan, Bernard (1972), *Land Use without Zoning*. Lexington, MA: Heath.

39. Buchanan and Tullock, *Calculus of Consent*, 58.

40. Ibid., 61, emphasis added.

# REFERENCES

Barnett, William II (1989), "Subjective Cost Revisited," *Review of Austrian Economics* 3: 137–138.

Benson, Bruce L. (1989), "Enforcement of Private Property Rights in Primitive Societies: Law without Government," *Journal of Libertarian Studies* 9(1): 1–26.

—— (1989), "The Spontaneous Evolution of Commercial Law," *Southern Economic Journal* 55: 644–661.

—— (1990), *The Enterprise of Law: Justice without the State.* San Francisco, CA: Pacific Research Institute for Public Policy.

Bernard, Jesse (1962), *Academic Women.* University Park, PA: Pennsylvania State University Press.

Block, Walter (1979), "Free Market Transportation: Denationalizing the Roads," *Journal of Libertarian Studies* 3(2): 209–238.

—— (1980), "Congestion and Road Pricing," *Journal of Libertarian Studies* 4(3): 299–330.

—— (1983), "Public Goods and Externalities: The Case of Roads," *Journal of Libertarian Studies* 7(1): 1–34.

—— (1983), "Theories of Highway Safety," *Transportation Research Record* 912: 7–10.

—— (1996), "Road Socialism," *International Journal of Value-Based Management* 9: 195–207.

—— (1994), "Libertarianism vs. Libertinism," *Journal of Libertarian Studies* 11(1): 117–28.

——. "Another look at the *Calculus of Consent.*" *Forthcoming*

——. "A Comment on Professor James Buchanan's *What Should Economists Do?*" *Forthcoming*

Block, Matthew, and Walter Block (1996), "Roads, Bridges, Sunlight, and Private Property Rights: Reply to Gordon Tullock," *Journal Des Economistes et des Etudes Humaines* 7(2/3): 315–26.

Block, Walter, and Walter Williams (1981), "Male-Female Earnings Differentials: A Critical Reappraisal," *Journal of Labor Research* 2(2): 383–388.

Buchanan, James M. (1969), *Cost and Choice: An Inquiry into Economic Theory.* Chicago, IL: Markham.

Buchanan, James M., and G. F. Thirlby (1981), *L.S.E. Essays on Cost.* New York: New York University Press.

Buchanan, James M., and Gordon Tullock (1962), *The Calculus of Consent: Logical Foundations of Constitutional Democracy.* Ann Arbor, MI: University of Michigan Press.

Burr, Richard E. (1986), "Rank Injustice: The Arbitrary Record of Comparable Worth," *Policy Review* Fall: 73–74.

Cadin, Michelle, and Walter Block (1997), "Privatize the Public Highway System," *The Freeman* 47(2): 96–97.

DiLorenzo, Thomas J., and Walter Block (2000), "Is Voluntary Government Possible? A Critique of Constitutional Economics," *Journal of Institutional and Theoretical Economics* 156(4): 567–582.

—— (2001), "*The Calculus of Consent* Revisited," *Journal of Public Finance and Management* 1(3): 305–321.

Epstein, Richard A. (1985), *Takings: Private Property and the Power of Eminent Domain.* Cambridge, MA: Harvard University Press.

Friedman, Milton (1962), *Capitalism and Freedom.* Chicago, IL: University of Chicago Press.

Friedman, David (1989), *The Machinery of Freedom: Guide to a Radical Capitalism*. 2nd ed. LaSalle, IL: Open Court.

Gornick, Vivian (1978), *Essays in Feminism*. New York: Harper and Row.

Gunderson, Gerald (1989), "Privatization and the 19th-Century Turnpike," *Cato Journal* 9(1): 191–200.

Gunderson, Morley (1982), *The Female-Male Earnings Gap*. Toronto: Ontario Ministry of Labor.

Hirsch, Werner Z. (1979), *Law and Economics*. New York: Academic Press.

Hoppe, Hans-Hermann (1989), *A Theory of Socialism and Capitalism: Economics, Politics, and Ethics*. Boston, MA: Kluwer.

—— (1993), *The Economics and Ethics of Private Property: Studies in Political Economy and Philosophy*. Boston, MA: Kluwer.

Klein, Dan (1990), "The Voluntary Provision of Public Goods? The Turnpike Companies of Early America," *Economic Inquiry* October: 788–812.

Klein, Dan, and G. J. Fielding (1992), "Private Toll Roads: Learning from the Nineteenth Century," *Transportation Quarterly* July: 321– 41.

—— (1993), "How to Franchise Highways," *Journal of Transport Economics and Policy* May: 113–30.

—— (1993), "High Occupancy/Toll Lanes: Phasing in Congestion Pricing a Lane at a Time," *Reason Foundation Policy Study* 170, November.

Klein, Dan, J. Majewski, and C. Baer (1993), "Economy, Community, and the Law: The Turnpike Movement in New York, 1797–1845," *Journal of Economic History* 53(3): 106–122.

—— (1993), "From Trunk to Branch: Toll Roads in New York, 1800–1860," *Essays in Economic and Business History* XI: 191–209.

Levin, Michael (1984), "Comparable Worth: The Feminist Road to Socialism." *Commentary*, September.

—— (1987), *Feminism and Freedom*. New York: Transaction Books.

Machan, Tibor (1975), "Law, Justice, and Natural Rights," *Western Ontario Law Review* 14: 119–126.

—— (1989), *Individuals and their Rights*. LaSalle, IL: Open Court.

Novak, Michael (1978), *The Spirit of Democratic Capitalism*. New York: Simon and Schuster.

Nozick, Robert (1974), *Anarchy, State, and Utopia*. New York: Basic Books.

Robb, Roberta E. (1978), "Earnings Differentials between Males and Females," *Canadian Journal of Economics* 11(2): 350–359.

Roth, Gabriel (1987), *The Private Provision of Public Services in Developing Countries*. Oxford: Oxford University Press.

—— (1966), *A Self-financing Road System*. London: Institute of Economic Affairs.

—— (1967), *Paving for Roads: The Economics of Traffic Congestion*. Middlesex: Penguin.

Rothbard, Murray N. (1973), *For a New Liberty*. New York: Macmillan.

—— (1982), *The Ethics of Liberty*. Atlantic Highlands, NJ: Humanities Press.

Siegan, Bernard H. (1970), "Non-Zoning in Houston," *Journal of Law and Economics* 13(1): 71–147.

—— (1972), *Land Use Without Zoning*. Lexington, MA: Heath.

Sowell, Thomas (1982), "*Weber* and *Bakke* and the Presuppositions of 'Affirmative Action,'" in *Discrimination, Affirmative Action, and Equal Opportunity*, eds. Walter Block and Michael Walker. Vancouver: The Fraser Institute.

Woolridge, William C. (1970), *Uncle Sam the Monopoly Man*. New Rochelle, NY: Arlington House.

# Part 4:
# Austrians and Public Choicers
# on Antitrust

# Chapter 9
# The Truth about Sherman

## 1. Introduction

Today regulation is generally recognized as a mechanism by which special interests lobby the government to create barriers to entry or other special privileges. Research has shown, for example, that the Civil Aeronautics Board cartelized the airline industry, the Interstate Commerce Commission helped monopolize the railroad and the trucking industries, the Federal Deposit Insurance Corporation sharply limited entry into the banking business, and occupational licensing created entry barriers into hundreds of occupations. Much of the history of regulation chronicles monopoly privileges procured through the auspices of the state, as Adam Smith pointed out more than 200 years ago in The Wealth of Nations.

Oddly, antitrust regulation is still widely viewed as government's benevolent response to the "failures" and "imperfections" of the marketplace. Even economists who are usually skeptical of regulations enacted in the name of the public interest seem to lose their perspective when it comes to antitrust. George Stigler, for example, has stated: "So far as I can tell, [the Sherman Act] is a public-interest law ... in the same sense in which I think having private property, enforcement of contracts, and suppression of crime are public-interest phenomena.... I like the Sherman Act" [Quoted in Thomas Hazlett, "Interview with George Stigler," *Reason*, January 1984: 46).

A 1984 survey of professional economists revealed that 83% of the respondents believed that "antitrust laws should be used vigorously to reduce monopoly power from its current level." (Bruno Frey, et al. (1984), "Consensus and Dissension Among Economists," *American Economic Review* May: 986–84.) His opinion is widespread despite common knowledge among antitrust scholars that in practice the antitrust laws restrain output and the growth of productivity have contributed to a deterioration of the competitive position of U.S. industry, and are routinely used to subvert competition.

Why then do the antitrust laws continue to command such powerful support among economists and legal scholars when the pervasive failures are so well known? There are several possible explanations. Antitrust consultants and expert witnesses often stand to make a good deal of money, so financial self-interest may preclude criticism of antitrust. Many economists are also unable to voice informed opinions on antitrust. If it is not their area of expertise, they may not have kept up with research over the past 30 years, or excessive concentration on mathematical models may have left some economists somewhat detached from economic reality. Finally, it is widely believed that there was once a "golden age of antitrust" during which the public was protected from rapacious monopolists by benevolent public servants. According to this perspective, although mistakes have been made, more knowledgeable and public-spirited regulators can successfully reform antitrust. Once reformed, antitrust policy can then perform its original purpose and defend competition and free enterprise.

Unfortunately, the Sherman Act was never intended to protect competition. It was a blatantly protectionist act designed to shield smaller and less efficient businesses from their larger competitors. There never was a golden age of antitrust. The standard account of the origins of antitrust is a myth.

## 2. Interest Group Politics and the Sherman Act

In the late 1880s, widespread economic change produced myriad pleas from relatively small – but politically active – farmers who sought protection from larger, corporate competitors. Historian Sanford Gordon offered an example: "Perhaps the most violent reaction [against industrial combinations] of any single special interest group came from farmers.... They singled out the jute bagging and alleged binder twine trust, and sent petitions to both their state legislators and to Congress demanding some relief. Cotton was suggested as a good substitute for jute to cover their cotton bales. In Georgia, Mississippi, and Tennessee the [farmers'] alliances passed resolutions condemning the jute bagging trust and recommended the use of cotton cloth." (Gordon, Sanford (1963), "Attitude toward the Trusts Prior to the Sherman Act," *Southern Economic Journal* July: 158).

Southern farmers were annoyed that consumers increasingly preferred jute to the cotton cloth they produced, and they sought antitrust legislation that would dissolve their competition. Such special-interest behavior was characteristic of the farm lobby. During the 51st Congress, Gordon notes that "64 petitions and memorials were recorded in the *Congressional Record,* all calling for action against combinations. These were almost exclusively from farm groups.... The greatest vehemence was expressed by representatives from the Midwest" (p. 162).

Farmers complained to their national representatives that the products they bought from the trust were increasingly expensive relative to the prices of farm products, but the facts do not support this contention. From 1865 to 1900 farm prices were falling, but at a slower rate than the general price level. This produced real income gains for farmers. In addition, the rapidly increasing quality of manufactured goods further improved the farmers' standard of living. The volatility of farm prices caused the farmers to be politically active.

Many other groups joined the antitrust coalition: small business organizations, academics (though not economists), and journalists. They argued that the "giant monopolies" were creating a "dangerous concentration of wealth" among the capitalists of the day. Although the conspicuous wealth of entrepreneurs such as Rockefeller, Vanderbilt, Mellon, and Morgan added fuel to this charge, it does not appear to be true. In fact, economic historians have concluded that from 1840 to 1900, the division of national income between labor and property owners (capital and natural resource suppliers) remained in a 70-to-30 ratio." (Gray, R., and J. Peterson (1965), *Economic Development in the United States.* New York: Irwin, 1965.) Over the same time span, both capital and developed natural resources increased faster than the labor force. This means that labor income per unit of labor rose compared with profit and interest per unit of property input.

Although there was no significant redistribution of wealth from labor to capital owners in the aggregate, competitive markets always alter the distribution of income in ways that some do not like. There was no "dangerous concentration of wealth," but many supporters of antitrust legislation found that their own income had fallen (or not increased rapidly enough). The push for antitrust legislation was an attempt to use the powers of the government to improve their economic status.

Economic conditions were changing rapidly in the latter part of the nineteenth century. Expansion of the railroad and inland shipping industries greatly reduced the cost of transportation. Technological developments led to large-scale (and lower-cost) production of steel, cement, and other goods. Communications technology rapidly expanded, especially the use of the telegraph. And the capital markets became more sophisticated. The United States also underwent a rapid transition from a predominantly agrarian to an industrial society. In 1810 the ration of farm to non-farm labor was approximately 4.0. This ratio fell to 1.6 by 1840, and by 1880 the labor force was about equally divided between farm and non-farm endeavors. Meanwhile, individuals and groups uncomfortable with rapid change were becoming increasingly adept at using the regulatory powers of the state. In this increasingly mercantilist atmosphere, the Sherman Act was passed in 1890.

## 3. Were the Trusts Monopolistic?

In introducing federal "antitrust" legislation, Sen. Sherman and his congressional allies claimed that combinations or trusts tended to restrict output and thus drive up prices. If Sherman's claims were true, then there should be evidence that those industries allegedly being monopolized by the trusts had restricted output. By contrast, if the trust movement was part of the evolutionary process of competitive markets responding to technological change, one would expect an expansion of trade or output. In fact, there is no evidence that trusts in the 1880s were restricting output or artificially increasing prices.

The *Congressional Record* of the 51st Congress provides a list of industries that were supposedly being monopolized by the trusts. Those industries for which data are available are salt, petroleum, zinc, steel, bituminous coal, steel rails, sugar, lead, liquor, twine, iron nuts and washers, jute, castor oil, cotton seed oil, leather, linseed oil, and matches. The available data are incomplete, but in all but two of the 17 industries, output increased – not only from 1880 to 1890, but also to the turn of the century. (The following discussion is based on DiLorenzo, Thomas J. (1985), "The Origins of Antitrust: An Interest-Group Perspective," *International Review of Law and Economics* June: 73–90.) Matches and castor oil, the only exceptions to the general rule, hardly seem to be items that would cause a national furor, even if they were monopolized.

As a general rule, output in these industries expanded more rapidly than GNP during the 10 years preceding the Sherman Act. In the nine industries for which nominal output data are available, output increased on average by 62%; nominal GNP increased by 16% over the same period. Several of the industries expanded output by more than 10 times the increase in nominal GNP. Among the more rapidly expanding industries were cottonseed oil (151%), leather goods (133%), cordage and twine (166%), and jute (57%).

Real GNP increased by approximately 24% from 1880 to 1890. Meanwhile, the allegedly monopolized industries for which a measure of real output is available grew on average by 175%. The more rapidly expanding industries in real terms included steel (258%), zinc (156%), coal (153%), steel rails (142%), petroleum (79%), and sugar (75%).

These trends continued from 1890 to 1900 as output expanded in every industry but one for which we have data. (Castor oil was the exception.) On average, the allegedly monopolized industries continued to expand faster than the rest of the economy. Those industries for which nominal data are available expanded output by 99%, while nominal GNP increased by 43%. The industries for which we have data increased real output by 76% compared with a 46% increase in real GNP from 1890 to 1900.

As with measures of output, not all of the relevant price data are available, but the information that is at hand indicates that falling prices accompanied the rapid expansion of output in the "monopolized" industries. In addition, although the consumer price index fell by 7% from 1880 to 1890, prices in many of the suspect industries were falling even faster.

The average price of steel rails, for example, fell by 53 percent from $68 per ton in 1880 to $32 per ton in 1890. The price of refined sugar fell from 9 cents per pound in 1880, to 7 cents in 1890, to 4.5 cents in 1900. The price of lead dropped 12%, from $5.04 per pound in 1880 to $4.41 in 1890. The price of zinc declined by 20%, from $5.51 to $4.40 per pound from 1880 to 1890.

The sugar and petroleum trusts were among the most widely attacked, but there is evidence that these trusts actually reduced prices from what they otherwise would have been. Congress clearly recognized this. During the House debates over the Sherman Act, Congressman William Mason stated, "*Trusts have made products cheaper, have reduced prices;* but if the price of oil, for instance, were reduced to one cent a barrel, it would not right the wrong done to the people of this country by the 'trusts' which have destroyed legitimate competition and driven honest men from legitimate business enterprises." (Congressional Record, 51st

Congress, House, 1st Session, June 20, 1890: 4100.) Sen. Edwards, who played a key role in the debate, added, "Although for the time being *the sugar trust has perhaps reduced the price of sugar, and the oil trust certainly has reduced the price of oil immensely,* that does not alter the wrong of the principle of any trust" (ibid., 2558.] Perhaps it would be more accurate to describe the Sherman Act as an anti-price-cutting law.

One final argument could be made that the trusts were practicing predatory pricing, that is, that they were pricing below their costs to drive out competitors. But in more than a century of looking for a proven real-world monopoly actually created by predatory pricing, an example has yet to be found. Moreover, prices charged by the nineteenth-century trusts continued to fall for more than a decade. What rational businessman would continue to price below cost for more than ten years?

In sum, the nineteenth-century trusts were not guilty of the charge levied against them by Sen. Sherman. There is no consistent evidence that they restricted output to raise prices.


## 4. Government: The True Source of Monopoly

It appears that one function of the Sherman Act was to divert public attention from a more certain source of monopoly-government. In the late nineteenth century, tariffs were a major source of trade restraints, but the Sherman Act made no provision for attacking tariffs or any other government-created barriers to competitive entry. In fact, evidence exists that a major political function of the Sherman Act was to serve as a smoke screen behind which politicians could grant tariff protection to their big business constituents while assuring the public that something was being done about the monopoly problem.

In a particularly revealing statement during the debates over the antitrust act, Sen. Sherman attacked the trusts on the ground that they "subverted the tariff system; they undermined the policy of government to protect ... American industries by levying duties on imported goods." (4100). This is certainly an odd statement from the author of the "Magna Carta of free enterprise." But increased output and reduced prices in these increasingly efficient industries apparently dissipated the monopoly profits previously generated by the tariffs. This worked against the objectives of the protected industries and their legislative champions, including Sen. Sherman.

Even more damning is the fact that just three months after the Sherman Act was passed, Sen. Sherman, as chairman of the Senate Finance Committee, sponsored legislation popularly known as the "Campaign Contributors' Tariff Bill" that sharply raised tariff rates. On October 1, 1890, the *New York Times* reported: "The Campaign Contributors' Tariff Bill now goes to the president for his signature, which will speedily be affixed to it, and the favored manufacturers, many of whom

... proposed and made the [tariff] rates which affect their products, will begin to enjoy the profits of this legislation."

The *New York Times* further reported that "the speech of Mr. Sherman on Monday [September 29, 1890] should not be overlooked, for it was one of confession." Apparently, Sen. Sherman withdrew his speech from the *Congressional Record* for "revision," but a reporter obtained an unabridged copy of the original. *The New York Times* reported:

> We direct attention to those passages [of Sherman's speech] relating to combinations of protected manufacturers designed to take full advantage of high tariff duties by exacting from consumers prices fixed by agreement after competition has been suppressed.... Mr. Sherman closed his speech with some words of warning and advice to the beneficiaries of the new tariff. He was earnest enough in his manner to indicate that he is not at all confident as to the outcome of the law. The great thing that stood in the way of the success of the bill, he said, was whether or not the manufacturers of this country would permit free competition in the American market. The danger was that the beneficiaries of the bill would combine and cheat the people out of the benefits of the law. They were now given reasonable and ample protection, and if they would resist the temptation attaching to great aggregations of capital to combine and advance prices, they might hope for a season of great prosperity... He did hope, the Senator concluded, that the manufacturers would open the doors to fair competition and give its benefits to the people.... He hoped the manufacturers would agree to compete one with another and would refuse to take the high prices that are so easily obtained.

It was absurd, of course, for Sen. Sherman to say that a protective tariff would actually help consumers if only manufacturers could be trusted to refrain from raising prices. The whole purpose of tariff protection is to allow domestic manufacturers to raise prices, or at least to avoid reducing them. Such hypocrisy led the *New York Times* to withdraw its support of antitrust legislation. *The Times* concluded: "That so-called Anti-Trust law was passed to deceive the people and to clear the way for the enactment of this ... law relating to the tariff. It was projected in order that the party organs might say to the opponents of tariff extortion and protected combinations, 'Behold! We have attacked the Trusts. The Republican party is the enemy of all such rings.' And now the author of it can only 'hope' that the rings will dissolve of their own accord." Thus, the Sherman Act seems to have been passed to help draw public attention away from the process of monopolization through tariff protection.

The Sherman Act won legislators votes and campaign contributions from farmers and small businessmen who thought antitrust regulation would protect them from their more efficient competitors, and the tariff bill was supported by all U.S. manufacturers, both large and small. In a political sense, then, the Sherman

Act was very efficient. Congress itself seems to have been one of the principal special-interest groups to benefit from antitrust legislation.

## 5. Economists and the Emergence of Antitrust

Although most economists today favor stricter antitrust regulation, from the 1880s until the 1920s the economics profession expressed nearly unanimous opposition to antitrust. When Sanford Gordon surveyed professional journals in the social sciences and articles and books written by economists before 1890, he found, "A big majority of the economists conceded that the combination movement was to be expected, that high fixed costs made large-scale enterprises economical, that competition under these new circumstances frequently resulted in cut-throat competition, that agreements among producers was a natural consequence, and the stability of prices usually brought more benefit than harm to the society. They seemed to reject the idea that competition was declining, or showed no fear of decline." (Gordon, Sanford, "Attitudes toward the Trusts," p. 158.)

George Stigler has also noted economists' initial disapproval of antitrust: "For much too long a time students of the history of antitrust policy have been at least mildly perplexed by the coolness with which American economists greeted the Sherman Act. Was not the nineteenth century the period in which the benevolent effects of competition were most widely extolled? Should not a profession praise a Congress which seeks to legislate its textbook assumptions into practice?" (Stigler, George (1982), "The Economists and the Problem of Monopoly," *American Economic Review* May: 1.) Stigler offered three possible explanations. First, economists did not appreciate the importance of tacit collusion. Second, they had too much confidence in other forms of regulation as a means of dealing with monopoly. Third, they underestimated the income they would receive as antitrust consultants.

These explanations are plausible, but there may be an even more important reason for the transformation of economists' attitudes toward antitrust. In the late nineteenth century most economists viewed competition as a dynamic, rivalrous process, similar to the theory of competition embodied in the work of Adam Smith and today's Austrian economists. Consequently, they tended to regard mergers as a natural consequence of the competitive struggle and not something that should be interfered with by antitrust legislation. (The following discussion is based on DiLorenzo, T. J., and Jack C. High (1988), "'Antitrust and Competition,' 'Historically Considered,'" *Economic Inquiry* 26(3): 423–435). Although some industries were becoming more concentrated in the late nineteenth century, rivalry was still as strong as ever, as the rapid expansion of output and the decline in prices attest. Thus, the economists of the time saw no reason to interfere in market processes with antitrust regulation.

Beginning in the 1920s, mathematical economists developed the so-called perfect competition model, and it replaced the older theory. To economists competition no longer meant rivalry and enterprise. Instead, it meant the equation of price and marginal cost. Most important, it meant that there must be "many" firms in "unconcentrated" industries. Once economists began to define competition in terms of market structure, they became more and more enamored with antitrust regulation as a way of forcing the business world to conform to their admittedly unrealistic theory of competition.

Economist Paul McNulty has noted: "The two concepts [of competition] are not only different; they are fundamentally incompatible. Competition came to mean, with the mathematical economists, a hypothetically realized situation in which business rivalry ... was ruled out by definition." (McNulty, Paul (1967), "A Note on the History of Perfect Competition," *Journal of Political Economy* August: 398.) F. A. Hayek has made an even stronger statement: "What the theory of perfect competition discusses has little claim to be called competition at all and ... its conclusions are of little use as guides to policy." (Hayek, F. A. (1948), "The Meaning of Competition," in his *Individualism and Economic Order.* Chicago, IL: University of Chicago Press, 92.) Moreover, wrote Hayek, "If the state of affairs assumed by the theory of perfect competition ever existed, it would not only deprive of their scope all the activities which the verb 'to compete' describes but would make them virtually impossible." Advertising, product differentiation, and price undercutting, for example, are all excluded by definition from a state of "perfect" competition which, according to Hayek, "means indeed the absence of all competitive activities."

Those economists who use market structure to measure competition are likely to have a favorable attitude toward antitrust regulation. Stigler asserted more than 30 years ago, "One of the assumptions of perfect competition is the existence of a Sherman Act." (Stigler, George (1957), "Perfect Competition, Historically Contemplated," *Journal of Political Economy* February: 1.) To the nineteenth-century economists, however, an antitrust law was incompatible with rivalry and free enterprise. The perfect competition model and its corollary, the structure-conduct-performance paradigm of industrial organization theory, have seriously misled the economics profession, at least as far as antitrust policy is concerned.

## 6. Conclusion

The two principal reasons for the "antitrust economists' paradox," then, are the lack of historical knowledge – particularly about actual economic events in the late nineteenth century – and the failure to appreciate that competition is best viewed as a dynamic discovery procedure, as Hayek contends. Economists who believe that there was once a "golden age of antitrust" have never produced any evidence of such an age. As this paper has shown, the Sherman Act was a tool used to regulate some of the most competitive industries in America, which were rapidly expanding their output and *reducing* their prices, much to the dismay of their less efficient (but politically influential) competitors. The Sherman Act, moreover, was used as a political fig leaf to shield the real cause of monopoly in the late 1880s-protectionism. The chief sponsor of the 1890 tariff bill, passed just three months after the Sherman Act, was none other than Sen. Sherman himself.

In the late nineteenth century most economists viewed competition as a dynamic, rivalrous process, much like the contemporary Austrian theory. Accordingly, they nearly unanimously opposed antitrust on the grounds that such a law would be inherently incompatible with rivalry, Once the economics profession embraced the "perfect" competition theory which, as Hayek has said, means "the absence of all competitive activities," it also embraced antitrust regulation. For once competition came to mean "many" firms and the equation of price to marginal costs, rather than dynamic rivalry, most economists became convinced that antitrust laws were needed to force markets in the direction of their idealized model of "perfect" competition. Consequently, antitrust has for over a century been a tremendous drag on competition, rendering American industry less productive and less competitive in world markets. Robert Bork might not have been exaggerating when, writing in his book, *The Antitrust Paradox,* he remarked that if government were to somehow force the economy into "competitive equilibrium," it would have approximately the same effect on personal wealth as several strategically placed nuclear explosions.

# Chapter 10
# The Myth of Natural Monopoly

The very term 'public utility' ... is an absurd one. *Every* good is useful 'to the public,' and almost every good ... may be considered 'necessary.' Any designation of a few industries as 'public utilities' is completely arbitrary and unjustified. -- Murray Rothbard, *Power and Market*.

## 1. Introduction

Most so-called public utilities have been granted governmental franchise monopolies because they are thought to be "natural monopolies." Put simply, a natural monopoly is said to occur when production technology, such as relatively high fixed costs, causes long-run average total costs to decline as output expands. In such industries, the theory goes, a single producer will eventually be able to produce at a lower cost than any two other producers, thereby creating a "natural" monopoly. Higher prices will result if more than one producer supplies the market.

Furthermore, competition is said to cause consumer inconvenience because of the construction of duplicative facilities, e.g., digging up the streets to put in dual gas or water lines. Avoiding such inconveniences is another reason offered for government franchise monopolies for industries with declining long-run average total costs.

It is a myth that natural monopoly theory was developed first by economists, and then used by legislators to "justify" franchise monopolies. The truth is that the monopolies were created decades before the theory was formalized by intervention-minded economists, who then used the theory as an *ex post* rationale for government intervention. At the time when the first government franchise monopolies were being granted, the large majority of economists understood that large-scale, capital intensive production did *not* lead to monopoly, but was an absolutely desirable aspect of the competitive process.

The word "process" is important here. If competition is viewed as a dynamic, rivalrous process of entrepreneurship, then the fact that a single producer happens to have the lowest costs *at any one point in time* is of little or no consequence. The enduring forces of competition-including potential competition-will render free-market monopoly an impossibility.

The theory of natural monopoly is also a-historical. There is no evidence of the "natural monopoly" story ever having been carried out, of one producer achieving lower long-run average total costs than everyone else in the industry and thereby establishing a permanent monopoly. As discussed below, in many of the so-called public utility industries of the late eighteenth and early nineteenth centuries, there were often literally dozens of competitors.

## 2. Economies of Scale during the Franchise Monopoly Era

During the late nineteenth century, when local governments were beginning to grant franchise monopolies, the general economic understanding was that "monopoly" was caused by government intervention, not the free market, through franchises, protectionism, and other means. Large-scale production and economies of scale were seen as a competitive virtue, not a monopolistic vice. For example, Richard T. Ely, co-founder of the American Economic Association, wrote that "large scale production is a thing which by no means necessarily signifies monopolized production."[1] John Bates Clark, Ely's co-founder, wrote in 1888 that the notion that industrial combinations would "destroy competition" should "not be too hastily accepted."[2]

Herbert Davenport of the University of Chicago advised in 1919 that only a few firms in an industry where there are economies of scale does not "require the elimination of competition,"[3] and his colleague, James Laughlin, noted that even when "a combination is large, a rival combination may give the most spirited competition."[4] Irving Fisher[5] and Edwin R.A. Seligman[6] both agreed that large-scale production produced *competitive* benefits through cost savings in advertising, selling, and less cross-shipping.

Large-scale production units unequivocally benefited the consumer, according to turn-of-the-century economists. For without large-scale production, according to Seligman, "the world would revert to a more primitive state of well-being, and would virtually renounce the inestimable benefits of the best utilization of capital."[7] Simon Patten of the Wharton School expressed a similar view that "the combination of capital does not cause any economic disadvantage to the community. ... Combinations are much more efficient than were the small producers whom they displaced."[8]

Like virtually every other economist of the day, Columbia's Franklin Giddings viewed competition much like the modern-day Austrian economists do, as a dynamic, rivalrous process. Consequently, he observed that "competition in some form is a permanent economic process. ... Therefore, when market competition seems to have been suppressed, we should inquire what has become of the forces by which it was generated. We should inquire, further, to what degree market competition actually is suppressed or converted into other forms."[9] In other words, a "dominant" firm that underprices all its rivals at any one point in time has not suppressed competition, for competition is "a permanent economic process."

David A. Wells, one of the most popular economic writers of the late nineteenth century, wrote that "the world demands abundance of commodities, and demands them cheaply; and experience shows that it can have them only by the employment of great capital upon extensive scale."[10] And George Gunton believed that "concentration of capital does not drive small capitalists out of business, but simply integrates them into larger and more complex systems of production, in which they are enabled to produce ... more cheaply for the community and obtain a larger income for themselves . ... Instead of concentration of capital tending to destroy competition the reverse is true. ... By the use of large capital, improved machinery and better facilities the trust can and does undersell the corporation."[11]

The above quotations are not a selected, but rather a comprehensive list. It may seem odd by today's standards, but as A.W. Coats pointed out, by the late 1880s there were only ten men who had attained full-time professional status as economists in the U.S.[12] Thus, the above quotations cover virtually every professional economist who had anything to say about the relationship between economies of scale and competitiveness at the turn of the century.

The significance of these views is that these men observed firsthand the advent of large-scale production and did not see it leading to monopoly, "natural" or otherwise. In the spirit of the Austrian School, they understood that competition was an ongoing process, and that market dominance was always necessarily temporary in the absence of monopoly-creating government regulation. This view is also consistent with my own research findings that the "trusts" of the late nineteenth century were in fact dropping their prices and expanding output faster than the rest of the economy-they were the most dynamic and competitive of all industries, not monopolists.[13] Perhaps this is why they were targeted by protectionist legislators and subjected to "antitrust" laws.

The economics profession came to embrace the theory of natural monopoly after the 1920s, when it became infatuated with "scientism" and adopted a more or less engineering theory of competition that categorized industries in terms of constant, decreasing, and increasing returns to scale (declining average total costs). According to this way of thinking, engineering relationships determined market structure and, consequently, competitiveness. The meaning of competition was no longer viewed as a behavioral phenomenon, but an engineering relationship. With the exception of such economists as Joseph Schumpeter, Ludwig von Mises, Friedrich Hayek, and other members of the Austrian School, the ongoing *process* of competitive rivalry and entrepreneurship was largely ignored.


### 3. How "Natural" Were the Early Natural Monopolies?

There is no evidence at all that at the outset of public utility regulation there existed any such phenomenon as a "natural monopoly." As Harold Demsetz has pointed out:

> Six electric light companies were organized in the one year of 1887 in New York City. Forty-five electric light enterprises had the legal right to operate in Chicago in 1907. Prior to 1895, Duluth, Minnesota, was served by five electric lighting companies, and Scranton, Pennsylvania, had four in 1906. ... During the latter part of the nineteenth century, competition was the usual situation in the gas industry in this country.

> Before 1884, six competing companies were operating in New York
> City ... competition was common and especially persistent in the tele-
> phone industry ... Baltimore, Chicago, Cleveland, Columbus, Detroit,
> Kansas City, Minneapolis, Philadelphia, Pittsburgh, and St. Louis,
> among the larger cities, had at least two telephone services in 1905.[14]

In an extreme understatement, Demsetz concludes that "one begins to doubt that scale economies characterized the utility industry at the time when regulation replaced market competition."[15]

A most instructive example of the non-existence of natural monopoly in the utility industries is provided in a 1936 book by economist George T. Brown entitled *The Gas Light Company of Baltimore*, which bears the misleading subtitle, "A Study of Natural Monopoly."[16] The book presents "the study of the evolutionary character of utilities" in general, with special emphasis on the Gas Light Company of Baltimore, the problems of which "are not peculiar either to the Baltimore company or the State of Maryland, but are typical of those met everywhere in the public utility industry."[17]

The history of the Gas Light Company of Baltimore figures prominently in the whole history of natural monopoly, in theory and in practice, for the influential Richard T. Ely, who was a professor of economics at Johns Hopkins University in Baltimore, chronicled the company's problems in a series of articles in the *Baltimore Sun* that were later published as a widely-sold book. Much of Ely's analysis came to be the accepted economic dogma with regard to the theory of natural monopoly.

The history of the Gas Light Company of Baltimore is that, from its founding in 1816, it constantly struggled with new competitors. Its response was not only to try to compete in the marketplace, but also to lobby the state and local government authorities to refrain from granting corporate charters to its competitors. The company operated with economies of scale, but that did not prevent numerous competitors from cropping up.

"Competition is the life of business," the *Baltimore Sun* editorialized in 1851 as it welcomed news of new competitors in the gas light business.[18] The Gas Light Company of Baltimore, however, "objected to the granting of franchise rights to the new company."[19]

Brown states that "gas companies in other cities were exposed to ruinous competition," and then catalogues how those same companies sought desperately to enter the Baltimore market. But if such competition was so "ruinous," why would these companies enter new-and presumably just as "ruinous"-markets? Either Brown's theory of "ruinous competition" - which soon came to be the generally accepted one - was incorrect, or those companies were irrational gluttons for financial punishment.

By ignoring the *dynamic* nature of the competitive process, Brown made the same mistake that many other economists still make: believing that "excessive" competition can be "destructive" if low-cost producers drive their less efficient rivals from the market.[20] Such competition may be "destructive" to high-cost competitors, but it is beneficial to consumers.

In 1880 there were three competing gas companies in Baltimore who fiercely competed with one another. They tried to merge and operate as a monopolist in 1888, but a new competitor foiled their plans: "Thomas Alva Edison introduced the electric light which threatened the existence of all gas companies."[21] From that point on there was competition between both gas and electric companies, all of which incurred heavy fixed costs which led to economies of scale. Nevertheless, no free-market or "natural" monopoly ever materialized.

When monopoly did appear, it was solely because of government intervention. For example, in 1890 a bill was introduced into the Maryland legislature which "called for an annual payment to the city from the Consolidated [Gas Company] of $10,000 a year and 3 percent of all dividends declared in return for the privilege of enjoying a 25-year monopoly."[22] This is the now-familiar approach of government officials colluding with industry executives to establish a monopoly that will gouge the consumers, and then sharing the loot with the politicians in the form of franchise fees and taxes on monopoly revenues. This approach is especially pervasive today in the cable TV industry.

Legislative "regulation" of gas and electric companies produced the predictable result of monopoly prices, which the public complained bitterly about. Rather than deregulating the industry and letting competition control prices, however, public utility regulation was adopted to supposedly appease the consumers who, according to Brown, "felt that the negligent manner in which their interests were being served [by legislative control of gas and electric prices] resulted in high rates and monopoly privileges. *The development of utility regulation in Maryland typified the experience of other states.*"[23]

Not all economists were fooled by the "natural monopoly" theory advocated by utility industry monopolists and their paid economic advisers. In 1940 economist Horace M. Gray, an assistant dean of the graduate school at the University of Illinois, surveyed the history of "the public utility concept," including the theory of "natural" monopoly. "During the nineteenth century," Gray observed, it was widely believed that "the public interest would be best promoted by grants of special privilege to private persons and to corporations" in many industries.[24] This included patents, subsidies, tariffs, land grants to the railroads, and monopoly franchises for "public" utilities. "The final result was monopoly, exploitation, and political corruption."[25] With regard to "public" utilities, Gray records that "'between 1907 and 1938, the policy of state-created, state-protected monopoly became firmly established over a significant portion of the economy and became the keystone of modern public utility regulation."[26] From that time on, "the public utility status was to be the haven of refuge for all aspiring monopolists who found it too difficult, too costly, or too precarious to secure and maintain monopoly by private action alone."[27]

In support of this contention, Gray pointed out how virtually every aspiring monopolist in the country tried to be designated a "public utility," including the radio, real estate, milk, air transport, coal, oil, and agricultural industries, to name but a few. Along these same lines, "the whole NRA experiment may be regarded as an effort by big business to secure legal sanction for its monopolistic practices."[28] Those lucky industries that were able to be politically designated as "public utilities" also used the public utility concept to keep out the competition.

The role of economists in this scheme was to construct what Gray called a "confused rationalization" for "the sinister forces of private privilege and monopoly," i.e., the theory of "natural" monopoly. "The protection of consumers faded into the background."[29]

More recent economic research supports Gray's analysis. In one of the first statistical studies of the effects of rate regulation in the electric utilities industry, published in 1962, George Stigler and Claire Fried land found no significant differences in prices and profits of utilities with and without regulatory commissions from 1917 to 1932.[30] Early rate regulators *did not* benefit the consumer, but were rather "captured" by the industry, as happened in so many other industries, from trucking to airlines to cable television. It is noteworthy-but not very laudable-that it took economists almost 50 years to begin studying the actual, as opposed to the theoretical, effects of rate regulation.

Sixteen years after the Stigler-Friedland study, Gregg Jarrell observed that 25 states substituted state for municipal regulation of electric power ratemaking between 1912 and 1917, the effects of which were to *raise* prices by 46% and profits by 38%, while reducing the level of output by 23%.[31] Thus, municipal regulation failed to hold prices down. But the utilities wanted an even more rapid increase in their prices, so they successfully lobbied for state regulation under the theory that state regulators would be less pressured by local customer groups, than mayors and city councils would be.

These research results are consistent with Horace Gray's earlier interpretation of public utility rate regulation as an anti-consumer, monopolistic, price-fixing scheme.

## 4. The Problem of "Excessive Duplication"

In addition to the economies of scale canard, another reason that has been given for granting monopoly franchises to "natural monopolies" is that allowing too many competitors is too disruptive. It is too costly to a community, the argument goes, to allow several different water suppliers, electric power producers, or cable TV operators to dig up the streets. But as Harold Demsetz has observed:

> [T]he problem of excessive duplication of distribution systems is attributable to the failure of communities to set a proper price on the use of these scarce resources. The right to use publicly owned thoroughfares is the right to use a scarce resource. The absence of a

price for the use of these resources, a price high enough to reflect the opportunity costs of such alternative uses as the servicing of uninterrupted traffic and unmarred views, will lead to their overutilization. The setting of an appropriate fee for the use of these resources would reduce the degree of duplication to optimal levels.[32]

Thus, just as the problem with "natural" monopolies is actually caused by government intervention, so is the "duplication of facilities" problem. It is created by the failure of governments to put a price on scarce urban resources. More precisely, the problem is really caused by the fact that governments own the streets under which utility lines are placed, and that the impossibility of rational economic calculation within socialistic institutions precludes them from pricing these resources appropriately, as they would under a private-property competitive-market regime. Contrary to Demsetz's claim, rational economic pricing in this case is impossible precisely because of government ownership of roads and streets. Benevolent and enlightened politicians, even ones who have studied at the feet of Harold Demsetz, would have no rational way of determining what prices to charge.

Murray Rothbard explained all this more than 25 years ago:

> The fact that the government must give permission for the use of its streets has been cited to justify stringent government regulations of 'public utilities,' many of which (like water or electric companies) must make use of the streets. The regulations are then treated as a voluntary *quid pro quo.* But to do so overlooks the fact that governmental ownership of the streets is itself a permanent act of intervention. Regulation of public utilities or of any other industry discourages investment in these industries, thereby depriving consumers of the best satisfaction of their wants. For it distorts the resource allocations of the free market.[33]

The so-called "limited-space monopoly" argument for franchise monopolies, Rothbard further argued, is a red herring, for how many firms will be profitable in any line of production "is an institutional question and depends on such concrete data as the degree of consumer demand, the type of product sold, the physical productivity of the processes, the supply and pricing of factors, the forecasting of entrepreneurs, etc. Spatial limitations may be unimportant."[34]

In fact, even if spatial limitations do allow only one firm to operate in a particular geographical market, that does not necessitate monopoly, for "monopoly" is "a meaningless appellation, unless monopoly price is achieved," and "*All* prices on a free market are competitive."[35] Only government intervention can generate monopolistic prices.

The only way to achieve a free-market price that reflects true opportunity costs and leads to optimal levels of "duplication" is through free exchange in a genuinely free market, a sheer impossibility without private property and free markets.[36] Political fiat is simply not a feasible substitute for the prices that are determined by the free market because rational economic calculation is impossible without markets.

Under private ownership of streets and sidewalks, individual owners are offered a tradeoff of lower utility prices for the temporary inconvenience of having a utility company run a trench through their property. If "duplication" occurs under such a system, it is because freely-choosing individuals value the extra service or lower prices or both more highly than the cost imposed on them by the inconvenience of a temporary construction project on their property. Free markets necessitate neither monopoly nor "excessive duplication" in any economically meaningful sense.

## 5. Competition for the Field

The existence of economies of scale in water, gas, electricity, or other "public utilities" in no way necessitates either monopoly or monopoly pricing. As Edwin Chadwick wrote in 1859, a system of competitive bidding for the services of private utility franchises can eliminate monopoly pricing as long as there is competition "for the field."[37] As long as there is vigorous bidding for the franchise, the results can be both avoidance of duplication of facilities and competitive pricing of the product or service. That is, bidding for the franchise can take place in the form of awarding the franchise to the utility that offers consumers the lowest price for some constant-quality of service (as opposed to the highest price for the franchise).

Harold Demsetz revived interest in the concept of "competition for the field" in a 1968 article.[38] The theory of natural monopoly, Demsetz pointed out, fails to "reveal the logical steps that carry it from scale economies in production to monopoly price in the market place."[39] If one bidder can do the job at less cost than two or more, "then the bidder with the lowest bid price for the entire job will be awarded the contract, whether the good be cement, electricity, stamp vending machines, or whatever, but the lowest bid price need not be a monopoly price . ... The natural monopoly theory provides no logical basis for monopoly prices."[40]

There is no reason to believe that the bidding process will not be competitive. Hanke and Walters have shown that such a franchise bidding process operates very efficiently in the French water supply industry.[41]

## 6. The Natural Monopoly Myth: Electric Utilities

According to natural monopoly theory, competition cannot persist in the electric utility industry. But the theory is contradicted by the fact that competition has in fact persisted for decades in dozens of U.S. cities. Economist Walter J. Primeaux has studied electric utility competition for more than 20 years. In his 1986 book, *Direct Utility Competition: The Natural Monopoly Myth,* he concludes that in those cities where there is direct competition in the electric utility industries:

• Direct rivalry between two competing firms has existed for very long periods of time-for over 80 years in some cities;

• The rival electric utilities compete vigorously through prices and services;

• Customers have gained substantial benefits from the competition, compared to cities where there are electric utility monopolies;

• Contrary to natural monopoly theory, costs are actually lower where there are two firms operating;

• Contrary to natural monopoly theory, there is no more excess capacity under competition than under monopoly in the electric utility industry;

• The theory of natural monopoly fails on every count: competition exists, price wars are not "serious," there is better consumer service and lower prices with competition, competition persists for very long periods of time, and consumers themselves prefer competition to regulated monopoly; and

• Any consumer satisfaction problems caused by dual power lines are considered by consumers to be less significant than the benefits from competition.[42]

Primeaux also found that although electric utility executives generally recognized the consumer benefits of competition, they personally preferred monopoly!

Ten years after the publication of Primeaux's book, at least one state – California - is transforming its electric utility industry "from a monopoly controlled by a handful of publicly held utilities to an open market."[43] Other states are moving in the same direction, finally abandoning the baseless theory of natural monopoly in favor of natural competition:[44]

• The Ormet Corporation, an aluminum smelter in West Virginia, obtained state permission to solicit competitive bids from 40 electric utilities;

• Akan Aluminum Corp. in Oswego, New York has taken advantage of technological breakthroughs that allowed it to build a new power generating plant next to its mill, cutting its power costs by two thirds. Niagara Mohawk, its previous (and higher priced) power supplier, is suing the state to prohibit Alcan from using its own power;

• Arizona political authorities allowed Cargill, Inc. to buy power from anywhere in the West; the company expects to save $8 million per year;

• New federal laws permit utilities to import lower-priced power, using the power lines of other companies to transport it;

• Wisconsin Public Service commissioner Scott Neitzel recently declared, "free markets are the best mechanism for delivering to the consumer . . . the best service at the lowest cost";

• The prospect of future competition is already forcing some electric utility monopolies to cut their costs and prices. When the TVA was faced with competition from Duke Power in 1988, it managed to hold its rates steady without an increase for the next several years.

The potential benefits to the U.S. economy from de-monopolization of the electric utility industry are enormous. Competition will *initially* save consumers at least $40 billion per year, according to utility economist Robert Michaels.[45] It will also spawn the development of new technologies that will be economical to develop because of lower energy costs. For example, "automakers and other metal benders would make much more intensive use of laser cutting tools and laser welding machines, both of which are electron guzzlers."[46]

## 7. The Natural Monopoly Myth: Cable TV

Cable television is also a franchise monopoly in most cities because of the theory of natural monopoly. But the monopoly in this industry is anything but "natural." Like electricity, there are dozens of cities in the U.S. where there are competing cable firms. "Direct competition ... currently occurs in at least three dozen jurisdictions nationally."[47] The existence of long-standing competition in the cable industry gives the lie to the notion that that industry is a "natural monopoly" and is therefore in need of franchise monopoly regulation. The cause of monopoly in cable *TV* is government regulation, not economies of scale. Although cable operators complain of "duplication," it is important to keep in mind that "while overbuilding an existing cable system can lower the profitability of the incumbent operator, it unambiguously improves the position of consumers who face prices determined not by historical costs, but by the interplay of supply and demand."[48]

Also like the case of electric power, researchers have found that in those cities where there are competing cable companies prices are about 23 percent below those of monopolistic cable operators.[49] Cablevision of Central Florida, for example, reduced its basic prices from $12.95 to $6.50 per month in "duopoly" areas in order to compete. When Tulestat entered Riviera Beach, Florida, it offered 26 channels of basic service for $5.75, compared to Comcast's 12-channel offering for $8.40 per month. Comcast responded by upgrading its service and dropping its prices.[50] In Presque Isle, Maine, when the city government invited competition, the incumbent firm quickly upgraded its service from only 12 to 54 channels.[51]

In 1987 the Pacific West Cable Company sued the city of Sacramento, California on First Amendment grounds for blocking its entry into the cable market. A jury found that "the Sacramento cable market was not a natural monopoly and that the claim of natural monopoly was a sham used by defendants as a pretext for granting a single cable television franchise ... to promote the making of cash payments and provision of 'in-kind' services ... and to obtain increased campaign contributions."[52] The city was forced to adopt a competitive cable policy, the result of which was that the incumbent cable operator, Scripps Howard, dropped its monthly price from $14.50 to $10 to meet a competitor's price. The company also offered free installation and three months free service in every area where it had competition.

Still, the big majority of cable systems in the U.S. are franchise monopolies for precisely the reasons stated by the Sacramento jury: they are mercantilistic schemes whereby a monopoly is created to the benefit of cable companies, who share the loot with the politicians through campaign contributions, free air time on "community service programming," contributions to local foundations favored by the politicians, stock equity and consulting contracts to the politically well connected, and various gifts to the franchise authorities.

In some cities, politicians collect these indirect bribes for five to ten years or longer from multiple companies before finally granting a franchise. They then benefit from part of the monopoly rents earned by the monopoly franchisee. As former FCC chief economist Thomas Hazlett, who is perhaps the nation's foremost authority on the economics of the cable TV industry, has concluded, "we may characterize the franchising process as nakedly inefficient from a welfare perspective, although it does produce benefits for municipal franchisers."[53] The barrier to entry in the cable TV industry is not economies of scale, but the political price-fixing conspiracy that exists between local politicians and cable operators.


## 8. The Natural Monopoly Myth: Telephone Service

The biggest myth of all in this regard is the notion that telephone service is a natural monopoly. Economists have taught generations of students that telephone service is a "classic" example of market failure and that government regulation in the "public interest" was necessary. But as Adam D. Thierer recently proved, there is nothing at all "natural" about the telephone monopoly enjoyed by AT&T for so many decades; it was purely a creation of government intervention.[54]

Once AT&T's initial patents expired in 1893, dozens of competitors sprung up. "By the end of 1894 over 80 new independent competitors had already grabbed 5 percent of total market share ... after the turn of the century, over 3,000 competitors existed."[55] In some states there were over 200 telephone companies operating simultaneously. By 1907, AT&T's competitors had captured 51 percent of the telephone market and prices were being driven sharply down by the competition. Moreover, there was no evidence of economies of scale, and entry barriers were obviously almost nonexistent, contrary to the standard account of the theory of natural monopoly as applied to the telephone industry.[56]

The eventual creation of the telephone monopoly was the result of a conspiracy between AT&T and politicians who wanted to offer "universal telephone service" as a pork-barrel entitlement to their constituents. Politicians began denouncing competition as "duplicative," "destructive," and "wasteful," and various economists were paid to attend congressional hearings in which they somberly declared telephony a natural monopoly. "There is nothing to be gained by competition in the local telephone business," one congressional hearing concluded.[57]

The crusade to *create* a monopolistic telephone industry by government fiat finally succeeded when the federal government used World War I as an excuse to nationalize the industry in 1918. AT&T still operated its phone system, but it was controlled by a government commission headed by the Postmaster General. Like so many other instances of government regulation, AT&T quickly "captured" the regulators and used the regulatory apparatus to eliminate its competitors. "By 1925 not only had virtually every state established strict rate regulation guidelines, but local telephone competition was either discouraged or explicitly prohibited within many of those jurisdictions."[58]

The complete demise of competition in the industry, Thierer concludes, was brought about by the following forces: exclusionary licensing policies; protected monopolies for "dominant carriers"; guaranteed revenues or regulated phone companies; the mandated government policy of "universal telephone entitlement" which called for a single provider to more easily carry out regulatory commands; and rate regulation designed to achieve the socialistic objective of "universal service."

That free-market competition was the source of the telephone monopoly in the early twentieth century is the biggest lie ever told by the economics profession. The free market never "failed"; it was government that failed to permit free-market competition as it concocted its corporatist scheme to the benefit of the phone companies, at the expense of consumers and potential competitors.

## 9. Conclusions

The theory of natural monopoly is an economic fiction. No such thing as a "natural" monopoly has ever existed. The history of the so-called public utility concept is that the late-nineteenth- and early-twentieth-century "utilities" competed vigorously and, like all other industries, they did not like competition. They first secured government-sanctioned monopolies, and *then,* with the help of a few influential economists, constructed an *ex post* rationalization for their monopoly power.

This has to be one of the greatest corporate public relations coups of all time. "By a soothing process of rationalization," wrote Horace M. Gray more than 50 years ago, "men are able to oppose monopolies in general but to approve certain types of monopolies. ... Since these monopolies were 'natural' and since nature is beneficent, it followed that they were 'good' monopolies. ... Government was therefore justified in establishing 'good' monopolies."[59]

In industry after industry, the natural monopoly concept is finally eroding. Electric power, cable TV, telephone services, and the mail, are all on the verge of being deregulated, either legislatively or *de facto,* due to technological change. Introduced in the U.S. at about the same time communism was introduced to the former Soviet Union, franchise monopolies are about to become just as defunct. Like all monopolists, they will use every last resource to lobby to maintain their monopolistic privileges, but the potential gains to consumers of free markets are too great to justify them. The theory of natural monopoly is a nineteenth-century economic fiction that defends nineteenth-century (or eighteenth century, in the case of the U.S. Postal Service) monopolistic privileges, and has no useful place in the twenty-first-century American economy.

# REFERENCES

1. Ely, Richard T. (1990), *Monopolies and Trusts*. New York: MacMillan, 162.

2. Bates Clark, John, and Franklin Giddings (1888), *Modern Distributive Processes*. Boston, MA: Ginn & Co., 21.

3. Davenport, Herbert (1919), *The Economics of Enterprise*. New York: MacMillan, 483.

4. Laughlin, James L. (1902), *The Elements of Political Economy*. New York: American Book, 71.

5. Fisher, Irving (1912), *Elementary Principles of Economics*. New York: MacMillan, 330.

6. Seligman, E. R. A. (1909), *Principles of Economics*. New York: Longmans, Green, 341.

7. Ibid., p. 97.

8. Patten, Simon (1889), "The Economic Effects of Combinations," *Age of Steel* Jan. 5: 13.

9. Giddings, Franklin (1887), "The Persistence of Competition," *Political Science Quarterly* March: 62.

10. Wells, David A. (1889), *Recent Economic Changes*. New York: DeCapro Press, 74.

11. Gunton, George (1888), "The Economics and Social Aspects of Trusts," *Political Science Quarterly* Sept.: 385.

12. Coats, A. W. (1961), "The American Political Economy Club," *American Economic Review* Sept.: 621–637.

13. DiLorenzo, Thomas J. (1985), "The Origins of Antitrust: An Interest-Group Perspective," *International Review of Law and Economics* Fall: 73–90.

14. Behling, Burton N. (1938/1989), "Competition and Monopoly in Public Utility Industries" in Harold Demsetz, ed., *Efficiency, Competition, and Policy*. Cambridge, MA: Blackwell, 78.

15. Ibid.

16. Brown, George T. (1936), *The Gas Light Company of Baltimore: A Study of Natural Monopoly*. Baltimore, MD: Johns Hopkins University Press.

17. Ibid., p. 5.

18. Ibid., p. 31.

19. Ibid.

20. Ibid., p. 47.

21. Ibid., p. 52.

22. Ibid., p. 75.

23. Ibid., p. 106. Emphasis added.

24. Gray, Horace M. (1940), "The Passing of the Public Utility Concept," *Journal of Land and Public Utility Economics* Feb.: 8.

25. Ibid.

26. Ibid., p. 9.

27. Ibid.

28. Ibid., p. 15.

29. Ibid., p. 11.

30. Stigler, George, and Claire Friedland (1962), "What Can Regulators Regulate? The Case of Electricity," *Journal of Law and Economics* October: 1–16.

31. Jarrell, Gregg A. (1978), "The Demand for State Regulation of the Electric Utility Industry," *Journal of Law and Economics* October: 269–295.

32. Demsetz, *Efficiency, Competition, and Policy*, 81.

33. Rothbard, Murray N. (1977), *Power and Market: Government and the Economy.* Kansas City, MO: Sheed, Andrews and McMeel, 75–76.

34. Rothbard, Murray N. (1993), *Man, Economy, and State: A Treatise on Economic Principles.* Auburn, AL: Ludwig von Mises Institute, 619.

35. Ibid., 620.

36. Ibid., 548.

37. Chadwick, Edwin (1859), "Results of Different Principles of Legislation and Administration in Europe of Competition for the Field as Compared with Competition within the Field of Service," *Journal of the Statistical Society of London* 22: 381–420.

38. Demsetz, Harold (1968), "Why Regulate Utilities?," *Journal of Law and Economics* April: 55–65.

39. Ibid.

40. Ibid.

41. Hanke, Steve, and Stephen J. K. Walters (1987), "Privatization and Natural Monopoly: The Case of Waterworks," *The Privatization Review* Spring: 24–31.

42. Primeaux, Jr., Walter J. (1986), *Direct Electric Utility Competition: The Natural Monopoly Myth.* New York: Praeger, 175.

43. (1995), "California Eyes Open Electricity Market," *The Washington Times,* May 27: 2.

44. The following information is from Toni Mack, "Power to the People," *Forbes,* June 5, 1995, pp. 119–126.

45. Ibid., p. 120.

46. Ibid., p. 126.

47. Hazlett, Thornas (1990), "Duopolistic Competition in Cable Television: Implications for Public Policy," *Yale Journal on Regulation* 7(1): 65–120.

48. Ibid.

49. Ibid.

50. Ibid.

51. Hazlett, Thomas (1985), "Private Contracting versus Public Regulation as a Solution to the Natural Monopoly Problem," in Robert W. Poole, ed., *Unnatural Monopolies: The Case for Deregulating Public Utilities.* Lexington, MA: Lexington Books, 104.

52. *Pacific West Cable* Co. v. *City of Sacramento,* 672 F. Supp. 1322 1349-40 (E.D. Cal. 1987), cited in Hazlett, "Duopolistic Competition."

53. Hazlett, Thomas, "Duopolistic Competition in Cable Television."

54. Thierer, Adam D. (1994), "Unnatural Monopoly: Critical Moments in the Development of the Bell System Monopoly," *Cato Journal* Fall: 267-85.

55. Ibid. 270.

56. Ibid.

57. Loeb, G. H. (1978), "The Communications Act Policy Toward Competition: A Failure to Communicate," *Duke Law Journal* 1: 14.

58. Thierer, "Unnatural Monopoly: Critical Moments in the Development of the Bell System Monopoly," 277.

59. Gray, "The Passing of the Public Utility Concept," 10.

# Chapter 11
# Monopolistic Competition and
# Macroeconomic Theory by Robert Solow

Robert Solow's *Monopolistic Competition and Macroeconomic Theory* is a short collection of three essays based on lectures that he gave at the University of Rome in 1996. Solow introduces the essays by asking: "How can one explain the fact that Keynesian ideas and methods have survived for sixty years despite their theoretical weaknesses and analytical crudities?" (1). Good question. Solow offers two reasons for the survival of Keynesian ideas: (1) The "usual alternatives" ask us to believe things that appear not to be true; and (2) Keynes's *General Theory* was premised on the assumption of perfectly competitive goods markets, and economists tend to be enamored of such models.

Reason number 1 seems farcical. It was *Keynesianism*, was it not, that argued that the state can spend us into prosperity, ignoring the concept of opportunity cost; taking a dollar from a citizen and having government spend it will magically turn it into more than a dollar (the "balanced-budget multiplier"); there is a tradeoff between inflation and unemployment; savings and capital accumulation are impoverishing because of the "paradox of thrift"; deficit spending is desirable; government debt is nothing to worry about because "we owe it to ourselves"; macroeconomic central planners will faithfully serve the "public interest" by "stabilizing" the economy and ignoring all political pressures; and countless other absurdities and falsehoods?

Solow doesn't name names when he criticizes "alternatives" (to Keynesian) theories other than to disparage "misperceptions stories." He could well be referring to the Austrian business cycle theory, however, with its emphasis on government-induced mal-investment. If so, it takes a great deal of *chutzpah* on his part to criticize this, or any, theory on the grounds that it is less realistic than Keynesianism. The author pathetically defends Keynesianism on the grounds that there are still economists who spend their time estimating "consumption functions, demand-for- money equations, and slow-price adjustment relations" (3).

Solow may be on more solid footing in arguing that macroeconomists have invested a great deal of time in "modeling" goods markets as perfectly competitive and are hesitant to abandon their old ways. But he completely ignores what is perhaps the main reason why Keynesian ideas and methods have survived despite their "theoretical weaknesses and analytical crudities" — the rational self-interest of economists and policymakers.

As explained by Keynes's biographer, Roy Harrod (1951: 192–193), Keynes himself believed that "the government ... was and could continue to be in the hands of an intellectual aristocracy. ... Keynes tended till the end to think of the really important decisions being reached by a small group of intelligent people, like the group that fashioned the Bretton Woods plan." Arthur Smithies (1951: 493–94) also discussed the authoritarian–central planning mindset of Keynes when he wrote that "Keynes hoped for a world where monetary and fiscal policy, carried out by *wise men* in authority, could ensure conditions of prosperity, equity, freedom, and possibly peace."

Solow himself championed this view of the economist as central planner in a very influential article co-authored with Paul Samuelson in the *American Economic Review* (1960) which laid out the Phillips Curve framework of having an enlightened elite choose for the country the "appropriate" mix of inflation and unemployment. Macroeconomic stabilization policy, guided by Keynesian dogma, catapulted interventionist-minded economists into positions of power and prominence as apologists for state power. These economists, and the academic institutions that employed them, have also benefited financially from this relationship through generous government funding of their academic research. As Rothbard wrote in *The Ethics of Liberty* (1998: 172), the state subsists by "engineering the support of a majority ... through securing an alliance with a group of opinion-moulding intellectuals whom it rewards with a share in its power and pelf."

Yet another reason for the popularity of Keynesian ideas and methods that Solow completely ignores is the rational self-interest of politicians. Politicians have always viewed Keynesianism as providing intellectual cover for what they always want to do anyway: spend as much of the taxpayers' money as possible on programs that benefit special-interest groups (in return for the groups' political support) while dispersing and disguising the costs with debt finance.

Solow is such a thoroughgoing interventionist that he seems incapable of acknowledging that government intervention is ever a cause of economic instability. In his introductory chapter he ponders the question of why price reduction does not always seem to occur during recessions or depressions and presents five possible reasons, based on pure speculation about the possible motives of business firms (the words "might," "could," and "perhaps" proliferate in his prose). One obvious reason for price inflexibility that is nowhere mentioned in Solow's book is minimum wage and other labor laws that have been designed specifically to artificially prop up compensation levels, especially in unionized industries. In this regard, Professor Solow would do well to read *Out of Work* (1993) by Richard Vedder and Lowell Gallaway, but I am not optimistic. Solow's writing is extraordinarily narrow in that his references include almost exclusively his M.I.T. colleagues and former students who all share the same overly mathematical methodology.

As with so much of mainstream economic "model building" – especially in macroeconomics – the sometimes bizarre assumptions Solow makes virtually guarantee that the models will give him the mathematical "results" that he desires. For example, on p. 44 he assumes that "nothing changes from one year to the next." On p. 34 he assumes away the price system: "There is no force that automatically works to eliminate excess supply of or excess demand for labor."

"Investment goods are produced by labor alone" and they "disappear completely after one period of use" (34). As he candidly admits at the end of the introductory chapter, "the particular results depend on those assumptions" (5).

The essence of Solow's three essays is to replace the fundamentally flawed equilibrium model of perfect competition (flawed from an Austrian perspective, that is) with an equally flawed equilibrium model of "monopolistic competition" in his macroeconomic model building. He is deeply distressed over the fact that "economists have been scared away from Keynesian-sounding conclusions over the past fifteen years or so" (25) and believes that incorporating long-ago discredited theories of monopolistic competition will somehow salvage Keynesian economics.

Solow's rigid refusal to consider government intervention as the source of economic instability leads him to pose a number of questions which he believes are profound puzzles but which in reality are quite elementary, if not simplistic. "When a modern industrial economy is struck by a real disturbance, like a sudden reduction in the perceived profitability of investment or a sudden increase in the propensity to save," he asks, "why does it take so long to return to full-employment equilibrium?" (15).

Of course, a "reduction in the perceived profitability of investment" is what is caused by monetary expansion and the mal-investment that it breeds, but Solow mentions nothing of this. Such "disturbances" are simply assumed to occur, like magic, without explanation. Moreover, an "increase in the propensity to save" is nothing to be alarmed about and usually just reflects individual choices guided by rates of time preference. But Solow, like all other Keynesian central planners, believes that he knows the "correct" rate of time preference for all citizens as well as the "correct" or "optimal" savings rate and that the state should use its coercive powers to force us into this state of economic bliss.

There is a mountain of history that would help Solow understand why it sometimes takes an economy so long to "return to full employment." I would start with Murray Rothbard's *America's Great Depression* (1963), which explains how, in economic crises prior to the Great Depression of the 1930s that were *not* responded to with massive government intervention, recovery was quite rapid. Government intervention – especially in labor markets – is the reason why recessions and depressions last longer than they otherwise would. Solow ignores history and pretends that such events are a Great Mystery that can only be unraveled by a garble of exquisite mathematical trivia. In a sense, mathematical economics is but a branch of hermeneutics – the "truth" is whatever these mathematical hermeneuticists say it is regardless of facts, history, and even logic.

At one point Solow seems ready to temporarily suspend his reliance on un-realistic mathematical models that admittedly explain very little about the economy and embark upon a path that will actually improve our economic understanding. Such a passage occurs on p. 19, where he makes the Kirznerian statement that "it is very important to know something about the forces that lead the economy to

148

'choose' one equilibrium configuration rather than another." But one is quickly disappointed. He says nothing about entrepreneurship – or about human action for that matter. Instead, he talks about mysterious "historical, accidental, sociological, and even psychological factors" without offering any hint as to just what these "factors" might be. Not a reference, not a footnote. Again, there is no mention at all of how government itself affects the market system other than as a benevolent tool of "stabilization policy": "One function of economic policy may be to help or induce the economy to choose a better rather than a worse equilibrium." This really is a naive child's view of government.

Solow at times descends into what Mises might have called the "cloud cuckoo land" when he presents theories of how "animal spirits" supposedly guide investment behavior ("What we have . . . constructed is a theory in which animal spirits . . . drive investment," he says on p. 25). He also makes a mountain out of a mole hill in referring to a "literature" that describes markets as "thick" (there are lots of trading partners) or "thin" (there are fewer trading partners). In Solow's theoretical world, if one wants to sell one's used car and is not immediately deluged with hundreds of offers, then there is a "thin-market externality" that needs to be "corrected" by state intervention. No such "imperfections" are *ever* hinted at with regard to the behavior of politicians and bureaucrats.

Solow considers his major "contribution" in this selection of essays to be his introduction of monopolistic competition, rather than perfect competition, into a macroeconomic model. In keeping with what appears to be an M.I.T. tradition of never reading anything but pure mathematical models and studiously ignoring history, philosophy, most alternative economic theories or schools of thought, and real-world economic events, Solow proceeds as though there have never been any criticisms of monopolistic competition theory.

But, of course, there have been so many criticisms that the theory has become an historical artifact (Kirzner, 1973; Rothbard, 1993). Monopolistic competition is a static equilibrium model that claims to distinguish itself from the equally absurd, static equilibrium model of perfect competition. But in perfect competition there is no genuine competition, as price cutting, advertising, product differentiation, and other genuinely competitive actions are simply assumed away. It is therefore not a valid "benchmark," regardless of how often economists may assume that it is.

Even Edward Chamberlin, the "father" of monopolistic competition theory, admitted that his theory was useless if one assumes that product differentiation – the key assumption of the theory – occurs in response to a desire on the part of businesses to cater to diverse consumer demands. Competition is a dynamic, rivalrous, discovery procedure that helps facilitate plan coordination among market participants, and advertising and product differentiation are essential elements of that process. The "excess capacity" story that is told by monopolistic competition theorists is contrived nonsense, but is nevertheless the keystone of Solow's model.

Just how absurd it is to label product differentiation as "monopolistic" is amplified by the development in recent years of what the management literature refers to as "mass customization" (Pine, 1993). Thanks to computer technology, manufacturers have been able to create an ever-increasing variety of goods and services tailored to the individual preferences of consumers. Just since the early 1970s the number of new car models has expanded from 140 to 260; soft drinks from 20 to 87; and television channels from 5 to 185. There are now 340 kinds of breakfast cereals, 3,000 different beers, and even 50 brands of bottled water.

All of this (and much more) has resulted from the combination of a fiercely competitive global marketplace and the application of information technology to manufacturing. Economists like Solow who still insist that product differentiation is a sign of "monopolistic" behavior are mired in an interventionist mindset that is not even remotely in touch with reality.

Murray Rothbard wrote in *Man, Economy, and State* (1993: 643) that "we must never let reality be falsified in order to fit the niceties of mathematics" but, of course, that is exactly what Solow and most other mathematical economists do. It is the coin of their theoretical realm. In Solow's case, he ignores or falsifies reality so that his contrived model can help him arrive at the conclusion that central bank monetary expansion will have nothing but benign effects. "If the money supply is increased," he writes, "the output of consumption goods increases more than proportionally, . . . output per worker increases, and so does the real wage" (49). Can the cure for the common cold be far behind?

Equally contrived is the model discussed in ch. 3 which concludes, in complete contradiction to sound economic logic, that "wage cutting in the presence of unemployment would be a step in the wrong direction" if one wishes to increase employment (59). No evidence is offered in support of this conclusion, only the gobbledygook of mathematical economics. The model is said to be "a version of the Hotelling–Lancaster–Salop model of monopolistic competition with a circular product space, and the equilibrium concept is symmetric Chamberlinian" (60). (Attention graduate students: Talk like this in job interviews and you could land a faculty spot at M.I.T.!).

Solow seems to have no conception of human action as a process of plan coordination, although he uses Austrian-sounding language at one point in discussing "coordination failure" in the marketplace. He sees the job of the economist as the construction of obtuse mathematical theories to ostensibly explain this alleged "failure," but not to inquire how market participants act to overcome coordination problems. He doesn't appear to be the least bit interested in how markets actually work; only to "model" them as inherently "flawed" in order to stroke his own ideological predilections.

It speaks ill of the economics profession that one of its gray eminences, Robert Solow, who has been "building models" for some fifty years, offers a macro-economic model that fails to incorporate a discussion of asset and labor markets.

Deep down, I suspect that he must recognize the absurdity of it all. On p. 35 he confesses: "I can talk about unemployment in this model, but I have not earned the right to talk about it seriously."

## REFERENCES

Harrod, Roy (1951), *The Life of John Maynard Keynes.* London: Macmillan.

Kirzner, Israel (1973), *Competition and Entrepreneurship.* Chicago, IL: University of Chicago Press.

Pine, Joseph B. (1993), *Mass Customization: The New Frontier in Business Competition.* Boston, MA: Harvard Business School Press.

Rothbard, Murray N. (1963). *America's Great Depression.* New York: Richardson and Snyder.

-- (1962/1963), *Man, Economy, and State.* Princeton, NJ: Richardson and Snyder.

-- (1998), *The Ethics of Liberty.* New York: New York University Press.

Smithies, Arthur (1951), "Reflections on the Work and Influence of John Maynard Keynes," *Quarterly Journal of Economics* 65(4): 578–601.

Solow, Robert, and Paul Samuelson (1960), "Analytical Aspects of Anti-Inflation Policy," *American Economic Review* 50 May: 177–194.

Vedder, Richard, and Lowell Gallaway (1993), *Out of Work: Unemployment and Government in Twentieth-Century America.* New York: Holmes and Meier.

# Chapter 12
## The Origins of Antitrust:
## An Interest-Group Perspective

Major political agitation for "antimonopoly" laws such as the Sherman Act was first led by farmers' organizations such as the Grangers and the Farmers' Alliance, who were among the most powerful political interests of the day. . . In seeking government regulation to hinder the development of large-scale farming, farm organizations were apparently seeking protection from pressures of competition, despite the rhetoric about "land monopolies." That farmers simultaneously complained about *falling* farm prices belied the notion that the farm industry was becoming monopolized...

Farmers also hoped to secure wealth transfers through the regulation of railroad rates, having accused the railroads of monopolistic pricing. But the view that the railroad industry prior to 1887 (when the ICC was created) was becoming monopolized is inaccurate, for the fall in railroad rates during that time is striking. The decline in railroad rates nationwide was even greater than the fall in the general price level from 1865 to 1900, so that farmers received substantial benefits from the competitiveness of that industry. In seeking governmental price regulation they were apparently trying to secure additional benefits beyond what a competitive railroad market would give them. For instance, the railroads gave rebates to their large-volume customers, as most competitive businesses must do. It is likely that smaller-scale farmers who did not receive rebates sought regulation to prohibit their competitors from receiving them.

In lobbying for antitrust legislation the farmers' organizations claimed that trusts and combinations were monopolies so that the things they bought (from the trusts) were becoming increasingly expensive relative to the prices of farm products. Thus the trusts were allegedly "exploiting" the farm population. But the facts do not support this interpretation. From 1865 to 1900 agricultural terms of trade improved from the farmers' perspective. While there was a declining general price level during much of this period, farm prices fell less than all other prices, producing real gains for farmers. Farm prices were, however, quite volatile which may explain why farmers became so politically active. A strong case can be made that such volatility explains why farm lobbyists have been among the most active (and effective) throughout history. Also, the quality of many manufactured goods was improving because of technological changes in the manufacturing sector so that the agricultural terms of trade were even better for farmers. Thus, it is difficult to fathom that the farm lobby was attempting to avoid rather than create monopoly rents by lobbying for "antimonopoly" or antitrust legislation.

Many other groups soon became part of the antitrust coalition- - small business organizations, academics (although not economists), and especially "progressive" journalists. The *Congressional Record* of the 51st Congress is replete with examples of congressmen voicing complaints of small businesses (especially agricultural businesses) in their districts who were allegedly being subjected to "unfair" competition by the trusts. These groups all claimed that the "giant monopolies" were creating a "dangerous concentration of wealth" among the capitalists of the day. Even though the conspicuous wealth of entrepreneurs such as Rockefeller, Mellon and Morgan added fuel to this charge, it does not appear that this was generally true. . . Although there was no general redistribution of wealth from labor to capital owners, dynamic, competitive markets always alter the distribution of income in ways that some do not like. There was no "dangerous concentration of wealth" taking place, but many supporters of antitrust probably found their own incomes lower than they liked and sought to use the powers of the state to alter that situation.

Despite the facts regarding income distribution, it is relevant that perceptions are often more important than reality in politics. The news media and popular press of the 1880s successfully nurtured the notion that the wealth of a small handful of successful entrepreneurs (the "robber barons") was coming at the expense of farmers, laborers and consumers, and was therefore the "legitimate" domain of governmentally-imposed redistribution. In short, they denied that business activity and free market exchange involving the "trusts" was mutually advantageous, but was rather a zero-sum game, at best. As one historian concluded:

> Trusts, it was said, threatened liberty, because they corrupted civil servants and bribed legislators; they enjoyed privileges such as protection by tariffs; they drove out competitors by lowering prices, victimized consumers by raising prices, defrauded investors by watering stocks, and somehow or other abused everyone. The kind of remedy that the public desired was also clear enough: it wanted a law to destroy the power of the trusts.

This statement of the standard account of the "trust problem" is quite revealing. If trusts bribed legislators and were protected by tariffs, then the source of the problem is government itself and the solution is less government regulation and the enforcement of laws against bribery and fraud, not bans on industrial combinations. Further, lowering prices and closing unprofitable plants is perfectly consistent with competitive behavior and any laws prohibiting these actions must hinder, not help competition. Moreover, the statement that trusts simultaneously lowered prices and raised prices, victimizing both competitors and consumers, is nonsensical. In sum, one may object to lower prices and plant closings on arbitrary distributional grounds: They may temporarily hurt less efficient businesses and necessitate the movement of capital and labor changes individuals may not wish to undertake. But to criticize these phenomena on the grounds that they are "monopolistic" is misleading. Hayek noticed that the benefits of competitive markets

> . . . are the results of such changes, and will be maintained only if the changes are allowed to continue. But every change of this kind will hurt some organized interests; and the preservation of the market order will therefore depend on those interests not being able to prevent what they dislike. All the time it is thus the interest of most that some be placed under the necessity of doing something they dislike (such as changing their jobs or accepting a lower income), and this general interest will be satisfied only if the principle is recognized that each has to submit to changes when circumstances. . . determine that he is the one who is placed under such a necessity.

Hayek pointed out another inherent difficulty in maintaining competitive markets in democratic societies: "In a society in which . . . the majority has power to prohibit whatever it dislikes, it is most unlikely that it will allow competition to arise."

There is no doubt that economic conditions were changing very rapidly in the latter part of the nineteenth century. Rapid expansion of the railroad and inland shipping industries greatly reduced the cost, both pecuniary and non-pecuniary, of transportation. Technological developments in the latter part of the century led to large-scale (and lower cost) production of steel, cement, and many other goods; communications technology rapidly expanded, especially with the use of the telegraph; and the capital markets became much more sophisticated. In addition, the nation underwent a rapid transition from a predominantly agrarian to an industrial society. In 1810 the ratio of farm to non-farm labor was approximately 4.0. This ratio fell to 1.6 by 1840 and by 1880 the labor force was about equally divided. It is also apparent that individuals and groups uncomfortable in an atmosphere of rapid change were becoming increasingly adept at using the regulatory powers of the stare to their own advantage, to slow or eliminate such change. It is in this atmosphere that the Sherman Antitrust Act was passed in 1890.

The Sherman Act was passed after 13 states had already instituted their own antitrust laws. The essential claim made by Senator John Sherman and his colleagues was that combinations or trusts tended to restrict output which drove up prices. . . If this is true, then one would expect to have observed restrictions of output in those industries that were allegedly being monopolized by the trusts and combinations. By contrast, if the trust movement was part of the evolutionary process of competitive markets responding to technological change, one would expect an expansion of trade or output. The data offer no support for the contention that in the 1880s trusts were restricting output and thereby increasing prices. From the *Congressional Record* of the 51st Congress a list of industries that were accused of being monopolized by the trusts was compiled. Those industries for which data were available . . . shows output growth from 1880 to 1900. The available data are incomplete, but one striking feature. . . is that of the 17 industries listed, there were increases in output not only from 1880 to 1890, but also to the turn of the century in all but two industries, matches and castor oil. These are hardly items that would cause a national furor, even if they were monopolized.

In addition, output in these industries generally expanded more rapidly than output in all other industries during the ten years preceding the Sherman Act. Data are available for some industries only in terms of nominal output, while measures of real output are available in others. In the nine industries for which nominal output data were available, output increased on average by 62% compared to an increase in nominal GNP of 16% during that time period-almost four times greater. Several of the industries expanded output by more than ten times the overall increase in nominal GNP. Some of the more rapidly expanding industries were cotton seed oil (151%), leather goods (133%), cordage and twine (166%), and jute (57%).

Real GNP increased by approximately 24% from 1880 to 1890, while those allegedly monopolized industries for which some measure of real output is available grew on average by 175% – seven times the rate of growth of the economy as a whole. Again, some of the industries grew more than ten times faster than real GNP. These included steel (258%), zinc (156%), coal (153%), steel rails (142%), petroleum (79%) and sugar (75%).

These trends continued to the turn of the century. Output expanded in each industry except castor oil, and, on average, output in these industries grew at a faster rate than the rest of the economy. Those industries for which nominal output data were available expanded by 99% compared to a 43% increase in nominal GNP, while the other industries increased real output by 76% compared to a 46% rise in real GNP from 1890 to 1900.

In sum, the data call into question the notion that those industries singled out by Senator Sherman and his colleagues were creating a "rising tide of monopoly power," if one judges by Senator Sherman's own measuring rod of monopoly power, output restriction. These industries were expanding much faster than the economy as a whole, a phenomenon that has been overlooked by those who adhere to the standard account of the origins of antitrust. To my knowledge this fact has not been revealed previously: It is usually *assumed*, without evidence, that the trusts were restricting output.

It is possible that even though the trusts were actually expanding output, they were doing so less rapidly than if such combinations did not exist, thereby increasing prices and profits. The data, however, do not support this interpretation. Prices in these industries were generally falling, not rising, even when compared to the declining general price level. Price data on these items are very scattered and some are simply unavailable. But the data that are available indicate that falling prices accompanied the rapid output growth in these industries. For example, the average price of steel rails fell from $68 to $32 between 1880 and 1890, or by 53%. The price of refined sugar fell by 22%, from 9 cents per pound in 1880 to 7 cents in 1890. It fell further to 4.5 cents by 1900. The price of lead dropped by 12%, from

$5.04 per pound in 1880 to $4.41 in 1890. The price of zinc declined by 20%, from $5.51 to $4.40 per pound from 1880 to 1890, and the price of bituminous coal remained steady at about $3.10 per pound, although it fell by 29%, to $2.20 from 1890 to 1900. Although the consumer price index fell by 7% from 1880 to 1890 this was proportionately less than all of these items except coal.

Perhaps the most widely-attacked trusts were those that existed in the sugar and petroleum industries. But there is evidence that the effect of these combinations or mergers was to reduce the prices of sugar and petroleum. Moreover, Congress clearly recognized this. . .

Thus the Congress acknowledged that combinations were actually responsible for improving the lot of the consumer by dropping prices "immensely." They objected, however, to the fact that less efficient (smaller) businessmen ('honest men') were driven out of business. The fact that these and other businessmen voted and contributed in other ways to political campaigns surely helps to explain this stance taken by the Republican-controlled Congress. At the time nearly every Congressional district had large numbers of small businesses (and farmers) so that one would have expected them to carry considerable political clout compared to the trusts which were far fewer in number and whose ownership was more dispersed... It was generally recognized that, despite the facts, the strong emotional opposition to the trusts fostered by journalists, politicians, and others meant that speaking in favor of them could mean political suicide.

In summary, the Sherman Act may possibly be viewed as special-interest legislation, the purpose of which was at least two-fold. First, to isolate certain groups, especially small businesses, from the rigors of competition. If the trusts were restricting output (or slowing its expansion) and raising prices, small businesses would not have objected, for they would have benefited from the (higher) price umbrella. This point is of considerable importance. It is widely acknowledged that small businesses have always initiated antitrust cases against their larger (and often more efficient) competitors . . . these actions typically protect small businesses from competition and inevitably lead to higher prices. If the larger businesses in these cases were colluding and raising industry prices, it stands to reason that smaller businesses would also benefit and would not have brought antitrust suits against them. The point is, just as small businesses have often benefited from the enforcement of the antitrust laws over the years (at the expense of larger businesses and consumers) they are likely to have been a major force behind the creation of the laws in the first place. By this interpretation their interest was not to prohibit monopoly from occurring but to protect themselves from competition. In short, they wanted an "antimonopoly" law to reduce competitive pressures in their industries.

A second purpose of the Sherman Act was to satisfy voters who had become increasingly envious of the economic success earned by nineteenth-century entrepreneurs and who were upset over rapidly-changing relative prices and wages. As mentioned in the above quotation of Hayek, changing relative prices are often characteristic of a dynamic, competitive market economy. But groups whose relative wages and incomes fall (at least temporarily) often protest to the government by lobbying for protectionist measures of various sorts, including antitrust laws. It is not unusual for economic instability (i.e., deflation) caused largely by the government's monetary policies to be blamed on a small handful of private corporations.

One objection to this interpretation may be that even though the trusts were dropping prices, couldn't they have been engaging in predatory pricing? This is possible, but not probable. Studies of predatory pricing over the past several decades have found that it is not likely to be a profitable practice and that there is no evidence that Standard Oil, which was sued for predatory pricing in the famous 1911 decision, was actually engaged in any such practice . . . Moreover, with respect to the trusts of the late nineteenth century, it is inconceivable that they would have allowed prices to fall for more than an entire decade, as they did, to 'temporarily' undercut the competition. That would have been irrational.

These statements are not meant to imply that there was no monopoly power in American industry during the late nineteenth century. It appears that one function of the Sherman Act was to divert public attention away from a more certain source of monopoly power, the state. It is well known that the Interstate Commerce Commission, established three years before the Sherman Act in 1887, served as the mechanism for the legal cartelization of the railroad industry. Here, and in many other instances, it was government regulation itself that was the source of monopoly power. Tariffs imposed by Congress were probably the major source of restraints of trade in the late nineteenth century, but the Sherman Act made no provision for them or for any other form of government-sanctioned monopoly. Nor should one expect vote-maximizing politicians to have done so, for they are major beneficiaries of such legislative privileges. In bestowing them, they win votes and campaign contributions from the beneficiaries. The political costs, on the other hand, are rather hidden, for the average voter has little or no financial incentive to discover the true costs of protectionism. Moreover, even though the aggregate costs of protectionism may be large, they are relatively small to each individual voter.

In a particularly revealing statement Senator Sherman attacked the trusts during the Senate debates over his bill on the grounds that they

> . . . subverted the tariff system; they undermined the policy of government to protect. . . American industries by levying duties on imported goods.

This is certainly an odd statement by the man who has been called the champion of free enterprise. However, the evidence cited above is consistent, with the Senator's political fears. Increased output and reduced prices in these industries apparently dissipated the monopoly rents previously procured by protective tariffs. This worked against the objectives of some in the protected industries and of their legislative allies such as Senator Sherman. Further, just three months after the Sherman Act was passed Senator Sherman, as Chairman of the Senate Finance Committee, sponsored a bill popularly known as the "Campaign Contributors" Tariff Bill. As reported in the *New York Times* on 1 October 1890:

> 'The Campaign Contributors' Tariff Bill now goes to the president for his signature, which will speedily be affixed to it, and the favored manufacturers, many of whom... proposed and made the [tariff] rates which affect their products, will begin to enjoy the profits of this legislation.

The *New York Times* further reported that "the speech of Mr. Sherman on Monday [29 September 1890] should not be overlooked, for it was one of confession." Apparently, Senator Sherman withdrew his speech from the *Congressional Record* for "revision," but a *New York Times* reporter obtained an unabridged copy of the original. As reported in the *New York Times*:

> . . . we direct attention to those passages [of Sherman's speech] relating to combinations of protected manufacturers designed to take full advantage of high tariff duties by exacting from consumers prices fixed by agreement after competition has been suppressed . . . Mr. Sherman closed his speech with some words of warning and advice to the beneficiaries of the new tariff. He was earnest enough in his manner to indicate that he is not at all confident as to the outcome of the law. The great thing that stood in the way of the success of the bill, he said, was whether or not the manufacturers of this country would permit free competition in the American market. The danger was that the beneficiaries of the bill would combine and cheat the people out of the benefits of the law. They were now given reasonable and ample protection, and if they would resist the temptation attaching to great aggregations of capital to combine and advance prices, they might hope for a season of great prosperity . . . . He did hope, the Senator concluded, that the manufacturers would open the doors to fair competition and give its benefits to the people . . . . He hoped the manufacturers would agree to compete one with another and would refuse to take the high prices that are so easily obtained.

For Senator Sherman to say that a protective tariff would not harm consumers or would actually help them if only manufacturers could be trusted to refrain from raising prices is contradictory, to put it mildly. It led to a complete reversal of the views of the *New York Times* which had for years been one of the foremost proponents of antitrust legislation. After observing the behavior of Senator Sherman and his colleagues during the months following the passage of the Sherman Act the *New York Times* concluded:

> That so-called Anti-Trust law was passed to deceive the people and to clear the way for the enactment of this . . . law relating to the tariff. It was projected in order that the party organs might say to the

> opponents of tariff extortion and protected combinations, 'Behold! We
> have attacked the Trusts. The Republican party is the enemy of all
> such rings.' And now the author of it can only 'hope' that the rings will
> dissolve of their own accord.

These suspicions are certainly justified. Monopoly has long been associated with governmental entry restrictions such as tariffs, quotas, licenses, monopoly franchises, and grandfather clauses, hut this type of activity has been immune from antitrust law. It is not unlikely that the Sherman Act was passed to help draw public attention away from the actual process of monopolization in the economy, among the major beneficiaries of which have always been the legislators themselves. The Sherman Act won votes and campaign contributions from small businesses, while the tariff bill was supported by all manufacturers, large and small. Tollison and McCormick argue that the essential role of legislators is precisely this: to act as "brokers" of legislation. By interfering with the competitive process the Congress became perhaps the chief interest group benefiting from the Sherman Act. Similar views were also voiced by many economists during that time, although they were almost completely ignored by the legislature.

# Chapter 13
# Total Repeal of Antitrust Legislation:
# A Critique of Bork, Brozen, and Posner

## 1. Introduction

The premise underlying laissez-faire capitalism is that the only actions which should be illegal are those which involve an initiation of aggression against another person or his property. Antitrust law is clearly in violation of this principle, because it prohibits business practices no one even alleges constitute such depredations.

The economists mentioned in the title of this paper are widely and properly celebrated for upholding the virtues of the free marketplace. However, there is one lacunae in their defense: antitrust legislation. Although they have done yeoman work in helping us to understand the beneficial effects of much commercial conduct which is prohibited by these enactments, their critique of this law is less than full. They each see a small but important role for the Antitrust Division of the Justice Department. They advocate reduction in the power and scope of this law, but not, unfortunately, total repeal.

It is as if they are a football team which has succeeded in bringing the pigskin to the three yard line, but can make no further progress. This paper is an attempt to help them over the goal line. To continue our football analogy, the present paper will not comment on the 97% of their work which is responsible, in large part, for the scholarly contribution to the cause of keeping antitrust law from being even more intrusive than it now is. In focusing on the 3 percent of disagreement, this paper may give the impression that there are large differences of perspective in public policy conclusions between these authors and their present critic. Nothing could be further from the truth.

## 2. Robert Bork

### 2.1 Merger
Robert Bork (1978) maintains that some entrepreneurial choices in the market lead to efficiency, while others merely serve to restrict output. His main thesis is that antitrust has thus far insufficiently distinguished between these two situations. This is important, he contends, because if consumer welfare is to be enhanced, the restriction of output must be prohibited, while wealth enhancing activities must be promoted (or at least allowed.)[1]

This can be shown by a consideration of Bork's "two vectors" hypothesis, representing, at least in the first instance, a merger. This is depicted in Figure 1.

As Bork explains:

> The diagram assumes that the merger reduces the long-run average costs of the two firms from $AC_1$ to $AC_2$ but that the increased market power created by the merger results in a restriction of output so that the rate moves from $Q_1$ to $Q_2$. We then see that consumers have lost output – for which they would have been willing to pay an amount above cost equal to the area labeled $A_1$ – and have gained in resource savings an amount equal to the area $A_2$. Obviously, if $A_2$, the cost savings, is larger than $A_1$, the dead-weight loss, the merger represents a net gain to all consumers. If $A_1$ is larger than $A_2$, a net loss results.
>
> This diagram can be used to illustrate all antitrust problems, since it shows the relationship of the only two factors involved, allocative inefficiency and productive efficiency. The existence of these two elements and their respective amounts are the real issues in every properly decided antitrust case. They are what we have to estimate-whether the case is about the dissolution of a monopolistic firm, a conglomerate merger, a requirements contract, or a price fixing agreement . . .
>
> It must also be remembered that there need not always be a tradeoff [between $A_1$ and $A_2$]. In most cases, in my opinion, economic analysis will show that one of the areas does not exist, and a decision of the case is therefore easy. Some phenomena involve only a dead-weight loss and no, or insignificant, cost savings. That is the case with the garden-variety price-fixing ring. Output is restricted so that $Q_2$ is to the left of $Q_1$, creating the area $A_1$, but there is no downward shift of costs, no line $AC_2$, and hence no area $A_2$. (p. 108; material in brackets added by present author)

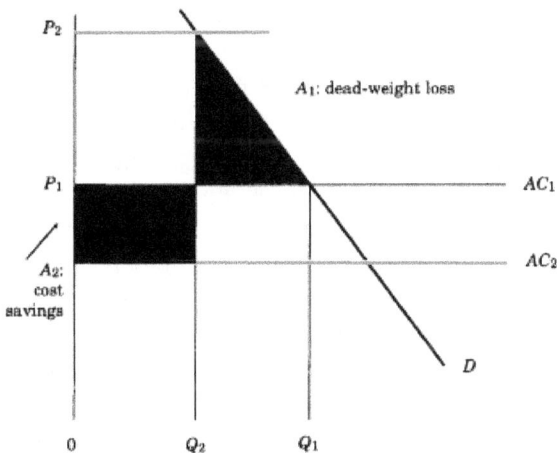

**Figure 1**

Source: Robert Bork, *The Antitrust Paradox: A Policy at War with Itself* (New York: Basic Books, 1978), p. 107

161

One problem with the foregoing is that it pushes the courts into the role of determining whether or not any particular type of industrial organization or contract is or is not "cost saving." But the judiciary has no comparative advantage in making any such determinations.[2] Its members are not selected on the basis of being able to do so. Their salaries and promotions are not in any way tied to success in distinguishing efficient arrangements from inefficient ones. Failures are not punished with demotions. Achievement is not automatically rewarded with promotion, or with the awarding of bigger, more important or precedent setting cases. Why, then, should we expect this behavior from the courts?

Indeed, if Bork himself is to be believed on this issue, jurists, all throughout the history of antitrust, have made findings which show them to be either unconcerned, or incompetent with regard to this issue. Says the author of this book:

> most of the mergers the Supreme Court strikes down and the 'price discriminations' the Robinson-Patman Act is intended to stamp out . . . are examples . . . which involve only efficiency gain and no dead-weight loss. (108–9)

A second difficulty has to do with the interpretation of the demand curve. In Bork's neoclassical construal, the demand curve is seen as an existing entity. True, this author concedes that "we do not know the location of any of the sides of the triangular area $A_1$," (one of which is the demand curve), but this is only an inconvenience. "They are what we have to estimate" (p. 108) is the way to get around this annoyance. But this will not do.[3] Demand curves are not "out there," ready to be measured by the modern econometric tools of analysis. Rather, they are, except for one dot ($P_2Q_2$, in this case), hypothetical alternatives which never come into play. Demand curves answer the question, Suppose that everything else in the universe were exactly the same as it now is, with the one exception that price, instead of being at $P_2$, is at some other level; then, how much would the customer be willing to buy at that other price. In the event, the price however, was $P_2$ and the consumer wished to purchase $Q_2$. That is all we know, or indeed, can know. The other points on this demand curve never come into play at all. They are contrary to fact conditionals. There is no sense in the notion that we can "estimate" them. There is no doubt that economists can look at other instances (other times, places, people) where different quantities of this item were purchased at different prices (and even attempt to control for the fact that the prices and quantities of substitutes and complements have altered, to say nothing of changing incomes, inflation, employment and even the weather) and in that way trace out a "demand curve." But this has little or nothing to do with what is depicted in that diagram. The point is, a demand curve is a unique non-repeatable hypothetical "event." All attempts to "measure" it are thus doomed to failure.

So far, we have been implicitly assuming that it is legitimate to make interpersonal comparisons of utility. It is now time to relax this assumption. In point of fact, this methodology is not tenable. It is perfectly reasonable to maintain that all trade benefits both parties in the *ex ante* sense. This is the reason they engage in such an activity, and this conclusion is part of the bedrock of the science of economics. It is quite another matter, however, to deduce from the failure of a trade to take place (in the free marketplace, $Q_1Q_2$ remains unsold, because it is not offered for sale) that had occurred, the buyer's welfare would have exceeded the loss to the seller. This contrary to fact conditional implies that interpersonal comparisons of utility indeed can be made-without offering any evidence or reason for such an assertion-and moreover that the consumer's benefit exceeds the producer's loss. The latter contention would remain unproven even if interpersonal utility comparisons were valid in the first place. And yet, unless this assertion is true, the value of $A_1$ would be negative, not positive as claimed by Bork. If a "garden-variety price-fixing ring"[4] succeeds in raising prices from $P_1$ to $P_2$, there is thus nothing within the strict science of economics that can be used to show that this will reduce social (as opposed to consumer) welfare.

Still another fallacy of the two vectors approach lies behind the very drawing of the cost curves in this diagram, $AC_1$ and $AC_2$. There is nothing untoward about using them for textbook illustration purposes only. Bork, however, is attempting to justify antitrust, a legislative enactment which can fine or even jail businessmen for the "crime" of price fixing, on the basis of this analysis. Under such circumstances it is reasonable to look more closely into these cost curves, an integral part of the analysis.

Cost, in economic theory, is not by any means limited to out of pocket expenses, even including implicit rent. These are part of the concept, but in its most sophisticated interpretation, cost is equivalent to the next best opportunity foregone by making any particular choice. As such, cost can only be a subjective notion (Buchanan, 1969; Buchanan and Thirlby, 1981; Mises, 1963). The next best opportunity foregone by the choice to sell $Q_1$ need not be anywhere close to $P_1$. In any case, it can never be known by a third party, for example by the Antitrust Division of the Justice Department, the government bureau charged with punishing or incarcerating price fixers.

More radically, the cost of all saleable items is actually zero, and therefore can have no effect in any case. States Rothbard (1962: 604):

> there is no such thing as costs (apart from speculation on a higher future price) once the stock has been produced. Costs take place along the path of decisions to produce – at each step along the way that investments (of money and effort) are made in factors. The allocations, the opportunities foregone, take place at each step as future production decisions must be taken and commitments made. Once the stock has been produced, however (and there is no expectation of a price rise), the sale is costless, since there are no advantages foregone by selling the product (costs in making the sale being here considered negligible for purposes of simplification). There-fore, the stock will tend to be sold at whatever price is obtainable.

163

> There is no such thing, then as 'selling below costs' on stock already produced.

One can go even further. Not only is the sale costless when it occurs, it may even occur at less than zero costs. For example, if I have piled up a horde of tomatoes, or shoes, or steel, or tires, and I cannot find a customer for them, then, at least in a strictly private property rights-no trespassing world (Rothbard, 1973: 1082), I will have to pay for their removal. Under such conditions the costs of the sale will be negative. That is, if the disposal costs are $500 (I have to pay $500 to rid myself of this unwelcome stock), then, *ceteris paribus,* I should be willing to sell it to a customer at any negative price above this level. For example, if I sell at $200, then I make a profit of $300. Even though I have to pay a customer $200 to cart away my merchandise, I am better off by $300 because the private sanitation hauler would have charged me $500.

### 2.2 Sovereignty

Yet another problem arises with regard to the issue of individual versus consumer sovereignty. Let us allow Bork to articulate this thesis in his own words. As far as consumer welfare is concerned, he states it as follows:

> (antitrust) can only increase collective wealth by requiring that any lawful products, whether skis or snowmobiles, be produced and sold under conditions most favorable to consumers. (91)
> Productive efficiency, like allocative efficiency, is a normative concept and is defined and measured in terms of consumer welfare. (104–5)

But this rendition of the goal is problematic. Why should the goal of antitrust be to enhance *consumer* welfare alone? Why, for that matter, should the aim of any public policy be so narrowly defined? If it is taken for granted that some sort of welfare be maximized by legislation, why not attempt to maximize *total* welfare, that is, the welfare derived by *both* producer and consumer.

It is possible to employ a *reductio ad absurdum* in this regard. If we really want to enhance the welfare of consumers only, as opposed to both consumers and producers, all sorts of other enactments become justifiable which would not have been otherwise. For example, if there were any producer's surplus (economic rents earned by manufacturers) then these should be summarily seized, and handed over to consumers. Needless to say, however, no warrant for any such action has ever been given.

This policy, moreover, is internally inconsistent, for it will tend to counteract Bork's own goal of augmenting consumer welfare. We cannot safely ignore people as producers if we are attempting to maximize their well-being as consumers. People are people, and typically play a dual role as both consumers and producers. If we hurt them in one role, they are necessarily hurt in the other as well.

Rothbard's remarks (1962: 560–561) seem to be addressed directly to the Bork hypothesis, although they were written almost two decades beforehand:

164

We have seen that in the free market economy people will tend to produce those goods most demanded by the consumers. Some economists have termed this system 'consumers' sovereignty.' Yet there is no compulsion about this. The choice is purely an independent one by the producer; his dependence on the consumer is purely voluntary, the result of his own choice for the 'maximization' of utility, and it is a choice that he is free to revoke at any time. We have stressed many times that the pursuit of monetary return (the con-sequence of consumer demand) is engaged in by each individual *only to the extent that other things are equal.* These other things are the individual producer's psychic valuations, and they may counteract monetary influences. An example is a laborer or other factor-owner engaged in a certain line of work at less monetary return than elsewhere. He does this because of his enjoyment of the particular line of work and product and/or his distaste for other alternatives. Rather than 'consumers' sovereignty,' it would be more accurate to state that in the free market there is *sovereignty of the individual:* the individual is sovereign over his own person and actions and over his own property. This may be termed *individual self-sovereignty.* To earn a monetary return, the individual producer must satisfy consumer demand, but the extent to which he obeys this expected monetary return, and the extent to which he pursues other, nonmonetary factors, is entirely a matter of his own free choice.

The term 'consumers' sovereignty' is a typical example of the abuse, in economics, of a term ('sovereignty') appropriate only to the *political* realm and is thus an illustration of the dangers of the application of metaphors taken from other disciplines. 'Sovereignty' is the quality of ultimate political power; it is the power resting on the use of violence. In a purely free society, each individual is sovereign over his own person and property, and it is therefore this self-sovereignty which obtains on the free market. No one is 'sovereign' over anyone else's actions or exchanges. Since the consumers do not have the power to coerce producers into various occupations and work, the former are not 'sovereign' over the latter.

To this it may be added, in order to bring it into more direct relevance with Bork, that not only do the "consumers not have the power to coerce producers into various occupations and work," but in the free society they do not have the power to coerce the producers to locate at $Q_1$, as opposed to their preferred point, $Q_2$. How does Bork describe the distance $Q_2Q_1$? He claims that this is a quantity of product the consumers are willing to purchase, at a price above the costs of production, and yet, because of nefarious or at least questionable doings on the part of the seller, the customer is disappointed in this desire. The area between $Q_2$ and $Q_1$, above the cost curve $AC_1$ and below the demand curve is defined as $A_1$, the dead-weight loss. This is the amount of welfare that could have been enjoyed by the consumer, but is not.

It is only by focusing on the buyer at the expense of the seller that Bork is able to characterize $A_1$ as a region of dead-weight loss. In order to see this, imagine for a moment that this author had subscribed to the notion of individual, not consumer sovereignty. If so, then how could we most accurately characterize the distance $Q_2Q_1$? No longer can we depict this merely as an amount of quantity that the consumer wishes, but is unable to buy. For under our present assumptions, there are two sides to this transaction, not just one. Now we can more accurately delineate $Q_2Q_1$ as a quantity that the consumer wishes to purchase, alright, but also as an amount that *the manufacturer does not wish to sell*. Similarly, our description of $A_1$ can no longer be one of unambiguous "dead-weight loss." Now, it must be characterized as an amount of welfare contended over by two different parties. If the sale takes place at $Q_1$, yes, Bork is correct;[5] the consumer will gain this amount of welfare. But the producer will also lose (presumably, he is unwilling to sell any more than $Q_2$ because past that point, his marginal revenue lies below his marginal cost). So, it is by no means an unambiguous dead-weight loss $A_1$ which must be set against a clear gain in cost savings of $A_2$; rather, $A_1$ is a loss only to one side of the trade, but a gain to the other.

It is possible for the Borkian side of this debate to articulate several objections to the Rothbard perspective on individual versus consumer sovereignty. First, it might be maintained, following Hutt (1940), that producers are themselves consumers. For example, whenever a seller acts in a way other than to maximize money returns, he is really "buying" services from himself. Therefore, the concept of consumers' sovereignty is wide enough to incorporate both producers and consumers.

If we adopt this way of looking at the matter, there are now two sets of consumers. The first, call them the consumer-consumers, are the people for whom Bork drew his demand curve. These are the ones who are purportedly suffering from the output restriction from $Q_1$ to $Q_2$. The second, call them the producer-consumers, the ones engaged in this (unwarranted, improper, according to the neoclassical school) restricting of output. These two sets of consumers, according to Bork, are acting incompatibly with one another.

As Rothbard (1962: 562) trenchantly states,

> In the aforementioned general sense, 'consumption' rules in any case. But the critical question is: *which* 'consumer?' The market consumer of exchangeable goods who buys these goods with money, or the market producer of exchangeable goods who sells these goods for money?

The point is, noticing that the producer, too, engages in consumption does not help one bit in determining whether we should force, through the majesty of the law, the producer-consumer to locate at $Q_1$ instead of $Q_2$, in behalf of the consumer-consumer. Rather, it sets up an infinite regress.

A second possible objection Bork could resort to was used by Hutt. As Rothbard notes (quoting Hutt), this is to distinguish between

> when a producer withholds his person or property out of a desire to use it for enjoyment *as a consumers' good* . . . in which case it. . . is a legitimate act, in keeping with rule by the consumer. On the other hand, when the producer acts to withhold his property in order to attain more monetary income than otherwise . . . then he is engaging in a vicious infringement on the consumers' will (Rothbard, 1962: 563).

This, too, however, has been answered by Rothbard. He notes that it is not difficult, but rather impossible, to distinguish between these two motives. Secondly, the only reason more profit can be earned at $P_2Q_2$ than at $P_1Q_1$ is because of the inelasticity of demand between the two points. But this arises out of consumer (consumer-consumer, that is) choice! If the consumers were unhappy with this state of affairs, they could

> easily make their demand curves *elastic* by *boycotting* the producer and/or by increasing their demands at the 'competitive' production level (Rothbard, 1962: 564).[6]

### *2.3 Predation*

If it is impossible, not merely difficult, to distinguish between psychic income and profitability as motives for "withholding," this applies as well to that between "deliberate aggression" in order to drive rivals from the market and in order to profit maximize. Here are Bork's views (144) on the subject:

> Predation may be defined, provisionally, as a firm's deliberate aggression against one or more rivals through the employment of business practices that would not be considered profit maximizing except for the expectation either that (1) rivals will be driven from the market, leaving the predator with a market share sufficient to command monopoly profits, or (2) rivals will be chastened sufficiently to abandon competitive behavior the predator finds inconvenient or threatening.

But the employment of the word "predation" is surely another illegitimate abuse of a metaphor taken from another discipline. Predation is what the lion does to the zebra. Strictly speaking, there can be no such activity in the free economy. For there is not even the hint of a charge, in Bork or anywhere else, that the business firms who have in this way gained the attention of the Antitrust Division have initiated violence against their competitors. If "predation" is to be given a commercial implication, it would be reasonable to confine it to such activities as fraud, theft, extortion, or "making him an offer he cannot refuse" in the parlance of a Mafia Godfather. The contrast between this and the acts of the Borkian "predator" are stark indeed. The latter "deliberately aggresses" against his competitors by offering his *customers* a better deal than they can obtain elsewhere. If this is predation, then the consumer, for whom Bork seems to have an unlimited regard, would presumably ask for more of it.

Our author lists three forms of predation. They are price cutting, disruption of distribution patterns, and misuse of government processes. Only the second is important to discuss, and we shall concentrate our remarks on it. This is because of the first, price cutting, Bork spends thousands of words (144–55) showing that neither economic theory nor economic history give support to the contention[7] that this is an efficacious way of engaging in predatory behavior.[8] As to the third, this is indeed "predation" of the sort mentioned above. Here, Bork properly castigates the initiation of frivolous lawsuits "in order to harm an actual or potential business rival" (p. 159). But the answer is not antitrust; it is the awarding of severe damages to those victimized by this practice. Under this rubric we can also add false and fraudulent advertising. This, too, is a legitimate role for the forces of law and order; but it cannot be used to justify the continued existence of a Federal Trade Commission, most of whose activities are aimed at suppressing legitimate commercial endeavors.

What, then, is "disruption of distribution patterns?" Bork (p. 156) explains:

> In any business, patterns of distribution develop over time; these may reasonably be thought to be more efficient than alternative patterns of distribution that do not develop. The patterns that do develop and persist we may call the optimal patterns. By disturbing optimal distribution patterns one rival can impose costs upon another, that is, force the other to accept higher costs. This may or may not be a serious cost increase, but if it is (and the matter can only be determined empirically), the imposition of costs may conceivably be a means of predation. The predator will suffer cost increases, too, and that sets limits to the types of cases in which this tactic will be used for predation. There is a further complication, moreover, in that the behavior involved will often be capable of creating efficiencies. Thus, the law cannot properly see predatory behavior in all unilaterally enforced changes in patterns of distribution.

There are several difficulties here. First, Bork must have in mind an exceedingly static world. That is the only situation in which his scenario could even roughly approximate the truth. Pattern persistence, however, is surely impossible in the modern day, under a regime of even limited economic freedom, where people are able to introduce new products (e.g., computers), implement new selling strategies (e.g., supermarkets), initiate new forms of business organization (e.g., franchising). Further, just because a distribution pattern has "persisted" in the past does not mean that it is optimal today, and certainly not tomorrow (Kirzner, 1973).

Second, the "further complication" is problematic. If this pattern of disruptive behavior is "often . . . . capable of creating efficiencies" how then can we distinguish between those alterations in business procedure which emanate from "predation," and those which come about due to enhanced efficiency? The empirical determination called for in this regard is no comfort; without any criterion for distinguishing between these phenomena, number crunching for the sake of number crunching will amount to nothing more than a full employment bill for out of work econometricians.

Third, there is no such thing as a "unilateral" change in the market. The market is no more and no less than the concatenation of all voluntary trades which take place in a given area. But all commercial exchange is, by its very nature, bilateral, not unilateral. It takes two to tango, and it takes two to trade.

Fourth, there are no "enforced" changes in patterns of distribution, or of anything else for that matter with regard to the market. If there is any initiation of physical force or violence, it is necessarily not part of the market (Rothbard, 1962).

Another disappointment with Bork's treatment of this subject is that he offers only two instances of disruption of distribution patterns that can be predatory, and there are difficulties with each. First is the use of exclusive dealing contracts. But he undermines this example with the concession that (156) "it is far more probable that . . . exclusive dealing is more efficient and has (been) adopted . . . for that reason." Further undermining this case is the statement (157):

> The law can usefully attack this form of predation only when there is evidence of specific intent to drive others from the market by means other than superior efficiency and when the predator has overwhelming market size, perhaps 80 or 90%.

The problem is not that it is difficult if not impossible to attain evidence of such specific intent. It is, more radically, that *all* commercial endeavors are, in effect, an attempt to drive others from the market through superior efficiency. The drawback to this perspective is that Bork refuses to define "efficiency" broadly enough so as to include producer's welfare as well as that of consumers.

The second example vouchsafed to us is that of the board of trade. Boards of trade, it would appear, can act capriciously. But such organizations are, at bottom, only private clubs. They have no special legal dispensations. If members do not like the way that board of trade A is handling its affairs, they are free to set up another, competing, board of trade, B. This threat will usually serve to compel the extant trade board to act reasonably.

Apart from these specific difficulties with Bork's theory of predation, there is the underlying philosophical problem[9] that it attempts to make distinctions where there are no discernible differences, Let us, in order to illustrate this point, attempt to construct several new analogues to economic "predation" in other, unrelated, fields.

The bottom line for Borkian "predation" is that it is legitimate to actively compete in order to earn profits; even "deliberate aggression" is allowed. However, one must act so as to earn profits directly; one may not indulge in business practices that sacrifice present profits, the sole purpose of which is to bankrupt a competitor, in order to earn profits later on, in the absence of the competition which would otherwise have been supplied by it.

Right now, in football, the goal is to move the pigskin in a forward direction, in order to score points. This is analogous to earning profits. If we were to adopt

Bork's philosophy to this context, we would have to ban any and all actions which undermine this end, in the short run, such as the quarterback dropping back (and *losing* valuable territory) in order to pass. Even the handoff from the center to the quarterback would have to be re-evaluated in the light of this legal philosophy. And what are we to make, in this context, of the sacrifice fly in baseball, or the bunt to advance a base runner. Surely, the purposeful loss of a valuable commodity (one of the three outs) even for the long-run good purpose of scoring an extra run would have to be regarded as illegal. Similarly, the sacrifice of a queen or some other valuable piece in chess would have to be ruled out of court. Is there really that much difference between such short-run counter-productive behaviors in the sporting world and their counterparts in the world of commerce such as local price cutting[10] or selling some goods at a loss (loss leaders) in order to attract customers into the store?

Take another case. You are the author (composer, producer) of book (song, movie) A, I am the author of book B. These books are on the same subject; they are rivals, or competitors. I am in this for the money; I have written this book in order to maximize profits. I have been asked to review your book in a newspaper, magazine, or journal. I give it a sharply critical negative review. An implication of Bork's analysis is that this act of mine ought to be proscribed by law, for it is "the employment of a business practice that would not be considered profit maximizing except for the expectation . . . that [a] rival will be driven from the market." Surely the implication which arises from Bork's analysis is intolerable; just as assuredly, it follows the logic of his interpretation. Did I not have a competing book in the market, I would not have so denigrated your effort; thus, my review would not have been profit maximizing but for the expectation that I could thereby entice potential book buyers from you to me.

Generalizing still further, from business to the world of interpersonal relations, what are we to make of the man who denigrates his rival for the affections of a woman? In the ordinary course of events, if Roger tells Elaine that Joe is a cad, a blunderer, a lazy incompetent moocher, we would just write it down to the rights of free speech. But the Borkian perspective applies here as well, provided that Roger would have said no such thing were Joe not competing with him for Elaine's hand in marriage.

But if this scenario applies, again we have a case where there is

> deliberate aggression against one or more rivals through the employ-
> ment of (interpersonal) practices that would not be considered profit
> maximizing except for the expectation that (1) rivals will be driven from
> the (marriage) market, leaving the predator with (the object of his
> desires), or (2) rivals will be chastened sufficiently to abandon com-
> petitive behavior the predator finds inconvenient or threatening.

## 3. Yale Brozen

### 3.1 Proper targets
Yale Brozen (1982), while not so vociferous in his defense of antitrust as Bork, clearly sees a positive role for this "curious institution." In his view (14):

> The antitrust agencies should be devoting themselves . . . to detecting and prosecuting the types of explicit collusion that restrain output. In devoting investigatory and prosecutorial effort to persistently concentrated industries, increasingly concentrated industries, and dominant firms, the agencies selected exactly the wrong targets. They are themselves restraining output and the growth of productivity.

This statement embodies the theme of the book. The Antitrust Division should not be rescinded. It should not be eliminated, root and branch. Rather, it has a legitimate role to play. If it could but free itself from concern with the red herring of high concentration, and focus instead on "explicit collusion," and "output restraint," it could make a positive contribution to society.

The problem with this perspective is not that Brazen has failed to put his finger on an egregious policy (attacking concentration); he has, in a thorough going and incisive way. This course of action has lead to a far poorer and less efficient economy than otherwise would have obtained. The difficulty is, rather, that there are *good* targets that the trustbusters should instead be aiming their fire at, in his view.

We have already discussed the issue of restraining output in the context of interpersonal comparisons of utility. But we can also call into question Brozen's opposition to "restraining output and the growth of productivity" under the rubric of welfare economics. Why should these goals be the *sine qua non* of economic public policy? G.D.P., physical output, and productivity growth, however important, are, still, themselves derivable from a principle even more consequential: individual choice. If the economic actor wishes, say, to pursue leisure instead of money income, human welfare will be better enhanced by allowing that decision to stand than by rescinding it, even for the persons "own good," and by coercively bringing about a situation where there are more goods and services in the economy than are compatible with his initial determination.

This is precisely what has occurred on the part of those chosen as proper targets for the Antitrust Division by Brozen. They are guilty of no more than explicitly agreeing, among themselves, to produce less than Brozen, an outside observer, would compel them to produce.

### 3.2 Concentration
The next bone of contention to be raised has to do with concentration. There is hardly a commentator more critical with regard to the way in which concentration ratios are used in U.S. jurisprudence than Brozen. For example:

> In order to find Alcoa guilty of violating the antitrust laws, Judge Learned Hand had to find that Alcoa 'controlled' the secondary aluminum market, despite the production of secondary aluminum by many suppliers, as well as that it had a 'monopoly' of primary aluminum. But he never considered whether aluminum competes with galvanized sheet metal, copper, magnesium, zinc, tinplate, glass, tin, and other materials used for some of the same purposes as aluminum. (46)

And again:

> The measure commonly used is total shipments from plants 'assigned' to an industry by the Bureau of the Census. A plant's entire output is assigned to the industry whose products make up the plurality of total shipments from the plant. If a plant belonging to a leading firm produces trucks and refrigerators, and more than half the value of its shipments is trucks, all the plant's shipments are assigned to the motor vehicle industry. That firm will then show a higher share of motor vehicle industry shipments tha[n] its actual share. (50)

Here is a further example:

> Industry definitions are generally based on technology or on inputs employed, not on markets. Separate concentration ratios are reported for beet and sugar cane refiners, for example. But since beet and sugar cane refiners compete with each other for the same customers, these ratios mean little in market terms. Their outputs are indistinguishable. In addition, glucose, dextrose, and fructose sugars are produced by the corn wet milling industry. Maple syrup and honey are produced by still two more industries. Artificial sweeteners are produced by still another industry. There is no concentration figure reported for the sweetener market. Although cane refiners compete with beet refiners and both compete with corn millers, maple sap boilers, beekeepers and chemical firms, no account is taken of this in measuring concentration. (51)

But the case is even worse than this. For artificial sweeteners *also* compete against the Jane Fonda Workout Tapes, against vacations at fat farms, and indeed, against just about everything else, such as chess sets, shoes, paper clips and light bulbs, in the sense that the family budget can stretch only so far, and thus any increased expenditure on practically *anything* means a reduction in spending on virtually everything else.

Unfortunately, Brozen's criticism of concentration measures is limited to such Census Bureau practice. He does not take the more radical step of condemning the logical coherence of concentration ratios *per se*.

In order to define a concentration ratio, an "industry," "line of commerce," or relevant "market" must first be defined. In the view of Brozen, and indeed, of virtually the entire economics profession,[11] this can be accomplished in a non-arbitrary manner through the use of cross elasticities. But these statistics are not objective "facts" of economics; they are not constants, akin to gravity in physics. Rather, they are necessarily limited as to scope and time dimension, and this leads to intractable problems. For example, it is well known that the greater the length of run, the higher the elasticity. If the price of x rises, the quantity demanded of substitutes cannot rise by very much, if at all, immediately; in the short run, it can rise by more; in the long run, and particularly in the very long run, it can increase by a very much greater amount. So, which is the "proper" length of run? Merely to ask this question is to see the utter arbitrariness of any answer, and thus of any such measure.

Even if this objection can somehow be answered, there is still the problem of the limited nature of any and all cross elasticity measures. A spurious objectivity is lent to the whole enterprise by stating that the cross elasticity of y with respect to x is 3.0. A more meaningful way of articulating this information is to say something along the lines of "In Ohio, in 1967, allowing a length of run of one year, the cross elasticity of y with respect to x was found to be 3.0." The former allows for easy generalizability; not so, the latter.

### 3.3 Conspiracy

On numerous occasions throughout his book, Brozen attacks conspiracy. For example, if express conspiracy occurs, present laws are adequate, and there is no need to outlaw concentration to make this actionable (140).

"Antitrust should focus its attention on improper exclusionary devices rather than on concentration or dominance *per se* .... [I]t should seek out trade restraining, explicit collusion" (405).

This author (147) also characterizes price fixing as "commercial conspiracy." Apart from being rather excessive, this verbiage amounts to mere emotivism. For a conspiracy is nothing more than an agreement opposed by the speaker. Bertrand Russell once said "I'm firm, you're stubborn, he's a pig-headed fool." Cognitively, these three expressions all mean the same thing; they only have different emotional content. Similarly, we can now say, "I [straightforwardly] agree, you [disreputably] connive, he engages in [criminal] conspiracy." There's not a dime's worth of difference between these three modes of expression on the factual plane; emotionally, they are worlds apart. The point is, *every* agreement or contract of which the speaker disapproves can be a conspiracy; the term is without intellectual or cognitive merit.

Brozen (1982: 151) even goes so far as to describe price fixing as a "defrauding" of customers. But why should this be so? I own a widget; Joe owns a widget. Each of the two widgets is the private property of myself and Joe, respectively. We agree (connive? conspire?) not to sell our own widgets, those over which we each have legitimate control, at less than $1 each. We do not compel other sellers to go along with this plan. Even less do we compel buyers to

173

make purchases at this price. Why should this be considered a fraudulent act-a veritable act of theft-upon our customers?

Perhaps this point can best be made in another context. Our author correctly analyzes advertising, and defends this practice from the charge of being an illegitimate barrier to entry. In the following passage (159), each time the word "advertising" is mentioned in the text, "conspiracy" has been added in parentheses. Try the mental experiment of substituting the latter for the former:

> The essence of the argument that advertising (conspiracy) constitutes a barrier to entry is that a new firm finds it difficult to gain customers because advertising (conspiracy) ties them to existing firms. A new entrant, it is argued, faces the 'prohibitively' expensive task of advertising (conspiring) to offset the prior advertising (conspiracy) of existing firms. This view is naive and, in some of its renditions, moralistic. Presumably, firms advertise (conspire) because it is in their interest to do so. But advertising (conspiracy) is expensive to existing firms as well as to potential entrants. It must be productive in some way to be justified. It is not a net social loss; if it were, other firms could provide the same service without advertising (conspiracy) and charge less. If a new firm finds it necessary to advertise (conspire), it is because whatever advertising (conspiracy) does, customers want done.

This exercise can also be performed substituting "collude" or "price fix" or "horizontally merge" for "advertise." If so, the chief conclusion reads as follows: If a new firm finds it necessary to price fix (horizontally merge), it is because whatever price fixing (horizontally merging) does, customers want done.

## 4. Richard Posner

Posner's (1986) contribution to the case for antitrust is truly remarkable. In most instances, authors who favor this public policy content themselves with marshalling the strongest arguments they can in its behalf, usually leave criticism of the points they make to their intellectual opponents. Our present author, in contrast, not only makes as strong a case for government intervention in this regard as anyone else, but, very unexpectedly, also furnishes us with some of the sharpest criticism of it to be found anywhere. At the end of the day, the careful reader is forced to conclude that Posner is indeed an enthusiastic supporter of government meddling with the free enterprise system, but cannot help but wonder exactly why this should be so.

At the outset, however, before we deal with his brief in behalf of government bashing successful business (for that is what, at bottom, antitrust is all about), let us attempt to anticipate, Posner's reaction to our characterization of his work. This will provide a good introduction to his treatment of antitrust, insofar as he employs the same methodology in the one instance as in the other: after stating his thesis, he undermines it himself.

In his view:

> Monopoly . . . and other unhappy by-products of the market are conventionally viewed as failures of the market's self-regulatory mechanisms and therefore as appropriate occasions for public regulation. But this way of looking at the matter is misleading. The failure is ordinarily a failure of the market *and* of the rule of the market prescribed by the common law. . . . The choice is rarely between a free market and public regulation. It is between two methods of public control-the common law system of privately enforced rights and the administrative system of direct public control-and should depend upon a weighing of their strengths and weaknesses in particular contexts (343).

In other words, it is improper for the present author to characterize Posner as an interventionist because of his justification of the antitrust system. Why? Because public policy always[12] involves one or the other method of public control. Notice how neatly, with this highly unusual definition, Posner retires one of his harshest critics from the field: the economist who insists upon the efficacy of the laissez-faire capitalist system. One in which there is no public control whatsoever, neither in defining the rights of person or property, nor in defending them. (For examples, see Benson, 1989, 1990; Friedman, 1989; Hoppe, 1989, 1992a, 1992b, 1992c; Rothbard, 1970, 1973, 1982.)

But this simply will not do. It is one thing to reject a philosophy due to its flaws. It is quite another matter to make it a definitional issue. Despite Posner, we continue to maintain that in addition to his two methods of public control, there is a third option: no public control at all. This is at least a potentially viable option, which should sink or swim based on its own merits. It does not deserve to be ruled out of court, definitionally, before the process of analysis even begins, as Judge Posner would have it.

Our best authority for this stance, somewhat paradoxically, is Posner himself. That is to say, he, on numerous other occasions, does make the more usual distinction between free markets and governmental meddling in them. He allows for a third alternative, apart from the "two methods of public control-the common law system and the administrative system" mentioned above, namely, full free enterprise. He must do so, otherwise government meddling is an impossibility. All intervention must fall into one or the other of these two categories.

Consider the following:

> The problem . . . with using one government intervention in the marketplace (subsidizing workplace injuries and illnesses) to justify another (regulating workplace safety and health {through OSHA}) is that it invites an indefinite and unwarranted expansion in government. (312)
>
> [or,] if as generally assumed, the private sector is more efficient than the public. (493)

Based on his statement of p. 343, on monopoly, this is incomprehensible. How can the private sector be more efficient than the public sector (or the reverse) if there is no distinction between public and private because there are, really, only two different kinds of public sectors? How can there be government intervention into the economy, if "this way of looking at the matter is misleading?"

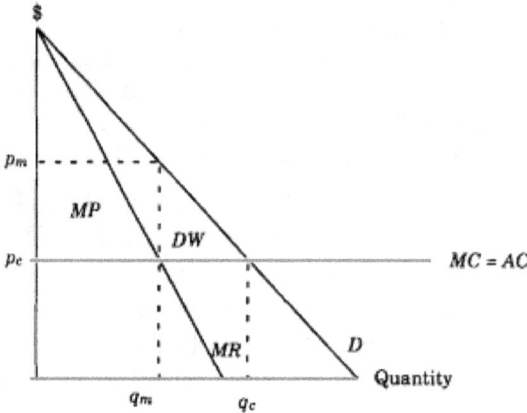

**Figure 2**

*Source*: Richard Posner. *Economic Analysis of Law*, 3rd ed. (Boston: Little Brown, 1986), p. 256.

With this brief introduction, we are now ready to consider the rather weak Posnerian argument for antitrust, and then, paradoxically, his very strong and emphatic intellectual rejection of it, and on the basis of it, somehow, his championing of this public policy.

Our author starts off with the same overused diagram, used by virtually all neoclassical economists. We are treated, once again, to the specter of the downward sloping demand, an *MR* curve which lies below *AR*, a flat *MC=AC*, on the basis of which we derive the dead weight loss due to "monopoly."[13]

But no sooner does Posner make this traditional presentation than he begins the process of subtly undermining it. He says one thing in one place, and the contrary in another, sometimes stating the thesis and the antithesis on virtually the same page. At the very outset, even before the introduction of his analysis, Posner states,

> the monopoly price . . . is the price that a firm having no competition or *fear thereof* would charge. Competition would make the price untenable. (252, emphasis added)

The problem with this is that it is the rare businessman, "monopolist" or not, who has not even the *fear* of competition, let alone some actual competition or other itself. If attainment of "monopoly" price is restricted to such people, it really is an "academic concept" (253) with little or no practical implication. Further, Posner enhances this criticism by conceding that "the establishment of a monopoly price creates an incentive for new sellers to come into the market" (p. 270). However, no sooner has he entertained the point that antitrust may be of only academic interest, but that he reverses field and takes it all back:

> The possibility of entry may seem to make monopoly an academic concept. But sometimes entry takes a long time, or is forbidden, or the new entrant is not able to produce at so low a cost as the exiting firm. (253)

For our purposes, we may safely ignore the case where entry is forbidden. In the modern context, entry can only be prohibited by the state, and if this occurs, we are clearly no longer in the realm of laissez-faire capitalism, the institution we wish to defend against the Posnerian attack.[14]

As well, the worry about entry taking a long time is also without merit. If all Posner wants to do is to show that the market does not always rationally allocate resources,[15] he need not resort to "monopoly." All he need do is point to the fact that the market is rarely if ever in even partial equilibrium, to say nothing of general equilibrium. But unless it is, there are always opportunities for reallocation of resources which are wealth enhancing (Kirzner, 1973). If so, then by stipulation the market misallocates resources continuously. The only problem with this approach is that it gives no reason to expect that any system can do better. And indeed, if we have learned anything from the demise of the Soviet Empire, it is clear that some systems do far worse.

But we may be doing Posner an injustice here.[16] Assume (as neoclassicals do) that price conspiracy has no redeeming virtues for consumers or for anyone else. Also assume that such agreements tend to fail over time. The issue, then, is: how *long* does it really take? If the law can put an end to an activity (without redeeming virtue) *immediately,* then why wait for the "market to work"?

There are two responses to this. First, the less radical argument, which is highly compatible with the neoclassical world view: the market works faster than government. The government typically suffers from bureaucratic and political arteriosclerosis: hearings must be held, rent seeking bribes arranged, sometimes political votes or referenda must be conducted. Even without unusual postponements, the market functions more quickly than the state. If we have learned anything from Hayek (1973), it is that a price system is by far the best communicator known to man.

The more radical response must leave the neoclassical realm and enter that of the Austrian. Here, we must withdraw the previously made assumptions. We can no longer accept the view that "conspiracy" has no redeeming social values. On the contrary, we assert, all commercial agreements between two consenting parties benefit the both of them, at least in the *ex ante* sense. Of the three grounds mentioned by Posner, he is on the firmest foundation with regard to cost, the subject to which we now turn. On this subject Posner states: "The conclusion that *DW* in figure 2 is a net social cost rests on the assumption that a dollar is worth the same to consumers and producers" (256).

Note the position in which this supposition places the analysis. The whole-neoclassical-case against "monopoly" is that it misallocates resources. Deadweight loss is Exhibit A in the brief. But the existence of net social costs rest upon the claim that "a dollar is worth the same to consumers and producers." But what is the status of this claim? It is a mere "assumption." Not a scintilla of evidence is given in its behalf. Not only is this claim merely assumed, not proven, it is not even discussed. Further, it is called into question in a different context by its very author, who states, "the shape and height of people's marginal utility curves are unknown, and probably unknowable" (436).[17]

Let us be clear on what is being said. We are not claiming that Posner has committed a blatant contradiction here. He is not saying in one place that marginal utility is unknowable, and in another that we know it well enough at least to fashion public policy on the basis of it. Nor does he hold that interpersonal comparisons of utility are, and elsewhere also are not, possible. However, what he does, is, if anything, even more problematic.[18] For surely knowledge of interpersonal comparisons of utilities are more risky and difficult than about the size and shape of a single person's marginal utility function. Posner throws up his hands in defeat at the prospect of obtaining information on the less complex of this pair, and bases his justification of antitrust policy on the more complex. The laws of logic would appear to indicate that if proposition A (interpersonal comparisons of utilities) is less secure than proposition B (the size and shape of a single person's marginal utility function), and if public policy cannot be grounded on the basis of B, then it certainly cannot be founded on the basis of A.

Nor does this exhaust the incompatibilities between Posner's defense of antitrust and his statements in other contexts. In the former case, he relies heavily on the existence of an objective, presumably measurable set of cost curves. What then, are we to make of the following quotes:

> Yet it would be difficult for a court to compute the firm's marginal cost. (286)
>
> Suppose a firm makes many different products, and some of the inputs – the time of its executives, for example – are the same for the different products. If the firm cuts the price of just one product, how should executive salaries be treated, in both the short and the long run, in deciding whether the price cut is predatory? (288)
>
> An important but invisible cost of a natural resource such as gas is the foregone opportunity to use it in the future. (338)

These statements present difficulties. This is because foregone opportunities are, by their very nature, subjective. No one can know, judging from actions[19] what the next best alternative was to any decision. If a man buys A at the cost of $1, we know he preferred this item to the money he paid for it. But we don't know his alternative cost: what he would have done with this financial resource had he not just purchased A. Would he have put it in the bank? bought B instead? purchased a stock or bond? placed it under his mattress? Only the man himself can know anything about this contrary to fact conditional.

And yet Posner (and all neoclassicals) makes bold to draw cost curves of other people, purportedly based on their foregone opportunities. But he can never know these even in principle! Does this stop him from weaving apologetics for government intervention on the basis of these curves? Not a bit of it.

States Posner: "Theft is also 'just' a transfer payment; the victim's loss is the thief's gain." But this is not true, unless it can be shown that the subjective evaluation placed on the item by the thief and his victim is identical, a manifest impossibility. Given that there are no utils (they are only a figment of the imagination of the neoclassical economists) and thus that there is no way of comparing the satisfaction of two different people, the thief and the property owner, Posner's statement cannot be true. He asks (258, n. 4), "Is this clearly so when the theft is of a good other than money?" It would appear that the implication here is that it is true that the victim's loss equals the thief's gain, when the good is other than money. If this is what Posner has in mind, he is quite correct. If the thief takes a bicycle or an oxygen tent, for example, he and the victim might place quite different evaluations on the good in question. But, contrary to Posner, the same analysis applies to money. Suppose the thief steals $100. Then, to be sure, the victim loses the $100, and the criminal gains an identical amount. But they may have used these funds for very different purposes, and derived very different amounts of satisfaction from this money, for all we know. We as outside third parties are in no position to distinguish between alternative uses. Suppose that the victim (the thief) were to use the $100 for successful cancer research – this $100 is the straw that breaks the back of the problem and uncovers a cure – and the thief (victim) for tying one on. Can we assert that the former brings about more utility than the latter? Not unless there are utils which may be interpersonally compared.

We have seen no reason to suppose that there is anything on the market deserving of the appellation, "monopoly." The revenue and cost curve argument, and the geometry upon which it is based, has been found wanting. Nevertheless, we must now leave the realm of high neoclassical theory for the moment, and turn to the practical question of how to determine whether "monopoly" power exists in certain specific circumstances. That is, we now assume, just for the sake of argument, that Posner's analysis of the economics of monopoly was correct, and our own critique either non-existent or fallacious.

The basic answer given to this practical question is elasticities. To put this in biblical terminology, by their elasticities shall thee be able to distinguish the "monopolistic" sheep from the competitive goats. In particular, cross elasticities of demand tell all. They indicate how competitive is one good with another. Thanks to them, we can give a non-arbitrary definition to the extent of an industry, without which concentration ratios, market shares, "monopoly" "power" – and all the other accouterments of modern antitrust philosophy – would all become unintelligible.

There are several problems with this tidy scenario. For one thing, elasticities are slippery characters. It is by no means clear which of the many alternative definitions is reasonable. Once again we are aided in our quest to undermine Posnerian economics by Posner himself, who instructs us as follows: Just as in the case of "the calculation of variable cost and therefore of marginal cost," elasticities, too, are "highly sensitive to the time period" (287). In the very short run, elasticities are small and hence "monopoly" is easy to perceive. As the length of the run under consideration increases, however, so does the elasticity, and with it the likelihood of finding "competitive" markets.

So which should be used? There are problems for the Posner thesis either way. In the long run then, elasticities are high, and the finding of "monopoly" unlikely. If our interests are confined to the short run, a determination of "monopoly" is attained more easily, but at the cost of relevance. That is, "monopoly" is only a short run or temporary problem. Posner admits as much, in the context of yet another discussion, this one not on "monopoly" but rather "monopsony." In his view,

> monopsony is a problem only where an input consumes resources that would be less valuable in other uses. Normally this condition is fulfilled only in the short run. (292)
>
> And again, monopsony pricing would have only short run effectiveness. (293)

We must conclude, then, that either "monopoly" is non-existent, or it presents no serious problem, hardly a ringing endorsement for antitrust policy.

There is yet another criticism of elasticity criterion. It arises even if we could somehow overcome the intractable difficulty of length of run: this measure does not have the attributes of a constant in the physical sciences, such as gravity. Rather, elasticity is merely a shorthand numerical summation of an act which took place in a specific geographical locale and at a certain point in history. In other words, we are never entitled to say that the cross-elasticity of y with regard to x is 4.7. At best, we can only say something along the lines[20] of "In Cleveland, in 1991, the cross elasticity of y with respect to x was 4.7." In Posner's view, we should fine people, and perhaps haul them off to jail,[21] on the strength of a statistic, measurement of which has all the likelihood of success as in nailing jello to a tree.

There is also the problem of a "chilling effect" concerning the victims of the anti-"monopoly" law. These businessmen, who have been more successful in attracting customers than deemed appropriate by the Posnerites, will tend to have diminished enthusiasm for a whole host of economically productive practices.[22] Lowering prices, improving product quality, more reliable delivery, better insurance, etc., will all tend to increase consumer satisfaction. But they will also invite the negative attention of the trust busters.

There is also the possibility of mistakes, ordinary human error, either in defining the markets, or calculating the elasticities, or in interpreting them. Again, Posner himself leads the way in pointing out the risks:

> As one might expect, errors are frequent in attempting to define the market for antitrust purposes. A good example is the celebrated cellophane monopolization case, in which the Supreme Court held that cellophane was not a relevant market because there was a high cross elasticity of demand between cellophane and other flexible packaging materials. (281)
>
> The courts have often mishandled economic evidence in antitrust cases. For example, in the U.S. Steel monopoly case, the Supreme Court, in ruling for the defendant, was impressed by the fact that U.S. Steel's market share had declined steadily after the combination of competing steel manufacturers to form the corporation (and that its competitors had not complained about its competitive tactics). The Court failed to recognize monopoly behavior. (270)

One would think that this would give him pause for thought. If we couldn't rely upon the courts "to do the right thing" in this case, from whence springs the optimism that they will do so in future? And yet, the bottom line for Posner is that upon this foundation of sand it is reasonable, it is responsible, to erect a policy affecting virtually the entire economy of the country.

Elsewhere, Posner launches a devastating critique of:

> direct regulation-which itself may be radically imperfect. For one thing, it tends to be more costly than common law regulation, because it is continuous; the common law machinery is invoked only if someone actually is hurt. ... For another thing, direct regulation tends to be more politicized than common law, because it relies more heavily on the public sector and because judges, although public officials, are more protected from political reward and retribution than administrators are. ... A related point is that regulation involves serious information problems. If accident victims have nothing to gain from bringing an unsafe condition to the government's attention, the regulators may have difficulty finding out what exactly the problem is. (345)

But why doesn't Posner realize that antitrust too constitutes "direct regulation"?

As far as information costs are concerned, our author gives an additional reason for preferring "monopoly:"

> An individual margarine producer may be reluctant to advertise the low cholesterol content of his product because his advertising will benefit his competitors, who have not helped defray its expense. (349)

Yet another series of Posner's remarks – this time on the cost reducing proclivities of "monopoly" – undercuts his argument in behalf of antitrust:

Sometimes monopoly will persist without any legal barriers to entry. Maybe the monopolist's costs are so much lower than those of any new entrant that the monopoly price is lower than the price that a new entrant would have to charge in order to cover his costs. (262)

The conditions of supply and demand in a market may be such that one firm can supply, at lower average cost than two or more firms, the entire output demanded; or one firm may have a superior management in whose hands the assets of all the other firms would be worth more than they now are. Either situation could lead to a monopoly through merger that might generate cost savings greater than the costs of the monopoly pricing that would result. *Unfortunately, it is exceedingly difficult to distinguish situations of this kind from the case of a merger to create a monopoly that involves few or no cost savings.* (278; emphasis added)

It is hard to base any conclusions on market share alone, even ignoring the substantial probability that if a firm has grown to a large size other than by recent . . . mergers, it probably is more efficient than its competitors, and its lower costs may outweigh the social costs resulting from its charging a monopoly price. Indeed, its monopoly price may be lower than the competitive price would be. (283)

Further argument given by Posner to undermine his antitrust contention concerns potential competition:

We know that the higher the elasticity of demand facing a firm, the less market power it has; and we also know that if an increase in price will evoke new output from other firms, i.e., if the elasticity of supply is positive, then the firm's elasticity of demand will be higher than it would otherwise be. This suggests, however, that there is no need for a separate doctrine of 'potential' competition. All that is necessary is to define markets broadly enough so that they include firms that, although they do not currently sell in the market in question, would do so if price rose slightly. (284)

But no sooner does he call for a way of incorporating potential competition into the antitrust analysis, on the very same page, he offers a succinct and well chosen criticism of it:

since collusion is largely a short run phenomenon, . . . maybe the elimination of such (new entry) threats is not important enough to warrant antitrust concern, especially since it will be difficult to compute market shares for firms that do not yet have any productive capacity. Indeed, it will be quite difficult to identify which firms are likely to build productive capacity to enter the market if the market price rises above the competitive level. (284)

In summary, let us be clear on what is being said here. We do not claim that these quotes from Posner contradict his case in behalf of antitrust. In his own mind, whether antitrust is justified or not depends upon a "balancing" of the grounds for and against; his conclusion is that the former outweigh the latter. The point being made here is that the support he gives for the case against antitrust is so strong, and in its behalf so weak, that despite his own explicit conclusion, the burden of his analysis vitiates this law.

There are two discernible hypotheses concerning antitrust which may be found in the *Economic Analysis of Law*. First, the neoclassical one given by Posner in those sections of his book dealing with the subject: the market is inefficient, veering off to "monopoly," in all too many cases. The function, purpose, motive, and result of antitrust is to negate this market failure, thereby increasing wealth, efficiency and economic welfare.

Despite the overwhelming popularity of the foregoing thesis in the journal and especially textbook literature, there is actually a second perspective which has some currency within the profession, that of rent seeking.[23] This alternative, in the tradition of the public choice school, tends to be somewhat underplayed by Posner, at least in those sections of his book dealing with "monopoly." It would be unfair to claim, however, that he is unaware of it. Consider the following:

> The deficiencies of public utility regulation viewed as a method of regulating profits, the degree to which it seems deliberately to maintain inefficient rate structures, and the frequency with which it has been imposed in naturally competitive industries and also used to dis- courage competition in industries that have some, but not pervasive, natural monopoly characteristics (railroads, for example) may lead one to wonder whether the actual purpose of public utility regulation is to respond to the economist's concern about the inefficient consequences of unregulated natural monopolies. Maybe instead regulation is a product, much like other products except supplied by the government, that is demanded by and supplied to effective political groups. Under this view there is no presumption that regulation is always designed to protect the general consumer interest in the efficient supply of regulated services. (339)

No, the problem with Posner is not that he is unaware of the public choice thesis; it is, rather, that he chooses not to apply it to antitrust policy. As we have seen, he has waxed eloquent about the court's many shortcomings in this regard (e.g., U.S. Steel, cellophane, etc.). One would think, then, that he would apply the same public choice analysis to antitrust law in general, as he does to public utility regulation, one particular aspect of this legislation. Tragically, he does not.

Why not apply this insight not only to public utility regulation, where it is very apropos, but also to antitrust, where it is equally applicable? Indeed, there is an important literature which views anti-"monopoly" legislation, and the attendant law suits, as nothing but the despoilization of, or takings (Epstein, 1985) from, private property owners (Kolko, 1963).

Posner, instead of calling for the repeal of antitrust, recommends that cartel contracts not be enforced (266). Actually, he goes further than that, characterizing this as an inadequate remedy, and advocates even more stringent controls. Nevertheless, he may have overlooked a better means to the end he favors. It is possible, that is, that strict enforcement will do more to undermine cartel agreements than non-enforcement.[24]

Consider the following. Suppose that the cartel fixes its price, through contract, at a level higher than "normal." This will necessitate an agreement to cut back on quantity, according to some agreed upon formula. If this plan is enforced by law, all will be well for the cartel provided that no outsider comes in. (The cheating cartel member is now little or no problem because, we may suppose, there are very stiff penalties for such behavior written into the contract.) But if one does, and can bribe at least one of the members of the cartel to insist that its cutback provisions be adhered to,[25] all members of the cartel can be put into serious jeopardy of bankruptcy. For if newcomers enter, even without undercutting the price, the first instinct of the cartel will be to produce more, thus lowering prices, in order to meet the competition. But if they are prevented from doing so by one "Trojan Horse" member of the cartel, the new entrants may be able to sweep all before them.

But this scenario will be anticipated by all firms thinking of signing on with a cartel. It will put a serious crimp in all such arrangements. These organizations may still spring up, but an extra cost will clearly be imposed upon them. They will be disadvantaged by having to act so as to exclude the "Trojan Horse," or any member who can be converted into this status by being bought out.

## 5. Conclusion

We have discussed the works of three eminent, conservative, "free market" oriented economists. Certainly, they constitute a reasonable sample of this universe of discourse. We have found that however profoundly they defend market institutions in other contexts, they fail to do so in the case of antitrust. Why this lacunae should exist on the part of people otherwise concerned with economic freedom is for another day's analysis. But that this is so is the only conclusion that may be fairly drawn from the discussion above.

### NOTES

1. Bork's discussion of "allocative efficiency" depends intimately on the "benchmarks" provided by the purely competitive model. But the entire notion of "output restriction" depends logically upon some reference point: "restriction" relative to what? I owe this point to an anonymous referee.

2. This applies, in spades, to the administrative commissions which do the lion's share of antitrust work, such as the Federal Trade Commission. At least there is some check and

balance on the former; they are subject to recall, and great scrutiny in the process of their initial appointments. These controls are greatly attenuated, if not virtually nonexistent, in the case of the civil service. I owe this point to an anonymous referee.

3. Bork also states: "Passably accurate measurement of the actual situation is not even a theoretical possibility; much less is there any hope of arriving at a correct estimate. ... Nobody knows these curves. Even the companies involved do not. The clarity of the graphs misleads many people" (108). In short, Bork himself knows that the demand curves are not "out there." The real mystery is why Bork conveniently forgets his own excellent and essentially Austrian criticism when he addresses himself to policy issues. (I owe this point to an anonymous referee.)

4. The use of the "ring" in this context is rather pejorative; it is akin to describing the ancient and honorable profession of price fixing along the lines of a car theft "ring."

5. Subject to further objections to be made below.

6. Rothbard (1962: 562) seems to have fully anticipated Bork when he talks of an economist who "hold(s) up 'consumers' sovereignty' as an *ethical ideal against which the activities of the free market are to be judged.* Consumers' sovereignty becomes almost an Absolute Good, and any action by producers to thwart this ideal is considered as little less than moral treason."

7. However, he does note that (154) "These considerations do not demonstrate that price cutting could never under any circumstances be a successful method of predation."

8. However, according to the logic of the argument, it should still be prohibited. Failing attempts at murder (rape, robbery, etc.) are still properly illegal, even though they do not accomplish their goals.

9. For a complementary critique of Bork which discusses dynamic and non-equilibrium considerations, see High (1984–1985).

10. Price cutting is illegal because it can be part of a strategy aimed at monopolizing. Raising prices is illegal because it is a way of cutting back on production; it is monopolistic withholding, e.g., the move from P1Q1 to P2Q2. The third alternative, selling at the same price as everyone else can also be held against the law on the grounds of collusion. This highlights yet another intrinsic difficulty with antitrust no matter how circumscribed and limited in application: any law which prohibits all possible choices is not compatible with the rule of law (Hayek, 1973). It is, rather, an aspect of totalitarian dictatorship-in this case, paradoxically to some, on the part of the democratic majority.

11. Exceptions are Rothbard (1962), Armentano (1972, 1982, 1991), High (1984–1985), Block (1977).

12. If we can ignore Posner's "rarely," which appears to be a rhetorical flourish. This we can safely do, since he vouchsafes us no example of a case where the choice *is* between a full free market and public regulation. Indeed, he denies this possibility outright.

13. This word appears in quotation marks to indicate the present author's view that real monopoly is always and ever part and parcel of government grants of special privileges. Fake monopoly, or neoclassical "monopoly," in contradistinction, is solely related to sellers facing downward sloping demand curves. See also Posner (1976).

14. For a critique of patents, the restriction of entry typically defended by neoclassical economists, see Rothbard (1962: 652–660).

15. That is, that the allocation of resources deviates from perfection, or could have been improved were we smarter, or had more time, or were somehow guaranteed arrival at equilibrium.

16. I owe the inclusion of this point to an anonymous referee.

17. "Probably unknowable" is curious. Does Posner believe that one day, with advanced scientific techniques, we will discover the shape and height of these curves?

18. Alternatively, we could interpret Posner's statement (436) as a claim about inter-personal comparisons of utility, in that it is couched in the plural. If so, there is the great danger of an incompatibility in the two views.

19. Human actions (Mises, 1963) and their implications are the only reliable way of ascertaining truth in economics. Merely asking an economic actor to specify the next best alternative foregone as the price of making any given choice is hardly a guarantee of determining it. He could be lying.

20. Posner (281, n. 1) cites Hanushek, Eric A., and John M. Quigley (1980), "What Is the Price Elasticity of Housing Demand?," *Review of Economics and Statistics* 62(3): 449–454. A more accurate title for this article would have been "What *was* the Price Elasticity of Housing Demand?"

21. Cf. the electrical case, where businessmen were actually incarcerated on the basis of this law; in the more ordinary case of treble damages, there is still the threat of a jail sentence if the fine is not, or cannot be paid.

22. Given that businessmen know the elasticity-market share test to which they will be subjected, they will be able, to some degree at least, to act so as to alter these statistics. Surely, this is a misallocation of resources. Yet from the private perspective of businessmen, they will do so as long as the costs are less than the possible losses which result from fighting off antitrust law suits.

23. This is a misnomer, and a very misleading one. Literally, apart from what landlords do, rent seeking applies to the seeking after economic rent, e.g., the difference between the price someone would have been willing to sell for (buy at) and the price at which the deal was actually consummated. To be sure there are "rent seekers" in this sense, zillions of them, because all one has to do to be one is to be an entrepreneur. The real "rent seekers," the ones who attempt to use government and regulatory means for their own ends (and, unfortunately, all too often succeed) would better and more accurately be categorized as booty seekers, or as thieves who work through the political process. Examples of such legalized theft include agricultural land reserves (theft from farmers), heritage preservation laws (theft from owners of hold homes), tariffs (theft from traders), minimum wages (theft from unskilled workers and potential employers), rent control laws (theft from landlords).

24. Nothing stated herein should be taken to indicate agreement with this goal of reining in cartel agreements. From the perspective of the present author, these arrangements, as in the case of all other "capitalist acts between consenting adults" such as the trade of $1.00 for a newspaper, enrich the parties who take part in it, at least in the *ex ante* sense (why else would they agree to do so).

25. We assume that if the members of a cartel unanimously wish to end it, no contract enforcement will deny them this right.

## REFERENCES

Armentano, Dominick T. (1972), *The Myths of Antitrust.* New Rochelle, N.Y.: Arlington House.

-- (1982), *Antitrust and Monopoly: Anatomy of a Policy Failure.* New York: Wiley.

-- (1991), *Antitrust Policy: The Case for Repeal.* Washington, D.C.: Cato Institute.

Benson, Bruce L. (1989), "Enforcement of Private Property Rights in Primitive Societies: Law without Government," *Journal of Libertarian Studies* 9: 1–26.

-- (1990), *The Enterprise of Law: Justice Without the State.* San Francisco, CA: Pacific Research Institute for Public Policy.

Block, Walter (1977), "Austrian Monopoly Theory-A Critique," *Journal of Libertarian Studies* 1(4): 271–279.

Bork, Robert H. (1978), *The Antitrust Paradox: A Policy at War with Itself.* New York: Basic Books.

Brozen, Yale (1982), *Concentration, Mergers, and Public Policy.* New York: Macmillan.

Buchanan, James M. (1969), *Cost and Choice: An Inquiry into Economic Theory.* Chicago, IL: Markham.

--, and G. F. Thirlby (1981), *L.S.E. Essays on Cost.* New York: New York University Press.

Friedman, David (1989), *The Machinery of Freedom: Guide to a Radical Capitalism.* 2nd edn. La Salle, IL: Open Court.

Hayek, F. A. (1973), *Law, Legislation and Liberty.* Chicago, IL: University of Chicago Press.

High, Jack (1984/1985), "Bork's Paradox: Static vs. Dynamic Efficiency in Antitrust Analysis," *Contemporary Policy Issues* 3: 21–34.

Hoppe, Hans-Hermann (1989), *A Theory of Socialism and Capitalism.* Norwell, MA: Kluwer.

-- (1992a), *A Theory of Socialism and Capitalism: Economics, Politics and Ethics.* Boston, MA: Kluwer.

-- (1992b), "The Economics and Sociology of Taxation," in *Taxation: An Austrian View.* Llewellyn H. Rockwell, Jr., ed. Norwell, MA: Kluwer.

-- (1992c), *The Economics and Ethics of Private Property: Studies in Political Economy and Philosophy.* Norwell, MA: Kluwer.

Hutt, W. H. (1940), "The Concept of Consumers' Sovereignty," *Economic Journal* 50: 66–77.

Kirzner, Israel M. (1973), *Competition and Entrepreneurship.* Chicago, IL: University of Chicago Press.

Mises, Ludwig von (1963), *Human Action.* Chicago, IL: Regnery.

Posner, Richard (1976), *Antitrust Law: an Economic Perspective.* Chicago, IL: University of Chicago Press.

Rothbard, Murray N. (1962), *Man, Economy, and State.* Los Angeles, CA: Nash.

-- (1970), *Power and Market: Government and the Economy.* Menlo Park, CA: Institute for Humane Studies.

-- (1973), *For a New Liberty.* New York: Macmillan.

-- (1982), *The Ethics of Liberty.* Atlantic Highlands, NJ: Humanities Press.

Stigler, George (1968), *The Organization of Industry.* Homewood, IL: Richard D. Irwin.

Telser, Lester (1987), *A Theory of Efficient Cooperation and Competition.* Cambridge: Cambridge University Press.

# Part 5:
# Rent Seeking

# Chapter 14
# Property Rights, Information Costs, and the Economics of Rent Seeking

> Although many economists are quick to label the . . . opinions of others . . . as mere prejudice (when they disagree), they cannot recognize ethical bias in themselves. They have convinced themselves that ethical bias is not there – because it 'ought not' to be there: scientists 'ought not' to allow ethical judgments of any kind to enter their work . . . The situation has become so bizarre that output and growth in output are often viewed as if they were ends in themselves, without regard to the uses to which they are put. – G. Warren Nutter, *Journal of Economic Issues*, July 1968

## 1. Introduction

An implicit (and sometimes explicit) assumption in the rent-seeking literature is that rent-seeking behavior can be objectively identified and that "waste" due to rent seeking can be empirically measured (Krueger, 1974; Posner, 1975; Cowling and Mueller, 1978).[1] However, one must carefully distinguish between rent seeking and profit seeking. The former supposedly reduces "social wealth" and is therefore wasteful, whereas the latter increases it. "Profit seeking is used in the rent-seeking literature to distinguish socially productive competition from socially unproductive rent seeking" (Lee, 1985: 212). Making such a distinction is plagued with difficulties, for "it is difficult to determine when 'profit seeking' ends and rent seeking begins" (Lee, 1985: 202).

In this paper I argue that the problem of objectively identifying "wasteful" rent seeking is intractable, and that rent-seeking waste can only be identified by introducing one's own subjective standards of value. This is not to say that the problem of rent seeking is unimportant, but to suggest that identifying rent seeking waste lies outside the boundaries of economic theory. The value judgments used are often hidden or unrecognized in the rent-seeking literature.

I do not argue that economists have nothing to say about rent seeking – that it is all subjective. To the contrary, making the value judgments more explicit is likely to advance economic understanding. The value judgments often involve implicit statements about the "appropriate" system of property rights; considering the economic consequences of alternative property rights systems is essential to understanding political economy.

## 2. Conceptual Problems with the Economics of Rent Seeking

Most students of public choice seem to agree that lobbying governmental authorities for income transfers entails a social cost since resources devoted to rent seeking could have alternatively been used to produce more goods and services. One need not disapprove of the particular lobbying effort to acknowledge this social cost. One who prefers more governmental spending on welfare may favor lobbying to promote that objective, but can still acknowledge that the lobbying itself is socially costly. Similarly, one who advocates a larger defense budget must acknowledge that lobbying by the military-industrial complex also entails a rent-seeking cost.

Designating such activities as "wasteful," however, is arbitrary, subjective, and not very illuminating. Consider the example of businesses and their unions lobbying for protectionism. Such activity has been criticized by economists because of the well-known benefits of free trade and because of its rent-seeking costs (Krueger, 1974). The criticisms cannot be based purely on economic grounds, however, for a fundamental economic reason: benefits and costs are subjective. To the economist, cost is opportunity cost and utility is not measurable.

Protectionism usually benefits a relatively small, well-organized group at the expense of the general public. But because benefits and costs are subjective, economic theory provides little guidance regarding whether or not such activities are wasteful. One may be able to roughly identify the winners and losers in the protectionist game, and to estimate the magnitude of the benefits and costs. Since interpersonal utility comparisons are impossible, however, gains and losses in utility by different individuals cannot be weighed against each other. As Pasour (1985: 131) has said, "utilitarian approaches do not present a way of determining which activities are wasteful . . . [w]hether or not an activity is considered to be rent seeking hinges on one's view of the legitimate role of the state." And as Buchanan (1979: 161) pointed out: "the economist can identify waste in the actions of other people only by imposing his own standard of value." The case against protectionism (and in favor of rent seeking to eliminate it) must be based on one's normative views of the "appropriate" system of property rights. Economic analysis may help form those views, but the analysis itself is not what determines whether protectionism is "good" or "bad."

Bhagwhati (1980) has shown that by eliminating market distortions, some types of rent seeking, i.e., lobbying to eliminate a tariff, increase production possibilities. In these instances rent seeking is supposedly desirable. Even the case for eliminating a tariff, however, cannot be made on purely economic grounds. Transitional losses will be imposed on firms and workers within the protected industry, even though consumers may benefit. Since the welfare loss to protected businesses and workers cannot be objectively compared to the utility gain to consumers, the elimination of a tariff cannot unequivocally be called welfare enhancing. It may lead to increased production of goods and services, but that's not the same as saying that social welfare will increase. Production is merely a criterion imposed by economists as one of *their* standards of evaluation. As discussed in every elementary economics text, *GNP* is at best a measure of economic activity, not necessarily of human welfare (Ekelund and Tollison, 1986: 113).

Lee (1985) has argued similarly that rent seeking can be beneficial if it helps expand the level of public goods provision to the socially optimal level. For example, "farmers engage in political competition aimed at securing funds for water projects . . . up to some point the construction of water projects may be efficiency enhancing . . . It would only be . . . construction of dams that cost more than they are worth that . . . would be considered (wasteful) rent seeking" (207). This is the standard welfare economics approach applied to the problem of rent seeking. One problem with welfare economics, however, is that it assumes costs and benefits are objective and measurable. But only the farmers themselves know the value of irrigation subsidies; outside observers cannot credibly claim such knowledge. Furthermore, if more water is used for irrigation (due to the lobbying efforts), less will be used for other purposes. And who is to say that the foregone uses of water are unworthy if the potential users value them? In short, since the optimal amount of governmental irrigation projects is unknowable to economists or other outside observers, "efficient rent seeking" to achieve such a state is not a very useful concept. It does not make sense to discuss "society's" welfare without accounting for revealed preferences and opinions of those who comprise the society.

Welfare economics poses other fundamental problems for rent-seeking theory, as described by Nutter (1968: 43):

> The trouble with [welfare economics] is clear: the optimum state is never achievable. Society is not only never there; it can never get there. In the first place, the optimum state is constantly changing as wants, resources, and technology . . . change. In the second place, . . . such a state cannot be defined independently of the path through which it is to be approached.

Thus, the use of the pejorative word wasteful to describe rent-seeking behavior is not based on sound theoretical grounds. It is based on implicit value judgments embodied in neoclassical economics regarding the legitimate role of the state and the "correct" structure of property rights.

It is worth repeating that I am not arguing that economists have nothing important to say about rent seeking. I only wish to point out that there are serious conceptual problems that have not yet been resolved.

## 3. Free-Market Monopoly and the Economics of Rent Seeking

The early literature on rent seeking emphasized the social costs of rent seeking through the aegis of the state, particularly the social costs of monopoly. The concept has now been expanded to include many genuinely free-market business activities. Cowling and Mueller (1978), for instance, include in their definition of rent-seeking waste business investment in excess production capacity, excessive accumulation of advertising good-will stocks, excessive product differentiation through R & D, and the entire market for corporate control. To these authors (and others) the social costs of monopoly entail much more than the resources used to lobby governmental authorities for monopolistic privileges; they also include myriad business practices. There is no analytical distinction between public (i.e., political lobbying) and private business behavior.

Littlechild (1980) has provided a powerful subjectivist critique of this approach to the economics of rent seeking. He argues that if one views competition as a dynamic process rather than a static equilibrium condition, and concedes that costs and benefits are subjective, then these activities are likely to be interpreted as a consequence of imperfect information, not monopolistic rent seeking. Furthermore, writes Littlechild, the profits that Cowling and Mueller measure as monopoly waste can be interpreted as the efficiency gains from entrepreneurship. For example, temporary monopoly profits may be the reward for entrepreneurial insight and innovation. Without the reward there will be no innovation, which would itself be costly to society.

Littlechild's critique has been largely ignored by public choice theorists who seem determined to expand the domain of rent-seeking behavior to include nearly every form of private business behavior. Tollison (1982), for example, includes "non-price competition in imperfectly competitive markets" in his list of rent-seeking activities. Colander (1985: 201) includes "the cost of establishing barriers to entry through product differentiation, advertising, marketing or product design ...; the cost of buying up excess capacity; the cost of temporarily using strategic pricing to keep rivals from entering the market; or the establishment of . . . factor market conditions which are optimal for the existing firms but are non-optimal for potential entrants." Salop and Scheffman (1982: 267) go even further by including any "conduct that raises rivals costs." Since it is difficult to imagine *any* competitive business practice that doesn't raise rivals' costs (if rivals choose to compete), the entire private enterprise sector would appear to be plagued with rent-seeking waste according to this definition. Following this reasoning, some economists have concluded that the social costs of monopoly may be far greater than is generally believed, and urge stricter governmental regulation of business to thwart such wasteful behavior.

By developing a world view that sees rent seeking everywhere[2] – a rent-seeking *society* – the theory risks explaining nothing by attempting to explain everything. Furthermore, by ignoring subjectivist insights, the rent-seeking literature gives a misleading view of the social costs of monopoly. It is therefore important that public choice theorists become more aware of the limitations of the economics of rent seeking. The following examples illustrate some of the conceptual difficulties of discussing the social (i.e., rent-seeking) costs of monopoly. I have intentionally chosen of the most extreme examples, that is, ones that are supposedly blatant and obvious instances of rent-seeking waste. I have also chosen examples from recent literature that, to my knowledge, have not yet been discussed by subjectivist critics of the economics of rent seeking.

### 3.1. Collusion to Restrict Output

Collusion to restrict output would appear to be among the least controversial forms of "free-market rent seeking," since economists have long believed that it is a source of monopoly. But even the very word collusion, as used by economists, is not objective. Many of the practices condemned by economists as "collusive" can alternatively be described as "cooperative." Collusion is generally used to describe a conspiracy against the public, implying that that activity is at best a zero-sum game. Since interpersonal utility comparisons are impossible, there are no clear guidelines for determining whether or not "society" benefits from cooperative/ collusive behavior. By the doctrine of revealed preference, all that is known with certainty is that the individuals who are cooperating benefit. Thus, the case for criticizing "collusive" business practices as wasteful rent seeking is not as strong as some may believe.

Cooperation among business rivals can entail social benefits as well as costs. Richardson (1965: 433), for example, has offered the following example of potential benefits of collusion:

> Let us suppose that the operation of a [trade] restriction reduces the uncertainty attaching to the yield from an investment, but at the same time provides greater scope for [monopoly] . . . The reduction of uncertainty should strengthen the willingness to invest, whereas the protection from competition should provide an incentive deliberately to restrict supply. Clearly, the net result cannot be predicted without some knowledge of the magnitude of the factors at work.

By reducing uncertainty, cooperation among business can possibly increase the incentive to invest. Furthermore, another alleged waste – investment in excess capacity – can also possibly be reduced by cooperative business agreements. Such cooperation, however, is often prohibited by antitrust or other regulations, especially in the U.S. Richardson recognized that the motive for collusion may often be to gain monopoly power. But such concerns reveal a further problem in determining whether or not collusion is "wasteful:" evaluating businessmen's motives is a task that seems more suited to mystics than economists.

### 3.2. Wasteful Mergers and Takeovers

Cowling and Mueller (1978: 745) assert that "managerial control over firm revenues is the reward for competing against . . . potential managers successfully" and that the use of resources to achieve these ends should be included in estimates of rent-seeking waste. They deny that the market for corporate control is a disciplining device, and view it as mere rent seeking by corporate management. Similarly, Ravenscraft and Sherer [1987] characterize the market for corporate control as "wasteful" on the basis of a study of 6,000 mergers that took place in the U.S. between 1950 and 1976. The study provided "little support for the hypothesis that the *average* merger or takeover yields significant improvements in efficiency and operating . . . performance" (18; emphasis added). They admit, however, that there are exceptions.

This research epitomizes the normative underpinnings of the rent-seeking perspective on the social costs of monopoly. Cowling and Mueller ignore evidence that mergers *are* often efficiency enhancing, not monopolizing, in arguing that mergers are socially wasteful. By ignoring the role of uncertainty Ravenscraft and Sherer may also be overstating the costs and understating the benefits of mergers. For example, they label most mergers socially wasteful because many acquired firms, after a period of years, are sold off. Acquisitions do not always work out as planned. This is only evidence of social waste, however, if one compares real-world markets with the perfectly competitive ideal where information is costless. But trial and error in the marketplace would appear to be the only way to learn which type of corporate structure is efficient. "Failed" acquisitions reveal which types of corporate structure are inefficient and need to be changed. Ina world of perfect certainty such activities are indeed wasteful; in the real world they are the only way such information can be obtained.

Finally, it is instructive to recall what Alchian and Allen (1967: 325) said about labeling mergers as wasteful:

> Economics gives no judgment about this . . . [A] proposal to prevent voluntary pooling of private wealth is denial of private-property rights. The criterion of 'misdirected' or inefficient use of resources is itself dependent on the normative premise that individuals should have the right to make the choices about use of goods. If we accept a criterion of efficiency relying on open market revelation of values we cannot logically deny full contracting rights to achieve efficiency . . . Yet that is what a refusal to allow mergers amounts to. Of course, there may be grounds *other* than efficiency for objecting to collusions and mergers – private property and individual choice may not be socially desirable institutions.

Thus, by labeling private, voluntary transactions as "wasteful" one is effectively, if not explicitly, stating one's preference for collectivized rather than individual property rights. If one accepts the normative premise that individuals should have rights to make decisions about the use of *their* property, write Alchian and Allen, then "individual freedom of choice is the ultimate test of value or 'proper' direction of resource use in *this* efficiency criterion" (p. 325). Furthermore, "the fundamental ethical question is what 'right' the rest of the public has to require by *law*" that individuals make different uses of their own personal property than they otherwise would.

This is more than just an ethical question. Once it is recognized that statements either in support or critical of mergers are ultimately based on normative premises regarding the "appropriate" system of property rights, it becomes important to investigate the possible economic consequences of alternative property rights systems. It is incumbent upon those who advocate greater governmental controls over merger activity to address the question of how the political authorities can be expected to perform. A public choice analysis of the governmental institutions that regulate corporate mergers would be more enlightening than merely denouncing them as wasteful because they may appear inconsistent with an idealized efficiency norm.

### 3.3. Price Fixing

These same questions apply to price-fixing conspiracies. Consider two salesmen, for instance, who agree to fix the prices of their television sets at a level higher than the existing price. Criticism of that behavior must be based on a belief that the salesmen should not be able to do whatever they wish with their own property - the television sets. Thus, the notion that price fixing is a wasteful activity is based on an implicit premise that favors collectivized property rights over an alternative structure of rights that would protect individual freedom of choice. It is not clear, however, where the moral authority would come from that would "legitimize" legal bans on voluntary price fixing arrangements. Nor is it clear that there are sound *economic* criteria that can be followed. Even if the price fixers succeed in earning monopoly profits – an unlikely occurrence if there are substitute goods and competition, actual and potential – it is not possible to determine the *net* effects on social welfare without making interpersonal utility comparisons.[3]

Whether price fixing is a wasteful activity is a matter of ethics, not economics, as Adam Smith recognized more than 200 years ago. One of the most widely quoted passages from the *Wealth of Nations* is the one about price conspiracies: "People of the same trade seldom meet together, even for merriment and diversion, but the conversation ends in a conspiracy against the public, or in some contrivance to raise prices" (Smith, 1776/1981: 145). But in *the very next sentence* Smith added: "It is impossible indeed to prevent such meetings by any law which either could be executed, or would be consistent with liberty and justice." Smith recognized the potential for price conspiracies, but did not condemn them as "wasteful" and did not think that "social welfare" could be improved by outlawing them.

### 3.4. Raising Rivals' Costs

Business decisions that raise rivals' costs have also been categorized as wasteful rent seeking (Salop and Sheffman, 1983). There is, of course, government-inspired rent seeking that raises rivals costs, such as mandatory product standards and other types of regulation (Maloney and McCormick, 1982). But Salop, Sheffman, and Schwartz (1984: 2) maintain that "analytically, it makes no difference whether rivals' costs are raised privately or by government intervention." Thus, the market process is supposedly the analytic equivalent of the political process, and government-imposed cost increases are just as wasteful and monopolistic as privately procured ones. Among the examples of free-market rent seeking offered in this context are exclusive dealing contracts, advertising and R & D expenditures, vertical mergers, and other forms of non-price competition.

Because the models of "raising rivals' costs" ignore the role of property rights and information costs they face many of the same problems the other theoretical examples of free-market rent seeking face. This is not the place to examine the models in detail, but some fundamental issues are worth discussing.

The literature on raising rivals' costs as a form of rent seeking dwells on the problem of "competitor injury." Businesses are always "injured," however, by the superior performance of their competitors. If such activity is legally restrained, injury will not be eliminated, but reallocated. For example, governmentally-imposed limits on R & D will harm the would-be innovators (the owners, managers and employees of those firms) as well as the potential customers. Thus, to condemn R & D spending as wasteful rent seeking is to implicitly favor one system of property rights over another – one that stifles innovation over one that encourages it. The latter system would inflict governmentally-imposed injury on "dominant firms" that undertake R & D because of a concern about "consumer welfare reduction" (Salop and Scheffmann, 1983: 270). This is a very narrow definition indeed of consumer welfare.

The literature on raising rivals' costs is based on the premise that "exclusionary strategies" are wasteful since they benefit a business at the expense of the business's rivals (Salop and Scheffman, 1983: 270). But this approach may be disputed on the grounds that competition "is the action of endeavoring to gain what another endeavors to gain at the same time" (Hayek, 1948: 96). To the extent this is true, "exclusionary" business strategies are competitive actions, and to condemn them as "wasteful" is to condemn competition.

Rent seeking by raising rivals costs becomes even more questionable once one realizes that legislative bans on such behavior *create* monopoly power. For example, lobbying for advertising *restrictions,* limits on certain R & D spending (i.e., that which is undertaken by one's competitors), and opposition to efficiency-enhancing vertical mergers by one's competitors are examples of government-inspired rent seeking. Rivals always prefer not to have their costs raised by being forced to compete; that's why they often respond to competition by lobbying for protectionist legislation and regulation.

In summary, these examples are only meant to illustrate the inherent difficulties of objectively measuring the rent-seeking costs of monopoly. They are not intended to imply that monopoly is not a problem worthy of academic attention, but to demonstrate the limitations of the economics of rent seeking.


## 4. Rent Seeking and Property Rights

It appears that the problem of objectively identifying "wasteful" rent-seeking activities is indeed intractable, for as Ricketts (1987: 463) stated, "a subjectivist approach to economics makes 'rent seeking' an extremely elusive concept." Ricketts suggests an alternative approach to the study of rent seeking that would "define rent seeking as the use of resources to challenge existing property rights" (462). One advantage of this definition, according to Ricketts, is that it makes a clear distinction between rent seeking and entrepreneurship. Specifically:

> Entrepreneurs accept the status quo distribution of property rights and rent seekers do not. Entrepreneurs trade in property rights. Rent seekers steal, infringe, or attempt to change by political means the established rights of others.

Ricketts's "status quo" approach admittedly has its problems, not the least of which is how to clearly define the status quo. One can imagine numerous instances where ill-defined property rights lead to gaming or "rent-seeking" activity. But it does seem to avoid many of the contradictions of the objectivist approach to the economics of rent seeking.

Another approach Ricketts cites is to stipulate some ideal property rights assignment that is used as a benchmark against which to compare existing arrangements. Ricketts is not very optimistic about this approach, however, for "it is not clear how we can find out what this ideal structure of rights involves" (462).

Granted, defining an "ideal" structure of rights is normative and is likely to be difficult and controversial. But so is agreeing on a definition of the status quo structure of property rights. The efficacy of alternative property rights structures is an arguable and a researchable issue. There is nothing particularly "unscientific" about investigating the economic consequences of alternative property rights structures and then, based on that research, trying to persuade others of what one believes to be a more "ideal" structure of rights. Moreover, this can be accomplished without denigrating "inferior" property rights structures as wasteful. This would involve value judgments, of course, but would make them explicit. This approach would emphasize making greater efforts to understand the *tradeoffs* involved in political economy. An example is Hayek's (1976) discussion of protectionism. Rather than denouncing lobbying for protectionist policies as wasteful,

Hayek explained that the benefits received from competitive markets and economic growth

> are the results of [economic change] and will be maintained only if the changes are allowed to continue. But every change of this kind will hurt some organized interests; and the preservation of the market order will therefore depend on those interests not being able to prevent what they dislike. All the time it is thus the interest of most that some be placed under the necessity of doing something they dislike (such as changing jobs...), and this general interest will be satisfied only if the principle is recognized that each has to submit to changes when circumstances ... determine that he is the one who is placed under such a necessity (94).

Protectionism may provide some individuals with valuable benefits, but at great cost to society, including the rent-seeking costs. That is the tradeoff, and Hayek asserts that an "ideal" property rights system that would serve "the interest of most" would limit such policies, perhaps by constitutional means. There is a long history of this type of research, which was the focus of so-called "classical political economy," or the political economy of Adam Smith.

### 4.1. Rent Seeking and Classical Political Economy

Leland Yeager has succinctly described one important element of so-called classical political economy. The essential task of political economy, says Yeager (1976: 560), is "*not* to maximize social welfare, somehow conceived, *not* to achieve specific pattern of outputs, prices, and incomes." Political economy is concerned instead "with a framework of institutions and rules within which people can effectively cooperate in pursuing their own diverse ends through decentralized coordination of their activities." Yeager (1985: 278) favors an approach to political economy that tries

> to form a conception of the good society by contemplating and comparing alternative sets of mutually compatible social institutions, [The] ideal is whatever arrangements best facilitate the success of individuals seeking to make good lives for themselves in their own diverse ways. Strictly speaking, [the] ultimate criterion is human happiness, however best served. It is a researchable and discussable empirical judgment that happiness is served by institutions that facilitate voluntary cooperation, including ones that secure the rights [to 'life, liberty, and the pursuit of happiness'] mentioned in the U.S. Declaration of Independence. This approach recognizes the importance of mutually beneficial cooperation among individuals ... through the gains from specialization and exchange... The approach recommended here appraises particular principles, rules, institutions, and policies according to whether they are likely to serve or subvert social cooperation in the sense just indicated.

Buchanan (1979] has also recommended that economists follow the approach of classical or "Smithian" political economy. According to Buchanan, Smith's famous discussion of "man's propensity to truck, barter, and exchange one thing for another . . . surely is [Smith's] answer to what economics or political economy is all about" (19).

This approach does not simply advocate voluntary cooperation and deplore coercion, however, but "investigates and compares the types of society likely to emerge from having alternative sets of institutions and rules and, in particular, from whether or not personal rights are recognized and respected" (Yeager, 1985: 279). The emphasis on the protection of personal rights would not preclude governmental intervention. For example, governmental action to deal with externality problems, a system of justice, and the provision of public goods, among other things, would be appropriate. After all, negative externalities are an imposition on the rights of those who are harmed by them. Without unanimous agreement one could not *prove* that such interventions did not involve some "waste," or "political externalities," but such proof would not be required. It is a matter of comparing alternative sets of (imperfect) institutions and evaluating them, the best one can, according to how well they accommodate individuals in "seeking to make good lives for themselves."

An emphasis on property rights structures that encourage human cooperation and limit (but not prohibit) coercion would avoid many objectivist contradictions of rent-seeking theory (as the status quo approach does). It would recognize that the production of goods and services is something that members of society value, but it is not the only (or necessarily the most important) thing. It would also recognize that "wealth" is not only enhanced by producing or physically shaping or growing things, but also by exchanging them. If individual freedom is accepted as an appropriate *ethical* standard, then individuals "should" have the right to enter into what they perceive as mutually beneficial contracts, provided that they do not violate the equal rights of others. This is not to imply that all private behavior is necessarily "good," but that much of it – especially business behavior – has been prematurely condemned because it interferes with some narrow and arbitrary standard of efficiency. Whether such behavior benefits "the society" and if so, to what extent, is researchable and debatable.

Classical political economy would differ in some important ways from the status quo approach. For instance, if a law banned certain types of corporate mergers, lobbying to repeal the law would be labeled rent seeking by the status quo approach since it sought to alter the existing distribution of property rights through political action. But the repeal of such a law would be more consistent with an "ideal" property rights structure that placed a high value on individual cooperation and freedom of contract. One of the "costs" of legal prohibitions on mergers is the abrogation of freedom of contract. One may not value freedom of contract very highly, but it is useful to pose the tradeoff in this way.

Another difference between the two approaches is that classical political economy would place more emphasis on what has been the primary concern of the economics of rent seeking – the effects on economic growth. To the extent that Olson (1982) is correct in his view that rent seeking is a major cause of economic stagnation, a change in the status quo that would limit the power of interest groups (and government itself) would be deemed highly valuable by the classical political economy approach but not necessarily by the status quo approach.

The two approaches also differ in how they would view political attempts to achieve "justice." According to the status quo approach, "ordinary political activity designed to protect an interest group . . . would not be rent seeking because it would be accepted that all property rights are held subject to the existing rules governing the legitimate ways that others may attempt to change them" (Ricketts, 1987: 463).

By contrast, classical political economy is more prone to advocate constitutional restrictions on interest group activity.[4] The roots of this reasoning are in Madison's (1787/1961) philosophical defense of the U.S. Constitution. "Widespread injustice," wrote Madison, is caused by governmental measures that "are too often decided, not according to the rules of justice and the rights of the minor party, but by the superior force of an interested and overbearing majority" coalition of interest groups. To "secure the public good" against the dangers of interest-group politics, wrote Madison, was the primary objective of the architects of the U.S. Constitution.

Finally, classical political economy reveals further contradictions in the economics of rent seeking. For example, writers who criticize rent seeking through the aegis of the state usually recommend – implicitly or explicitly – improved governmental enforcement of private property rights as a way of reducing such waste. "To reduce [rent seeking] waste . . . the . . . power of government is employed to help define and enforce private rights" (Anderson and Hill, 1980: 7). The contradiction is illustrated by so-called free-market rent-seeking. By designating advertising, R & D, price coordination, and other private, voluntary acts as wasteful (and recommending governmental regulation to reduce such waste), rent-seeking theorists implicitly or explicitly recommend that the power of government must be used to *attenuate* private rights, not protect them. Hence the contradiction.

Another contradiction is that greater governmental control over private business behavior will probably *increase* the types of social costs associated with rent seeking. Businesses subject to such controls are likely to devote resources toward influencing governmental decision makers. Businesses subject to American antitrust regulation, for example, have lobbied the antitrust authorities to permit their own mergers, pricing practices, and other business activities, but to prohibit those same activities when undertaken by their rivals (Armentano, 1982; Baumol and Andover, 1985).

# 5. Conclusions

A subjectivist view of costs and benefits makes the distinction between rent seeking and entrepreneurship non-operational. Consequently, whenever public choice scholars attempt to identify rent-seeking activities and to measure the social costs of rent seeking, they are *implicitly* making a statement about what the appropriate structure of property rights ought to be. This breeds confusion because what sometimes passes for scientific evidence is merely the expression of the researcher's own standard of value. One person's waste is another's cherished activity.

It would be beneficial if future research paid closer attention to the property rights implications inherent in discussions of the "rent-seeking costs" of various activities. There is nothing particularly "unscientific" about attempting to understand these implications and to clarify the tradeoffs they represent. In fact, one would think that merely labeling activities as "wasteful" without thoroughly investigating their economic consequences is somewhat of an unscientific practice.

This is not to suggest that rent seeking is not a serious economic problem. There is much evidence (Olson, 1982) that it can be quite costly in terms of stifling economic growth. Rent seeking "has been with us always" (Buchanan, 1980: 3), and has been a concern of scholars and statesmen for centuries. Over 200 years ago James Madison warned that interest-group politics, if not restrained by constitutional means, fostered "instability, injustice, and confusion," which are "the mortal diseases under which popular governments have everywhere perished." So-called rent seeking is an age-old problem of political economy that can be discussed more clearly once one is aware of the difficulties inherent in the concept.

## 5.1. Summary
So-called rent-seeking behavior can supposedly be objectively identified and measured. But since benefits and costs are subjective and interpersonal utility comparisons are impossible, rent-seeking "waste" can only be identified by introducing one's own standard of value. Economic understanding is likely to be improved by recognizing the limitations of the economics of rent seeking and making the value judgments embodied in it more explicit. The value judgments usually connote an "appropriate" structure of property rights; considering the economic consequences of alternative property rights structures is essential to understanding political economy.

## NOTES

1. This issue is also examined by Pasour (1986) and Ricketts (1987). Neither author, however, is primarily concerned with so-called free-market rent seeking, which is a prominent concern of this paper.

2. Buchanan (1983) extends the concept of rent seeking to the issue of bequests and inheritance, and there are other extensions as well, i.e. to the act of theft. The present discussion, however, deals exclusively with *business* practices that have been designated as wasteful in the rent-seeking literature.

3. Armentano (1986: 62) reviews the possible social *benefits* of price coordination that have been discussed in the economics literature. These include, for example, saving a firm from bankruptcy or merger, allowing for more non-price competition, reducing information costs to firms, reducing price uncertainty to buyers and sellers, reducing the uncertainties of market entry, thereby encouraging it, restricting non-price rivalry, and stimulating research and development, among other things.

4. Ricketts (1987: 463) recognizes this distinction when he writes: "For the purpose of establishing a definition of rent seeking ... it is necessary to distinguish between property rights in resources held at a given point in time (the status quo) and the constitutional rights ... to attempt to change the status quo."

## REFERENCES

Alchain, A. A., and W. Allen (1967), *University Economics.* Belmont, CA: Wadsworth.

Anderson, T., and P. J. Hill (1980), *The Birth of a Transfer Society.* Stanford, CA: Hoover Press.

Armentano, D. (1986), *Antitrust Policy.* Washington, D.C.: Cato Institute.

Bhagwati, J. (1980), "Lobbying and Welfare," *Journal of Public Economics* 14: 395–401.

Baumol, W., and J. Ordover (1985), "The Use of Antitrust to Subvert Competition," *Journal of Law and Economics* 28: 247–265.

Buchanan, J. (1979), "What Should Economists Do?," in G. Brennan and R. Tollison (eds.), *What Should Economists Do?* Indianapolis, IN: Liberty Press.

-- (1980), "Rent Seeking and Profit Seeking," in J. Buchanan, G. Tullock, and R. Tollison (eds.), *Toward a Theory of the Rent-Seeking Society.* College Station, TX: Texas A&M University Press, 3–15.

-- (1983), "Rent Seeking, Noncompensated Transfers, and Laws of Succession," *Journal of Law and Economics* 26: 71–85.

Colander, D. (1985), "Some Simple Geometry of the Welfare Loss from Competitive Monopolies," *Public Choice* 45: 199–206.

Cowling, K., and D. Mueller (1978), "The Social Costs of Monopoly Power," *Economic Journal* 88: 727–748.

Ekelund, R., and R. Tollison (1986), *Economics.* Boston, MA: Little, Brown & Co.

Hayek, F. A. (1948), *Individualism and Economic Order.* Chicago, IL: University of Chicago Press.

-- (1976], *Law, Legislation, and Liberty,* Vol. 3. Chicago, IL: University of Chicago Press.

Krueger, A. (1974), "The Political Economy of the Rent-Seeking Society," *American Economic Review* 64: 291–303.

Lee, D. (1985), "Marginal Lobbying Cost and the Optimal Amount of Rent Seeking," *Public Choice* 45: 206–213.

Littlechild, C. (1980), "Misleading Calculations of the Social Cost of Monopoly Power," *Economic Journal* 91: 348–363.

Madison, J. (1787/1961), *The Federalist Papers*, no. 10. New York.

Nutter, W. (1968), "Economic Welfare and Welfare Economics," *Journal of Economic Issues* 2: 166–172.

Olson, M. (1982), *The Rise and Decline of Nations*. New Haven, CT, and London: Yale University Press.

Pasour, E. C. (1986), "Rent Seeking: Some Conceptual Problems and Implications," *Review of Austrian Economics* 1: 123–143.

Posner, R. (1975), "The Social Cost of Monopoly and Regulation," *Journal of Political Economy* 83: 807–827.

Ravenscraft, D., and F. Sherer (1987), "The Long-Run Performance of Mergers and Takeovers," in K. Chilton and M. Weidenbaum (eds.), *Public Policy toward Corporate Takeovers*. New Brunswick, NJ: Transaction Publishers.

Richardson, G. B. (1965), "The Theory of Restrictive Trade Practices," *Oxford Economic Papers* 17: 432–449.

Ricketts, M. (1987), "Rent Seeking, Entrepreneurship, Subjectivism, and Property Rights," *Journal of Institutional and Theoretical Economics* 143: 457–466.

Salop, S., and D. Scheffman (1983), "Raising Rivals' Costs," *American Economic Review* 73: 267–271.

--, and W. Schwartz, [1984], "A Bidding Analysis of Special Interest Regulation: Raising Rivals' Costs in a Rent-Seeking Society," U.S. Federal Trade Commission Bureau of Economics Working Paper.

Smith, A. (1776/1981), *An Inquiry Into the Nature and Causes of the Wealth of Nations*. Indianapolis, IN: Liberty Fund.

Tollison, R. D. (1982), "Rent Seeking: A Survey," *Kyklos* 35: 575–602.

Tullock, G. (1967), "The Welfare Costs of Tariffs, Monopoly, and Theft," *Western Economic Journal* 5: 224–232.

Yeager, L. (1976), "Economics and Principles," *Southern Economic Journal* 42: 559–570.

-- (1985), "Rights, Contract, and Utility in Policy Espousal," *Cato Journal* 5: 259–294.

# Chapter 15
# All Government is Excessive: A Rejoinder to Dwight Lee's "In Defense of Excessive Government"

## 1. Introduction

Given Dwight Lee's stalwart free enterprise credentials, it is more than passingly curious that the title of his 1998 Presidential Address to the Southern Economic Association was "In Defense of Excessive Government."[1]

After all, Lee is Professor of Economics and holder of the Bernard B. and Eugenia A. Ramsey Chair of Private Enterprise Economics at the University of Georgia. In addition to holding a named chair in "Private Enterprise Economics," he is also the former president of the Association of Private Enterprise Educators, a group devoted to not only the study of markets, private enterprise, property rights, and capitalism, but one which

> is largely, but not exclusively, made up of academic economists with strong free market views and strong skepticism of government actions (it started many years ago as an association of free enterprise chair holders but has expanded to include anyone with a strong free enterprise perspective).[2]

As well, Lee has been associated with another group that claims a market orientation, the Center for Study of Public Choice, both at George Mason University and at Virginia Polytechnic Institute & State University. Other like-minded organizations with which he is connected include the Mont Pelerin Society, the Center for the Study of American Business at Washington University, the Earhart Foundation, and the Olin Foundation. In his association with the Foundation for Economic Education, he writes a regular commentary on free enterprise economics, previously in *The Freeman*, and now for its *Ideas on Liberty*. To top it all off, he has been included on the free-enterprise-oriented Templeton Honor Roll for Education in a Free Society.

If there were any doubt that Lee has had a long and illustrious career in promoting and defending the institutions of economic freedom, a brief perusal of the titles of his publications in his three-dozen-page-long vitae will convince any reader otherwise. Nor is it controversial to claim that as well as being widely interpreted as an exponent of economic freedom, this author sees himself in precisely this light. In fact, Lee announces at the very outset of his article, "I don't have much practice defending government," and mentions

> those with whom I have long identified, classical liberals working in the field of public choice who advocate if not a minimal government, certainly one that is limited far more than any existing democracy.[3]

All of this makes Lee's title incomprehensible, in that it would appear to be a 180-degree shift from nearly all of his past publication record. Further, the title is not a misnomer; Lee actually defends not only government intervention into the economy, but even intervention to an admittedly "excessive" degree.

Before I launch into a critique of this article, I would like to make several introductory remarks. First, I admire the extremism of this article. If one is going to defend government, why be a moderate? No, go "whole hog" and defend the most extreme version of this philosophy.[4]

Second, as a critic of the claims of the Public Choice School to be a spokesman for economic freedom and capitalism,[5] I am delighted that Lee announces himself as intending to "use arguments drawn from, and consistent with, the public choice perspective to make my case."[6] Of all those who explicitly defend public choice, Lee, alone in my opinion, clearly appreciates its (coercive) socialistic and interventionistic core. In contrast, all other advocates of this school of thought mistakenly see it as on the side of the free enterprise angels.[7] In other words, if public choice underlies his essay, and it clearly does, then so much the worse for public choice.

Third, Lee writes "I certainly would not have written this article if it were going to be subjected to a rigorous review process."[8] This gives me pause; I would not want to criticize an ill-considered, half-thought-out article, preferring to "hold my fire" for the best work of an intellectual opponent. On the other hand, this was Lee's 1998 Presidential Address to the Southern Economic Association, and does appear in the *Southern Economic Journal* (albeit without benefit of refereeing). Either of these considerations alone, and, certainly, both of them together, suggest that the article is "fair game" for criticism. In addition, authors are responsible for all of their work, including op-ed pieces, chapters in books, and published speeches, none of which are refereed.

Fourth, Lee announces that the reason he accepts, even urges, retaining admittedly inefficient government programs is because we cannot rid ourselves of them without also being forced to make do without being able to "secur(e) advantages that only government action can provide." He writes that "to get government to provide things we want, like the Washington Monument, we will have to put up with excessive spending on other government activities that cost more than they are worth."[9] In contrast, to foreshadow my rejoinder, I shall claim that there are no desirable goods or services that "only government action can provide," and that, to the extent the public wishes to view things like the Washington Monument, the market is fully capable of providing them.[10]

Further, to the extent that it is true that "only government action can provide" certain things, this concerns mass murder[11] and only mass murder.[12] Every other government function (defense, courts, police, helping the poor, etc.) has been accomplished by private individuals.

Fifth, Lee is guilty of misusing several economic phrases (e.g., "rent seeking" and "collective action"), and correcting him on these matters would alone render worthwhile a response to his essay.

I shall now proceed with my critique of this very interesting essay, following Lee's own outline.


## 2. Compared to What?

In this section, Lee claims that just because there are "inevitable market failures" does not mean that government ameliorative action is justified, because the proper comparison or yardstick for commerce is not perfection. He then goes on, paraphrasing James Buchanan, to make the identical point with regard to the latter:

> [my] argument might be taken as a criticism of the naiveté of both the market-failure welfare economists and the market-works-politics-fails stance of many modern public choice new neo-classical economists. By comparison with idealized standards, both markets and politics fail.[13]

In other words, rather than seeking a "moral equivalence" between market and state, Lee finds an "economic equivalence." Both market and state have been unduly attacked, by, in effect, extremists of either side.[14] Moderators of the ilk of Lee and Buchanan are needed to set the balance right by showing that *both* the critics of the market *and* the critics of the government are in error.

There are several problems with this analysis. Let us consider the concept of "market failure," since Lee uses it as a stick with which to beat up on free enterprise. It cannot be denied that there is "market failure" in the sense that not every decision made by all businessmen will always be correct. There is, after all, such a thing as entrepreneurial error. If we are to include under the rubric of "businessmen" all economic actors, including employees, investors, savers, etc., then room for error expands even more. But this is not at all what is commonly meant by "market failure," nor does it capture Lee's understanding of it, which is fully compatible with common usage within the economics profession. This concept is not a synonym for mistakes made by human beings in their bartering and trucking activities. Instead, at least within the realm of professional economics, it signifies particular "failures," such as monopoly, public goods, externalities, income inequality, discrimination, etc.

My point, in rejoinder, is that there is no such thing as market failure in this sense.[15]

Second, even if there were such a valid concept, Lee's assertion cannot be maintained. To show this, let us grant his claim that markets fail compared to some ideal situation that exists in the never-never land of neoclassical texts. Typically, this is the world of perfect competition. This makes it curious that Lee supportively cites Bork's extremely well-founded and insightful statement:

> A determined attempt to remake the American economy into a replica of the textbook model of competition would have roughly the same effect on national wealth as several dozen strategically placed nuclear explosions.[16]

But if perfect competition is not the standard Lee uses to find free enterprise wanting, then to what *would* he contrast it to achieve this end?

In sharp contrast, one does not need any such ideal to call into question governmental actions. The state stands condemned in and of itself, once it is realized that the public sector is based upon coercion. Indeed, government is the institutionalization of "coercion," as Lee himself acknowledges.[17] But if this is so, it raises a per se difficulty with these institutional arrangements, one which simply does not arise in markets.

If Mr. A trades an apple for Mr. B's berries, then each is made better off in the ex ante sense of anticipations. That is, neither would have agreed to the trade had not A preferred berries to apples, and B preferred apples to berries. A's profit is the difference to him between his valuations of the higher-ranked berries and the lower-ranked apples. B's profit, likewise, is the divergence in value to him between the more-valued apples and the less-valued berries. In every voluntary transaction, we can infer that all participants are better off, or else they would not participate. So much for markets.[18]

In the public sector, things are very different. Here, we may suppose that a tax of $100 is levied against Mr. C that will allow the government to engage in a service, call it mosquito abatement. Can we infer from this transaction that Mr. C values the service more than the costs? That he, for example, gains $150 from the spraying of swamps, and thus earns a profit of $50? In a word, no. This transaction is a coercive one, not a voluntary one,[19] so there need not be mutual gains.

Thus, to find fault with the free market, one has to create idealized models against which to compare the free market. We do not need to resort to any such concept as an "ideal government" to find fault with our own real government. To the contrary, governments stand condemned since they are intrinsically coercive, and for that reason alone are "economic failures."

## 3. The "Invisible Hand" Behind Rent Seeking Waste

There is perhaps no greater misnomer in all of economics than "rent-seeking" as employed by the Public Choice school, since, by that term, they mean nothing less than theft: the seizure, by force or the threat of force, of other people's property. Given that this is the case, and that Lee himself characterizes government behavior as "coercion,"[20] a far more descriptive phraseology for this behavior would be "booty seeking" or "theft seeking" or "piracy seeking" or "robbery seeking" or "larceny seeking." As it stands, "rent seeking" is an unwarranted attack on the ancient and honorable profession of garnering land, housing, or property rent, or, as in profit seeking, an attempt to gain economic rent. Lee admits that "the term 'rent seekers' is commonly used as a pejorative."[21] Why should such an innocent activity as seeking rent be used to depict something so highly problematic?

### 3.1 Private Interest Dominates the Political Process
A more substantive difficulty with Lee's treatment is that in his attempt to "defend ... rent seekers" he erroneously equates this activity with "self-interest."[22] Now a "great insight" of the Public Choice School is that people do not sprout angel's wings when they enter government service; rather, they take their self-interest right along with them into the bureaucracy. But to identify self-interest and "booty seeking" is to commit a serious logical error. As Adam Smith has shown, self-interest in the private sphere leads, through the invisible hand, to good effects. It is quite a leap in logic, however, to posit a similar phenomenon under statism. There is a world of difference between theft and self-interest, despite the fact that among the criminal class, the latter leads to the former. Similarly, sexual obsession can provoke rape, but we can certainly distinguish between the two phenomena.

It is as a result of these musings that Lee brings himself to declare that "we should (not be) particularly offended by rent seekers."[23] While he attempts to mitigate this rather ill-considered statement, he succeeds only partially,[24] and contents himself with noting that markets are more congruent with consumer desires than are political systems. But the problem goes far deeper than that. If we are correct in identifying "rent seeking" with outright (albeit legalized) theft, then to say that we should not be offended by "rent seekers" is to say that we should not be offended by robbers, provided that they have obtained warrants for their actions from legislatures.[25]

### 3.2 The Problem of Providing Public Goods
Lee maintains that "market incentives leave ... public goods ... greatly under-provided, if provided at all." This is problematic in that this author goes out of his way to present us with a joke: "How's your wife? Compared to whom?" The point is that economists think naturally in terms of alternatives, and that "pointing out that something is flawed is not a meaningful criticism of it unless better alternatives are possible."[26]

Yet, in the present context, Lee is doing precisely what he warned us against with his joke. He is pointing out that with markets, public good production is sub-optimal. In the spirit of his joke, we may reply, "So what?" Unless Lee can show that government, with all the flaws in it that he himself acknowledges, is an *improvement* over allegedly imperfect markets in this regard, his carping amounts to naught, by his own admission. But he does not even attempt to show this, let alone succeed in so doing.

Lee's claim that markets will under-optimally provide public goods may sound all right to the economic ear, but this is only because sentiments of this sort have continuously been drummed into our ears as undergraduates, graduate students, and beyond. Actually, for a profession that prides itself on basing all claims on empirical support,[27] Lee's claim, pivotal to his thesis, is embarrassingly short on statistical verification. Moreover, there is not a single solitary good or service characterized as a "public good" that has not been provided privately.[28] The common list of public goods provided privately includes defense (handled by private police forces and detective agencies),[29] courts and a judicial system (via such organizations as the American Arbitration Association),[30] roads and highways (provided by private firms, private communities, and other entities),[31] lighthouses (provided by long-shoremen's associations or dock owners),[32] mosquito spraying, welfare (through private charities including churches and non-profit organizations),[33] and more. As for markets providing less than optimal amounts of these goods and services, Lee, as well as the entire economics profession, has yet to provide any criterion for optimality other than mere "blackboard economics" (we are all familiar with marginal, average, and total private and social utility and cost curves).

However, a basic postulate of neoclassical economics is that its tenets are made up of falsifiable propositions. Yet, no such set of clearly falsifiable propositions has been offered, or can be offered, not least because of the essential subjectivity of cost and utility.[34] Nor does Lee even attempt to meet this challenge. Not only does he not specify any empirical measure for optimal government involvement in the economy, he also eschews any attempt to define a criterion for determining this measure. In this regard, he joins forces with that other advocate of free enterprise, John Kenneth Galbraith, who was forever complaining about niggardliness in the public sector, and opulence in the private.[35]

In behalf of the ballot box vote, Lee writes that "preferences are communicated candidly," since there need be no fear of "being exploited by free riders."[36] Both of these declarations are suspect.

As far as candidness is concerned, Lysander Spooner had the following to say:

> [V]oting is not to be taken as proof of consent. . . . On the contrary, it is to be considered that, without his consent having even been asked, a man finds himself environed by a government that he cannot resist; a government that forces him to pay money, render service, and forego the exercise of many of his natural rights, under peril of weighty punishments. He sees, too, that other men practice this tyranny over him by the use of the ballot. He sees further, that, if he will but use the ballot himself, he has some chance of relieving himself from this tyranny of others, by substituting them to his own. In short, he finds himself, without his consent, so situated that, if he use the ballot he may become a master; if he does not use it, he must become a slave.

And he has no other alternative than these two. In self-defense, he attempts the former.[37]

As concerns free riders, Lee has no way of demonstrating that any exist, nor, if this hurdle can somehow be overcome, that entrepreneurs cannot internalize any ensuing externalities. Instead, the author implicitly assumes that they exist and cannot be overcome in this manner. Yet, logically, this is not enough. If free riders do exist, then we are all free riders. For example, we all benefit from the existence of Mozart, but none of us have ever lifted a hand to help him. That is simply a part of civilization. To turn this into a market failure is highly problematic.

Lee writes the following: "without government action, we would find ourselves with less national defense, less crime prevention, and less environmental quality than we have."[38] Absent statistical justification, such a claim seems very rash. Indeed, the truth would appear to be the very opposite. For example, with the advent of the movie "Pearl Harbor" and several critical reviews of it, even the meanest intelligence is finally becoming aware of the fact that it was FDR, running on a "peace" platform,[39] who incited the Japanese into waging war on the United States.[40] Likewise, it was the U.S. government, recklessly ignoring President George Washington's insightful "Farewell Address" where he warned of "entangling alliances" and foreign adventurism, which got us into World War I, the Korean "police action," Viet Nam, and altogether too many other invasions of foreign countries in recent days to even mention. This is "national defense?" A case can easily be made to the effect that it is the very opposite: *offense*.

Further, the state is, on net balance, a creator of crime, not a preventer of it, even if we do not count its own acts as criminal. To consider a single case, the prohibition of drugs calls into serious question the direction of causation between the public sector and crime.[41] Then, too, government categorizes so many victimless "crimes" as illegal, each of which is responsible for yet more crime and "less crime prevention." Under this rubric, we must count laws against gambling, prostitution, markets in body parts,[42] pornography, and the prohibition of alcohol during previous epochs.

What of environmental protection? Here, too, it is difficult to make the case that the government is the solution, not the problem, Lee to the contrary notwithstanding. The state contributes to environmental despoliation in many ways. It contributes to the "tragedy of the commons" through the sheer extent of its land holdings,[43] and by not allowing for the privatization of endangered species. It exacerbates air pollution by not interpreting such behavior as trespass against private property.[44] Its much-vaunted so-called market-based solutions, tradable emissions rights, are but variants of socialism, and, thus, vulnerable to the familiar arguments against central planning.[45] If Lee wishes to base his defense of government upon its provision of environmental amenities, he will have a tough row to hoe.

Even if it were the case that government made a positive net contribution to national defense, protection against crime, and promoting environmental quality, how can we account for his view that all this can be attained for "*certainly* less than people desire at the cost of providing them?"[46] Whence springs all the certainty? Without markets, one would have thought we were at sea without a rudder; there would no way of determining whether the citizens value government's "contributions" more than its costs. Implicitly, Lee has a method for determining this, but he seems curiously unwilling to vouchsafe this method to the rest of us.

In his effort to be even handed and balanced, Lee concedes that "public provision of public goods is plagued with the same type of free-rider problems as private provision."[47] He mentions in this regard "rational ignorance" and "expressive voting." This is all well and good as far as it goes, but it does not go far enough. Another advantage enjoyed by the dollar vote vis-à-vis the ballot box vote is that in the former but not the latter system, there are entrepreneurs with an invisible hand incentive to internalize externalities. If and to the extent that the concept of spill-over effects is a coherent one,[48] markets can solve them.

In fact, it is no exaggeration to say that such "market failures" stem not from the market itself, but from failures to allow private property to extend far enough. For example, the so-called external economy offered by traffic lights to motorists or by street lights to passers-by is solely a function of the fact that roads, highways, and streets are owned and managed by the public sector in the first place. Were this not the case, that is, were these amenities allowed to be offered to customers by entrepreneurs, the entire difficulty would vanish in a trice. Traffic and street lights would be provided as they now are, by private gated communities, super markets, shopping malls, etc. Disneyland, for example, is not exactly bereft of this type of street furniture, and all of it comes entirely courtesy of the voluntary sector. There is not one modicum of coercion involved, as occurs via government roads.

The essence of Lee's thesis is that

> because transmitting demands for public goods to government suppliers is so difficult, not only is much of this waste [excessive and inefficient government programs] understandable, it can also serve a useful purpose. . . . Attempts to reduce the inefficiency that comes inevitably with supplier control over providing public goods can easily result in greater inefficiency by reducing the amount of public goods provided.[49]

Difficulties abound, here. For one thing, in the absence of voluntary markets, we never have incontrovertible evidence that consumers wish to have public goods at their disposal. Consider a park in this regard. If it is private, and if the enterprise shows a profit, then we know that customers value this amenity more than the cost of bringing it to them. But in the case of the public park, we know no such thing, and cannot know it. In a democracy, all we know is that certain people were forced, either directly or indirectly on the basis of tyranny of the majority, to pay for this park. Some of them may even use it. But there is no preference that can be objectively revealed, demonstrating for one and all to see, that the people value the park more than its alternative costs.[50]

For another, markets are perfectly capable of providing any and all goods and services characterized by Lee as "public." Firms may not do so to the extent that Lee deems optimal, but, as he never offers any criterion on the basis of which this may be objectively judged, we are justified in ignoring him on this point, just as we do with Galbraith, and for similar reasons on similar issues.

For a third thing, there is no logical stopping point in this thesis. If we take it at face value (and how else can we take it), the theory can justify *any* level of government intervention.[51] Once allow the cloven hoof of admittedly excessive state depredations with no stipulated stopping point, where does it end? It can theoretically culminate with 100% totalitarian government, of the sort the bad old USSR only dreamed about.

### 3.3 The Case of the Military-Industrial Complex

In this section, Lee tries to show that even the vast waste attendant upon the Military-Industrial Complex (MIC) can be justified. After all, without this great inefficiency, which is accounted for by the "rent seeking" payment which goes to the bureaucrats responsible for it, we would not have an army at all, or far too small an army, and that would be intolerable. Lee writes: "The case for the MIC then is based on the very real possibility that it is better to have an adequate supply of national defense at excessive cost than an inadequate supply at least cost."[52]

This sounds as if he makes these things up as he goes along. How does Lee know this is so? How can he defend against the claim that on the contrary, it is better to have a (slightly) inadequate supply of national defense at (moderate) cost than a (fully) adequate supply at (gargantuan excessive) cost? Whatever happened to marginal analysis? Surely, Lee would agree that if we devoted 100% of the GDP to defense, and none to food, and we all died as a result, that this would be inferior to a situation where we had an army slightly too small for our needs, but plenty of food. But this directly contradicts his statement.

Another problem is that only in the market can such marginal costs and benefits be compared with one another. Under ballot box voting, with no prices emanating from the process, it is impossible to make such comparisons. This is precisely the problem of central planning, which underlies the Austrian case against all such institutions.[53] Lee doesn't know, and cannot know, that the market is out of balance in this regard. He must ever be blind to the issue of whether or not the government allocates resources in the manner he describes.[54]

Lee delivers himself of this opinion: "Each [representative] would . . . know that his or her constituents could benefit from . . . national defense."[55] Yet, for all we know as disinterested scientists, the entire polity may be composed of pacifists who revile the idea of protecting themselves. People may *say* they wish to be defended, but they can be lying in a way they cannot be when they plunk down a dollar on the barrelhead and take away some apples. What would it *mean* for such a person to deny that he ranks the apples higher than the dollar he just voluntarily paid for them? People may *vote* for an army in a referendum, or in favor of politicians who promise to provide defense, but, as even Lee has conceded in his analysis of the weaknesses of the public sector, this does not definitively establish any such preference.

Lee continues with this problematic claim: "Residents of South Carolina receive as much protection from a submarine patrolling the oceans as do residents of California no matter whose taxes pay for it."[56] It is plausible that if the submarines were patrolling the eastern Pacific, the Californians would feel safer, and the South Carolinians neglected, and if the subs were in the western Atlantic, then the very opposite would be the case.[57] The point is that the country cannot necessarily be treated as one single unit. Even if it were not so vast, still, police or army manpower allocated to one area presumably has a higher marginal product there than somewhere else.

Consider Jude Wanniski's argument concerning the military-industrial complex:

> President Bush now is running around Europe trying to persuade our NATO allies and the Russians that the ABM Treaty is obsolete, because the Cold War is over. But why then abrogate that treaty and spend a trillion dollars on more exotic weapons? For the first time in the history of the world, we are at the tippy-top of the world political economy. There is not a single nation that shows the slightest interest in challenging that hegemony. Instead of debating new weapons systems, we should start from the other end of the spectrum and ask why we need a Defense Department at all. We should "sunset" the Pentagon. In other words, start with the assumption that we do not need ANY Pentagon, and ask that the Military-Industrial Complex tell us why they need to soak our taxpayers for astronomical sums of money when we have no visible adversaries.
>
> Why do we need an Army and an Air Force and Marines and a Navy, for goodness sakes? If we dissolved the whole shootin' match, the other nations of the world that now are forced to spend precious resources to protect themselves from threats from Uncle Sam would be able to follow our example and downsize from military empires to simple police forces. Doesn't that make sense? When Defense Secretary Don Rumsfeld took office a few months back, he undertook a reappraisal of Pentagon needs in this new era, but he did it in such secrecy that Republicans in Congress complained and your predecessor as Majority Leader, Trent Lott, had to call him on the carpet to get him to open up. Rumsfeld's approach was from the top down, guaranteed to add to the Pentagon's demands for resources when we already outspend the rest of the world *combined* on 'national defense.'[58]

### 3.4 The Case of the Environmental-Industrial Complex

Let us stipulate, if only for the sake of argument, and contrary to the criticisms mentioned above, that government is on net balance a force for environmental protection, not the very opposite. Even so, Lee's analysis is still marred by his inability to discern an "optimal" point for governmental interference with the economy. His only answer to the question of "How much role for the public sector" would appear to be "More."

Lee writes:

> But, as with the MIC, we are dealing with a public good, and one can
> defend the waste in environmental policy as providing the rents
> necessary to mobilize interest groups to take *more* political action on
> behalf of environmental protection than would be taken otherwise.

And again: "the MIC and the EIC may serve a useful function by *exaggerating* the threats to be protected against."[59] If "more" is the only answer, and Lee is instigating the EIC to exaggerate dangers so as to call forth yet even "more" government intervention, there really is no stopping place short of "all." This is a strange way to defend markets, one of Lee's ostensible goals.

### 3.5 The Case of Crime Control

Lee dismisses the role of private security guards in quelling crime, even though he admits there are more of them than public police officers, on the ground that "the former create primarily private goods."[60] This is difficult to understand. One would have thought, instead, that "a cop is a cop" and "security is security." If it looks like a cop, dresses like a cop, and acts like a cop, well, then, maybe it *is* a cop.

But no. It would appear, at least for Lee, that the financing of a service determines whether or not it is a private or public good. However, this is erroneous. According to his own neoclassical theory, whether a good is private or public depends solely upon its excludability (whether one consumer can exclude another) and rivalrousness (whether one consumer should exclude another), not at all upon how it is financed.

Consider chart 1.

|  | Should Exclude | Should Not Exclude |
|---|---|---|
| Can Exclude | A (shoes) | B (television signal) |
| Can Not Exclude | C (street) | D (defense) |

The columns (Should Exclude and Should Not Exclude) concern whether a good is rivalrous. The rows (Can Exclude and Can Not Exclude) consider whether a good is excludable. This two-by-two matrix gives rise to four possibilities, labeled as boxes A, B, C, and D. A is a pure private good, such as shoes or butter, since these goods are rivals in that if I use them, you are precluded from their utilization, unless you pay for them. Thus, there is reason to preclude you from their enjoyment, otherwise I cannot fully retain them, given that only one of us can do so.

214

As well, excluding non-payers can easily be done, making this category the only one of the four not characterized as a "failure."[61]

D is the pure public good, since, if I enjoy it, I am not able to exclude you from it, nor is it rivalrous, in that my use of it does not at all detract from yours. The usual examples given of this category are national defense and the lighthouse.[62] According to proponents of this doctrine, you should not be excluded from this benefit even though you do not pay for it, nor can you be precluded from enjoying it without payment; thus, it cannot be provided by a private firm on a profit-making basis.

An example of B is a television broadcast: this service is not rivalrous, in that one person's enjoyment of a program does not reduce that of another, but non-payers can be excluded from viewing it, given the advent of jamming devices which render feasible pay for view. However, since the marginal cost of adding one more viewer is zero, it would be inefficient to charge anyone for this benefit. Hence, profit-earning businesses cannot come into being, and the government must somehow engage itself in provision.

An illustration of C is the crowded street. Here, it is difficult or impossible to exclude passersby, but each of them impedes the free flow of all the others, so the good is rivalrous. Government must provide sidewalks, in this view, since people will free ride (or, rather, free "walk.")

It is this concept that is at the core of Lee's analytic framework. Without it, his entire range of proposals falls to the ground. Yet, it can easily be shown that this staple of mainstream economics is a tissue of fallacies. Coase is reputed to have already eliminated the lighthouse as member of category D by supposedly showing that boat owners did have incentive to pay off those who marked off dangerous rocks. The risk was that they should ever be turned off in an hour of need; this made it well worth-while to pay for this valuable service. Similarly, defense and crime prevention are not rivalrous; if a police station or a submarine is in one place, it is not so easy for it to cover another. Nor are they non-excludable: people who pay might be given signs saying that they are under the protection of the security firm, while those who do not pay do not receive such signs. In such a state, the latter would be natural targets for criminals, whether foreign or domestic.

At the other end of the spectrum, it is by no means clear that A is not a null set. If you purchase shoes and butter, for example, it might well be claimed that I am a beneficiary. To the extent that you are now healthier and more able to work, you will be less of a financial drain on me, and more able to enter into a division of labor with me. So, you cannot exclude me from enjoying your use of your own purchases, even though I do not pay for them.[63]


## 4. Some Criticisms

Lee takes time to consider three possible objections to or criticisms of his thesis: people voluntarily contribute to public goods production, people privately produce public goods, and the bad aspects of rent-seeking should be eliminated while the good aspects kept.

## 4.1 People voluntarily contribute

The first criticism against his thesis considered by Lee is that "people do contribute voluntarily to the provision of public goods." And his refutation of this objection? "[M]ost economists would agree that such voluntary action alone would leave us with woefully inadequate quantities of public goods such as national defense, environmental quality and crime control."[64]

There are difficulties here. First, there is no such thing as a "public good"; this is mere statist apologetics. As we have seen above, not even category A can be precluded from such characterization, and the members of the other three categories can all be so considered. Rivalrousness has a strong subjective element, and just because the state cannot exclude non-payers from service does not mean that more efficient entrepreneurs cannot.

Second, on the assumption that this is a coherent concept, there will be an under-allocation of resources to these goods under the pure market, but also an over-allocation under government control, given bureaucratic "rent seeking," and Lee gives no reason to suppose that the latter is preferable to the former.

Third, it is particularly unsatisfactory to "argue" in favor of a proposition that "most economists would agree" with it. This constitutes the informal fallacy of *argumentum ad populem*.[65]

Fourth, it is simply not true that public goods can only be provided by people "sacrificing private concerns"[66] in violation of Adam Smith's notion of the invisible hand. This overlooks the institution of internalizing externalities for fun and profit.

Fifth, to show that there is a core element of subjectivism inherent in the concept, Lee maintains that "family farming, medical care . . . [and] education are not public goods."[67] But "most economists," to resort to his own style of arguing for the nonce, would certainly disagree with this assessment. Indeed, education is one of the most highly utilized examples of a public good in the literature.

## 4.2 Private individuals create private, not public, goods

Lee's second criticism of the argument that private individuals can provide public goods is that to the extent they do, they are no longer private. He writes:

> Any arrangement that succeeds in providing a public good to many people, where excludability is a concern, requires some means of making collective decisions and then enforcing those decisions on those who either disagree with them or attempt to free rider [sic]. In other words, such a 'private' arrangement for providing public goods takes on characteristics of governments.[68]

Here, Lee is laboring under the belief that "collective decisions" equal "coercive decisions." Like virtually all other members of the Public Choice School, he fails to distinguish between acting collectively and acting coercively. But there is all the world of difference between a municipal pool and a private club which offers its members the use of the common swimming facilities. Both are "collective" activities, but the former is coercive, while the latter is voluntary. In the private club, if you don't pay, you cannot enjoy the amenity, which is the private property of all of those who have paid. As for the town recreational center, you are *forced* to subsidize it, through taxes. You may move away, only to the next town, but still, you are doing so at the point of a gun.

Contrary to Lee, there is no "continuum between private organizations, from which exit is easy, and governments, from which exit is difficult."[69] Either you are a victim of coercion, or you are not. If the former, it is necessarily a statist act.[70] To be sure, there is a continuum between coercion and non-coercion, between threats and non-threats. For example, just how far my fist must be from your nose before I am deemed to have committed an assault upon you is a matter of degree. But once that issue is settled, there is no further continuum of any relevance. Government financing of the swimming pool is coercive; the private counterpart is not.

There is an old joke that asks: "Do you know the difference between a bathroom and a living room?" If you reply in the negative, the punch line is, "Well, then, don't come to my house." In like manner we can say that if you don't know the difference between voluntary and coercive acts, then you might want to reconsider whether you really want to do political economics, since this is the most basic distinction in that entire field of endeavor. Boudreaux, Holcombe, and now Lee indicate that they are either unable or unwilling to make this most fundamental distinction.

This reply of Lee's sets up a catch-22 situation for his opponent. Either no individual person can (fully) supply a "public good," or, if he can, then he is really acting governmentally. Heads Lee wins, tails his opponent loses. But this cannot be allowed to stand. Lee cannot be allowed to win the debate with this trick of linguistic legerdemain. Very much to the contrary, there is no reason why a firm cannot supply a "public good." And if it does, there is no valid argument that automatically converts this into a governmental act. Methodologically, neoclassical economists live or die based on falsifiability. One must be able to mention a state of the world in which one's thesis can be untrue, at least in principle. In this case, Lee cannot do so. Hence, his thesis contradicts his own methodological principles.[71]

### 4.3 Keeping the good while eliminating the bad

The third objection that Lee considers is that in carrying out so-called invisible hand "rent-seeking,"[72] his argument "applauds the productive consequences of special-interest rent seeking while minimizing the counterproductive consequences." Here is his very charming response:

> But this criticism assumes we can get rid of the harmful rent seeking
> and keep that which is beneficial. That sounds good to me. I want to

go on record right now as being in favor of getting rid of the bad and keeping the good. But there is a small problem with this noble sentiment. How do we carry it out?[73]

The answer seems perfectly clear: privatize, and allow the invisible hand of the market to provide all goods and services that people can demonstrate they prefer, when compared to the costs necessary to produce them.

Lee goes on to deny he is "suggesting here that we can never get rid of bad government programs" and mentions the Civil Aeronautics Board, the Interstate Commerce Commission, and the Selective Service System as cases where we have done so successfully.[74] However, in welcoming airline, the draft, and other such deregulations, Lee is undermining his very own position. Had he remained true to it, he would have objected to these occurrences on the ground that these accretions to economic freedom would have put at undue risk all the wonderful things that government does for us, public-goods wise. What benefit to us is it to have slightly more economic freedom in the airline industry, etc., he would have said, if this reduces the "rent-seeking" that bureaucrats can garner; for if it does, then these people will employ the "Washington Monument" tactic and refuse to provide us with national defense, crime fighting, light houses, etc. It is surely penny wise and pound foolish to advocate *any* deregulation, based on this perspective.

But perhaps I speak too quickly. Perhaps there is *some* level of economic freedom, short of that which prevails in such capitalist bastions as Cuba and North Korea, which is both optimal and sustainable. The only problem with this surmise is that our guide in these matters, Prof. Lee, vouchsafes us no criterion on the basis of which we can make any such judgment. All he says on the matter, in effect, is that we must appreciate government excess, because it is only in this way that we can attain those elements of the state without which we as a society could not survive. But we are left hanging in the air, so to speak, as far as a roadmap that indicates just *how much* excessive government we must endure to retain for ourselves the "good bits." All we are told is that more government is better. It would appear that his motto would be "that government which governs most governs best," or "that government is best which governs most."

## 5. The Marginal versus the Total

Lee starts off this section reiterating his argument from authority:

I believe *most people*, public choice economists included, will accept that governments, at least those constrained by constitutional democracy, as imperfect as those constraints are, create positive net value in total. The citizens in the industrial democracies are better off with their existing levels of government than they would be without government.[75]

For all I know, this might even be true. But this is not a bar room brawl; rather, it is supposed to be an exercise in scholarship. In such contexts, mere assertions, even backed up by majority opinion amongst economists, will not suffice. It would be nice to know the *evidence* upon which Lee bases his claim, but such evidence is not forthcoming. It would be nice to know, at least in principle, how he recommends that we empirically or otherwise *test* this declaration, but that, too, is not provided. So much for the self-styled reliance upon data on the part of mainstream economists.

However, basing his argument on marginal, not total considerations, Lee now reverses field. Instead of calling for an ever-increasing bureaucracy and "more" government expenditure due to the invisible hand of politics, Lee now writes:

> the political process . . . results in government's expanding beyond the point where its marginal value equals its marginal cost. The recommendation is not for the elimination of government, but for the downsizing of government.[76]

I confess that I am confused. Now, and in the case of the "Civil Aeronautics Board, the Interstate Commerce Commission, and the Selective Service System" and, I presume, although he doesn't discuss them in this article, rent control, minimum wages, and tariffs, there is too much government and we must cut back. But all throughout the article we are told, again and again, that excessive government is justified in that if we don't have it, or if we try to quell it, we do so at the expense of forcing ourselves to do without (or with vast under-allocations of resources to) defense, crime fighting, environmental protection and other goods and services it is imperative that we avail ourselves of.

In this very section Lee illustrates this point with a diagram showing the necessity of putting up with "police brutality . . . a particularly offensive example of excessive government."[77] If there were any question about the desirability of tolerating excessive government for Lee, he continues:

> Give any agency of the government the power required to provide the maximum value over its ideal range of activity, and you have almost surely given it, and its special-interest clients, the power to expand its activity beyond that desirable range. . . . To obtain a reasonable level of inframarginal benefits from government activity, government has to have enough power to expand its activity beyond the point where, at the margin, that activity is destructive.[78]

But why are matters any different with regard to those aspects of government Lee recommends trimming?

The essence of this article is its advocacy of increased government, seemingly without end. Interspersed within it are a few adventitious claims for reducing the power of the state, but in the context of this essay, they are merely the emanations of lip service to a world-view with which Lee has long been associated.

## 6. Is a Desirable Minimal State Possible?

Lee maintains that if a minimal state were possible, it would not be desirable, and if it were desirable, it would not be possible. Let us consider these claims in reverse order. Why, first, given that a minimal government were desirable, would it be impossible to attain?

> The minimal state is considered desirable because the public cannot control political decisions to prevent government from being used by special interests to trump the public interest when it expands beyond minimal state limits. But the special-interest influence that makes a large government such a threat to the general public is also the dominant force behind the growth in government.[79]

But the latter statement is not true. Just as a matter of positive economics, if Lee's public-choice-based theory were a correct explanation of increasing government encroachment, there would be no possibility of the existence of the economies of Hong Kong or Singapore, which are not earmarked by excessive government, at least relative to most other countries in the world.[80]

Nor would this apply to the U.S. in its early days, where rarely was there to be found a government program that would be considered excessive, at least by today's standards. Some historians date the fall of the U.S. from Lyndon Johnson's "Great Society" welfare state.[81] Others go back to FDR's "New Deal." A better starting point would be the progressive period in the late nineteenth century.[82] An even better one would be Lincoln's War of Northern Aggression.[83]

In any event, if public choice considerations were definitive, these nations, areas and epochs of relative economic freedom could not have occurred, for we would have had to, in effect, bribe bureaucrats with the proceeds of excessive governmental "rent seeking" to induce them to produce needed statist programs.

A far better explanation of why we have sunk so low, economic freedom-wise, can be found in the role of the intellectuals. Their independence has been purchased by the forces of dirigisme, and their function is to weave apologetics for an ever-increasing role for the state.[84] The pen is indeed mightier than the sword, if only because, ultimately, it determines the direction in which the latter is pointed. As Rothbard notes:

> since the early origins of the State, its rulers have always turned, as a necessary bolster to their rule, to an alliance with society's class of intellectuals. The masses do not create their own abstract ideas, or indeed think through these ideas independently; they follow passively the ideas adopted and promulgated by the body of intellectuals, who become the effective 'opinion molders' in society. And since it is precisely a molding of opinion on behalf of the rulers that the State most desperately needs, this forms a firm basis for the age-old alliance of the intellectuals and the ruling classes of the State. The alliance is based on a *quid pro quo*: on the one hand, the intellectuals spread

among the masses the idea that the State and its rulers are wise, good, sometimes divine, *and at the very least inevitable and better than any conceivable alternative.* In return for this panoply of ideology, the State incorporates the intellectuals as part of the ruling elite, granting them power, status, prestige, and material security. Furthermore, intellectuals are needed to staff the bureaucracy and to 'plan' the economy and society.[85]

Later, in a passage seemingly addressed to Lee, although it was penned long before, Rothbard declares:

The rule of the State is . . . made to seem inevitable. Furthermore, any alternative to the existing State is encased in an aura of fear. Neglecting its own monopoly of theft and predation, the State raises the specter among its subjects of the chaos that would supposedly ensue if the State should disappear. The people on their own, it is maintained, could not possibly supply their own protection against sporadic criminals and marauders.[86]

Second, let us consider why if a minimal state were possible, it would not be desirable. In Lee's view, this is because:

if somehow the public acquired sufficient control over government to achieve a minimal state, the government would be subject to sufficient control to usefully address problems not within the purview of a minimal state. A government that is a good agent can obviously expand its reach farther with socially beneficial results than a government that is a poor agent. So the public control over government necessary to make a minimal state possible would render such a state no longer desirable.[87]

Let us suppose that libertarian ideology swept the country to a degree sufficient to achieve the minimal state,[88] although there was still not enough support to entrench laissez faire capitalism or free market anarchism.[89] This would satisfy the first of Lee's conditions: there would now be sufficient control over the "rent seeking" bureaucrats to forestall them in their aggrandizing efforts. But does this mean that this minimal government could "usefully address problems not within the purview of a minimal state"? It is difficult to see why this should be so, unless one adopts the (coercive) socialistic philosophy according to which the *only* thing holding government back from playing a positive role in the economy is "rent seeking." But surely the Austrian critic of centrally planned socialism encompasses far more than this.[90]

Further, "a government that is a good agent" is a veritable contradiction in terms, even if, *mirable dictu*, we somehow attain the power to achieve a limited version of it. Lee reckons without the insight that a limited evil is still an evil.[91]

When dealing with a fundamentalist archist[92] such as Lee, one must be careful to discern a belief system that is not at all open to the possibility that markets can function in areas traditionally reserved for the government. For him, the idea of a well-functioning society in the absence of the state is not merely impossible, it appears actually meaningless, so little credence does he give to this vision as a practical application of political philosophy. And yet, if the government of the U.S. is necessary since without it people would be in a relationship of anarchy with one another (there is no over-arching legal authority ruling them all), then it also follows that since the countries of the world are now in precisely the same state of anarchy with one another as would be citizens of the U.S. without this particular government (there is no over-arching legal authority ruling them all), then a world government (e.g., the U.N. with real power) would be justified on these grounds. Yet, few are the archists willing to derive this non-deniable conclusion from their own (implicit) premises.

Lee considers two objections to his argument. First:

> It might be argued that it is possible to exert the type of broad control over government necessary to achieve a minimal state, but not exert the detailed control required to make government a better agent at solving particular problems.

He follows with his response:

> The trouble that I see with this objection is that it presumes that government solutions require detailed involvement, or micromanaging. But this is not the case. Indeed, government can typically accomplish more by establishing a frame of incentives that motivates private action than by attempts to solve problems and provide services directly. For example, given the inefficiency associated with the command-and-control approach to pollution control, there are certainly pollution problems that it makes no economic sense for government to address but which could be beneficially addressed by market-incentive approaches.[93]

The difficulty with this reaction is that government is inefficient in *both* broad and narrow regulations, and this specifically includes "establishing a frame of incentives." The state has established "incentives" with 90% marginal tax rates and above, welfare programs which reward sloth, idleness, promiscuity, and child illegitimacy,[94] rent controls, minimum wages, and trade restrictions. This is supposed to be productive, just because it is not micromanaging. As for his example of tradable emissions rights as a solution to pollution control, this, too, has come under withering attack from free enterprise, private property quarters.[95]

The second objection considered by Lee emanates from adherents of natural rights. These people, benighted souls that they are:

> reject such efficiency-based arguments when it comes to determining the acceptable role of government. From this perspective, the only justification for government is as a means of protecting the natural rights of individuals, and the only acceptable way of providing this protection is in ways that do not violate anyone's natural rights.

Lee's response to these critics is mere dogmatism:

> To those who refuse to accept a positive connection between public control over government and the amount it is desirable for government to do, I have no response except to say I think they are wrong.[96]

## 7. Conclusion

After the serious mauling he has given them all throughout his article, Lee attempts to win back his free enterprise credentials in his concluding remarks by writing that "I hope no one takes my remarks as a defense of the status quo or as an argument against trying to rein in the size and scope of government activities."[97] Yet, that is exactly the implication to be drawn from Lee's article. Are we completely to ignore the very title of his article?

Further, Lee must have had some misgivings himself about his essay, compelling him to declare:

> At this point some of you may be wondering what happened to the Dwight Lee whose work has been largely devoted to pointing out and critiquing the excesses of government, not defending them. Let me make clear, the old Dwight Lee is still here.[98]

Nor will it help his resuscitation as a free enterpriser to declare at this late point that "I believe that government is larger than is warranted by my defense of excessive government."[99] After all, he fails to give even a scintilla of a reason for this claim.

Lee believes, also, that "public choice arguments can help restrain, and possibly reverse, government growth, at least marginally," by "reduc(ing) the influence of politically organized interest groups."[100] If so, then based on the gist of the entire corpus of his article, this school of thought is a very dangerous one. Remember, according to this article, government is good, and more government is even better, even "excessive" government, because without the excesses and inefficiencies, we cannot have the crucially important "public goods" programs that government and only government can provide. So if the Public Choice School succeeds at restraining, and possibly reversing, government growth, then it will put at risk the entire apparatus of the state.

Lee ends on the following note: "But with luck and public choice scholars attacking government excess rather than defending it, there will soon be less excess to defend." How this is possible to reconcile with an essay the burden of which is to extol excessive government, is beyond my ability to discern. Lee's is a brilliant and courageous essay in which he takes the insights of the Public Choice School rigorously to their logical conclusion. Nor does he shrink from embracing the implications of his own theory.[101] This is admirable, in a scholarly sense. But although economics boasts the beauty of mathematics or geometry, it is also a humane science with immediate political implications for our lives.

Lee's conclusions, in my view, are indistinguishable from those favored by advocates of totalitarian Communism or Nazism. His is a recipe for no less than the destruction of economic freedom. There is no logical stopping point for government intervention once we grant the existence of the invisible hand of the political system. The fact that Lee ended up in a place so inhospitable to the political economic philosophy he has been associated with all his career should have given him pause for thought. It did not. Hopefully, the present article will make a contribution in that direction.

## NOTES

1. See Lee, Dwight R. (1999), "In Defense of Excessive Government," *Southern Economic Journal* 65(4): 675–690.

2. Bruce Benson, current vice president of the Association of Private Enterprise Educators, in his letter of invitation to the 2002 APEE annual meeting.

3. Lee, "In Defense of Excessive Government," 675.

4. I could hardly be expected to take any other position on the matter, as is shown by my book *Defending the Undefendable.* New York: Fox and Wilkes, 1991. Lee is consistent in this regard, in that he announces himself willing to "irritate almost everyone," another sentiment with which I am in complete accord. See Lee, "In Defense of Excessive Government," 675.

5. See, e.g., Block, Walter, and Tom DiLorenzo (2000), "Is Voluntary Government Possible? A Critique of Constitutional Economics," *Journal of Institutional and Theoretical Economics* 156(4): 567–582; Block, Walter, and Tom DiLorenzo (2001), "The Calculus of Consent Revisited," *Public Finance and Management* 1(3): 305–321; and DiLorenzo, Tom, and Walter Block (2001), "Constitutional Economics and the Calculus of Consent," *Journal of Libertarian Studies* 15(3): 37–56. Also see DiLorenzo, Thomas J. (1988), "Competition and Political Entrepreneurship: Austrian Insights into Public Choice Theory," *Review of Austrian Economics* 2: 59–71; and Rothbard, Murray N. (1997), "Buchanan and Tullock's The Calculus of Consent," in *Applications and Criticism from the Austrian School*, vol. 2, The Logic of Action. Cheltenham: Edward Elgar 269–274.

6. Lee, "In Defense of Excessive Government," 675.

7. That Lee *welcomes* this (coercive) socialist core cannot properly be interpreted as a disparagement of this profound intellectual insight, although, to be sure, it calls into question his otherwise stellar pro-market credentials.

8. Lee, "In Defense of Excessive Government," 675.

9. Ibid., 675, 676.

10. The Disney Corporation and the hotel entrepreneurs of Las Vegas have erected far more spectacular structures than this; the Empire State Building alone puts it into the shade.

11. Ostrowski, James, "Killers Kill the Killer," *LewRockwell.com*, puts the number of civilians murdered by the U.S. government at 2,523,625. The greatest so-called private mass murderer in the U.S., Timothy McVeigh, killed fewer than 100 innocent people. However, I do not consider McVeigh a private killer. Rather, since he engaged in what is quintessentially a function of government, he should be seen in that light. A careful reading

of Lysander Spooner, *No Treason* (1870; reprint, Larkspur, CO: Pine Tree Press, 1966), will convince the fair-minded reader that the two are indeed members of the same "industry."

12. Think soccer hoodlums armed with weapons of mass destruction. See on this Courtois, Stephane, Nicols Werth, Jean-Louis Panne, Andrzej Paczkowski, Karel Bartosek, and Jean Louis Margolin (1999), *The Black Book of Communism: Crimes, Terror, Repression,* trans. Jonathan Murphy and Mark Cramer. Cambridge, MA: Harvard University Press; Rummel, R.J. (1994), *Death by Government.* New Brunswick, NJ: Transaction Publishers; Rummel, R.J. (1992), *Democide: Nazi Genocide and Mass Murder.* New Brunswick, NJ: Transaction Publishers; and Rummel, R.J. (1997), *Statistics of Democide.* Charlottesville, VA: Center for National Security Law, School of Law, University of Virginia. The "score" of millions of people killed is roughly the following: Mao's China: 60; Stalin's U.S.S.R.: 20; Hitler's Germany: 10; Pol Pot's Cambodia: 2. Thus, it can be seen that while the U.S. is a "player," it is not at the top of the rogue's gallery.

13. Lee, "In Defense of Excessive Government," 676; cf. Buchanan, James (1988), "Market Failure and Political Failure," *Cato Journal* 8(1): 12.

14. Not, presumably, of the "good" kind of extremists as indicative of Lee's philosophical stance, but of the "bad" kind who fail to agree with this "economic equivalence" perspective.

15. The idea of market failure has been thoroughly demolished in many places by many scholars. For a general overview, see Cowen, Tyler (ed.) (1988), *The Theory of Market Failure: A Critical Examination.* Fairfax, VA: George Mason University Press.

On monopoly as market failure, see Armentano, Dominick (1982), *Antitrust and Monopoly: Anatomy of a Policy Failure.* New York: Wiley; Armstrong, Donald (1982), *Competition versus Monopoly: Combines Policy in Perspective.* Vancouver, B.C.: Fraser Institute; Block, Walter (1982), *Amending the Combines Investigation Act.* Vancouver, B.C.: Fraser Institute; Block, Walter (1977), "Austrian Monopoly Theory – A Critique," *Journal of Libertarian Studies* 1(4): 271–79; Block, Walter (1994), "Total Repeal of Antitrust Legislation: A Critique of Bork, Brozen, and Posner," *Review of Austrian Economics* 8(1): 35–70; Barnett, William, and Jerry Dauterive (1985), "A Property Rights Approach to Natural Monopoly," paper presented at the annual meeting of the Southern Economic Association, 1985; DiLorenzo, Thomas J. (1997), "The Myth of Natural Monopoly," *Review of Austrian Economics* 9(2): 43–58; High, Jack (1984/1985), "Bork's Paradox: Static vs. Dynamic Efficiency in Antitrust Analysis," *Contemporary Policy Issues* 3: 21–34; McChesney, Fred (1991), "Antitrust and Regulation: Chicago's Contradictory Views," *Cato Journal* 10(3): 775–798; Rothbard, Murray N. (1970), *Man, Economy, and State.* Los Angeles, CA: Nash; Shugart, II, William F. (1987), "Don't Revise the Clayton Act, Scrap It!" *Cato Journal* 6: 925–932; and Smith, Jr., Fred L. (1983), "Why Not Abolish Antitrust?" *Regulation* 7: 23–28.

On externalities, spillovers, and public goods, see Hoppe, Hans-Hermann (1993), "Fallacies of the Public Goods Theory and the Production of Security," in *Economics and Ethics of Private Property: Studies in Political Economy and Philosophy.* Boston, MA: Kluwer; Hoppe, Hans-Hermann (1998), *The Private Production of Defense* (Auburn, AL: Ludwig von Mises Institute); Rogers Hummel, Jeffrey (1990), "National Goods vs. Public Goods: Defense, Disarmament, and Free Riders," *Review of Austrian Economics* 4: 88–122; Block, Walter (1983), "Public Goods and Externalities: The Case of Roads," *Journal of Libertarian Studies* 7(1): 1–34; Block, Walter (1989), "The Justification of Taxation in the Public Finance Literature: A Critique of Atkinson and Stiglitz, Due, Musgrave and Shoup," *Journal of Public Finance and Public Choice* 3 Fall: 141–158; Block, Walter (1993), "Canadian Public Finance Texts Cannot Justify Government Taxation: A Critique of Auld &

Miller; Musgrave, Musgrave, & Bird; McCready; and Wolf," *Canadian Public Administration* 36(1): 225–262.

Other so-called "market failures," such as inequality of wealth and racial and sexual discrimination, are hardly worth citing in this context.

16. Lee, "In Defense of Excessive Government," 677; Bork, Robert H. (1978), *The Antitrust Paradox: A Policy at War with Itself.* New York: Basic Books, 92.

17. Ibid., 677, 678, and 683.

18. Nozick, Robert (1974), *Anarchy, State, and Utopia.* New York: Basic Books, 163, has characterized them as the embodiment of "capitalist acts between consenting adults."

19. Some might argue that under democracy, the *society*, rather than the *individual*, has voluntarily acquiesced to this transaction. However, the institution of democracy is not without its critics. See Hoppe, Hans-Hermann (1997), "The Political Economy of Monarchy and Democracy and the Idea of a Natural Order," in *Values and the Social Order*, ed. Gerard Radnitzky, vol. 3. Aldershot: Avebury; Hoppe, Hans-Hermann (1994), "Time Preference, Government, and the Process of De-Civilization – From Monarchy to Democracy," *Journal des Economistes et des Etudes Humaines* 5(2/3): 319–352. Reprinted in Denson, John V. (ed.) (1997), *The Costs of War: America's Pyrrhic Victories.* New Brunswick, NJ: Transaction Publishers; and Hoppe, Hans-Hermann (2001), *Democracy, the God that Failed: The Economics and Politics of Monarchy, Democracy, and Natural Order.* New Brunswick, NJ: Transaction Publishers.

20. Lee, "In Defense of Excessive Government," 677, 678, and 683.

21. Ibid., 677.

22. Ibid., 678.

23. Ibid., 678.

24. Ibid., 678, note 3.

25. The Nazi incarceration of Jews was perfectly legal under German law of the time. This hardly renders it inoffensive.

26. Lee, "In Defense of Excessive Government," 678, 676.

27. The Austrian school of economics is an honorable exception to this rule.

28. With the exception of murder on a mass scale, as discussed above.

29. See Anderson, Terry and P.J. Hill (1979), "An American Experiment in Anarcho-Capitalism: The *not* so Wild, Wild West," *Journal of Libertarian Studies* 3(1): 9–29; Hoppe, Hans-Hermann (1998/1999), "The Private Production of Defense," *Journal of Libertarian Studies* 14(1): 27–52; Rothbard, Murray N. (1978), *For a New Liberty.* New York: Macmillan; Stringham, Edward (1998/1999), "Justice without Government," *Journal of Libertarian Studies* 14(1): 53–77; and Tinsley, Patrick (1998/1999), "Private Police: A Note," *Journal of Libertarian Studies* 14(1): 95–100.

30. For the general case that law, justice, courts, etc., could be provided in the absence of government, see Barnett, Randy E. (1998), *The Structure of Liberty: Justice and the Rule of Law.* Oxford: Clarendon Press; Benson, Bruce L. (1989), "Enforcement of Private Property Rights in Primitive Societies: Law without Government," *Journal of Libertarian Studies* 9(1): 1–26; Bernstein, Lisa (1992), "Opting out of the Legal System: Extralegal Contractual Relationships in the Diamond Industry," *Journal of Legal Studies* 21(1): 115–157; Cuzán, Alfred G. (1979), "Do We Ever Really Get Out of Anarchy?," *Journal of Libertarian Studies* 3(2): 151–158; Jasay, Anthony de (1997), *Against Politics: On Government, Anarchy, and Order.* London: Routledge; Friedman, David (1989), *The Machinery of Freedom: Guide to a Radical Capitalism*, 2nd edn. La Salle, IL: Open Court; Hadfield, Gillian K. (2001),

"Privatizing Commercial Law," *Regulation* 24(1): 40–45; Hoppe, Hans-Hermann (1989), *A Theory of Socialism and Capitalism: Economics, Politics, and Ethics*. Boston, MA: Kluwer; Hoppe, Hans-Hermann (1993), *The Economics and Ethics of Private Property: Studies in Political Economy and Philosophy*. Boston, MA: Kluwer; Kinsella, N. Stephan (1995), "Legislation and the Discovery of Law in a Free Society," *Journal of Libertarian Studies* 11(2): 132–181; Macey, Jonathan, and Maureen O'Hara (1999), "Regulating Exchanges and Alternative Trading Systems: A Law and Economics Perspective," *Journal of Legal Studies* 28: 17–54; Rothbard, Murray N. (1978), "Society Without a State," in *Anarchism: Nomos XIX*, eds. J.R. Pennock and J.W. Chapman. New York: New York University Press, 191–207; Skoble, Aeon J. (1995), "The Anarchism Controversy," in *Liberty for the 21st Century: Essays in Contemporary Libertarian Thought*, eds. Tibor Machan and Douglas Rasmussen. Lanham, MD: Rowman and Littlefield, 77–96; Sechrest, Larry J. (1999), "Rand, Anarchy, and Taxes," *Journal of Ayn Rand Studies* 1(1): 87–105.

31. Beito, David T. (1993), "From Privies to Boulevards: The Private Supply of Infrastructure in the United States during the Nineteenth Century," in *Development by Consent: The Voluntary Supply of Public Goods and Services*, ed. Jerry Jenkins and David E. Sisk. San Francisco, CA: Institute for Contemporary Studies, 23–48; Block, Walter (1979), "Free Market Transportation: Denationalizing the Roads," *Journal of Libertarian Studies* 3(2): 209–238; Block, Walter (1980), "Congestion and Road Pricing," *Journal of Libertarian Studies* 4(3): 299–330; Block, Walter (1983), "Public Goods and Externalities: The Case of Roads," *Journal of Libertarian Studies* 7(1): 1–34; Block, Walter (1983), "Theories of Highway Safety," *Transportation Research Record* 912: 7–10; Block, Walter (1996), "Road Socialism," *International Journal of Value-Based Management* 9: 195–207; Block, Walter, and Matthew Block (1996), "Roads, Bridges, Sunlight, and Private Property Rights," *Journal des Economistes et des Etudes Humaines* 7(2/3): 351–362; Block, Walter (1998), "Roads, Bridges, Sunlight, and Private Property: Reply to Gordon Tullock," *Journal des Economistes et des Etudes Humaines* 8(2/3): 315–326; Foldvary, Fred (1994), *Public Goods and Private Communities: The Market Provision of Social Services*. Aldershot: Edward Elgar; Cadin, Michelle, and Walter Block (1997), "Privatize the Public Highway System," *The Freeman* 47(2): 96–97; Cobin, John M. (1999), "Market Provisions of Highways: Lessons from Costanera Norte," *Planning and Markets* 2(1) September; Klein, Dan, John Majewski, and C. Baer (1993), "Economy, Community, and the Law: The Turnpike Movement in New York, 1797–1845, *Journal of Economic History* March: 106–122; Klein, Dan, and G.J. Fielding (1993), "How to Franchise Highways," *Journal of Transport Economics and Policy* May: 113–330; Lemennicier, Bertrand (1996), "La Privatisation des rues," *Journal Des Economistes et des Etudes Humaines* 7(2/3): 363–76; and Semmens, John (1987), "Intraurban Road Privatization," *Transportation Research Record* 1107.

32. The classic article on this topic is Coase, Ronald H. (1974), "The Lighthouse in Economics," *Journal of Law and Economics* 17: 357–376. For an argument that Coase has not succeeded in showing that markets can provide lighthouse services, the opinion on this matter of most economists notwithstanding, see Barnett, II, William, and Walter Block, "Coase and Van Zandt on Lighthouses," (Loyola University New Orleans, photocopy).

33. See Rothbard, *For a New Liberty*; Hughes, Mark (1988), review of *The Nonprofit Sector: A Research Handbook*, ed. Walter W. Powell, *The Philanthropist* 7(4): 61–65; and Hughes, Mark (1990), "Counterpoint: A Response to Bennet and DiLorenzo," *The Philanthropist* 9(3): 43–56.

34. Nobel-prize-winning economist James Buchanan, in his Austrian persona, is fully aware of subjectivism. See, e.g., Buchanan, James M., and G.F. Thirlby (1981), *L.S.E. Essays on Cost.* New York: New York University Press; and Buchanan, James M. (1969), *Cost and Choice: An Inquiry into Economic Theory.* Chicago, IL: Markham. See also von Mises, Ludwig (1966), *Human Action*, 3rd rev. ed. Chicago, IL: Regnery; Rothbard, *Man, Economy, and State*; and Barnett, II, William, "Subjective Cost Revisited," *Review of Austrian Economics* 3: 137–138. It is too bad that when Buchanan wears his Public Choice hat, he forgets all about his qualifications and scientific modesty in this regard. On this, see footnote 5, above.

35. Galbraith, John Kenneth (1958), *The Affluent Society.* Boston: Houghton-Mifflin.

36. Lee, "In Defense of Excessive Government," p. 679. Yet, no sooner does he make this claim than he attempts to moderate it to a degree by his characterization of this view as "simplistic." Further, his discussion of "expressive voting" constitutes another qualification. Nonetheless, Lee does not completely divorce himself from this viewpoint.

37. Spooner, *No Treason*, p. 15.

38. Lee, "In Defense of Excessive Government," p. 679.

39. Old joke: How can you tell if a politician is lying? If he moves his lips. So much for Lee's claim about "preferences [being] communicated candidly." How can they be communicated candidly if politicians lie?

40. See, e.g., Stinnett, Robert B. (1999), *Day of Deceit: The Truth about FDR and Pearl Harbor.* New York: Touchstone.

41. See Block, *Defending the Undefendable*, pp. 39–49; Block, Walter (1993), "Drug Prohibition: A Legal and Economic Analysis," *Journal of Business Ethics* 12: 107–118; Block, Walter (1996), "Drug Prohibition, Individual Virtue, and Positive Economics," *Review of Political Economy* 8(4): 433–436; Boaz, David (ed.) (1990), *The Crisis in Drug Prohibition.* Washington, D.C.: Cato Institute; Cussen, Meaghan, and Walter Block (2000), "Drug Legalization: A Public Policy Analysis," *American Journal of Economics and Sociology* 59(3): 525–536; Friedman, Milton (1989), "An Open Letter to Bill Bennett," *Wall Street Journal* September 7; Hamowy, Ronald (ed.) (1987), *Dealing with Drugs: The Consequences of Government Control.* San Francisco, CA: The Pacific Institute; Rothbard, *For A New Liberty*; Szasz, Thomas (1985), *Ceremonial Chemistry: The Ritual Persecution of Drugs, Addicts and Pushers.* Holmes Beach, FL: Learning Publications; Szasz, Thomas (1992), *Our Right to Drugs: The Case for a Free Market.* New York: Praeger; and Thornton, Mark (1991), *The Economics of Prohibition.* Salt Lake City, UT: University of Utah Press.

42. On the case for a free market in this field, see, e.g., Barnett, Andy H., T. Randolph Beard, and David L. Kaserman (1996), "Scope, Learning, and Cross-Subsidy: Organ Transplants in a Multi-Division Hospital – An Extension," *Southern Economic Journal* 62(3): 76–67; Barnett, II, William, Michael Saliba, and Deborah Walker (2001), "A Free Market in Kidneys: Efficient and Equitable," *Independent Review* 5(3): 373–385; Barnett, William (1988), "The Market for Used Human Body Parts," *The Free Market* 6(2); Block, Walter, Roy Whitehead, Clint Johnson, Mana Davidson, Alan White, and Stacy Chandler (1999–2000), "Human Organ Transplantation: Economic and Legal Issues," *Quinnipiac College School of Law Health Journal* 3: 87–110; and Block, Walter (1988), "The Case for a Free Market in Body Parts," in *Essays in the Economics of Liberty: The Free Market Reader*, ed. Llewellyn Rockwell. Auburn, AL: Ludwig von Mises Institute, 266–272.

43. See Block, Walter (1990), "Environmental Problems, Private Property Rights Solutions," in *Economics and the Environment: A Reconciliation*, ed. Walter Block. Vancouver, B.C.: Fraser Institute, 282–322.

44. Rothbard, Murray N. (1990), "Law, Property Rights, and Air Pollution," in *Economics and the Environment: A Reconciliation*, ed. Walter Block. Vancouver, B.C.: Fraser Institute; and Horwitz, Morton J. (1977), *The Transformation of American Law: 1780–1860*. Cambridge, MA: Harvard University Press.

45. See Dauterive, Jerry W., William Bennett, and Everett White (1985), "A Taxonomy of Government Intervention," *Journal of the Southwestern Society of Economists* 12(1): 127–130. Also see McGee, Robert W., and Walter Block (1994),, "Pollution Trading Permits as a Form of Market Socialism, and the Search for a Real Market Solution to Environmental Pollution," *Fordham University Law and Environmental Journal* 6(1): 51–77.

46. Lee, "In Defense of Excessive Government," 679, emphasis added.

47. Ibid., 679.

48. This is a perfectly rational concept in ordinary language, but not in technical economics. For more on this see Block, Walter (1980), "On Robert Nozick's 'On Austrian Methodology'," *Inquiry* 23(4): 397–444; and Block, Walter (1999), "Austrian Theorizing: Recalling the Foundations," *Quarterly Journal of Austrian Economics* 2(4): 21–39.

49. Lee, "In Defense of Excessive Government," 680.

50. Rothbard, Murray N. (1997), "Toward a Reconstruction of Utility and Welfare Economics," in *Method, Money, and the Austrian School*, vol. 1 of *The Logic of Action*. Cheltenham: Edward Elgar.

51. See Dauterive, Bennett, and White, "A Taxonomy of Government Intervention."

52. Lee, "In Defense of Excessive Government," 681.

53. See on this Armentano, Dominick T. (1969), "Resource Allocation Problems Under Socialism," in *Theory of Economic Systems*, ed. William P. Snavely. New York: Charles E. Merrill, 129–139; Block, Walter (1992), "Socialist Psychology: Values and Motivations," *Cultural Dynamics* 5(3): 260–286; Boettke, Peter J. (1991), "The Austrian Critique and the Demise of Socialism: The Soviet Case," in *Austrian Economics: Perspectives on the Past and Prospects for the Future*, vol. 17, ed. Richard M. Ebeling. Hillsdale, MI: Hillsdale College Press, 181–232; Chaloupek, Günther K. (1990), "The Austrian Debate on Economic Calculation in a Socialist Economy," *History of Political Economy* 22(4): 659–675; Conway, David A. (1987), *A Farewell to Marx: An Outline and Appraisal of His Theories*. Middlesex: Penguin Books; Cubeddu, Raimondo (1993), *The Philosophy of the Austrian School*. New York: Routledge, 109–158; Dorn, James (1978), "Markets True and False in Yugoslavia," *Journal of Libertarian Studies* 2(3): 243–268; Ebeling, Richard M. (1993), "Economic Calculation Under Socialism: Ludwig von Mises and His Predecessors," in *The Meaning of Ludwig von Mises*, ed. Jeffrey Herbener. Norwell, MA: Kluwer Academic Press, 56–101; Foss, Nicolai Juul (1995), "Information and the Market Economy: A Note on a Common Marxist Fallacy," *Review of Austrian Economics* 8(2): 127–136; Gordon, David (1990), *Resurrecting Marx: The Analytical Marxists on Freedom, Exploitation, and Justice*. New Brunswick, NJ: Transaction Publishers; Hayek, Friedrich A. (1978), "The New Confusion About Planning," *New Studies in Philosophy, Politics, Economics, and the History of Ideas*. Chicago, IL: University of Chicago Press, 232–246; Heilbroner, Robert (1990), "Analysis and Vision in the History of Monetary Economic Thought," *Journal of Economic Literature* 28: 1097–1114; Herbener, Jeffrey M. (1996), "Calculation and the Question of Mathematics," *Review of Austrian Economics* 9(1): 151–62; Hoff, Trygve J.B. (1981), *Economic Calculation*

in a Socialist Society. Indianapolis, IN: Liberty Press; Hoppe, Hans-Hermann (1996), "Socialism: A Property or Knowledge Problem?" *Review of Austrian Economics* 9(1): 147–54; Horwitz, Steven (1996), "Money, Money Prices, and the Socialist Calculation Debates," *Advances in Austrian Economics* 3: 59–77; Keizer, Willem (1997), "Schumpeter's Walrasian Stand in the Socialist Calculation Debate," in *Austrian Economics in Debate*, ed. Willem Keizer, Bert Riben, and Rudy Van Zijp. London: Routledge; and Kirzner, Israel M. (1988), "The Economic Calculation Debate: Lessons for Austrians," *Review of Austrian Economics* 2: 1–18.

54. For more on the Austrian arguments related to this topic, see Klein, Peter G. (1996), "Economic Calculation and the Limits of Organization," *Review of Austrian Economics* 9(2): 3–28; Lavoie, Don (1981), "A Critique of the Standard Account of the Socialist Calculation Debate," *Journal of Libertarian Studies* 5(1): 7–22, 41–87, and 89–97; Lewin, Peter (1998), "The Firm, Money, and Economic Calculation," *American Journal of Economics and Sociology* 57(4): 499–513; Maltsev, Yuri N. (1993), *Requiem for Marx*. Auburn, AL: Ludwig von Mises Institute; von Mises, Ludwig (1981), *Socialism*. Indianapolis, IN: Liberty Press; Murrell, Peter (1983), "Did the Theory of Market Socialism Answer the Challenge of Ludwig von Mises? A Reinterpretation of the Socialist Controversy," *History of Political Economy* 15(1): 92–105; O'Driscoll, Gerald P. (1977), *Economics as a Coordination Problem*. Kansas City: Sheed Andrews and McMeel, 1–15; O'Neill, John (1996), "Who Won the Socialist Calculation Debate?" *History of Political Thought* 17(3): 431–442; Persky, Joseph (1991), "Retrospectives: Lange and von Mises, Large-Scale Enterprises, and the Economic Case for Socialism," *Journal of Economic Perspectives* 5(4): 229–36; Reisman, George (1996), *Capitalism: A Treatise on Economics*. Ottawa, IL: Jameson Books, 135–139, 267–282; Reynolds, Morgan O. (1998), "The Impossibility of Socialist Economy," *Quarterly Journal of Austrian Economics* 1(2): 29–43; Rothbard, Murray N. (1991), "The End of Socialism and the Calculation Debate Revisited," *Review of Austrian Economics* 5(2): 51–70; Salerno, Joseph T. (1990), "Ludwig von Mises as a Social Rationalist," *Review of Austrian Economics* 4: 26–54; Salerno, Joseph T. (1990), "Postscript: Why a Socialist Economy is 'Impossible'," in *Economic Calculation in the Socialist Commonwealth*, by Ludwig von Mises. Auburn, AL: Ludwig von Mises Institute, 51–71; Schultz, Helen E. (ed.) (1976), *Economic Calculation Under Inflation*. Indianapolis, IN: Liberty Press; Ramsey Steele, David (1992), *From Marx to Mises: Post-Capitalist Society and the Challenge of Economic Calculation*. La Salle, IL: Open Court; Ramsey Steele, David (1981), "Posing the Problem: The Impossibility of Economic Calculation under Socialism," *Journal of Libertarian Studies* 5(1): 99–111; Stiebler, Reinhard (1999), "A Pre-History of Misesian Calculation: The Contribution of Adolphe Thiers," *Quarterly Journal of Austrian Economics* 2(4): 41–47; Tamedly, Elizabeth (1969), *Socialism and the International Economic Order*. Caldwell, ID: Caxton Printers; Vaughn, Karen I. (1980), "Economic Calculation under Socialism: the Austrian Contribution," *Economic Inquiry* 18(20): 535–554; Yeager, Leland B. (1994), "Mises and Hayek and Calculation and Knowledge," *Review of Austrian Economics* 7(2): 93–110.

55. Lee, "In Defense of Excessive Government," 680.

56. Ibid.

57. I assume away for the sake of argument the possibility that the citizens in either state might see the sub's presence as a provocation, and thus a greater danger to themselves.

58. Jude Wanniski, "Sunset the Pentagon," polyconomics.com.

59. Lee, "In Defense of Excessive Government," 681, emphasis added.

60. Ibid., 682.

61. To be fair to mainstream economists, this category contains most goods and services in an economy. They advocate coercive socialism for the relatively few remaining members of the other three categories, at most.

62. The lighthouse has somewhat and very gradually fallen out of favor as an example of a pure public good since the publication of Coase, "The Lighthouse in Economics." Note that Lee nowhere mentions this case, but he does prominently use crime, the environment, and national defense. Why is it that although the lighthouse can no longer be used for this purpose in polite economic circles, the same fate has not (yet) befallen these three cases? I speculate that this phenomenon is due solely to the fact that it was Coase, a widely respected mainstream economist, who obliterated the public goods aspect of the lighthouse. The other cases have been demolished by Rothbard and others, but to no avail so far.

Here is a contrary-to-fact conditional to consider: had it been Rothbard and other libertarians who had done for lighthouses what Coase is widely seen as having done, and had it been Coase who had shown that defense, crime stopping, and environmental protection were not public goods, Lee and others of his ilk would now be using the lighthouse to illustrate the idea of public goods, and would be eschewing these other examples for that purpose.

63. For a critique of the mainstream economic view on externalities and public goods see Rogers Hummel, Jeffrey (1990), "National Goods Versus Public Goods: Defense, Disarmament, and Free Riders," *Review of Austrian Economics* 4: 88–122; and Morriss, Andrew P. (1998), "Miners, Vigilantes, and Cattlemen: Overcoming Free Rider Problems in the Private Provision of Law," *Land and Water Law Review* 33(2): 581–696.

64. Lee, "In Defense of Excessive Government," 682.

65. For examples of the case against the Austrian school of economics based on the argument from authority, see Laband, David N., and Robert D. Tollison (2000), "On Secondhandism and Scientific Appraisal," *Quarterly Journal of Austrian Economics* 3(1): 43–48; Rosen, Sherwin (1997), "Austrian and Neoclassical Economics: Any Gains from Trade?" *Journal of Economic Perspectives* 11(4): 139–52; and Vedder, Richard, and Lowell Gallaway (2000), "The Austrian Market Share in the Marketplace for Ideas, 1871–2025," *Quarterly Journal of Austrian Economics* 3(1): 33–42. For rejoinders, see Anderson, William L. (2000), "Austrian Economics and the 'Market Test': A Comment on Laband and Tollison," *Quarterly Journal of Austrian Economics* 3(3): 63–73; Block, Walter (2000), "Austrian Journals: A Critique of Rosen, Yeager, Laband and Tollison, and Vedder and Gallaway," *Quarterly Journal of Austrian Economics* 3(2): 45–61; Yeager, Leland (1997), "Austrian Economics, Neoclassicism, and the Market Test," *Journal of Economic Perspectives* 11(4): 153–63; and Yeager, Leland (2000), "The Tactics of Secondhandism," *Quarterly Journal of Austrian Economics* 3(3): 51–61.

66. Lee, "In Defense of Excessive Government," 682.

67. Ibid., 683.

68. Ibid. On this point, Lee cites Holcombe, Randall (1994), *The Economic Foundations of Government*. New York: New York University Press; and Boudreaux, Donald J., and Randall G. Holcombe (1989), "Government by Contract," *Public Finance Quarterly* 17(3): 264–280. For a reply to this line of reasoning, see Block, Walter, "National Defense and the Theory of Externalities, Public Goods, and Clubs" (Loyola University of New Orleans, photocopy).

69. Lee, "In Defense of Excessive Government," 683.

70. This must be qualified somewhat. A government is correctly defined as an institution with a legal monopoly over initiatory coercion in a given geographical area. Strictly speaking, then, a "free enterprise" or private gunman is not a government, since he has no such legal monopoly. Nonetheless, he is engaged in a statist type of act, given that the quintessential element of the government is the initiation of force or the threat thereof, and he resembles them in that.

71. On this, see Hoppe, Hans-Hermann (1988), *Praxeology and Economic Science*. Auburn, AL: Ludwig von Mises Institute; Rothbard, Murray N. (1976), "Praxeology, Value Judgments, and Public Policy," in *The Foundations of Modern Austrian Economics*, ed. Edwin G. Nolan. Kansas City, MO: Sheed and Ward; and Selgin, George A. (1988), "Praxeology and Understanding: An Analysis of the Controversy in Austrian Economics," *Review of Austrian Economics* 2: 19–58.

72. Lee, "In Defense of Excessive Government," 684. This phrase is a strong candidate for internal contradiction of the year honors.

73. Ibid., 683.

74. Ibid., 684.

75. Ibid., 684–85, emphasis added.

76. Ibid., 685.

77. Ibid.

78. Ibid., 686.

79. Ibid.

80. See Gwartney, James, Robert Lawson, and Walter Block (1996), *Economic Freedom of the World, 1975–1995*. Vancouver, B.C.: Fraser Institute.

81. See Murray, Charles (1984), *Losing Ground: American Social Policy from 1950 to 1980*. New York: Basic Books; Carlson, Allan C. (1988), *Family Questions*. New Brunswick, NJ: Transaction Publishers; and Tucker, William (1985), "Black Family Agonistes," *American Spectator* July: 14–17.

82. See Kolko, Gabriel (1963), *Triumph of Conservatism*. Chicago, IL: Quadrangle Books.

83. See, e.g., Rogers Hummel, Jeffrey (1966), *Emancipating Slaves, Enslaving Free Men: A History of the American Civil War*. Chicago, IL: Open Court; and DiLorenzo, Thomas J. (2002), *The Real Lincoln: A New Look at Abraham Lincoln, His Agenda, and an Unnecessary War*. Roseville, CA: Prima Publishing.

84. Sadly, the present piece under consideration, Lee, "In Defense of Excessive Government," can be considered a paradigm case in this regard. It is obvious that in weaving new and clever apologetics for the growth of the state, Lee worsens the status of economic freedom, a goal that he purports to favor, at least in some points in his missive, e.g., regarding the Civil Aeronautics Board, the Interstate Commerce Commission, the Selective Service System, etc.

85. Rothbard, *For a New Liberty*, 59, emphasis added.

86. Ibid., 61.

87. Lee, "In Defense of Excessive Government," 687.

88. Oh happy day!

89. Doh!

90. In particular, the Austrian position stresses lack of information and deficiency in prices and appraisement, due to a lack of private property rights.

91. Nozick, *Anarchy, State, and Utopia*, suffered from a similar problem. For an anarcho-capitalist critique of Nozick's position, see Barnett, Randy (1977), "Whither

Anarchy? Has Robert Nozick Justified the State?" *Journal of Libertarian Studies* 1(1): 15–22; Childs Jr., Roy A. (1977), "The Invisible Hand Strikes Back," *Journal of Libertarian Studies* 1(1): 23–34; Evers, Williamson M. (1977), "Toward a Reformulation of the Law of Contracts," *Journal of Libertarian Studies* 1(1): 3–14; Rothbard, Murray N. (1977), "Robert Nozick and the Immaculate Conception of the State," *Journal of Libertarian Studies* 1(1): 45–58; and Sanders, John T. (1977), "The Free Market Model versus Government: A Reply to Nozick," *Journal of Libertarian Studies* 1(1): 35–44.

92. The archist is the opposite of the anarchist. The anarchist maintains that the absence of government is ideal; the archist that its presence is ideal.

93. Lee, "In Defense of Excessive Government," 687, 688.

94. See Gwartney, Lawson, and Block, *Economic Freedom of the World, 1975–1995*.

95. See, e.g., Rothbard, "Law, Property Rights, and Air Pollution"; also McGee and Block, "Pollution Tradings Permits as a Form of Market Socialism."

96. Lee, "In Defense of Excessive Government," 688. One may be excused for wondering if such fulminations belong in a supposedly prestigious scholarly journal.

97. Ibid.

98. Ibid.

99. Ibid.

100. Ibid., 688, 689.

101. Apart, of course, from his conclusion, and from a few inconsistent gestures in the direction of free enterprise sprinkled throughout his paper, where he attempts to deny his thesis.

## REFERENCES

Anderson, Terry, and P.J. Hill (1979), "An American Experiment in Anarcho-Capitalism: The *not* so Wild, Wild West," *Journal of Libertarian Studies* 3(1): 9–29.

Anderson, William L. (2000), "Austrian Economics and the 'Market Test': A Comment on Laband and Tollison," *Quarterly Journal of Austrian Economics* 3(5): 63–73.

Armentano, Dominick (1982), *Antitrust and Monopoly: Anatomy of a Policy Failure*. New York: Wiley.

——— (1969), "Resource Allocation Problems under Socialism," in *Theory of Economic Systems*, edited by William P. Snavely. New York: Charles E. Merrill.

Armstrong, Donald (1982), *Competition versus Monopoly: Combines Policy in Perspective*. Vancouver, B.C.: Fraser Institute.

Barnett, Andy H., T. Randolph Beard, and David L. Kaserman (1996), "Scope, Learning, and Cross-Subsidy: Organ Transplants in a Multi-Division Hospital – An Extension," *Southern Economic Journal* 62(3): 760–767.

Barnett, Randy E. (1998), *The Structure of Liberty: Justice and the Rule of Law*. Oxford: Clarendon Press.

——— (1977), "Whither Anarchy? Has Robert Nozick Justified the State?" *Journal of Libertarian Studies* 1(1): 15–21.

Barnett, William (1988), "The Market for Used Human Body Parts." *The Free Market* 6(2).

Barnett, William, and Jerry Dauterive (1985), "A Property Rights Approach to Natural Monopoly." Paper presented at the annual meeting of the Southern Economic Association.

Barnett, William, II (1989), "Subjective Cost Revisited." *Review of Austrian Economics* 3(1): 137–138.

Barnett, William, II, and Walter Block, "Coase and Samuelson on Lighthouses." Loyola University New Orleans. Photocopy.

Barnett, William, II, Michael Saliba, and Deborah Walker (2001), "A Free Market in Kidneys: Efficient and Equitable," *Independent Review* 5(3): 373–385.

Beito, David T. (1993), "From Privies to Boulevards: The Private Supply of Infrastructure in the United States during the Nineteenth Century," in *Development by Consent: The Voluntary Supply of Public Goods and Services*, edited by Jerry Jenkins and David E. Sisk. San Francisco, CA: Institute for Contemporary Studies.

Benson, Bruce L. (1989), "Enforcement of Private Property Rights in Primitive Societies: Law Without Government," *Journal of Libertarian Studies* 9(1): 1–26.

Bernstein, Lisa (1992), "Opting out of the Legal System: Extralegal Contractual Relationships in the Diamond Industry," *Journal of Legal Studies* 21: 115–157.

Block, Walter (1982), *Amending the Combines Investigation Act*. Vancouver, B.C.: Fraser Institute.

—— (2000), "Austrian Journals: A Critique of Rosen, Yeager, Laband and Tollison, and Vedder and Gallaway," *Quarterly Journal of Austrian Economics* 3(2): 45–61.

—— (1977), "Austrian Monopoly Theory – A Critique," *Journal of Libertarian Studies* 1(4): 271–279.

—— (1999), "Austrian Theorizing: Recalling the Foundations," *Quarterly Journal of Austrian Economics* 2(4): 21–29.

—— (1993), "Canadian Public Finance Texts Cannot Justify Government Taxation: A Critique of Auld & Miller; Musgrave, Musgrave, & Bird; McCready; and Wolf," *Canadian Public Administration* 36(2): 225–262.

—— (1988), "The Case for a Free Market in Body Parts." In *Essays in the Economics of Liberty: The Free Market Reader*, edited by Llewellyn Rockwell. Auburn, AL: Ludwig von Mises Institute.

—— (1980), "Congestion and Road Pricing," *Journal of Libertarian Studies* 4(3): 299–330.

—— (1991), *Defending the Undefendable*. New York: Fox and Wilkes.

—— (1993), "Drug Prohibition: A Legal and Economic Analysis," *Journal of Business Ethics* 12(9): 689–700.

—— (1996), "Drug Prohibition, Individual Virtue, and Positive Economics," *Review of Political Economy* 8(4): 433–436.

—— (1990), "Environmental Problems, Private Property Rights Solutions," in *Economics and the Environment: A Reconciliation*, edited by Walter Block. Vancouver, B.C.: Fraser Institute.

—— (1979), "Free Market Transportation: Denationalizing the Roads," *Journal of Libertarian Studies* 3(2).

—— (1989), "The Justification of Taxation in the Public Finance Literature: A Critique of Atkinson and Stiglitz, Due, Musgrave and Shoup," *Journal of Public Finance and Public Choice* 3 Fall: 141–158.

—— (2003), "National Defense and the Theory of Externalities, Public Goods and Clubs," in *The Myth of National Defense: Essays on the Theory and History of Security Production*, ed. Hans-Hermann Hoppe. Auburn, AL: Mises Institute, 301–334.

—— (1980), "On Robert Nozick's 'On Austrian Methodology'," *Inquiry* 23(4): 397–444.

234

—— (1983), "Public Goods and Externalities: The Case of Roads," *Journal of Libertarian Studies* 7(1): 1–34.

—— (1996), "Road Socialism," *International Journal of Value-Based Management* 9: 195–207.

—— (1998), "Roads, Bridges, Sunlight, and Private Property: Reply to Gordon Tullock," *Journal des Economistes et des Etudes Humaines* 8(2/3): 315–326.

—— (1992), "Socialist Psychology: Values and Motivations," *Cultural Dynamics* 5(3): 260–282.

—— (1983), "Theories of Highway Safety," *Transportation Research Record* 912: 7–10.

—— (1994), "Total Repeal of Anti-Trust Legislation: A Critique of Bork, Brozen, and Posner," *Review of Austrian Economics* 8(1): 35–70.

Block, Walter, and Matthew Block (1996), "Roads, Bridges, Sunlight, and Private Property Rights," *Journal des Economistes et des Etudes Humaines* 7(2/3): 351–362. qw

Block, Walter, and Tom DiLorenzo (2000), "Is Voluntary Government Possible? A Critique of Constitutional Economics," *Journal of Institutional and Theoretical Economics* 156(4): 567–582.

—— (2001), "The Calculus of Consent Revisited," *Public Finance and Management* 1(3): 305–321.

Block, Walter, Roy Whitehead, Clint Johnson, Mana Davidson, Alan White, and Stacy Chandler (1999–2000), "Human Organ Transplantation: Economic and Legal Issues." *Quinnipiac College School of Law Health Journal* 3: 87–110.

Boaz, David (ed.) (1990), *The Crisis in Drug Prohibition*. Washington, D.C.: Cato Institute.

Boettke, Peter J. (1991), "The Austrian Critique and the Demise of Socialism: The Soviet Case," in *Austrian Economics: Perspectives on the Past and Prospects for the Future*. Vol. 17, edited by Richard M. Ebeling. Hillsdale, MI: Hillsdale College Press, 181–231.

Bork, Robert H. (1978), *The Antitrust Paradox: A Policy at War with Itself*. New York: Basic Books.

Boudreaux, Donald J., and Randall G. Holcombe (1989), "Government by Contract," *Public Finance Quarterly* 17(3): 264–280.

Buchanan, James (1988), "Market Failure and Political Failure," *Cato Journal* 8(1): 1–13.

Buchanan, James M. (1969), *Cost and Choice: An Inquiry into Economic Theory*. Chicago, IL: Markham.

Buchanan, James M., and G. F. Thirlby (1981), *L.S.E. Essays on Cost*. New York: New York University Press.

Cadin, Michelle, and Walter Block (1997), "Privatize the Public Highway System," *The Freeman* 47(2): 96–97.

Carlson, Allan C. (1988), *Family Questions*. New Brunswick, NJ: Transaction Publishers.

Chaloupek, Günther K. (1990), "The Austrian Debate on Economic Calculation in a Socialist Economy," *History of Political Economy* 22(4): 659–675.

Childs, Roy A., Jr. (1977), "The Invisible Hand Strikes Back," *Journal of Libertarian Studies* 1(1).

Coase, Ronald H. (1974), "The Lighthouse in Economics," *Journal of Law and Economics* 17(2): 357–376.

Cobin, John M. (1999), "Market Provisions of Highways: Lessons from Costanera Norte." *Planning and Markets* 2(1).

Conway, David A. (1987), *A Farewell to Marx: An Outline and Appraisal of His Theories*. Middlesex: Penguin Books.

Courtois, Stephane, Nicols Werth, Jean-Louis Panne, Andrzej Paczkowski, Karel Bartosek, and Jean Louis Margolin (1999), *The Black Book of Communism: Crimes, Terror, Repression*. Translated by Jonathan Murphy and Mark Cramer. Cambridge, MA: Harvard University Press.

Cowen, Tyler (ed.) (1988), *The Theory of Market Failure: A Critical Examination*. Fairfax, VA: George Mason University Press.

Cubeddu, Raimondo (1993), *The Philosophy of the Austrian School*. New York: Routledge.

Cussen, Meaghan, and Walter Block (2000), "Drug Legalization: A Public Policy Analysis," *American Journal of Economics and Sociology* 59(3): 525–536.

Cuzán, Alfred G. (1979), "Do We Ever Really Get Out of Anarchy?," *Journal of Libertarian Studies* 3(2): 151–158.

Dauterive, Jerry W., William Bennett, and Everett White (1985), "A Taxonomy of Government Intervention," *Journal of the Southwestern Society of Economists* 12(1): 127–130.

DiLorenzo, Thomas J. (1988), "Competition and Political Entrepreneurship: Austrian Insights into Public Choice Theory," *Review of Austrian Economics* 2(1): 59–71.

—— (1997), "The Myth of Natural Monopoly," *Review of Austrian Economics* 9(2): 43–58.

—— (2002), *The Real Lincoln: A New Look at Abraham Lincoln, His Agenda, and an Unnecessary War*. Roseville, CA: Prima Publishing.

DiLorenzo, Tom, and Walter Block (2001), "Constitutional Economics and the Calculus of Consent," *Journal of Libertarian Studies* 15(3): 37–56.

Dorn, James (1978), "Markets True and False in Yugoslavia," *Journal of Libertarian Studies* 2(3): 243–268.

Ebeling, Richard M. (1993), "Economic Calculation under Socialism: Ludwig von Mises and His Predecessors," in *The Meaning of Ludwig von Mises*, edited by Jeffrey Herbener. Norwell, MA: Kluwer Academic Press.

Evers, Williamson M. (1977), "Toward a Reformulation of the Law of Contracts," *Journal of Libertarian Studies* 1(1): 3–13.

Foldvary, Fred (1994), *Public Goods and Private Communities: The Market Provision of Social Services*. Aldershot: Edward Elgar.

Foss, Nicolai Juul (1995), "Information and the Market Economy: A Note on a Common Marxist Fallacy," *Review of Austrian Economics* 8(2): 127–136.

Friedman, David (1989), *The Machinery of Freedom: Guide to a Radical Capitalism*. 2nd edn. La Salle, IL: Open Court.

Friedman, Milton (1989), "An Open Letter to Bill Bennett." *Wall Street Journal*, September 7.

Galbraith, John Kenneth (1958), *The Affluent Society*. Boston, MA: Houghton-Mifflin.

Gordon, David (1990), *Resurrecting Marx: The Analytical Marxists on Freedom, Exploitation, and Justice*. New Brunswick, N.J.: Transaction Publishers.

Gwartney, James, Robert Lawson, and Walter Block (1996), *Economic Freedom of the World, 1975–1995*. Vancouver, B.C.: Fraser Institute.

Hadfield, Gillian K. (2001), "Privatizing Commercial Law," *Regulation* 24(1): 40–45.

Hamowy, Ronald (ed.) (1987), *Dealing with Drugs: The Consequences of Government Control*. San Francisco, CA: The Pacific Institute.

Hayek, Friedrich A. (1978), "The New Confusion About Planning," in *New Studies in Philosophy, Politics, Economics, and the History of Ideas*. Chicago, IL: University of Chicago Press.

Heilbroner, Robert (1990), "Analysis and Vision in the History of Monetary Economic Thought," *Journal of Economic Literature* 28(3): 1097–1114.

Herbener, Jeffrey M. (1996), "Calculation and the Question of Mathematics," *Review of Austrian Economics* 9(1): 151–162.

High, Jack (1984), "Bork's Paradox: Static vs. Dynamic Efficiency in Antitrust Analysis," *Contemporary Policy Issues* 3(2): 21–34.

Hoff, Trygve J. B. (1981), *Economic Calculation in a Socialist Society*. Indianapolis, IN: Liberty Press.

Holcombe, Randall (1994), *The Economic Foundations of Government*. New York: New York University Press.

Hoppe, Hans-Hermann (2001), *Democracy, the God that Failed: The Economics and Politics of Monarchy, Democracy, and Natural Order*. New Brunswick, NJ: Transaction Publishers.

—— (1993), *The Economics and Ethics of Private Property: Studies in Political Economy and Philosophy*. Boston, MA: Kluwer.

—— (1993), "Fallacies of the Public Goods Theory and the Production of Security," in *Economics and Ethics of Private Property: Studies in Political Economy and Philosophy*. Boston, MA: Kluwer.

—— (1997), "The Political Economy of Monarchy and Democracy and the Idea of a Natural Order," in *Values and the Social Order*, edited by Gerard Radnitzky. Vol. 3. Aldershot: Avebury.

—— (1988), *Praxeology and Economic Science*. Auburn, AL: Ludwig von Mises Institute.

—— (1999), "The Private Production of Defense," *Journal of Libertarian Studies* 14(1): 27–52.

—— (1998), *The Private Production of Defense*. Auburn, AL.: Ludwig von Mises Institute.

—— (1996), "Socialism: A Property or Knowledge Problem?" *Review of Austrian Economics* 9(1): 143–149.

—— (1989), *A Theory of Socialism and Capitalism: Economics, Politics, and Ethics*. Boston, MA: Kluwer.

—— (1997), "Time Preference, Government, and the Process of De-Civilization – From Monarchy to Democracy," In *The Costs of War: America's Pyrrhic Victories*, edited by John V. Denson. New Brunswick, NJ: Transaction Publishers.

Horwitz, Morton J. (1977), *The Transformation of American Law: 1780–1860*. Cambridge, MA: Harvard University Press.

Horwitz, Steven (1996), "Money, Money Prices, and the Socialist Calculation Debates," *Advances in Austrian Economics* 3: 59–77.

Hughes, Mark (1990), "Counterpoint: A Response to Bennet and DiLorenzo," *The Philanthropist* 9(3): 43–56.

—— (1988), Review of *The Nonprofit Sector: A Research Handbook*, edited by Walter W. Powell. *The Philanthropist* 7(4).

Hummel, Jeffrey Rogers (1996), *Emancipating Slaves, Enslaving Free Men: A History of the American Civil War*. Chicago, IL: Open Court.

—— (1990), "National Goods versus Public Goods: Defense, Disarmament, and Free Riders," *Review of Austrian Economics* 4(1): 88–122.

Jasay, Anthony de (1997), *Against Politics: On Government, Anarchy, and Order*. London: Routledge.

Keizer, Willem (1997), "Schumpeter's Walrasian Stand in the Socialist Calculation Debate," in *Austrian Economics in Debate*, edited by Willem Keizer, Bert Riben, and Rudy Van Zijp. London: Routledge.

Kinsella, N. Stephan (1995), "Legislation and the Discovery of Law in a Free Society," *Journal of Libertarian Studies* 11(2): 132–181.

Kirzner, Israel M. (1988), "The Economic Calculation Debate: Lessons for Austrians," *Review of Austrian Economics* 2(1): 1–18.

Klein, Dan, and G. J. Fielding (1993), "How to Franchise Highways," *Journal of Transport Economics and Policy* 27(2): 113–130.

Klein, Dan, John Majewski, and C. Baer (1993), "Economy, Community, and the Law: The Turnpike Movement in New York, 1797–1845," *Journal of Economic History* March: 106–122.

Klein, Peter G. (1996), "Economic Calculation and the Limits of Organization," *Review of Austrian Economics* 9(2): 3–28.

Kolko, Gabriel (1963), *Triumph of Conservatism*. Chicago: Quadrangle Books.

Laband, David N., and Robert D. Tollison (2000), "On Secondhandism and Scientific Appraisal," *Quarterly Journal of Austrian Economics* 3(1): 43–48.

Lavoie, Don (1981), "A Critique of the Standard Account of the Socialist Calculation Debate," *Journal of Libertarian Studies* 5(1): 41–87.

Lee, Dwight R. (1999), "In Defense of Excessive Government," *Southern Economic Journal* 65(4): 674–690.

Lemennicier, Bertrand (1996), "La Privatisation des rues," *Journal Des Economistes et des Etudes Humaines* 7(2/3): 363–374.

Lewin, Peter (1998), "The Firm, Money, and Economic Calculation," *American Journal of Economics and Sociology* 57(4): 499–512.

Macey, Jonathan, and Maureen O'Hara (1999), "Regulating Exchanges and Alternative Trading Systems: A Law and Economics Perspective," *Journal of Legal Studies* 28: 17–53.

Maltsev, Yuri N. (1993), *Requiem for Marx*. Auburn, AL: Ludwig von Mises Institute.

McChesney, Fred (1991), "Antitrust and Regulation: Chicago's Contradictory Views," *Cato Journal* 10: 775–798.

McGee, Robert W., and Walter Block (1994), "Pollution Trading Permits as a Form of Market Socialism, and the Search for a Real Market Solution to Environmental Pollution," *Fordham University Law and Environmental Journal* 6(1): 51–77.

Mises, Ludwig von (1966), *Human Action*. 3rd rev. edn. Chicago, IL: Regnery.

——— (1981), *Socialism*. Indianapolis, IN: Liberty Press /Liberty Classics.

Morriss, Andrew P. (1998), "Miners, Vigilantes, and Cattlemen: Overcoming Free Rider Problems in the Private Provision of Law," *Land and Water Law Review* 33(2): 581–696.

Murray, Charles (1984), *Losing Ground: American Social Policy from 1950 to 1980*. New York: Basic Books.

Murrell, Peter (1983), "Did the Theory of Market Socialism Answer the Challenge of Ludwig von Mises? A Reinterpretation of the Socialist Controversy," *History of Political Economy* 15(1): 92–105.

Nozick, Robert (1974), *Anarchy, State, and Utopia*. New York: Basic Books.

O'Driscoll, Gerald P. (1977), *Economics as a Coordination Problem*. Kansas City, MO: Sheed Andrews and McMeel.

O'Neill, John (1996), "Who Won the Socialist Calculation Debate?" *History of Political Thought* 17(3): 432–442.

Ostrowski, James (2001), "Killers Kill the Killer." *LewRockwell.com*.

Persky, Joseph (1991), "Retrospectives: Lange and von Mises, Large-Scale Enterprises, and the Economic Case for Socialism," *Journal of Economic Perspectives* 5(4): 229–236.

Reisman, George (1996), *Capitalism: A Treatise on Economics*. Ottawa, IL: Jameson Books.

Reynolds, Morgan O. (1998), "The Impossibility of Socialist Economy," *Quarterly Journal of Austrian Economics* 1(2): 29–44.

Rosen, Sherwin (1997), "Austrian and Neoclassical Economics: Any Gains from Trade?" *Journal of Economic Perspectives* 11(4): 139–152.

Rothbard, Murray N. (1997), "Buchanan and Tullock's *The Calculus of Consent*," in *Applications and Criticism from the Austrian School*. Vol. 2 of *The Logic of Action*. Cheltenham: Edward Elgar.

—— (1991), "The End of Socialism and the Calculation Debate Revisited," *Review of Austrian Economics* 5(2): 51–76.

—— (1978), *For a New Liberty*. New York: Macmillan.

—— (1990), "Law, Property Rights, and Air Pollution," in *Economics and the Environment: A Reconciliation*, edited by Walter Block. Vancouver, B.C.: Fraser Institute.

—— (1970), *Man, Economy, and State*. Los Angeles, CA: Nash.

—— (1976), "Praxeology, Value Judgments, and Public Policy," in *The Foundations of Modern Austrian Economics*, edited by Edwin G. Nolan. Kansas City, MO: Sheed and Ward.

—— (1977), "Robert Nozick and the Immaculate Conception of the State," *Journal of Libertarian Studies* 1(1): 45–57.

—— (1978), "Society without a State," in *Anarchism: Nomos XIX*, edited by J.R. Pennock and J.W. Chapman. New York: New York University Press.

—— (1997), "Toward a Reconstruction of Utility and Welfare Economics," in *Method, Money, and the Austrian School*. Vol. 1 of *The Logic of Action*. Cheltenham: Edward Elgar.

Rummel, R.J. (1994), *Death by Government*. New Brunswick, NJ: Transaction Publishers.

—— (1992), *Democide: Nazi Genocide and Mass Murder*. New Brunswick, NJ: Transaction Publishers.

—— (1997), *Statistics of Democide*. Charlottesville, VA: Center for National Security Law, School of Law, University of Virginia.

Salerno, Joseph T. (1990), "Ludwig von Mises as a Social Rationalist," *Review of Austrian Economics* 4(1): 26–54.

—— (1990), "Postscript: Why a Socialist Economy Is 'Impossible'," in *Economic Calculation in the Socialist Commonwealth*, by Ludwig von Mises. Auburn, AL.: Ludwig von Mises Institute.

Sanders, John T. (1977), "The Free Market Model versus Government: A Reply to Nozick," *Journal of Libertarian Studies* 1(1): 35–44.

Schultz, Helen E. (ed.) (1976), *Economic Calculation under Inflation*. Indianapolis, IN: Liberty Press.

Sechrest, Larry J. (1999), "Rand, Anarchy, and Taxes." *Journal of Ayn Rand Studies* 1(1): 87–105.

Selgin, George A. (1988), "Praxeology and Understanding: An Analysis of the Controversy in Austrian Economics," *Review of Austrian Economics* 2: 19–58.

Semmens, John (1987), "Intraurban Road Privatization," *Transportation Research Record* 1107: 120–125.

Shugart, William F., II. (1987), "Don't Revise the Clayton Act, Scrap It!" *Cato Journal* 6: 925–932.

Skoble, Aeon J. (1995), "The Anarchism Controversy," in *Liberty for the 21st Century: Essays in Contemporary Libertarian Thought*, edited by Tibor Machan and Douglas Rasmussen. Lanham, MD: Rowman and Littlefield.

Smith, Fred L., Jr. (1983), "Why Not Abolish Antitrust?" *Regulation* January/February: 23–28.

Spooner, Lysander (1870/1966), *No Treason*. Reprint, Larkspur, CO: Pine Tree Press.

Steele, David Ramsey (1992), *From Marx to Mises: Post-Capitalist Society and the Challenge of Economic Calculation*. La Salle, IL: Open Court.

——— (1981), "Posing the Problem: The Impossibility of Economic Calculation under Socialism," *Journal of Libertarian Studies* 5(1): 1–15.

Stiebler, Reinhard (1999), "A Pre-History of Misesian Calculation: The Contribution of Adolphe Thiers," *Quarterly Journal of Austrian Economics* 2(4): 41–47.

Stinnett, Robert B. (1999), *Day of Deceit: The Truth about FDR and Pearl Harbor*. New York: Touchstone.

Stringham, Edward (1998/1999), "Justice without Government," *Journal of Libertarian Studies* 14(1): 53–77.

Szasz, Thomas (1985), *Ceremonial Chemistry: The Ritual Persecution of Drugs, Addicts, and Pushers*. Holmes Beach, FL: Learning Publications.

——— (1992), *Our Right to Drugs: The Case for a Free Market*. New York: Praeger.

Tamedly, Elizabeth (1969), *Socialism and the International Economic Order*. Caldwell, ID: Caxton Printers.

Thornton, Mark (1991), *The Economics of Prohibition*. Salt Lake City, UT: University of Utah Press.

Tinsley, Patrick (1998/1999), "Private Police: A Note," *Journal of Libertarian Studies* 14(1): 95–100.

Tucker, William (1985), "Black Family Agonistes," *American Spectator* July: 14–17.

Vaughn, Karen I. (1980), "Economic Calculation under Socialism: The Austrian Contribution," *Economic Inquiry* 18(20): 535–554.

Vedder, Richard, and Lowell Gallaway (2000), "The Austrian Market Share in the Marketplace for Ideas, 1871–2025," *Quarterly Journal of Austrian Economics* 3(1): 3–33.

Wanniski, Jude (2001), "Sunset the Pentagon," polyconomics.com.

Yeager, Leland (1997), "Austrian Economics, Neoclassicism, and the Market Test," *Journal of Economic Perspectives* 11(4): 139–165.

——— (1994), "Mises and Hayek and Calculation and Knowledge," *Review of Austrian Economics* 7(2): 93–109.

——— (2000), "The Tactics of Secondhandism," *Quarterly Journal of Austrian Economics* 3(3): 51–61.

# Chapter 16
# Watch Your Language

## 1. Introduction

Language is crucial to clear communication. It makes distinctions. We can hardly express ourselves without it. Our very thoughts can either be brought forth, or not, depending upon whether we have sufficient verbiage with which to attain this end. If the pen is mightier than the sword because it can determine the direction in which this weapon is aimed, then words are even mightier than the pen, for without the former the latter is useless.

Which words have we lost? Which have been thrust down our throats by the forces of socialism, statist feminism, and political correctness? What changes are imperative, if we are to even have a chance to turn things around in a more freedom oriented direction?

## 2. Ms.

Mrs. and Miss have been all but taken from us, and we have been given the execrable Ms. in their place. This is a crucial loss, for the modern language in this regard papers over, nay, obliterates, the distinction between the married and unmarried state for women, while the "archaic" words positively exult in this distinction. This alteration has become so well entrenched by the "inclusive" language movement that even some ostensibly conservative writers and periodicals have adopted it.

Why is this a tragedy? Because it is a disguised attack on the family. Whether the feminists accept this or not, virtually all heterosexual bondings are initiated by the male of the species. (There are good and sufficient sociobiological reasons why this should be the case). Anything that promotes this healthy and life affirming trend must be counted as a good; anything that impedes it as a bad. If it is easy to distinguish between married and unmarried females, male initiative is to that extent supported; if not, then the opposite.

If unmarried males are given incentive to approach unmarried females, this supports the institution of marriage and heterosexuality. To the extent they approach married women, this not only undermines marriage, one of the main bulwarks of society, but directly attacks civilization by exacerbating jealousy and intra male hostility.

Why have the feminists urged Ms. upon us? Ostensibly, because it is "unfair" to distinguish between women on the basis of marital status, but not men. If so, then far better to urge the analogous distinction Mister and Master for married and unmarried men, than to lose that for women. We live in a complex age; surely any institution which simplifies it, by costlessly giving us more information, not less, is to be applauded.

But the softening of this distinction between Mrs. and Miss has implications far removed from any questions of "fairness." This can be seen by asking "Quo bono" from Ms? Those who benefit from making single women less available to heterosexual men are homosexual women, plus all those concerned with the so called overpopulation problem. In economics, when there are large numbers of people or anything else involved, it is commonly assumed that at least some are on the margin.

In this case, there are males on the margin between approaching a female or not, and females on the margin between hetero and homo sexuality. Ms moves society in the diametric opposite direction from the desirable in both these dimensions.

One argument against refusing to adopt to this modern consensus is that people should have the right to choose their own names. If someone wants to change from Cassius Clay to Muhammad Ali, or from Don McCloskey to Deirdre McCloskey, that is their business. Polite people will refer to them by their chosen not their given names.

But this does not at all apply to titles. If I call myself King Block, or Emperor Block, no one need follow suit on this out of considerations of etiquette. Ms. is a title, not the name of any person. When in doubt, always use Miss, not Mrs. The latter is or at least should be an honorific, not lightly to be bestowed in ignorance.

And the same analysis applies to using "he" to stand for "he" or "she," or "him" for "him" or "her." Our writing has become convoluted, and singular and plural no longer match, in an attempt to defer to the sensibilities of self-styled feminists. There is nothing more pathetic than a conservative magazine, attempting to score points against a feminist idea, and yet feeling constrained to use such "inclusive" language.

Could we have as successfully criticized Marxism, had we felt constrained to couch our attacks in Marxist language?


## 3. Developing Countries

It is arrant leftism to call the underdeveloped countries of the world "developing." This is a triumph of will and good intentions over reality; many of these countries are retrogressing, not at all developing. Why not call a spade a spade and insist upon truth in political economy? Let us reserve the honorific "developing" for those countries which have, however imperfectly, embraced capitalism and are hence growing, and use "underdeveloped" or "retrogressing" for those, such as North Korea or Cuba which still cling to central planning and government ownership, and as a result are in the process of moving back to the economics of the Stone Age.

## 4. Rent Seeking

In the literature of the Public Choice school of economic thought, the phrase "rent seeking" is used to described what, even for them, is a rather despicable act: using the power of the state to capture wealth which would not be forthcoming through ordinary market transactions. Examples include minimum wages, farm subsidies, tariffs, etc.

But why use the rather innocuous word "rent" to indicate what is really (indirect) theft? Why not, instead, characterize such acts as loot seeking, booty seeking, pillage seeking, plunder seeking, swag seeking, ransack seeking, theft seeking or plain old robbery (via the intermediation of the government).

This Public Choice practice actually denigrates either one or two things that go by the same name. One is the ancient and honorable institution of collecting rent for land, or houses, or other property, instead of selling them outright. Is there supposed to be something wrong with being a landlord? The other is the concept of economic rent which depicts something that has no foregone alternative.

For example, when the price of Rembrandts increases, this does not call forth an additional supply of these paintings; their fortunate owners gain an economic rent. But why should this be denigrated? As a matter of justice, these particular people made these investments; why should they not profit from them? And as far as economic efficiency is concerned, these higher prices still play an allocative role.

To conflate either of these activities with running to government for special grants of privilege to undermine one's competitors is thus an unwarranted attack on rational language. With friends like these, the freedom philosophy hardly needs enemies.


## 5. Social Justice

For any rational person, "social justice" would indicate a subset of justice focused more narrowly that the entire concept on just, presumably on "social" issues, whatever they are. But in the real word, this phrase applies not to a subcategory of justice, but rather to one particular perspective on justice, namely, that articulated by our friends on the left.

This places opponents of socialism, multiculturalism, etc., in the position of having to say that they oppose social justice. Wonderful, just wonderful. Far better to stick to our guns, to attempt to use language in a way we prefer, rather than have it dictated to us by our intellectual enemies.

In my view, we, too, should embrace "social justice." However, of course, instead of taking an egalitarian position on the concept, we utilize our tried and true insights involving personal and private property rights, negative liberties, homesteading, etc.

## 6. Tax Subsidies

The government does not tax the churches. The government does not (yet) tax (and control) the internet. Is this fair? Not at all, maintain some. These are tax subsidies. The government is subsidizing churches and the e mail, forcing the rest of us to pay more as a result. That is one way to look at the matter.

Another, a far more appropriate way, is that these are not subsidies at all. When some of us are allowed to keep our own hard earned money in our pockets, to spend as we please and not as our masters in Washington D.C. wish, this is hardly a subsidy. Rather, this is part and parcel of private property rights. To take the opposite position is to implicitly acquiesce in the notion that the state really owns the entire wealth of the populace, and anything they leave us is an act of generosity, or subsidy.

This is nonsense on stilts. We are the legitimate owners of all we produce, and government doesn't have a penny they didn't first mulct from us.

# Part 6:
# Taxation

# Chapter 17
## Utility Profits, Fiscal Illusion, and Local Public Expenditures

## 1. Introduction

Economists have recently shown an interest in the relation between public finance and public regulation. Posner (1971) has developed a theory of "taxation by regulation" whereby rate regulation is used as an income redistribution device by charging prices above average cost to one group of customers and below cost to others. Posner's paper includes a detailed discussion of the probable efficiency and equity effects of this practice. Since utility profits often represent a sizable source of municipal revenues,[1] a number of other authors have investigated the allocative and distributive effects of taxation by regulation or "internal subsidization" in several of the public utilities industries. Mann (1977) has studied the effects of internal subsidization in the municipally owned water supply industry and has found that such practices entail substantial allocative and distributive effects. Hollas and Friedland (1980) and Primeau and Nelson (1980) have studied the municipally owned and privately owned electric utility industries respectively, and have found that the process of regulation results in internal subsidization in each case. Taking this research program one step further, Nelson (1980) has examined the effects of internal subsidization on enterprise efficiency. He tested the null hypothesis that revenue contributions to the general fund by municipally owned electric utilities has no effect on the average cost of production for contributing firms. His test results led him to reject this hypothesis and to accept the alternative that internal subsidization tends to decrease average production costs. Nelson speculated that revenue contributions as such may induce a greater degree of "x-efficiency" on the part of public utility management.

In the present paper we shall be concerned with yet another aspect of taxation by regulation that has been largely ignored. Namely, what effect, if any, does the use of utility profits to subsidize a municipality's general fund have on the consumer-taxpayer's perception of the tax price of local public goods and services and, consequently, on the level of local public expenditures? That is, does internal subsidization by municipally owned utilities sever the link between public benefits received and taxes paid, creating a fiscal illusion that causes the consumer-taxpayer to over- or underestimate the true tax price of local public goods and services?[2] In the following sections we shall examine and test the hypothesis stated by Colberg (1955: 386) over twenty-five years ago that

> ...raising a portion of municipal revenues by means of 'profits' on the sale of utility services ... is part of a trend toward concealing the actual

cost of government. Most consumers believe high utility rates are attributable to the high cost of producing service rather than to an indirect collection of taxes. Consumers, therefore, are forced to buy more government services than they realize.[3]

## 2. Utility Profits and Fiscal Illusion

In this section we shall briefly review the conceptual basis of fiscal illusion in order to clarify the above hypothesis.

What Pommerehne and Schneider (1978) call the "traditional" view of fiscal illusion asserts that fiscal illusion is mainly attributable to the cost of obtaining accurate information on the individual's tax burden, which varies depending upon the structure of the tax system. For example, individuals are likely to be more aware of their personal income taxes than of various excise, sales and corporate income taxes. Similarly, it has been hypothesized that individuals will not fully discount and capitalize future tax burdens, making debt finance seem less costly than tax finance. The overall complexity of the revenue system has also been shown to disguise the true cost of public goods and services (Wagner, 1976).

In essence, the idea of fiscal illusion is based not upon irrational behavior on the part of consumer-taxpayers, but rather on the fact that the individual faces positive and increasing costs of obtaining information on his fiscal burden, which is in turn a function of the structure of the tax system. Furthermore, as the economics of information (Stigler, 1961, 1962) would predict, individuals will not obtain perfect information, but rather the optimal amount. Since the rational individual does not expect to have more than a negligible effect on the size and composition of the public goods bundle he receives, investment in public sector benefit-cost information is not expected to yield much of a return (Downs, 1957; Tullock, 1967). Alternatively, the complexity of the tax system increases the cost of obtaining budgetary information which will, according to the traditional view, lead individuals to con-sistently underestimate their true fiscal burden. Such underestimation would increase the quantity of public output demanded.

Even though the traditional view of fiscal illusion predicts underestimation of tax burdens, and there is some empirical evidence in support of this proposition (Wagner, 1976; Green and Munley, 1977), it is theoretically possible that fiscal illusion could bias one's expectations in the opposite direction. As Pommerehne and Schneider point out, there may exist taxes that are well known but whose actual burden is not. In this case underestimation is equally as conceivable as overestimation. In light of this the ultimate effect of fiscal illusion becomes an empirical matter.[4]

Next, let us consider the effects of one particular element of the local tax structure, internal subsidization, on the *perceived* tax price of local public output. The following discussion is an application of a more general model developed by

Wagner (1976). In Figure 1 below, $T_2$ represents the perceived tax price of local public output facing the median voter in the absence of internal subsidization. In this instance the amount of tax revenues taken in will be $T_2 A Q_1 0$, with the desired level of output, $Q_1$. Now, according to Colberg's hypothesis, internal subsidization will decrease the perceived price of local public goods and services as the link

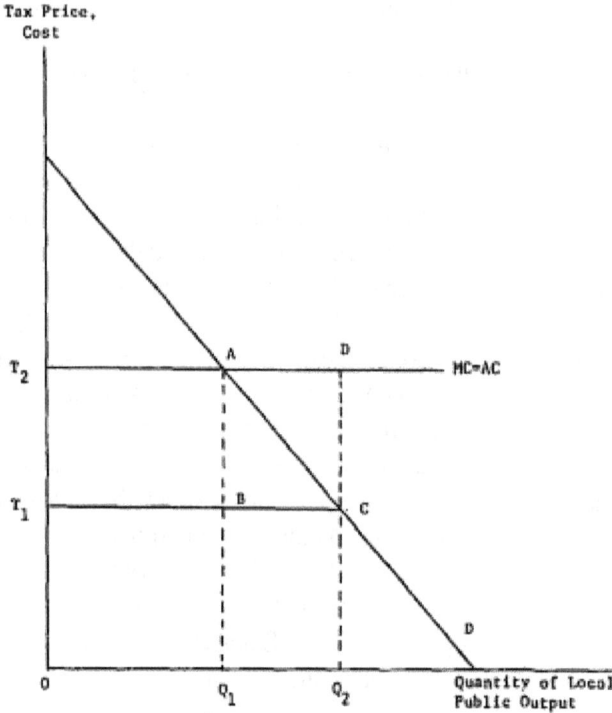

Figure 1.

between public benefits received and taxes paid is severed. The perceived tax price then becomes, say, $T_1$ where the quantity of public output demanded increases to $Q_2$ and the budget increases to $0 T_2 D Q_2$, since the actual price is still $T_2$. Thus internal subsidization leads individuals to underestimate the actual cost of government, inducing them to purchase more government services than they otherwise would.

## 3. Utility Profits and Local Public Expenditures: Empirical Evidence

In the previous section the hypothesis was deduced that internal subsidization decreased the perceived relative price of local public output, thereby increasing the level of local public expenditures. In this section several tests of this hypothesis are offered. The first test employed here involves the estimation of the following two reduced form public expenditure models as seen in equations (1) and (2) for a sample of 116 municipalities in New York State, fifty-two of which engage in the practice of internal subsidization.

$$E_i = \alpha + \sum_{i=1}^{n} b_i X_i + \beta_1 H_i + \beta_2 S_i + e_i \tag{1}$$

$$E_i - U_i = \alpha + \sum_{i=1}^{n} b_i X_i + \beta_1 H_i + \beta_2 S_i + e_i \tag{2}$$

where $E_i$ = per capita expenditures in the $i^{th}$ municipality
    $\alpha$ = constant term
    $b_i$ = vector of coefficients to be estimated
    $X_i$ = vector of independent supply and demand variables
    $H_i$ = Herfindahl index of concentration of revenue sources
    $S_i$ = dummy variable = 1 for municipalities practicing internal sub-
        sidization, zero otherwise
  $E_i - U_i$ = per capital expenditures exclusive of utility expenditures
    $e_i$ = random error term.

The models in equations (1) and (2) are reduced form public expenditure models similar to those used by Wagner and Weber (1975), Wagner (1976) and Greene and Munley (1977).[5] The independent variables are listed below in Table 1. The Herfindahl index is defined as

$$H = \sum_{i=1}^{3} R_i^2 \tag{3}$$

where $R_i^2$ = share in total city revenue generated by a particular revenue source. The data used for this study revealed three different sources-property taxes, sales taxes, and "other" revenues, *exclusive* of utility revenues. The purpose of this index is to measure and control for the overall simplicity of the revenue structure. The fiscal illusion hypothesis predicts a negative coefficient, which would indicate that increased simplicity or concentration in the revenue structure is associated with a reduced level of local public expenditures.

*Table 1.* Independent variables, equations (1) and (2)

| Variable | Description |
| --- | --- |
| POP | Population of the $i_{th}$ municipality in 1976 |
| PCI | Per capita income |
| PNW | Percent nonwhite population |
| IGR | Intergovernmental revenue |
| PWGE | Average monthly public wage |
| H | Herindahl index of tax concentration |
| S | Dummy variable = 1 for subsidy cities, zero otherwise |

249

As mentioned above, from available data[6] fifty-two municipalities in the state of New York were found to engage in the practice of using utility profits to subsidize the general fund. In these municipalities the average subsidy comprised approximately 7% of revenues from own sources while in one city, Plattsburgh, utility revenue contributions made up 85% of total revenues from own sources and another, Schenectady obtained 53% of its tax revenues from utility profits. These are non-trivial amounts as, on average in New York State municipal government revenue sources are categorized as follows: property tax (46%); sales taxes (16%); income taxes (16%); charges and miscellaneous (14%).

The empirical test involved estimating the public expenditure models in equations (1) and (2) for a pooled sample of the fifty-two subsidy cities and the sixty-four other municipalities for which data were available that did not make net contributions to the general fund with utility profits. The focus of this test is on the coefficient of the dummy variable, $S$. The null hypothesis is that ceteris paribus, there is no significant difference in public expenditure levels between subsidy and non-subsidy cities. That is, the null hypothesis can be written as $H_0$: $\beta_2 = 0$. The fiscal illusion model developed above leads us to expect a positive and significant sign for $\beta_2$ which would thereby reject the null hypothesis. The OLS estimates of equations (1) and (2) are seen below in Table 2 where t-statistics are in parentheses.

While the F-statistics indicate that equations (1) and (2) are generally signif-icant, they "explain" approximately 40 and 38% of the variance of the dependent variables respectively. The coefficient of the dummy variable, $S$, is positive and significant at the .001 level. This lends support to the proposition that, ceteris paribus, a municipality's revenue structure will have an effect on local public expenditures. In particular, those municipalities in the sample which subsidize their general fund with utility profits have larger expenditure levels, all other things equal, than in those cases where internal subsidization is absent. This evidence does support the general hypothesis that internal subsidization decreases the perceived tax price of local public output, thereby increasing local expenditures. It is interesting to note that the coefficient for the Herfindahl index was also negative as expected. Of course, there may be other factors related to different legal institutions in the sample cities which may have an additional effect on expenditures if they were controlled for, but taking the entire sample from a single state does limit this problem.[7]

*Table 2.* Estimates of equations (1) and (2).

| Variables | Eq. 1 | Eq. 2 |
|---|---|---|
| POP | .125[b] | .192[a] |
| | (2.50) | (3.846) |
| PCI | −9.90[a] | −1.745 |
| | (−9.612) | (−1.025) |
| PNW | −.527 | −2.56 |
| | (−.394) | (−1.912) |
| IGR | 10.526[c] | 13.33[a] |
| | (2.00) | (5.128) |
| PWGE | 1.585 | 2.17[d] |
| | (1.283) | (1.764) |
| H | −110.339[d] | −92.13 |
| | (−1.385) | (−1.156) |
| S | 146.46[a] | 157.97[a] |
| | (4.207) | (4.534) |
| CONSTANT | 256.25[a] | 211.86[b] |
| | (3.454) | (2.854) |
| $R^2$ | .404 | .376 |
| $F_{(5,111)}$ | 10.544 | 9.385 |

[a] significant at the .001 level.
[b] significant at the .01 level.
[c] significant at the .05 level.
[d] significant at the .10 level.

The preceding evidence indicates that by decreasing the perceived relative price of local public goods, internal subsidization induces the median voter to choose a larger bundle of public output and, consequently, a larger tax burden than if better benefit-cost information were available. As an additional piece of evidence consider the effects of internal subsidization on municipal "own tax revenues." Strauss and Wertz (1976) have studied this question in the context of internal subsidization by municipally owned electric utilities in North Carolina.[8] They estimated an equation of the following form to test for whether or not internal subsidization has an effect on per capita own revenues in a sample of North Carolina cities:

$$PCOR = \beta_1 + \beta_2 E + \beta_3 P + \beta_4 PCY + e_i \qquad (4)$$

where *PCOR* = per capita own revenues, exclusive of utility revenues; *E* = dummy variable = 1 for cities with internal subsidies by municipally owned electric utilities, zero otherwise; *P* = population, a measure of tax base; *PCY* = per capita income; $e_i$ = random error term. The focus of Strauss and Wertz' test was the $\beta_2$ coefficient which they found to be negative and significant, implying that electric utility profits in those North Carolina cities in their sample are a substitute for own revenues, primarily the property tax.

This equation is probably mis-specified, however, for a number of reasons. First, one would expect internal subsidization by other types of utilities, which are omitted, to have an effect on the composition and magnitude of local revenue contributions. Second, equation (3) omits the very important fact that a number of authors (Jackson, 1972; Gramlich and Galper, 1973; Inman, 1971) have found that intergovernmental aid has an effect on the composition of local revenue sources. Generally speaking, these researchers have found that some forms of aid are substitutes for local revenues while others actually stimulate local taxation, i.e., matching grants. Thus omitting intergovernmental revenue as an independent variable leads to a serious misspecification of equation (3). In light of this the following equation was estimated for the 116 New York municipalities to test for whether or not internal subsidization yields an increase in local tax burdens, as the fiscal illusion argument would predict.

$$PCOR = \beta_0 + \beta_1 POP + \beta_2 PCI + \beta_3 IGR + \beta_4 S + \beta_5 H_i + e_i \qquad (5)$$

The variables have all been defined above. The results of OLS estimates of equation (5) are seen below in equation (6) with t-statistics in parentheses.

$$PCOR = 139.07^a + 250.0\ POP + 19.92\ PCI^d + 90.91\ IGR^a$$
$$\phantom{PCOR = } (3.355) \qquad (.055) \qquad (1.454) \qquad (29.412)$$

$$+\ 83.485\ S^a - 51.47\ H$$
$$\phantom{+} (4.015) \qquad (1.067) \qquad\qquad\qquad\qquad (6)$$

$$R^2 \quad = \ .253$$

$$F_{(5,111)} = 7.536$$

[a] significant at .001 level.
[d] significant at .10 level.

While equation (6) explains approximately 25% of the variance in $PCOR$ and is generally significant, the coefficient of the dummy variable, $S$, has the expected positive sign and is significant at the .001 level. Intergovernmental revenue was also found to be positive and highly significant. This result is consistent with the evidence brought forth in Table 2 - that internal subsidization is conducive to increasing local expenditure levels and tax burdens. If internal subsidization in the sample cities is accompanied by any substitution of utility profits for other local tax sources it is likely that this "substitution effect" is outweighed by the positive "expenditure effect" induced by internal subsidization.

Next, the following model was estimated for the fifty-two subsidy cities to examine how the *amount* of the subsidy affects per capita own revenues.

$$PCOR = \beta_1 + \beta_2 POP + \beta_3 PCI + \beta_4 IGR + \beta_5 A + \beta_6 H + e_i \qquad (7)$$

where all the variables have been defined above except for A, which is the amount of the subsidy. The OLS estimates of equation (7) are seen in equation (8).

$$PCOR = 168.54^b + 19.23\,POP^a + 4.50\,PCI - 13.89\,IGR$$
$$\quad\quad\ (2.336)\ \ (10.964)\quad\quad\ (.486)\quad\quad (-.250)$$

$$+\ 1.67\,A^a\ -\ 184.40\,H^b \tag{8}$$
$$\quad (5.253)\quad\quad (2.158)$$

$$R^2 \quad = \ .306$$

$$F_{(5,48)} = 4.136$$

[a] significant at .001 level.
[b] significant at .05 level.

The sign of the subsidy variable, A, is positive, as expected, and significant at the .001 level which implies that a S1 increase in the internal subsidy results in about a $1.67 increase in per capita own tax revenues, exclusive of utility revenues.


## 4. Summary and Conclusions

The main purpose of this paper has been to examine, theoretically and empirically, the effects of internal subsidization by municipal utilities on local public expenditures and tax burdens. The hypothesis was deduced that internal subsidization severs the link between public benefits received and taxes paid, creating a fiscal illusion that induces consumer-taxpayers to underestimate the actual cost of government. This in turn would lead to larger expenditure levels than would otherwise be forthcoming. This hypothesis was tested statistically with a sample of fifty-two municipalities in the state of New York which use utility profits to subsidize the general fund and sixty-four other municipalities which do not. A reduced form public expenditure model was estimated which included a dummy variable to check for any differences in expenditures, *ceteris paribus,* between the 'subsidy cities' and others. It was found that subsidy cities had larger expenditure levels, all other things equal, which adds support for the main hypothesis. It was also found that while it is possible that utility profits may be substituted for other local revenue sources, in the sample of New York municipalities studied internal subsidization is likely to have stimulated expenditures, leading to an *increase* in local tax collections. This result adds further support for the main hypothesis.

# NOTES

1. In a sample of New York municipalities discussed below, utility profits comprise, on average, 7% of revenue from "own sources" and as much as 85% in some cities. Colberg (1955) reports that nearly every type of municipally owned utility industry in the U.S. contains a substantial number of firms that contribute subsidies to the general fund.

2. For a review of some of the fiscal illusion literature see Buchanan (1960, 1967), Goetz (1977) and Wagner (1976).

3. Colberg (1955) also investigated the prospect that above average cost pricing for utility services would reduce the amount demanded, thereby distorting the firm's long-run average cost curve as well as having various equity effects.

4. An empirical test of the "Colberg hypothesis" is the subject of the next section.

5. The linearity assumption for this model was found to be valid by Wagner (1976) and Greene and Munley (1977).

6. Data were obtained from New York State, Division of the Budget, 1976 and 1979–80, and U.S. Bureau of the Census, 1977.

7. Another test was performed to try to determine the effects of the amount of the subsidy on expenditures. The following two equations were estimated for the fifty-two subsidy cities:

$$E_i \quad = \alpha + \sum_{i=1}^{n} b_i X_i + \beta_1 A_i + \beta_2 H_i + e_i \tag{1'}$$

$$E_i - U_i = \alpha + \sum_{i=1}^{n} b_i X_i + \beta_1 A_i + \beta_2 H_i + e_i \tag{2'}$$

where $A$ = amount of subsidy. In each case the coefficient for $A$ was positive, as expected, but insignificant.

8. They were primarily interested in the effects on the composition of the local tax structure and the subsequent vertical and horizontal equity effects.

# REFERENCES

Buchanan, J. M. (1960), *Fiscal theory and political economy.* Chapel Hill, NC: University of North Carolina Press.

Buchanan, J. M. (1967), *Public finance in democratic process.* Chapel Hill, NC: University of North Carolina Press.

Colberg, M. (1955), "Utility profits: A substitute for property taxes," *National Tax Journal* 8 (December): 382–387.

Downs, A. (1957), *An economic theory of democracy.* New York: Harper and Row.

Goetz, C. J. (1977), "Fiscal illusion in state-local finance," in T. Borcherding (ed.), *Budgets and bureaucrats: The source of government growth.* Durham, NC: Duke University Press.

Gramlich, E., and Galper, H. (1973), "State and local fiscal behavior and federal grant policy," *Brookings Papers on Economic Activity* I: 15–58.

Greene, K. V., and Munley, V. G. (1977), "Fiscal illusion. the nature of public goods and equation specification," *Public Choice* 33: 95–100.

Hollas, D., and Friedland, T. (1980), "Price discrimination in the municipal electric industry," in R. Zerbe (ed.), *Research in law and economics*. Greenwich CT: JAI Press.

Inman, R. (1971), *Four essays on fiscal federalism*. Ph.D. Diss., Harvard University.

Jackson, J. (1972), "Polities and the budgetary process," *Social Science Research* 1 (April): 35–60.

Mann, P. (1977), "The interlocking of municipalities and publicly owned utilities," In P. B. Downing (ed.), *Local service pricing policies and their effect 011 urban spatial structure.* Vancouver: University of British Columbia Press.

Nelson, R. A. (1980), "Revenue contributions and efficiency in municipal utilities," *Economic Inquiry* June: 509–513.

New York State. Division of the Budget, (1976), *Special report on municipal affairs.*

New York State. (1979/80), Division of the Budget. *Statistical yearbook.* 1979–80.

Pommerehne, W., and F. Schneider (1978), "Fiscal illusion, political institutions and local public spending: Some neglected relationships," *Kyklos* 31: 381–408.

Posner, R. A. (1971), "Taxation by Regulation," *Bell Journal of Economics* 2(Spring): 22–50.

Primeau, W. J., and R. A. Nelson (1980), "An examination of price discrimination and internal subsidization by electric utilities," *Southern Economic Journal* July: 84–99.

Stigler, G. J. (1961), "The economics of information," *Journal of Political Economy* 69 June: 213–225.

Stigler, G. J. (1962), "Information and labor markets," *Journal of Political Economy* 70 Oct., Suppl.: 94–105.

Strauss, R. P., and K. L. Wertz (1976), "The impact of municipal electric profits on local public finance," *National Tax Journal* 22: 22–30.

Tullock, G. (1967), *Toward a mathematics of politics.* Ann Arbor, MI: University of Michigan Press.

U.S. Bureau of Census (1977), *Census of governments*, Vol. 3: *Public Employment.*

U.S. Bureau of the Census (1977), *Census of governments*, Vol. 4: *Finances of municipalities and township governments.*

Wagner, R. E. (1976), "Revenue structure, fiscal illusion and budgetary choice," *Public Choice* 25 Spring: 45–61.

Wagner, R. E., and W. Weber (1975), "Competition, monopoly and organization of government in metropolitan areas," *Journal of Law and Economics* 18 December: 661–684.

# Chapter 18
# The Expenditure Effects of Restricting Competition in Local Public Service Industries: The Case of Special Districts

## 1. Introduction

In the field of urban public finance, much effort has been put into the task of delineating what is meant by optimal jurisdiction size.[1] Such concepts have led various authors to suggest the restructuring of the organization of local government as a possible means of dealing with local fiscal problems. In contrast to these efforts to depict an optimal structure at a point in time, authors such as Wagner and Martin (1978), Bish and Nourse (1975), and Ostrom et al. (1976) have explored the positive economic effects of various rules and arrangements for facilitating structural change over time. For example, this research agenda has addressed questions such as: What are the expenditure effects of different arrangements for municipal incorporation and annexation, of the ability to contract for services, and of the availability of various revenue sources? This paper further pursues this approach by examining the expenditure effects of legislation in several states that has led to the restriction of the use of single-purpose special districts in the provision of local public services.

The next section describes the proclaimed rationale for why such restrictions have been adopted. The third section then examines the likely effects of these arrangements on the allocation of public resources from a public choice perspective. The hypothesis is deduced that restricting the growth of special districts will render the local government industry more monopolistic, thereby increasing the cost of providing local public services. This hypothesis is then tested by exploring the effects of special district growth restrictions on general per capita local governmental expenditures and on per capita expenditures on water supply, fire protection, sewage disposal, and housing and urban renewal in the two states that have reduced the growth of special districts most severely, California and Oregon.[2] The final section lists summaries and conclusions.

## 2. The Rhetoric of Local Governmental Reform

The "new reform tradition," a set of ideas about how local government "ought" to be organized, contends that the proliferation of special districts in urban areas creates costly administrative duplication as well as confusion among citizen-taxpayers with respect to how government is organized.[3] Such confusion is thought to lead to less responsive local government. Furthermore, it is alleged that special districts are not as capable of exhausting economies of scale in the provision of local public services as are consolidated, general purpose units of government and, therefore, contribute to higher-cost service provision. These views have been embraced by a number of public organizations such as the Advisory Commission on Intergovernmental Relations (ACIR), the National Municipal League, and the Committee for Economic Development (CED). The ACIR, for example, has presented the view that, in general, "... special districts ... inhibit efforts of district consolidation or annexation which would provide more effective and more efficient service to the whole area."[4]

Thus in assuming that centralized municipal service provision is most "efficient," special districts are held to be "inefficient" service providers *by definition.* This view is quite predominant in much of the literature of urban planning, public administration, and urban politics.[5] The legislators of several states have made use of this reasoning in adopting legislation that creates state regulatory agencies whose purpose is to restrain the growth of special districts. These regulatory agencies, staffed by local public service agency managers, local politicians, and citizen-representatives, have been quite effective in limiting the growth of special districts, as seen in Table 1.

## 3. Urban Reform from a Public Choice Perspective

Beginning with Tiebout (1956) and Stigler (1957), an alternative (to the reform tradition) economic approach to the organization of local government has been developed that views competition among local governmental units as being

*Table 1.* Effectiveness of state restrictions on special district growth

| State | 1962 | 1967 | % Change 62-67 | 1972 | % Change 67-72 | 1977 | % Change 72-77 |
|-------|------|------|--------|------|--------|------|--------|
| California | 1,962 | 2,168 | 10.5 | 2,223 | 2.5 | 2,227 | 0.2 |
| Oregon | 727 | 800 | 10.0 | 826 | 3.1 | 797 | -3.5 |
| Nevada | 85 | 89 | 4.7 | 134 | 50.6 | 132 | -1.5 |
| New Mexico | 102 | 97 | -5.0 | 99 | 2.1 | 100 | 10.0 |
| Washington | 867 | 937 | 8.1 | 1,021 | 9.0 | 1,060 | 3.8 |
| U.S.A. | 18,322 | 21,264 | 16.1 | 23,885 | 12.3 | 25,962 | 8.7 |

Source: U.S. Department of Commerce, Bureau of the Census, Census of Governments, 1962-77.

analogous to competition among firms in an industry. The well-known Tiebout hypothesis asserts that a fragmented local governmental environment comprised of competing jurisdictions can indeed be conducive to allocative efficiency under certain assumptions. Barzel (1969) and Buchanan (1970) have extended the Tiebout model by showing that local governmental consolidation leads to a loss in consumption efficiency, contrary to the reformists' assumption that fragmentation is synonymous with "unresponsiveness" on the part of local public supply institutions. Bradford and Oates (1974) have generated evidence that indicates that this welfare loss is likely to be quite large. In light of this research, one would expect special district growth restrictions to diminish, not enhance, consumption efficiency in the provision of local public services.[6]

While consumption efficiency is indeed enhanced by the creation of special districts, the major focus of the remainder of this paper will be on the expenditure effects of special district service provision.

First, consider the technological aspect of economies of scale in local government. A major argument put forth by consolidation proponents is that consolidation of special districts will enhance possibilities of the benefits of economies of scale in the provision of local public services. However, past research has found that there are not likely to be economies of scale for such services as police, fire protection, refuse collection, libraries, street maintenance, and primary and secondary education for jurisdictions beyond the size of 15,000–20,000 population.[7] It appears that there are economies of scale for such capital intensive services as water supply, sewage disposal, and electric power. Further research has found, however, that there also exist diseconomies of scale for water supply, sewage disposal, and electricity, due to diminishing returns as well as increased distribution costs as distance from facility site increases.[8] Thus whether or not consolidation can yield the technological advantage of economies of scale is by no means clear. Furthermore, in the absence of any empirical evidence, there is no a priori reason to believe that special districts are not just as capable as general purpose municipal governments in achieving economies of scale.[9]

Aside from the technological aspects of local public service provision, the economics of bureaucracy implies that alternative public supply institutions will have an effect on the cost of providing local public services. For example, restricting the growth of special districts renders the local government industry more monopolistic.[10] Wagner (1974) has shown that local governmental consolidation provides rational, self-interested local public managers with greater incentives to shirk their monitoring (of local public service provision) activities, which consequently increases the cost of providing local services. Another reason to suspect a greater degree of x-inefficiency as such on the part of local public managers in a consolidated local governmental environment is deduced from Tullock's (1965) theory of bureaucracy. Tullock contends that in public organizations rational, self-interested bureaucrats seeking to enhance their career opportunities will not transmit to their superiors any information that may be detrimental to their own career aspirations. In the absence of profit-loss statements in the public sector, it becomes difficult if not impossible to monitor the effectiveness of public managerial decision-making. Therefore, one expects that the information received by the ultimate decision-maker(s) will be incomplete, biased, and perhaps unreliable. Furthermore, as public agencies gain in size, this process becomes more widespread. Replacing single-purpose special districts with larger municipal departments that are a part of general-purpose units of government would intensify such information loss, increasing the cost of providing local public services.

Another relevant consideration is that the availability of public supply alternatives such as special districts dilutes the monopoly power of municipal or county bureaucracies and thus impairs the ability of public employee groups to expand the size of the local public sector.[11]

In essence, the hypothesis advanced here is that restricting the growth of special districts renders the local government industry more monopolistic, and such monopoly power will tend to increase the cost of providing local public services. In the next section, this hypothesis is tested empirically against the alternative (reformist) hypothesis that restricting special district growth improves the hierarchical organization of local government, enhances possibilities to attain economies of scale, and consequently decreases the cost of providing local public services.

## 4. An Empirical Test

The states of California and Oregon provide an experimental laboratory for the testing of the above hypothesis. As seen in Table 1, these are the two slates that have restricted the growth of special districts most severely. The number of SMSA special districts was even more severely restricted, as seen in Table 2.

The following procedure was used to test the hypothesis. A public expenditure model was employed to estimate per capita county expenditures, including expenditures by municipalities, county governments, townships, and special districts from a sample of pooled data from California and Oregon and from three control-group states. The control-group states chosen were Texas, Kentucky, and West Virginia. These states were chosen since (a) there is free entry by special districts, unlike in California and Oregon, and (b) these are the states for which data were available that experienced the greatest rates of growth in the number of special districts. Thus the local public service industries in these states are among the most competitive. The statistical test used involved the estimation of the following reduced form public expenditure model as seen in equation (1) first with general per capita expenditures as the dependent variable and then for per capita expenditures on water supply, fire protection, sewage disposal, and housing and urban renewal.[12] The independent variables are similar to those used by Wagner and Weber (1975). The major focus of this lest is on the coefficient of the dummy variable, which equals I for California and Oregon counties, zero otherwise.

Table 2. Growth rates of SMSA special districts in California and Oregon, 1962-72

| | Number of SMSA special districts | | | | |
|------|------|------|------|------|------|
| State | 1962 | 1967 | % Change 1962-67 | 1972 | % Change 1967-72 |
| California | 894 | 1300 | 45 | 1,279 | − 2 |
| Oregon | 247 | 350 | 42 | 257 | −27 |

Source: U.S. Department of Commerce, Bureau of the Census, *Census of Governments*, 1962-72.

259

The coefficient of the dummy variable enables us to distinguish any statistically significant differences in per capita expenditures, ceteris paribus, for the two groups of states both in 1967, before special district growth restrictions, and in 1977, after the local public service industries in California and Oregon had become more concentrated.[13] For example, a positive and significant coefficient in 1967 and 1977 but of a greater magnitude in 1977 would indicate that special district growth restrictions are likely to have increased the cost of providing local public services. This particular technique was used by Cook (1973) and Gusteley (1978) in separate studies of the expenditure effects of local governmental consolidation in Toronto, Canada, and Dade County, Florida, respectively.

$$E_i = \alpha + \sum_{j=1}^{n} b_j X_{ji} + \phi D + e_i \tag{1}$$

$E_i$ = per capita expenditures in county $i$, including expenditures by county governments, municipalities, townships, and special districts.

$\alpha$ = constant term

$b_j$ = vector of coefficients to be estimated

$X_{ji}$ = vector of independent variables for county $i$

$D$ = dummy variable = 1 for California and Oregon counties, zero otherwise

$\phi$ = coefficient of dummy variable

$e_i$ = independent and identically distributed error term with mean zero and finite variance $\sigma^2$.

The OLS estimates of this equation are seen in Tables 3–5. In the case of general expenditures, as shown in Table 3, per capita expenditures were estimated to be $14.79 higher in California and Oregon than in the control group states in 1967. In 1977, this difference became strikingly larger, thus lending support to the monopoly government hypothesis. Limiting the growth of special districts is likely to have led an increase in the cost of providing local public services, ceteris paribus.

Estimates of the expenditure model for those services most frequently provided by special districts are shown in Tables 4 and 5.[14] In the case of water supply, there was no significant difference between the two groups of states in 1967, but by 1977 per capita expenditures were estimated to be $11.43 greater in California and Oregon, ceteris paribus.

While fire protection expenditures were estimated to be $3.39 greater in California and Oregon in 1967, this difference increased by over 300% to $13.64 in 1977. In Table 5, we find that for sewage disposal the dummy variable coefficient increased fourfold over the ten-year period, but was not significant in 1977. Thus it is not clear whether per capita expenditures on sewage disposal increased, decreased, or remained constant as the local public service industries in California and Oregon became more concentrated. No significant differences were found between the two groups of states in either 1967 or 1977 for the housing and urban renewal function, although the (insignificant) coefficient of the dummy variable declined over that time period.

Table 3. Estimes of general expenditure coefficients

| Independent variable | $E_{67}$ | $E_{77}$ |
|---|---|---|
| Population | 0.38 (0.613) | 0.41 (0.590) |
| Total assessed property value | 1.30[b] (1.15) | 0.35 (0.739) |
| Aver. monthly public wage | −0.89[b] (−1.44) | −2.46[a] (−7.66) |
| Intergovernmental revenue | 0.40 (0.65) | 1.41[b] (1.620) |
| Percent urban population | 1.82[b] (1.562) | 0.10 (0.02) |
| Percent white population | −2.85 (−0.96) | −0.75[b] (−1.25) |
| Dummy variable | 14.79[b] (1.280) | 2263.13[a] (7.946) |
| Constant | 398.35 (1.260) | 5239.58[a] (11.74) |
| $R^2$ | 0.317 | 0.714 |
| Sample size | 51 | 51 |

[a] Significant at 0.01 level.
[b] Significant at 0.10 level.

Table 4. Water supply and fire protection expenditures

| Independent variable | Water supply | | Fire protection | |
|---|---|---|---|---|
| | $E_{67}$ | $E_{77}$ | $E_{67}$ | $E_{77}$ |
| Population | −0.48 (0.145) | −0.58 (−0.586) | −0.62 (−0.386) | −0.934 (−0.182) |
| Total assessed property value | −0.49[b] (−1.170) | 1.28 (1.050) | −1.67[a] (6.137) | 1.63[b] (1.57) |
| Aver. monthly public wage | −2.67 (−1.05) | 1.03[b] (1.290) | 0.980 (0.727) | 0.81[a] (4.274) |
| Intergovernmental revenue | 0.268 (0.888) | 0.17 (0.227) | 0.57 (0.347) | 1.04 (0.222) |
| Percent urban population | 0.100 (0.616) | −0.10 (0.05) | 0.11 (0.037) | 0.30[c] (2.40) |
| Percent white population | −0.24 (−0.614) | 1.39[a] (−13.90) | −0.10 (−0.07) | 1.82[b] (1.504) |
| Dummy variable | 2.710 (0.259) | 11.43[c] (2.125) | 3.39[c] (1.815) | 13.64[a] (2.952) |
| Constant | 30.98 (0.714) | 39.87[a] (8.591) | 1.58 (0.198) | 1.12 (0.114) |
| $R^2$ | 0.108 | 0.127 | 0.730 | 0.388 |
| Sample size | 47 | 47 | 48 | 48 |

[a] Significant at 0.01 level.
[b] Significant at 0.10 level.
[c] Significant at 0.03 level.

In essence, the evidence brought forth here shows a striking increase in per capita general expenditures, ceteris paribus, in those states that have imposed effective restrictions on the growth of single-purpose special districts. The increased cost of providing water supply and fire protection services contributed substantially to the overall increase in general expenditures.

## 5. Summary and Conclusions

The purpose of this paper has been to extend the type of positive economic analysis of the urban public economy that has been initiated by Wagner and Martin (1978), Wagner and Weber (1975), Ostrom et al. (1976), and others. The hypothesis was tested that restricting the growth of single-purpose special districts renders local service industries more monopolistic and should therefore increase local public expenditure levels. Evidence brought forth indicates that the effect of such restrictions imposed in two states, California and Oregon, was to increase general per capita expenditures, ceteris paribus. Per capita expenditures on water supply and fire protection, two services frequently provided by special districts, were also seen to increase dramatically after controlling for other supply and demand determinants of local public expenditures. Thus the empirical test of the last section supports the monopoly-enhancing view of special district growth restrictions and leads us to reject the alternative reformist hypothesis that consolidating or annexing special districts will lead to improved hierarchical organization of local government and diminish the cost of providing local public services.

Table 5. Sewage disposal and housing and urban renewal expenditures

| Independent variable | Sewage disposal $E_{67}$ | $E_{77}$ | Housing and urban renewal $E_{67}$ | $E_{77}$ |
|---|---|---|---|---|
| Population | −0.95 (0.768) | 0.46 (0.517) | 0.30$^d$ (1.689) | 1.44$^d$ (2.00) |
| Total assessed property value | 1.03 (1.153) | −1.361$^a$ (−2.927) | 0.28 (0.200) | 1.65$^b$ (1.450) |
| Aver. monthly public wage | 3.33$^c$ (2.237) | 4.63$^c$ (2.292) | 3.85 (2.353) | 8.33$^b$ (1.310) |
| Intergovernmental revenue | −0.619 (−0.506) | 0.54 (0.908) | 2.38$^d$ (1.684) | 0.23 (0.090) |
| Percent urban population | 4.44$^a$ (3.062) | −0.16 (−0.417) | −0.53 (−1.06) | 0.31$^b$ (1.600) |
| Percent white population | −3.95$^a$ (27.075) | −0.14 (−0.219) | 0.12 (0.132) | 2.38$^a$ (7.677) |
| Dummy variable | 6.96$^d$ (1.844) | 28.80 (0.936) | −7.97 (−0.378) | −11.02 (−0.925) |
| Constant | 3.73 (0.230) | 44.45 (0.516) | 49.78 (0.487) | 28.11 (0.676) |
| $R^2$ | 0.314 | 0.132 | 0.802 | 0.224 |
| Sample size | 49 | 49 | 41 | 41 |

[a] Significant at 0.01 level.
[b] Significant at 0.10 level.
[c] Significant at 0.03 level.
[d] Significant at 0.05 level.

As the economics of regulation would predict, regulating the growth of special districts is a way that local politicians and bureaucrats can use the powers of the state to limit entry into the local government industry, thereby enhancing their monopoly power.

## NOTES

1. See Henderson (1979) for a review of this literature.
2. These particular services were chosen as they are the services most frequently provided by single-purpose special districts.
3. See Bish (1971) for a discussion of "reform traditions" in urban politics.
4. ACIR (1964).
5. See, for example, Bollens (1957).
6. See Downing and DiLorenzo (1981) for a summary of some survey evidence regarding citizen satisfaction with services provided by local governmental units.
7. See Hirsch (1970) for a summary of such evidence.
8. See the articles by Downing and Gusteley and Wells in Downing (1977).
9. With respect to one particular service, sewage disposal, Downing (1969) has shown that a number of treatment and disposal facilities is likely to be superior to one regional authority on the basis of allocative efficiency.
10. See Savas (1974) and Margolis (1974) for a general discussion of the monopolistic tendencies of local governments that provide various local public services. Also, see Wagner and Weber (1975), who deduce (and test) the hypothesis that consolidated, general-purpose units of government practice full-line forcing that enables them to expand their budgets.
11. Greene and Munley (1979) review both theoretical and empirical work previously done on this "self-generating growth" hypothesis that was first derived by Tullock (1972). They also offer a further test of the hypothesis.
12. Per capita and not total public expenditures were used in an effort to avoid heteroskedasticity problems as noted in Munley and Green (1978).
13. Data were obtained from U.S. Department of Commerce, Bureau of the Census, *Census of Governments,* various volumes, and the *Census of Population.*
14. Much of the reform tradition literature asserts that consolidation or annexation of special districts will decrease the cost of providing these particular services. See ACIR (1964).

## REFERENCES

Advisory Commission on Intergovernmental Relations (1964), *The problem of special districts* in *American government.* Washington, D.C.: U.S. Government Printing Office.
Barzel, Y. (1969), "Two propositions on the optimum level of producing public goods," *Public Choice* 6(Spring): 270–279.
Bish, R. L. (1971), *The public economy of metropolitan areas.* Chicago, IL: Markham.
Bish, R. L., and H. Nourse (1975), *Urban economics and policy analysis.* New York: McGraw-Hill.
Bollens, J. C. (1957), *Special district government in the U.S.* Berkeley, CA: University of California Press.

Bradford, D. F., and W. E. Oates (1974), "Suburban exploitation of central cities and governmental structure," in H. Hochman and G. Peterson (eds.), *Redistribution through public choice*. New York: Columbia University Press, 43–92.

Buchanan, J.M. (1970), "Principles of urban fiscal strategy," *Public Choice* 8(Spring): 1–16.

Cook, G. A. (1973), "Effect of metropolitan government on resource allocation: The case of education in Toronto," *National Tax Journal* 26(December): 585–590.

Downing, P. B. (1969), *The economics of urban sewage disposal*. New York: Praeger.

Downing, P. B. (ed.) (1977), *Local service pricing policies and their effect on urban spatial structure*. Vancouver: University of British Columbia Press.

Downing, P. B., and DiLorenzo, Thomas J. (1981), "User charges and special districts," in R. Aranson and E. Schwartz (eds.), *Management policies in local government finance*. Washington, D.C.: International City Management Association.

Greene, K. V., and V. G. Munley (1979), "Generating growth in public expenditures: The role of employee and constituent demand," *Public Finance Quarterly* 7(January): 92–109.

Greene, K. V., and V. G. Munley (1978), "Fiscal illusion, the nature of public goods, and equation specification," *Public Choice* 33: 95–100.

Gusleley, R. D. (1978), "The allocational and distributional impacts of government consolidation: The Dade County experience," in R. L. Lineberry (ed.), *The politics and economics of urban services*. Beverly Hills, CA: Sage, 87–102.

Henderson, J. V. (1979), "Theories of group, jurisdiction and city size," in P. Mieszkowski and M. Straszheim (eds.), *Current issues in urban economics*. Baltimore, MD: Johns Hopkins Press.

Hirsch, W. Z. (1970), *The economics of state and local government*. New York: McGraw-Hill.

Margolis, J. (1974), "Public policies for private profits: Urban government," in H. Hochman and G. Peterson (eds.), *Redistribution through public choice*. New York: Columbia University Press, 289–319.

Ostrom. E. (ed.) (1976), *The delivery of urban services: Outcomes of change*. Beverly Hills, CA: Sage.

Savas, E.S. (1974), "Municipal monopolies versus competition in delivering urban services," in W. D. Hawley and D. Rogers (eds.), *Improving the quality of urban management*. Beverly Hills, CA: Sage.

Sligler, G. J. (1957), "The tenable range of functions of local government," in U.S. Congress, Joint Economic Committee on Federal Expenditure Policy for Economic Growth and Stability, 213–219.

Tieboul, C. (1956), "A pure theory of local government expenditures," *Journal of Political Economy* 64(October): 416–24.

Tullock, G. (1965), *The politics of bureaucracy*. Washington, D.C.: Public Affairs Press.

Tullock, G. (1972), "Review of Niskanen's bureaucracy and representative government," *Public Choice* 12(Spring): 119–124.

Wagner, R. E. (1974), "Supply-side aspects of the theory of local government: Owners, managers, and lake-over bids," Working paper CE-74-6-3, Center for Study of Public Choice, VPI & SU.

Wagner, R. E., and D. Martin (1978), "The institutional framework for municipal incorporation: An economic analysis of local agency formation commissions in California," *Journal of Law and Economics* 21(October): 404–425.

Wagner, R. E., and Weber, W. (1975), "Competition, monopoly and the organization of government in metropolitan areas," *Journal of Law and Economics* 18(December): 661–684.

# Chapter 19
# The Justification for Taxation in the Public Finance Literature: An Unorthodox View

## 1. Introduction

Public finance is the sub-discipline of economics that deals with taxes, fiscal policy and government enterprise in general. In order to assess the case in behalf of taxation commonly made in this field, I shall analyze the public finance textbooks of Atkinson and Stiglitz (1980), Due (1963), Musgrave (1959) and Shoup (1969).[1] I have chosen textbooks because they are a distillation of knowledge, methodology and perspective of an entire profession; they are the amalgamation of what is considered correct and important. I have chosen these four because they are a representative sample, and highly respected[2] amongst the practitioners of economic orthodoxy in this domain.

The category of economic study we shall consider is sometimes called government finance, sometimes public economics, and sometimes government economics. But whatever the name, this field is very different from all other subdisciplines of economics in one important respect. In every other case, whether it is micro or macro, trade or labor, business cycles or money, resources or growth, development or industrial organization, managerial or accounting, the practitioner plunges right into the subject matter.

In public finance, in contrast, and only in public finance, there is first an attempt to justify the very existence of the topic. In every textbook on this theme I have examined, plus the four to be scrutinized here in detail, there is always an introductory chapter, and in some cases two or three, where the author feels compelled to defend against the charge that the whole enterprise rests upon a foundation of sand.[3]

How can we account for this felt need to vindicate the very subject matter, though this can only be speculative, one possibility is that public finance is the only economic field studying activities to which the use of force is intrinsic.

Shoup, however, attempts to deny this. Or, rather, to mitigate this claim, by asserting that other institutions beside government also avail themselves to the use of force. He states (p. 4): "The government's system operates with the aid of a legal power of compulsion. But in many countries one or more members of a family or of a religious or charitable organization have possessed or still do possess legal power of compulsion over other members. The chief difference between the government's allocating system and that of the family, church, or other nonprofit institution lies in the degree of impersonality of the rules under which the government distributes its services and allocates the burden of covering the costs."

But this is unconvincing. For one thing, there is surely a great difference between the way a private charity engages in fund raising, and the government's tax system. In the former case, this is accomplished through purely voluntary means; in the latter, there is a resort to threats of incarceration.[4] Shoup, perhaps, could attempt to defend his position by claiming that families do exercise coercion over children. But this would not be definitive in the case of adults, where families, religious and charitable organizations treat their members on a voluntary basis. For another, while there is indeed an important difference between government and these charitable institutions with regard to impersonality, this doesn't begin to account for the distinction between the public and private sectors, to which the latter belongs.

If not impersonality, of what, then, does the justification for the tax system consist? Although each of our four authors places a different emphasis on the matter, a definite pattern emerges. On the whole, they all subscribe to the view that government action (i.e., taxation) is justified because of market failure. In what is to follow I shall consider the charge of market failure under seven different rubrics: 1. Perfect competition; 2. Externalities; 3. Growth and economic development; 4. Merit goods; 5. Equity; 6. Obstacles to charging a price and 7. Stability.

## 2. Perfect Competition

It is charged by the public finance community that the real world lacks the conditions which together comprise perfect competition: perfect, costless and full information; demand curves of infinite elasticity; numerous sellers and buyers in all markets; homogeneous products; equilibrium; futures markets and insurance for all conceivable goods and services.[5]

This absence of perfect competition is very important in the view of the public finance economists. Due, for example, goes so far as to assert that "freedom of choice is interfered with ... when competition ceases to be entirely perfect" (p. 11). But there is a serious objection with such a stance. It fails to distinguish between lack of free choice, and lack of numerous alternatives. An otherwise free man who has the unfortunate luck to live on a desert island, or to have been born thousands of years ago, has very few options, compared to most people in modern western industrialized countries. But unless he is under some sort of compulsion (i.e., in prison), he does not lack free choice. Rather, he merely has fewer alternatives than might be available to him under other situations.

Perfect competition, moreover, is unlikely to increase the number of options. To the extent that is meaningful to even discuss this model as a possible description of reality, the requirement that all goods be homogeneous would on the face of it practically guarantee fewer choices than at present. For the heterogeneity of foods and services is surely one of the greatest sources of variety.

Nor has the perfectly competitive model itself gone uncriticized.[6] Among the basic fallacies is that perfect competition, paradoxically, misconstrues competition. It is usually operationally defined in terms of four firm concentration ratios: the percentage of an industry's sales, profits, output, employment, etc., is accounted for by the largest four firms. If this ratio is "low", perfect competition is said to be approximated, but if it is "high", the market is said to be "imperfect." But all such measurements are entirely arbitrary.[7] No one has ever shown where "low" leaves off and where "high" begins. Equally arbitrary is the very definition of an industry. If narrowly conceived (i.e., colas) the ratio will be "high," but if broadly determined (i.e., all beverages) the ratio will be "low." But again we are vouchsafed no non-capricious delineation. And this is because no proper definition of an industry exists, despite the crucial need for it on the part of those who behave in the coherence of the perfectly competitive scheme. If anything in this murky field is certain, it is that were "perfect competition" ever attained, it would be the very opposite of rivalry. With zero profit, no innovations and product definition, no con-tinuing struggle to woo customers away from one another, "perfect competition" is no competition at all.

There is also the difficulty that the absolutely crucial concept of entry restrictions is all but ignored, despite protestations to the contrary. During the years that I.B.M. and ALCOA were the only sellers of computer services and aluminum, respectively, there was complete free entry; that is, no laws existed which prohibited or even discouraged competition. As a result, both companies acted competitively, that is, rivalrously, fending off *potential* competition by innovating, cost cutting, reducing prices, etc. In contrast, the organization of taxicabs in most cities resembles the perfectly competitive model: there are numerous buyers and sellers, and only one price is charged. But new entry is strictly prohibited. Para-doxically, then, advocates of "perfect competition" must see the highly regulated taxi industry as closer to their ideal than the almost completely free computer and aluminum industries.

In a sense, the lack of perfect competition justification for government action is almost too good. For it proves far too much. It argues, in effect, that

1) reality does not resemble an arbitrarily contrived model of the world;
2) reality should resemble this model; and therefore
3) the government should step in, to bring the world into closer conformity with the model.

But almost anything can be "proven" with this line of reasoning. Substitute for perfect competition objects moving faster than the speed of light, or people having more than two arms,[8] and further government intervention can easily be justified.

Even were it true, however, that the market is somehow deficient because the pinnacle of perfect competition has not been attained it by no means follows that further state encroachments on the economy would improve matters. It is entirely possible that the governmental "cure" might be worse than the free enterprise "disease." In reality, the so-called efforts to improve competition through anti-trust activity have soon degenerated into rent seeking, i.e., attacks on private property. Indeed, many have started off with that very intent (Kolko, 1963).

The most potent charge of the perfect competitionists is not that monopolistic firms earn excessive profits, but rather that they misallocate resources. But as Rothbard (1970) shows, this thesis depends entirely on the existence of an independent and objective measure of optimal production under perfect competition. There are curves and diagrams aplenty which illustrate such points, but nowhere is there a criterion for determining the exact price and quantity for each product in a perfectly competitive world.

In any case, there can be no optimal allocation of goods and services under government control. This, even the public finance writers concede. According to Due, for example, the only objective criterion for resource allocation would be the marginal social benefits equal to marginal social costs rule. However, he states (p. 21): "The comparison cannot be made on any meaningful basis. As a *practical matter,* there is no way in which the marginal social costs and benefits of activities which benefit the community as a whole can be measured; the MSB-MSC rule offers no *actual guidance* for policy determination (emphasis added)." In his view, the whole process of government production is reduced to arbitrariness: "In other words, the optimum levels of each activity are determined by the collective estimates of the community regarding relative desirability of particular degrees of attainment of various specific goals" (p. 22). In case you missed it, this means allocating resources by ballot-box voting.

Another aspect of the lack of perfect competition is the lumpiness of factors, or decreasing cost industries. Unused capacity, or conditions where marginal costs are lower than average costs, is a particularly irritating situation for the public finance theorists (Musgrave, p. 7; Due, p. 21), on the grounds, again, of resource misallocation. But there are several difficulties here. Costs are essentially a subjective phenomenon [Buchanan and Thirlby, 1981]. The most basic elemental concept of cost is alternative cost, the next best alternative foregone by the economic actor when he makes a choice. But these costs can only be known to the chooser himself, not to outside observers, such as public finance economists who wring their hands at the prospect of a wrong decision being made.

Moreover, the proponents of this doctrine are lead into a *reductio ad absurdum.* Consider the additional seats in a movie theater which are left unoccupied when there is less than a full house. The objective costs of seating these people, goes the argument, are zero. Allowing in additional people would add to their welfare, without reducing that of anyone else.[9] Pareto conditions are thus not met under real world conditions, because a positive price, any positive price, precludes movie attendance by at least some people.

But this is a recipe for nationalizing all industries which have high set-up or fixed costs, and low marginal costs. If positive prices are not allowed to be charged in the case of newspapers, books, theatres, automobiles, air travel, etc., these industries cannot possibly continue to exist in the private sector. Actually, however, the *reductio* is even more serious. It extends to *all* goods and services, whatever the concatenation of fixed and variable costs. For once a product is manufactured, and is just sitting there in the warehouse, or on the retailer's shelf, for all intents and purposes it has virtually no alternative costs at all. Thus, according to the perfectly competitive doctrine we are here considering, it should not be sold for any positive price. Rather, it should all be given away for free.

## 3. Externalities

Yet another source of private market resource misallocation are externalities, variously called: "neighborhood effects," "public goods," "non-excludability" and the "free rider" problem. These phenomena, too, justify taxation and the government regulatory activity, at least in the view of the public finance economists.

Consider first external economies. Musgrave states (p. 7): "Establishment of an expensive store may increase real estate values in the neighborhood, even though the store cannot collect for the services thus rendered. A railroad into new territory may lead to gains in economic development that greatly exceed the profits to the particular railroad. Since the market permits a price to be charged for only a part of the services rendered, the development may be unprofitable from the private, but profitable from the public, point of view."

However, the owner of the new expensive store is the only one who knows for sure its future location. He is therefore in a position to buy up large swatches of the surrounding real estate *before* its value rises, due to his own investment. (And the same reasoning, of course, applies to the railroad). Another way of internalizing this sort of externality is with the self-enclosed shopping center. There, virtually all of the supposed spillover benefits of retail commerce are captured by the owner of the mall.

Now consider the case of external diseconomies. According to Musgrave (p. 7), "Similarly, private operations may involve social costs that are not reflected in private cost calculations and, hence, are not accounted for by the market. A factory may pollute the air and damage an adjoining resort. The smoke nuisance is a cost to the particular community, yet it is not a private cost to the firm. The resort owners cannot collect from the firm since they cannot prevent its use of the common air. Thus, what is profitable to the private firm may be unprofitable from a social point of view."

These difficulties do abound, but they are not at all the fault of the marketplace, as the critics contend. The problem with this analysis is that it fails to take into account the institution of private property rights.[10]

In the early part of the 19th century, there were a spate of law suits which established the precedents which now inform pollution law (Horwitz, 1977). Before that time private property rights were all but sacrosanct. Plaintiffs were commonly granted injunctions against railroads, manufacturers, and other polluters. But then arose a doctrine according to which the private property right not to be invaded by smoke particles had to be "balanced" against the "public good." In effect, the courts began deciding that the public interest consisted of allowing polluters almost *carte blanche*. As a result industrial technology began switching from non-pollution intensive methodologies to pollution intensive ones. Even a particularly ecologically-minded manufacturer would be powerless to stop this oncoming tide. For if he refrained from unleashing pollutants, perhaps by investing in smoke prevention devices, he would be imposing a cost disadvantage upon himself. Other things equal, he would tend to drive himself toward bankruptcy.

The point is, despite the views of the public finance theorists, that market cannot exist in a vacuum. It rests on a foundation of law. If jurists will not protect property rights, "external diseconomies" will indeed abound. But this is an instance of government failure, not market failure (Rothbard, 1982).

The creed of externalities and public goods is also responsible for a frontal attack on the concept of methodological individualism. Due tells us (p. 12) that "there are various services, such as national defense, which yield substantial benefits to society over and above those which may accrue directly and separately to individuals." But it is difficult to envision what may exist "over and above... individuals." On the contrary, one is tempted to reply, there are only individuals in society; there is nothing that can accrue to any "society" which exists over and above the individuals who comprise it. There is certainly no such thing as a group mind or conscience which can experience benefits which somehow go unappreciated by mere individual citizens (Block, 1980).

Further, it is not true that all members of society benefit equally from government defense expenditures, as claimed by Musgrave.[11] On the contrary, some people are "hawks," who presumably demand ever-increasing military budgets; some are "doves," who call for cut backs. And others are pacifists, who don't benefit at all from armaments. For them weaponry – even limited to defensive purpose – is actually a harm.

We turn now to the claim of non-excludability. According to Musgrave (p. 8), "People who do not pay for the (social) services cannot be excluded from the benefits that result; and since they cannot be excluded from the benefits, they will not engage in voluntary payments. Hence, the market cannot satisfy such wants. (Government) budgetary provision is needed if they are to be satisfied at all." But excludability is just an example of internalizing externalities. It is merely a matter of common sense, and sometimes of research and investment into new "fence-building" technology. If the will is there, the job can usually be done. Of course, if it is legally prohibited, it usually cannot occur. In such a case, however, the fault does not lie with the market, but rather with the statist prohibitions on the functioning of the market.

270

Consider the case of the old-fashioned baseball stadiums. In days of yore, fans would congregate on the roofs of surrounding buildings to watch an important game, such as the world series. The baseball companies were thus unable to exclude these non-paying viewers, and, according to the theory, not only should not have been able to continue operations, but never should have been able to set up a business in the first place. In the event, however, the solution was simple: building higher fences; and ultimately, domed stadiums.

How could this work in the case of defense? One possibility might be a geographical in-gathering of like-minded people within the U.S. on grounds of compatibility on defense matters. For example, the hawks might more closely congregate in Orange Country, California, or in Texas; the doves might assemble in Greenwich Village, and on the upper west side of New York City; in Cambridge, Massachusetts, in Ann Arbor, Michigan, and in the People's Republic of Santa Monica. This tendency might be aided by legislation easing restrictive covenants, so that landlords and property owners would not rent or sell unless the tenant or purchaser agreed to contribute to a private defense agency (or not, as the case may be). Further, such private enterprise protection firms might issue buttons, stickers or signs to their clients, in this way better enabling the exclusion of all non-participants from the benefits (Block, 1983; Friedman, 1973].

Excludability is not inherent in goods - the public finance error, any more than value is inherent in goods – the Marxist error. The fashioning of better fences, jamming devices, and other ways to discriminate between payers and non-payers, is an entrepreneurial task. To be sure, it is sometimes hard to conceive of what business could accomplish in these areas, but this is only because markets are currently not allowed to operate in this regard.[12]

Sometimes the externalities argument is couched in terms of social wants and public goods. The complaint, here, is that the tie between payment and benefit is broken; the advantages of a would-be commercial enterprise are not (cannot be!) limited to customers, so no one is willing to pay. The contention is that we all benefit from national defense, courts, public health measures, etc., whether we contribute to their financing or not. As a result, a "Let George do it" attitude develops. Force, therefore, brutal naked force, must be resorted to if these services are to be produced.

In this regard Musgrave (p. 10) tells us: "The government must step in, and compulsion is called for." And again (pp. 10–11): "A political process must be substituted for the market mechanism, and individuals must be made to adhere to the group decision."

On this theory, however, it would be difficult to account for the existence of any charitable or civic organizations. Consider such groups as the NAACP, ASPCA, ACLU, Salvation Army, United Way, March of Dimes, Red Cross, MS Foundation, Public Radio and Television. In each case, all ties between benefit and payment are cut. None of these public benefactors is able to exclude non-payers from

271

receiving benefits (Hughes, 1989). Further, this view of the public finance ideologues is inconsistent with the creation of the very government they are so anxious to justify. For the state, on their view, is a public good. "We are all free riders. If I start a government, it will benefit you too; so I won't do it. Nor will you, for such activity will benefit me."[13] But this only points to a very flawed logic in the public finance lexicon. It is surely erroneous to defend government and its tax collections on a theory which implies that no such institution can be created in the first place.

## 4. Economic Growth

The market is also said to misallocate resources between present and future consumption. I.e., it is charged that the rate of growth is not optimal under free enterprise, and that this, too, is a justification for government taxation and expenditure policy. In the view of Musgrave (p. 7), "other discrepancies may arise from differences between public and private ... time preferences."[14] And Shoup maintains (pp. 38–39) that "the rate at which income per head will grow under full employment can be increased by public finance measures that restrain certain types of consumption, thus freeing resources for investment in the broadest sense, including education, medical care, and improvements in the pattern and level of nutrition for children and working age adults that increase their productive capacity, present or future, by more than the cost of these improvements (all discounted to a given date). Some of those whose consumption is restricted for this purpose will object, not agreeing that the present sacrifice is worth the gain, present and future, even if that gain materializes in time to be enjoyed by them rather than only by a future generation."

Surprisingly, all such public finance attempts to show non optimal growth patterns assert that standards of living will increase ton slowly. This is in sharp contrast to the view that growth is too *fast*, which is espoused equally firmly in the "limits to growth" literature (Ehrlich, Galbraith). Which is correct? The point is that neither one is; that the only firm basis upon which to judge whether or not economic growth is optimal is the time preference rates of the individual economic actors. But this is precisely the point rejected by both sets of critics of the marketplace! Neither, unfortunately, wrestles with this basic question. Neither proves that the saving consumption decisions made by the individual are "inefficient."

Let us focus on the public finance claim that growth is too slow in the capitalist system. Even granting this dubious proposition, it by no means follows that government, fiscal and other such policies are a good means toward attaining a higher growth rate. For as the best research in this area shows (Bauer, 1971, 1981, 1985), in reality the state actually retards economic development. If the public finance theorists really favor enhanced rates of progress, the last thing they should advocate is an expanded government sector.

## 5. Merit Goods

Let us review for a moment. So far, we have examined the public finance writer's treatment of perfect competition, externalities and growth. We have noted their attempt to justify taxes on the ground that the market, if left to its own devices, would misallocate resources in these three respects. It was contended that the *laissez-faire* system could not maximize welfare from the point of view of the average person, or consumer. That is to say, the vantage point of consumer sovereignty took center stage. It was made the core of the analysis.

And now, we arrive at their investigation of merit goods. Here, we shall see, there is a complete reversal of field. Instead of arguing that the market is deficient in that it misallocates resources, these writers now maintain that although the free enterprise system does *not* misallocate resources from the vantage point of consumer sovereignty, government should still be brought in, precisely for that purpose!

What are merit wants? According to Shoup (p. 43), "Certain private-sector outlays are deemed so laden with a public purpose that they are stimulated by tax laws or subsidies; philanthropic and religious outlays are examples." Musgrave (p. 13) holds that merit wants are "considered so meritorious that their satisfaction is provided for through the public budget, over and above what is provided for through the market and paid for by private buyers ... Public services aimed at the satisfaction of merit wants include such items as publicly furnished school luncheons, subsidized low-cost housing, and free education. Alternatively, certain wants may be stamped as undesirable, and their satisfaction may be discouraged through penalty taxation, as in the case of liquor... *The satisfaction of merit wants, by its very nature, involves interference with consumer preferences.* In view of this, does the satisfaction of merit wants have a place in a normative theory of public economy, based upon the premise of individual preference in a democratic society? A position of extreme individualism could demand that all merit wants be disallowed, but this is not a sensible view." Atkinson and Stiglitz (p. 8) describe merit wants as "a category of goods where the state makes a judgment that certain goods are 'good' or 'bad,' and attempts to encourage the former (e.g., education) and discourage the latter (e.g., alcohol). *This is different from the arguments concerning externalities and public goods, in that with merit wants, the 'public' judgment differs from the private evaluation, rejecting a purely individualistic view of society*" (emphasis added).

But this will not do at all. The public finance economists cannot have it both ways. If it was so important not to misallocate resources from the perspective of consumer sovereignty before (e.g., their analysis of perfect competition, externalities, growth) how can the very opposite now be required, namely a setting aside of the sovereign consumer's desire for alcohol, and wish to neglect education?

Alternatively, if resource allocation in service of the sovereign consumer is so unimportant that it can be set aside in favor of these paternalistic merit wants, why should anyone pay attention to arguments purporting to show that the market misallocates resources by being imperfectly competitive and subject to externalities and growth problems?

The public finance writers cannot both have their cake and eat it. Their merit want concept makes a mockery of their allocation concerns. The two are contradictory. At least one set of arguments must go by the board.


## 6. Income Redistribution

At first glance, it might be thought difficult for avowedly value-free economists to prove that income redistribution follows from the basic premises of their discipline. But such niceties do not for a moment dissuade the public finance theorists from this task. What are their arguments?

Atkinson and Stiglitz announce (p. 6) that "Pareto efficiency does not ensure that the distribution that emerges from the competitive process is in accord with the prevailing concepts of equity (whatever these may be)." One of the primary activities of the government is indeed redistribution. Indeed? Surely, before we accept any such conclusion we must be shown that there are certain specific concepts of equity[15] which alone follow from economic principles. Needless to say, this has not even been attempted, let alone accomplished. And why bring up Pareto efficiency? This is completely dependent upon the vantage point of consumer sovereignty, which has been rejected in the merit want analysis.

Musgrave's defense does not fare any better. He declares (p. 17) that "there was a time when the provision of public services was considered its [government's] only legitimate function, and it was argued that 'the fiscal problem pure and simple' should not be confused with 'alien considerations of social and economic policy.' Subsequently, *however, most people came to recognize* that the revenue-expenditure process of government is bound to have social and economic effects, and that these may be aimed usefully at purposes not directly connected with the immediate objective of satisfying public wants. Adjustments in the state of distribution are one such purpose" (emphasis added). This defense consists of a semi-reasonable opening statement, coupled with a gigantic "however," followed by no more than a bald assertion that "most people" in effect have changed their minds about this matter. No reasons are given for supposing that this change of heart was preferable to the opinions which originally prevailed.[16]

Shoup, in contrast, does attempt to base the normative standard of equity in the positive realm. He opines (p. 23) that "there is a generally accepted standard of equity, or fairness, with respect to public finance measures: equal treatment of those equally circumstanced. It is a principle predominantly founded in analogy with equal treatment before the law." But this analogy is only tenuously connected with present considerations. Justice would indeed be outraged if of two parties guilty of the same crime, one were hanged and the other set free. But is this sufficient ground for in effect robbing Peter to pay Paul?[17]

Due's analysis of this question is lengthy (pp. 9–10), but very informative, and worthy of quotation in full. He starts out in a quite reasonable manner, a vast improvement on the treatment accorded to this subject by many of his public finance colleagues, but then he takes it all back. He does so with a howler of a "however," which is probably the largest and most dramatic "however" in the entire history of economic thought.

"(A) generally accepted goal is that of a distribution of income which is regarded as equitable by the consensus of opinion in society. Since equity in income distribution, as in all matters, is based upon value judgments, economics can be of no real assistance in defining it. It is sometimes argued that economic welfare requires a distribution of income such that the marginal satisfactions of all persons are equal, since otherwise a shifting of income from some persons to others would increase total satisfaction. Actually, this statement has no significant meaning, because of the impossibility of making interpersonal utility comparisons, that is, of comparing relative satisfactions obtained by different persons. There is no way in which the satisfaction received by one person from the consumption of a particular good can be compared with that received by another person from the consumption of the same good. It is not possible *to* say that two persons with the same income, accumulated wealth, number of dependents, and other external circumstances receive the same satisfaction and thus are 'equally well off' in any subjective sense. It is impossible to show that a person with a million-dollar income receives less satisfaction from the expenditures of an additional dollar that does a person with an income of one thousand dollars."

So far, so good. Due has brilliantly closed the door on all sorts of government interventionism, in the name of unsubstantiated value judgments, and illicit inter-personal comparisons of utility. But now comes that infamous "however."

"However," Due continues, "persons make judgments about equity in the distribution of income, on the basis of which they evaluate the actual patterns which occurs with a market economy. Furthermore, in any particular society, there is a substantial consensus of opinion about an optimum pattern; while there are extremists at both ends of the scale, the differences in opinion would typically appear to extend over a relatively narrow range. There is widespread acceptance of the view that the actual distribution of income which develops in a market economy is excessively unequal, and thus that equity requires a closing-together of the extremes, the incomes of the very poor being increased and those of persons at the highest levels being reduced."

Although these passages follow directly one from the other in Due's text, it is as if they were written by two very different people. The first paragraph quoted above wields the basic tools of economic analysis into a coherent refutation of the case for redistribution; but the second is filled with every cliché which mars the usual public finance treatment of this subject. His earlier insights disappear in a welter of consideration for public opinion, and "widespread acceptance;" he seems to feel that truth consist of a sort of "golden mean" between extreme views; he swallows whole the view that incomes can be shown to be "excessively unequal," based solely on considerations of positive economics. All in all, a most disappointing discussion.


## 7. Obstacles to Charging a Price

At one time virtually all economists at least theoretically conceded the preferability of the market over the government bureaucracy on straight efficiency grounds. They did so, or were presumed to have done so, because of the profit and *loss* weeding out process which operates in the former case, but not the latter (Mises, 1969). But this, unfortunately, is far from true in the public finance literature.

Contends Due (p. 16): "It is generally presumed that private enterprise can produce more efficiently than governments, because of the effective stimulus provided by the profit motive. *However,* there are certain situations in which governmental production may be more efficient, in the broad sense of that term. In the first place, certain real costs to society may be avoided if the services are produced by the governments and provided free of charge to the users. The savings are due primarily to elimination of the costs of collecting the charges from the users; the administrative expenses of the taxes used to finance the activities may be much less. For example, if sidewalks were provided by private enterprise, the cost of collection of tolls would far exceed the present costs of collection of property taxes and special assessments to finance sidewalks. This is an extreme example, but the same considerations apply to the financing of highways, since the costs of collection of tolls on all roads must greatly exceed the costs of administering the gas tax" (emphasis added).

When Due uses the word "however," we have learned that we must tread carefully. The problem here is that he has in mind a very unsophisticated version of the free enterprise system. In sidewalk provision, for example, he seems to picture pedestrians stopping to pay at a toll booth set up near each home or store they pass. In actual point of fact many miles of private sidewalks now exist – in shopping malls, condominium developments – and there are no costs of collection; rather, the service is given away for free, as a package deal offered to shoppers, guests, owners and tenants. In the event, these private sidewalks are far more safer, cleaner and in better repair than their public counterparts; and this is because of the usual profit and loss considerations.

A similar analysis applies to the case of private highways [Block, 1983; Rothbard, 1973]. Under free enterprise, motorists would not have to stop every few feet at a toll booth, as Due implies. Rather, sophisticated electronic monitoring devices *could* be utilized as a low-cost collection technique. Alternatively, a leaf could be borrowed from the Singapore experience. That system utilizes differentially colored windshield display permits to indicate time of day and geographical area where travel is allowed. This works on a principle similar to the one used in coin-operated private parking lots.

It is undoubtedly true that *government* toll booth systems are vastly inefficient. As presently operated, limited access highway motorists are forced to stop their high speed travel every few miles in order to pay a few pennies. This system is as galling as it is costly. It is even likely that a gas or property tax may be a more efficient collection device.[18] But it by no means follows as Due seems to think it does that *private* collection costs would therefore be more expensive than either a tax or the present toll booth system. We cannot conclude that absence of collection costs can render public operation of commercial ventures more efficient than private.

## 8. Stabilization

A recurring claim all throughout the public finance literature is that the unencumbered market is subject to sudden bouts of depression, and that government intervention is thus needed to keep the economy on an even keel. Musgrave's statement (p. 22) is symptomatic of the genre: "A free economy, if uncontrolled, tends towards more or less drastic fluctuations in prices and employment; and apart from relatively short-term swings, maladjustments of a secular sort may arise towards unemployment or inflation. Public policy must assume a stabilizing function in order to hold within tolerable limits departures from high employment and price stability."

This view amounts to the reiteration of the old familiar standby, "market failure." But here, as in all other cases where t his charge is made, it is "government failure" which is really responsible for the flaw mistakenly seen in the market.

Unemployment, for example, is not intrinsic to the capitalist order. On the contrary, it is brought about through all sorts of unwise and mischievous government interventions: minimum .wage legislation; legal support tor unions to raise wage rates above productivity levels; the Davis-Bacon Act; "fair" labor standards; occupational licensure; excessive taxation (Williams, 1982).

Similarly, Musgrave to the contrary notwithstanding, inflation is always and ever a strictly governmental phenomenon [Friedman and Schwartz, 1963; Walker, 1976]. Price inflation depends crucially upon excessive monetary creation, and in the modern era of central banking this is solely a prerogative of the state. It can only be alleged that the market is responsible for inflation from a perspective that is innocent of basic economics.

The 1929 depression is commonly thought to be a product of the unhampered market place. This is perhaps "exhibit A" of the public finance point of view on this matter. But even here, despite widely accepted man in the street opinion, there is strong evidence which indicates that far from being a result of the working of the free economy, the great depression, too, came about because of unwise government policy: the Smoot-Hawley tariff; artificial controls on wages and prices, keeping them inflexible in a downward direction. Most important, Friedman and Schwartz (1963) lay a large part of the blame for this debacle at the door of the Federal Reserve System, which presided over the reduction of the money supply by one third in the short space of a few months.[19]

## 9. Conclusion

We are forced to conclude that the main task set for themselves by the public finance writers has not been met: they have failed to justify – without resorting to unsupported value judgments – the institution of taxation. We cannot infer, based on this examination, that taxes are *not* justified. We can only maintain that their self-imposed task has not been accomplished, and that the whole question of how and whether taxes may be justified is still unresolved.[20]

This is an unsatisfactory state of affairs for text book writers in a sub-discipline of economics. After all, a text is supposed to be an amalgamation of well-established doctrine in the field. Either this task should be acquitted with far greater success, or it is advisable that it be left off entirely from the table of contents. Then, public finance could address its proper task: a positive economic evaluation of the effects of taxation, and not a deeply flawed normative justification of the tax system.

### NOTES

1. Unless otherwise noted, all unmarked page · references refer to these four texts.

2. According to Due (p. 13), Musgrave's text "is the modern classic in the field of government finance."

3. For example, at the conclusion of his introductory chapter in this regard, Due (p. 17) states: "These considerations account for the undertaking of the great bulk of present-day government activities. Likewise, they provide a *justification* for replacement of the market mechanism by central decision making on the part of the government" (emphasis added).

4. This point can be interpreted in both a value-free (positive economic) and value-laden (normative economic) manner. From the latter perspective, it is usually stipulated as immoral for one person to demand funds from another against his will – for whatever purpose. Exceptions, however, are commonly made for state tax collections, but for an alternative view, see Spooner (1870, 1973). This distinction is also based on a positive economic category, our main focus of interest in the present paper. For there is all the difference in welfare economics between a forced interaction and a voluntary one. In the latter case we are entitled to deduce, at least *ex ante,* that both parties gain from the exchange. In the former, no such conclusion is ever warranted.

5. This latter condition is especially stressed by Atkinson and Stiglitz (pp. 7 and 349). But the lack of any specific market (say, that for mud pies) is no indication of inefficiency. Rather, it may be evidence that market actors contemplate receiving insufficient returns for setting up such markets. In any case, all academic critics of the non-existence of a given market are free to set up one on their own. That they do not do so, and instead cavil at the inactivity of *others,* is evidence not of market inefficiency, but of their own timidity.

6. See Armentano (1972, 1982, 1986); Block (1982); Rothbard (1970, chapter 10); 01 Lorenzo (1988); Brozen (1982), 144.

7. The two-firm concentration ratio in a boxing ring is 100%. Yet anyone who has ever entered this milieu knows just how competitive it is. See Armstrong (1982).

8. If one arm is useful, and two are even better, then do not three, four or even eight constitute a further improvement?

9. Presumably we should ignore the welfare of the proprietor. After all, he is only in business to earn a profit, a most despicable motive; so anything done to him need not be too carefully factored into our calculations.

10. Perhaps this is why Atkinson and Stiglitz go so far afield in their comprehension of the problem: they have made a decision to eschew consideration of property. In their view (pp. 7–8) "Even if the economy is well described by the competitive equilibrium model, the outcome may not be efficient because of externalities. There are innumerable examples where the actions of an individual or firm affect others directly (not through the price system). Because economic agents take into account only the direct effects upon themselves not the effects on others, the decisions they make are likely not to be 'efficient.' Air and water pollution are perhaps the most notable examples." However, they also state (p. 4) that their "coverage is selective. Some readers will no doubt be horrified or disappointed by the omissions, which include ... the economics of property rights."

11. He states (p. 12): "Social wants are those wants satisfied by services which must be consumed in equal amounts by all."

12. Note that we are not advocating that any such new industries be allowed to operate. Indeed, we are not advocating anything, for such would be the task of normative economics. To engage in such matters would take us away from our agenda, which is a positive economic criticism of the public finance case for taxation.

13. We are here discussing the *creation* of the government, not its continued *existence.* It is important to distinguish between these two situations because only the former, not the latter, is incompatible with the philosophy underlying the public finance literature. For once the state exists, it can force all people to pay taxes; thus there need not be any "spillover benefits." But this argument cannot apply to its very creation, *before* it is able to extract payments from all and sundry.

14. The following sentence reads: "Indeed, if we assume that any one person's welfare depends on that of all others – a case of keeping up with the Joneses – we must conclude that the satisfaction of all private wants involves gains and losses that are not accounted for in the market." But surely this involves a *reductio ad absurdum,* for this is a justification for a government takeover of *all* commercial activity. It proves far too much, and in doing so, exhibits yet again the fallacy of the argument.

15. Whatever concepts of equity there may be floating around in society will hardly do. For it is doubtless true that the income distribution which emerges as a result tor market place activity will not be in accord with many concepts of equity.

16. Due (p. 12) argues along similar lines; "The market economy, even with relatively free competition, has resulted in a pattern of income distribution among families which opinion in society has typically regarded as inequitable, because of the high degree of inequality." But is "opinion in society" correct? How much inequality is too high? Why should only money incomes be subject to forced egalitarianism? Suppose we had the ability to redistribute intelligence, or serenity, or health: is there anything in the axioms of economics that would force us to recognize the validity of coercive transfers of these characteristics? These are among the questions avoided by the public finance advocates of wealth transfers.

17. There is also the religious analogy. In the bible (Matthew, chapter 20, verses 1–16) there is a story of workers who begin their (equally productive) labors at different times of the day, and all end at the same time. Nevertheless, they are all paid the same amount of money at the end of the day. The moral of the story drawn by some left wing commentators is that this is unfair, because unequals are being treated equally. But the employment contract is an agreement between consenting adults. The employer, surely, can in effect make a free gift of money to those laborers who began later in the day, without being accused of anything untoward. This, as it happens, is in accord with the biblical interpretation.

18. The gas tax has the disadvantage that it cannot be used for peak-load pricing. The statist toll booth system now in operation *could* be used in this manner, but given bureaucratic arteriosclerosis, it is not.

19. As well, in the Austrian analysis, the previous bout of inflation during the 1920s artificially encouraged and overstimulated basic industries and round about methods of production: this, in their view, led to the debacle of the thirties (see Rothbard, 1975; Mises, 1966, 1971; Hayek, 1932, 1933; for a critique of this view, see Tullock, 1988).

20. Are there any public finance texts which conclude from their initial examination of these matters that taxes are not justified? Not to the knowledge of the present writer. The writers in this field act almost as if it would be awkward were any such conclusion to be drawn; that is such a case it would be exceedingly difficult for the remainder of the book to be written. But this is to conflate the normative and the positive. Surely one can engage in a positive analysis of the effect of a policy without concerning oneself with the moral justification of that policy.

## REFERENCES

Armentano, D. T. (1982), *Antitrust and Monopoly: Anatomy of a Policy Failure*. New York: Wiley.

-- (1972), *The Myths of Antitrust*. New Rochelle, N.Y.: Arlington House.

-- (1986), *Antitrust Policy: The Case for Repeal*. Washington D.C.: Cato.

Armstrong, D. (1982), *Competition vs. Monopoly*. Vancouver: The Fraser Institute.

Atkinson, A. B., and J. E. Stiglitz (1980), *Lectures on Public Economics*. New York: McGraw-Hill.

Bauer, P. (1971), *Dissent on Development: Studies and Debates on Development Economics*. London: Weidenfield.

-- (1981), *Equality, The Third World and Economic Delusion*. Cambridge, MA: Harvard University Press.

-- (1985), "Liberation Theology and Third World Development," *Theology, Third Wor* *Development and Economic Justice*. Block, W., and D. Shaw (eds.). Vancouver: Th Fraser Institute.

Block, W. (1982), *The Combines Investigation Act*. Vancouver: The Fraser Institute.

-- (1983), "Public Goods and Externalities: The Case of Roads," *Journal of Libertari* *Studies* 7(1): 1–34.

-- (1980), "On Robert Nozick's 'On Austrian Methodology,'" *Inquiry* 23(4): 397–444.

Brozen, Y. (1982), *Concentration, Mergers and Public Policy*. New York: MacMillan.

Buchanan, M., and G. F. Thirbly (eds.) (1980), *L.S.E. Essays on Cost,* New York, New Yo University Press.

Di Lorenzo, T. (1988), "Competition and Political Entrepreneurship: Austrian Insights in Public Choice Theory," *Review of Austrian Economics* II: 59–72.

Due, J. F. (1963), *Government Finance: An Economic Analysis*. 3rd edn. Homewood, Irwin.

Ehrlich, P. R. (1986), *The Population Bomb*. New York: Ballantine.

Friedman, D. (1973), *The Machinery of Freedom*. New York: Harper and Row.

Friedman, M., and A. J. Schwartz (1963), *A Monetary History of the U.S., 1867–19* Princeton, NJ: National Bureau of Economic Research.

Galbraith, J. K. (1967), *The Underdeveloped Country*. Toronto: CBC Publications.

-- (1958), *The Affluent Society*. Boston, MA: Houghton Mifflin.

-- (1972), *The New Industrial State*. Boston, MA: Houghton Mifflin.

-- (1956), *American Capitalism*. Boston, MA: Houghton Mifflin.

-- (1973), *Economics and the Public Purpose*. Boston, MA: Houghton Mifflin.

Hayek, F. A. (1932), *Prices and Production*. London: Routledge.

-- (1966/1933), *Monetary Theory and the Trade Cycle*. New York: A. M. Kelley.

Horowitz, M. J. (1977), *The Transformation of American Law, 1780–1860*. Cambridge, MA: Harvard University Press.

Hughes, M. (1989), *The Voluntary Service Sector in Canada*. Vancouver: The Fraser Institute.

Kolko, G. (1963), *The Triumph of Conservatism*. Chicago, IL: Quadrangle.

Von Mises, L. (1966), *Human Action*. 3rd edn. Chicago, IL: Regnery.

-- (1980), "Profit and Loss," in *Planning for Freedom*. South Holland, IL: Libertarian Press, 103–144.

-- (1971), *The Theory of Money and Credit*. New York: Foundation for Economic Education.

Musgrave, R. A. (1959), *The Theory of Public Finance: A Study in Public Economy*. New York: McGraw Hill.

Rothbard, M. N. (1970), *Man, Economy and State*. Los Angeles, CA: Nash.

-- (1982), "Law, Property Rights and Air Pollution," *Cato journal* 2(1): 55–99.

-- (1973), *For a New Liberty*. New York: MacMillan.

-- (1975), *America's Great Depression*. Kansas City, MO: Sheed and Ward.

Shoup, C. S. (1969), *Public Finance*. Chicago, IL: Aldine.

Spooner, L. (1973/1870), *No Treason*. Colorado Springs, CO: Ralph Myles.

Tullock, G. (1988), "Why the Austrians Are Wrong about Depressions," *Review of Austrian Economics* 2: 73–78.

Williams, W. (1982), *The State against Blacks*. New York: McGraw-Hill.

# Part 7:
# Other Topics in Public Choice

# Chapter 20
# A Constitutionalist Approach
# to Social Security Reform

## 1. Introduction

It is well known that the Social Security system embodies two basic functions: welfare and insurance. Another well-known fact, which is often ignored in popular and academic discussions of Social Security, is that the combination of the welfare and insurance functions creates an "inherent contradiction," as described by Peter Ferrara.[1] Because Social Security has always pursued welfare objectives as well as insurance goals, it operates on a pay-as-you-go basis – Social Security taxes paid into the system are not saved or invested as with real, private insurance, hut instead are paid out to current recipients, as in a welfare program. As a result, the Social Security system provides insurance benefits in a very inefficient and inequitable way, imposes major negative effects on the economy, and severely restricts individual freedom. Since Social Security diverts billions of dollars in savings to the current expenses of government, capital investment is much lower than it would otherwise be, and consequently economic growth, national income, and employment are also depressed.[2] Individual taxpayers are made worse off, since they lose the interest return they would receive if their money were invested – a return much higher than that earned on tax payments and benefits financed by future generations.[3]

Perhaps the most serious problem created by the Social Security system stems from its coercive and compulsory nature. Because of the welfare aspects of the benefit structure, some beneficiaries get more than they are (actuarially) entitled to, while others get less. If the system were voluntary, those getting less would opt out of the system, threatening it with bankruptcy. Because the program as it is now constructed must be compulsory if it is to survive, political decision makers insist that it must be run by the government, since the government is the only institution that has such powers of coercion. Thus, the program will always operate according to political rather than economic criteria. This politicization, in fact, is the basic cause of the program's inherent instability, as will be discussed below.

Many writers have recognized the inherent instability of the Social Security system and have prescribed various "solutions," many of which are aimed at separating the welfare and insurance functions.[4] Martin Feldstein seems to appreciate more fully than others the importance of separating the welfare and insurance elements. He has proposed placing the insurance portion of Social Security on a fully funded basis with a self-supporting trust fund. But this proposal is also hound to be disappointing, should it be adopted, for it leaves the insurance function of Social Security in the domain of the government sector and subject to the forces of political manipulation.

The objective of this paper is to explain the inherent advantages, in terms of equity and efficiency, of complete privatization or "denationalization" of the old-age insurance industry. As the title indicates, the discussion will present a "constitutionalist" perspective on Social Security reform. As in so many other areas, government's excursions into the old-age insurance industry have produced many undesirable results. I contend that this situation has come about neither because the "wrong" people were in office, nor because they were misinformed, but because our democratic institutions are constrained neither by law nor by strong traditions regarding the appropriate tasks of government.[5] Government has expanded far beyond its more limited role of protecting private property rights. It now thrives on the game of interest-group politics, whereby one group's rights are destroyed to accommodate another's in return for political support that helps keep the existing government in power. This widening of governmental powers is largely responsible for many of the destructive policies (such as Social Security) that we observe today.

The remainder of the paper will discuss the effects of the change in the constitutional setting that has allowed the nationalization of the old-age insurance industry. Section II presents some of the relevant conceptual issues from a constitutionalist perspective and discusses privatization of old-age insurance. Section III compares public and private provision of old-age insurance from a theoretical standpoint. Section IV explores the function of public advertising in the provision of Social Security and contrasts it with the role of private advertising. Section V examines the argument that compulsory governmental provision is needed because of "market failures," and section VI offers a summary and conclusions.

## 2. Private versus Political Provision of Old-Age Insurance: Some Conceptual Issues

The issue of whether old-age insurance is best allocated by market or by political criteria is moot to those who understand the negative consequences of the attenuation of private property rights under political resource allocation. Nevertheless, it is important to emphasize the profound differences between the market process and the political process as mechanisms for allocating resources.

The market is a process in which individuals voluntarily interact with one another in pursuit of their own interests. And with appropriately designed institutions such as well-defined, enforced, and respected property rights, freedom of contract, freedom of exchange, and the enforcement of contracts, self-interested behavior generates a spontaneous order – an order chosen by no one; yet it tends to maximize the subjective values of all the market participants. It is in this sense that the market order can be termed "efficient." The maximization of subjective values, as individuals themselves perceive them, is the result of the market process and is not something that can be defined or "maximized" by some outside observer. A point worth emphasizing is that self-interested behavior does provide individuals with incentives to cheat, to defraud, or to default, but as James Buchanan[6] has pointed out, laws, customs, traditions, or moral precepts have been constructed or have evolved to limit such behavior in the market. Thus an overriding function of government is to establish the "rules of the game," and to define and protect property rights, the freedom of exchange, and freedom of contract so as to facilitate mutually advantageous trade.[7] The successful performance of this function, along with generally agreed-upon norms regarding the illegitimacy of cheating and defrauding one's partners in exchange, strengthens the market process and enhances individual welfare.

By contrast, there simply are no such constraints imposed upon "political exchange." It is rare indeed that a politician is prosecuted for bribery, corruption, hand, or dishonesty. Who would create such laws, and who would enforce them but politicians themselves? In politics, ownership rights are not respected. In fact the state seems to operate on the notion that those within government lay claim to all property rights, and have the power to rearrange these rights as they see fit, this is not a "devil theory" of government. Politicians and bureaucrats are, as individuals, no different from the rest of us, they prefer more rights to the use of resources to fewer and are utility maximizers, just as we all are. But the utility of the politician or bureaucrat, operating in the world of "political exchange," is not necessarily enhanced primarily by ownership rights in some goods or services, as in the private market. Politicians and bureaucrats use their positions in government to bestow special rights or privileges on politically active individuals or groups in exchange for votes, campaign contributions, and other forms of political support.[8] Those whose rights are consequently abridged are usually those who are not well organized politically. The revocation or destruction of property rights is the business of modern politics, and politicians are continually seeking to expand the market for their "services." Stability in private property rights is anathema to politicians and bureaucrats, for it imposes constraints on their abilities to accumulate power and wealth.

The Social Security system currently consumes a large part of taxable income and therefore represents a significant infringement of individual rights by government. Since the system is compulsory, individuals are denied the right to control a large portion of their incomes. And, more important for our purposes, they are prohibited from choosing other means of purchasing old-age insurance. The important point is that by its very nature, compulsory government provision of old-age insurance is "inefficient" and therefore reduces individual welfare. If old-age insurance were provided privately, the appropriate role for government would be the more limited one of protecting economic liberties in that and other markets.

Currently the government has revoked those rights – rights that many throughout society have recognized as important. As Peter Ferrara has stated:

> It should be apparent that the coercive nature of social security violates all of these rights. It forces individuals to enter into contracts, exchanges, and associations with the government that they should have the right to refuse. It prohibits individuals from entering into alternative contracts, exchanges, and associations with others concerning the portion of their incomes that social security consumes. It prevents individuals from choosing courses of action other than participation in social security, although these courses of action will hurt no one ... The program ... operates by the use of force and coercion against individuals rather than through voluntary consent. The social security program thus restricts individual liberty in major and significant ways...[9]

From a constitutionalist perspective, it is the enforcement and protection of these rights through the rule of law that is necessary to prevent government from further abusing its power by manipulating the Social Security system for political gain. Such a rule of law may be either written or unwritten, but it will only be enforced if it has the approval of at least a majority of the electorate. In short, as argued below, what is essential to meaningfully address the Social Security dilemma is a change in the constitutional setting. Such a change would require that citizens come to realize the importance of economic liberties, such as the freedom to control a large portion of one's income, and to prohibit the further political plundering of these and other freedoms. For once the government extends its powers beyond the protection of basic rights and enters the realm of legislation and regulation, more and more freedoms are denied, and individual welfare is reduced.

## 3. The Political Economy of Privatization: The Case of Old-Age Insurance

Many taxpayers are made worse off because the old-age-insurance industry is monopolized by government. These individuals would therefore benefit if privatization were allowed. Unfortunately, taxpayers are generally poorly organized politically and will therefore find it difficult (though by no means impossible) to achieve privatization. Among the major beneficiaries of governmental control of the old-age insurance industry are Social Security Administration (SSA) bureaucrats. Bureaucrats are basically no different from other individuals; their primary objective is to enhance their own self-interest. Public employees, however, face a starkly different institutional setting than their private-sector counterparts. This difference explains why government provision of old-age insurance is likely to be more costly and of a lower quality than private provision. In the private sector, the manager (of an insurance company) who tries to minimize the cost to his customers is rewarded by profits, as cost reductions increase his price/cost margin. Profits may benefit the manager directly, should he be a part owner of the firm, or indirectly in the form of more frequent promotions and salary increases. Further, the private managers who do not strive to minimize costs and to produce a high quality product will be penalized by the loss of profits. Managerial labor markets also promote cost minimization, because the firms that do not reward managerial talent will lose that talent (along with the profit-making opportunities) to competing firms.

The market for corporate control is yet another device that creates pressure for cost-minimizing behavior, because managers who do not strive to maximize the value of the firm (by giving the consumers what they want at least cost) run the risk of being replaced through the mechanism of a takeover bid.[10] Finally, the survival principle dictates that the private firms that do not strive to provide high-quality products at least cost in competitive markets will, in the long run, simply not survive. In sum, private-sector institutions provide strong incentives for firms to offer old-age insurance in a least cost way and to cater to the preferences of their customers.

By contrast, no such institutional arrangements exist in the public sector. There are no profits, by definition, in the public sector. A growing body of literature on the economics of bureaucracy[11] explains, however, that in the absence of the profit incentive, utility-maximizing public bureaucrats will pursue the objective of increasing their consumption of perquisites such as staff, travel allowances, on-the-job leisure, and so on. And all of these items are more likely to be obtained with a larger budget for the bureau. Thus, public-sector bureaucrats such as those at the SSA are likely to act so as to maximize discretionary revenues – the excess revenues beyond the cost of providing old-age insurance – and to have a strong preference for on the job leisure, since the price of leisure is lowering the public sector than in the private sector. Consequently, the SSA has little incentive to make changes that will better serve the needs of its "customers." Such changes would be time consuming and costly for the SSA whereas the benefits, in terms of the probability of achieving a larger budget, would be very small. There is little, if anything, the SSA can gain by improving service to the taxpayers.

This bureaucratic attitude explains why the overall quality of government-provided services has the poor reputation it does. The SSA bureaucrats can more profitably spend their time (from their perspective) convincing the Congress and the public (through publications and advertisements) that government old-age insurance provides benefits far greater than what it actually provides, so as to make their own positions (and budget) more secure. These bureaucrats are among the major beneficiaries of the Social Security monopoly. Unlike private monopolists, however, they not only charge a monopoly price but also have the power to force consumers to pay it. Government has often been referred to as the monopolist par excellence, and the SSA lives up to that image.

In[...] to solving the problems of bureaucratic incentives and monopoly power, [th]e system would be a more effective way of permitting consumers to articul[at]e diverse demands for old-age insurance. Each individual could purcha[se differ]ent amounts and types of insurance, according to his preferences. By cont[rast, th]e current system entails a tremendous welfare loss, since it imposes one set [of ben]efit provisions on everyone. The inefficiency of this system is readily apparen[t: sing]le workers must pay for survivors insurance that they do not need – if an unm[arried] worker (with no children) dies, nothing is paid in his name, despite years of [contri]butions; single people must buy the same amount of insurance as married p[eople]; people without children pay the same as those with children; those in low-risk [occu]pations contribute as much as those who work in high-risk jobs, and so on. The [list i]s almost endless.

A furth[er p]roblem is that there is no relation between (tax) prices paid and benefits re[cei]ved. Unlike the private sector, where consumers could trade off different typ[es o]f insurance coverage and other goods depending on their incomes, preferences[, a]nd relative prices, the "price" of Social Security is determined by current bene[fit] levels, and no tradeoffs are allowed. Furthermore, the true price of Social Secu[rity] is well hidden from the average taxpayer, who is not likely to know that he hims[elf] pays for his "employer's contribution" in the form of lower wages. Not to ment[ion] the fact that the true opportunity cost would include the (private) return he co[uld] have earned under a private system and the effects of reduced capital accum[ul]ation and economic growth.

If individu[al]s prefer a change in the types of benefits provided by the Social Security syste[m], they must bear the costs of becoming informed about the current system and m[ust] discover what politicians are promising to do about it. Finally, they must hear the [c]ost of becoming part of an organized coalition powerful enough to influence legis[la]tion. These transactions costs are inordinately high compared to those in the [p]rivate market, which is far more conducive to making marginal adjustments.

Government provision of old-age insurance will also necessarily result in an inequitable distribution of benefits, since the distribution will be shaped according to the preferences of the groups with the most political clout. Those who are not well organized and well financed will always be the net losers. As Peter Ferrara has shown, this group includes women, blacks, the poor, the young, and, ironically, many of the elderly, who would be better off with the right to invest their finds as they see fit. By inflicting costs on these groups, the Social Security system may very well have sown the seeds of its own demise, for beyond some point the marginal benefits to these and other groups of securing truly effective reform via privatization will outweigh the marginal transactions costs. Perhaps then politicians will finally begin to feel the heat. And as the late Senator Everett Dirksen once said, "When politicians begin to feel the heat, they begin to see the light."

## 4. The Role of Public Advertising

One aspect of Social Security that has generated much criticism is the use of allegedly misleading advertising by the SSA. Advertising plays a prominent role in both the private and public sectors, although the net effects are quite different in the two settings. In the private sector, insurance companies advertise primarily to provide information regarding product quality and prices, since consumers typically have very limited knowledge of the alternative products available to them. Furthermore, the firms with the most reliable products are likely to advertise most heavily, for they have the most to gain from repeat sales.[12] There is also considerable evidence that advertising makes the economy more competitive by facilitating comparison shopping.[13] Economic research has revealed, in fact, that legislative restrictions on advertising tend to lessen competitive pressures and to raise prices. And, although much fraudulent or misleading advertising exists, as long as the consumer has the option of comparing and contrasting competing claims of advertisers he is unlikely to be continually misled or "exploited." Market competition protects the consumer from fraudulent advertising, although there are also legal restrictions on such behavior. In fact, private advertising is one of the most heavily regulated economic activities.

Is it also true that government advertising by agencies such as the SSA is on a par with private advertising? That is, does it aim to inform citizens of available alternatives? The answer to this question is an unequivocal no, since the consumers of Social Security have no market choice. Like most other services provided by government, old-age insurance is monopolized: The consumer has no choice between the SSA and a private insurance company. He must continue to pay Social Security taxes regardless of which alternative he may prefer.

Since the SSA does spend large sums on advertising, the question becomes: Are politicians and bureaucrats held legally liable for their promises, as they insist their private-sector counterparts should be? As Richard E. Wagner pointed out in a most original analysis of the role of public advertising:

> Politicians cannot be held liable for their promises. If a hot dog manufacturer's all-meat product turns out to be 30 percent chicken and bread crumbs, he will most likely encounter difficulty with the government, even if consumers buy the product. But when the government's comparable product turns out to be 60 percent baloney, no regulatory agency will take action.[14]

This, of course, is not to suggest that more regulation is needed. The point is that politicians and bureaucrats are not in fact held liable for false advertising, and the SSA is among the most serious offenders. In a now-famous statement from a booklet published by the SSA we are told:

> The basic idea of Social Security is a simple one: during working years employees, their employers, and self-employed people pay Social

Security contributions into special trust funds. When earnings stop or are reduced because the worker retires, dies, or becomes disabled, monthly cash benefits are paid to replace part of the earnings his family has lost.[15]

Similar statements are made through government campaigns, the press, and on radio and television. As Milton Friedman has said, however, it would be hard to pack a greater number of false and misleading statements into a single paragraph. Individuals do not pay Social Security "contributions." Contributions are voluntary; Social Security taxes are not – and failure to pay them will result in fines, imprisonment, or both. Furthermore, employers do not pay "their share" of Social Security taxes; the burden of taxation is ultimately shifted to the wage earner.[16] The above paragraph also gives one the impression that the "special trust funds" are actually sums of money that are saved and invested much like private pension funds, rather than being immediately paid out in benefits. Finally, one also gets the impression that one's future benefits will be paid from the "trust funds" and that such benefits are guaranteed. In reality, the only guarantee is the willingness and ability of future generations to pay Social Security taxes.

Apparently, the purpose of such advertising is to mislead the public into believing that Social Security is in fact equivalent to private insurance. Perhaps that is why we are told that Social Security cards are "the symbol of your insurance policy under the federal Social Security Law."[17] Because of the absence of market constraints, and because politicians and bureaucrats themselves are "responsible" for enforcing laws or standards regarding false and misleading advertising by government, such activities can be expected to continue throughout the SSA in particular and the government generally.

Another effect of misleading advertising by the SSA stems from the fact that Social Security benefits, like the benefits of most governmental services, fall into the category of goods economists call "credence services."[18] These are services whose quality is difficult to judge. Many private services, e.g., car repair, fall into this category, and individuals can be induced to pay more for the service if they are unsure about the quality. The unsuspecting motorist who thinks that all he needs is an oil change has more than once been counseled into an engine overhaul, although competitive pressures make this behavior costly to the station owner and will therefore limit it. One would expect this type of fraudulent behavior to be even more widespread in the public sector, however, because of the difficulty of evaluating services and the absence of market alternatives.

In light of all this, just what is the function of public advertising as practiced by the SSA? Richard Wagner seems to have it right:

> [The] principal function of public advertising would seem lobe to promote acquiescence about the prevailing public policies. The purpose of public advertising would he to reassure citizens that the fact that

290

their public goods are composed of 60 percent baloney indicates good performance.[19]

Thus, while the Social Security system impairs individual wealth and freedom and exerts a strong negative influence on the economy, the role of political advertising is to draw the public's attention away from these realities, so as to enhance the prospects for further growth of the Social Security bureaucracy. Such advertising hides the welfare aspects of the program. By emphasizing (contrary to fact) that Social Security is like an insurance program and that Social Security taxes are like insurance premiums, the SSA obscures the trite costs of the program. This increases the political acceptability of the current program and provides more security not for the elderly, but for the Social Security bureaucracy.

## 5. The Provision of Old-Age Insurance: A Case of Market Failure?

There have been numerous rationales advanced for the governmental provision of old-age insurance to the exclusion of private provision, including the "forced savings" argument, welfare and redistributionist rationales, the alleged superiority of a pay-as-you-go system that must be governmentally provided, and the desirability of intergenerational transfers. All of these rationales have been widely discussed elsewhere, but yet another is of particular relevance to the privatization issue and will therefore be dealt with here. Namely, the argument has been made that government provision of old-age insurance is necessary because of market imperfections that would make private-sector alternatives unattractive or unavailable. This is the classic "market failure" rationale for government intervention. One alleged market inefficiency stems from the fact that those who anticipate a long life may purchase annuities heavily, which will increase the rates charged these individuals and to others. The "average" person may therefore be treated "unfairly" or be priced out of the market and will be left without the protection provided him by Social Security. Thus it is alleged that an "adverse selection" problem exists. However, actuarial rates are based on characteristics of groups of purchasers, not on particular individuals. Those who are expected to live longer (i.e., women) can expect to be charged higher rates than those with lower expected life spans. Prohibiting such arrangements by government mandate, however, would cause what one might call a *government-induced* market "failure."[20]

Even if private markets would not emerge for certain groups of individuals (which is mere conjecture), one cannot argue for compulsory governmental provision on the grounds of economic efficiency. For in order for any change to be economically efficient, it must make someone better off without making anyone worse off. That is why voluntary trade is efficient, but it also explains why governmental provision of old-age insurance could never be, for that would require unanimous consent. In light of the fact that private alternatives would yield several times the return to Social Security, unanimous agreement to maintain the current system would be impossible. The case for prohibiting privatization can only be based on coercion, not efficiency, as conventionally defined.

A second "market failure" argument is based on the idea that since individuals do not have perfect information about market alternatives, and since information is costly, government provision is needed. Information is a public good, so it is said, so that the market "fails" in this respect to provide the optimum quantity. This particular line of reasoning commits what Harold Demsetz called the "nirvana fallacy": If one compares a world of perfection with the real world, the real world will invariably turn out to be imperfect or inefficient.[21] In fact, the market process best facilitates the use of knowledge in society.[22] No group of governmental planners at the Social Security Administration could ever make efficient use of all the constantly changing information that exists in the minds of consumers. Only individuals themselves can make such decisions, and the private market is the only known mechanism that can facilitate this process. Once individuals decided what the "appropriate" retirement age is, when to start buying old-age insurance, etc., private firms would meet the demand. Increased demand for certain types of policies would be reflected in higher relative prices, which would induce a greater supply.

By contrast, given that personal preferences vary widely, the uniform provision of one kind of old-age insurance by the government would satisfy the preferences of relatively few. It is the government that is a major source of inefficiency in the use of information. Governmental provision, by definition, cannot accommodate the diversity of preferences that exists in the world. More important, governmental provision totally subverts the role of the price system in conveying the relevant information. It simply substitutes the preferences of bureaucrats for those of consumers, as conveyed by the price system. When one judges the efficiency of the private insurance market by a benchmark of omniscience, one is quite naturally led to the conclusion that the market "fails." But from the standpoint of reality, it is well known that the private market is much more accommodating to diversity of preferences than the bureaucracy is.

In sum, it appears that the "market failure" arguments in favor of compulsory governmental provision of old-age insurance rest on very weak ground. They are, however, rather typical products of an entire industry that has evolved, wherein welfare economists concoct an ever-increasing volume of excuses for governmental coercion to promote ends with which they personally agree. It appears that such arguments are nothing but attempts to ease the consciences of those who make them.[23]

A radical departure from orthodox welfare economics, developed by Ken Shepsle,[24] provides what I believe to be a more accurate explanation of why the insurance component of Social Security is nationalized. While much has been made of the polar distinction between public and private goods and problems of externalities and other "market failures" in discussions of the "appropriate" role of

292

government in the economy, Shepsle notes that all goods are mixes of publicness and privateness, and most processes of production and consumption generate externalities. But the governmental response to these problems is generally idiosyncratic: Sonic externalities are regulated, others are not; some goods with attributes of publicness are provided by government, others are not; and many private goods are provided by government. In short, welfare economics has little to do with actual governmental decisions to intervene in private markets. Among the factors that are decisive, according to Shepsle, are the opportunities for coalition building by those who stand to benefit front the program, the abilities of political entrepreneurs to enact the programs (with which they hope to enhance their terms in office), and the ability to extol arguments exaggerating market failure and emphasizing the "need" for intervention.

Although Social Security has recently become somewhat of a political albatross, it was, for many years, a political goldmine. (Of course, it is still manipulated to secure votes.) For years the program has been a means of dispensing benefits to current voters at the expense of future generations, who of course cannot object. From the very start, the system was used by politicians to advance their political interests. Politicians convinced the public that the system would be run on a fully funded basis, hut that promise was soon broken. Congress has voted benefit increases without accompanying tax increases in nearly every election year,[25] so that the system is now on the verge of financial collapse. Allowing privatization would impair the empire building capacities of politicians; that is why the Greenspan Commission did not even consider it.

Special-interest groups have also played an important role in shaping the Social Security system, by lobbying for particularized benefits and for ideological benefits such as increased welfare spending. Of course, the most important interest group is current beneficiaries, who are arguably the strongest political force in the nation, and who provide opposition to any significant proposals for change.

Finally, as with all government programs, those who intend to run the program are the foremost lobbyists in support of it.[26] This was certainly true at the system's inception, and few would dispute the fact that the SSA bureaucracy spends much of its time and effort exaggerating the "necessity" of maintaining the status quo (but with a bigger budget) and discouraging privatization.

In summary, the market-failure arguments in support of governmental provision of the insurance element of Social Security do not stand up to close scrutiny. It is doubtful that a problem of adverse selection would be of any consequence under privatization, and even if it were, one could not argue for mandatory governmental provision on efficiency grounds, for efficiency requires unanimous consent. Nor can one claim that imperfect information is cause for governmental intervention, for private markets have proven to be far superior to government bureaucracies in the use of knowledge – knowledge that can be transmitted only via the price system. The case for compulsory governmental provision of old-age insurance is based on coercion, not efficiency or equity. In particular, the main impact of the current system is to redistribute wealth, not to provide insurance, and the motivation for this system is, I believe, that the people who benefit from the transfers want them and are adept at using the powers of the state to secure them.[27] The net losers are all those who do not receive particularized benefits but who must nevertheless continue to pay taxes and experience the effects of slower economic growth.[28]

## 6. Summary and Conclusions

It does not appear that the Social Security crisis can be dealt with by manipulating the benefit structure or the tax structure every five years or so. At best, this strategy postpones the day of reckoning and permits politicians to stand on the brink of disaster, piously claiming they have saved everyone's Social Security. As discussed above, a first step toward effective reform is the complete privatization of the insurance element of Social Security. Privatization would provide benefits more tailored to individual preferences and a higher return on investment, and would 'stimulate private savings, capital accumulation, and economic growth.

What are the prospects for real reform? The recent actions of the Reagan administration, Congress, and the Greenspan Commission convey pessimism. Politics-as-usual has produced yet another short-term remedy for a long-term illness. But I am not pessimistic. The key to understanding the nature of the problem is to recognize that a major reason for this and other government failures is that there has been a change in the constitutional setting. A skirmish in the battle of ideas, if you will, has been won by those who prefer more centralized control over the economy and a redistribution of wealth to themselves and to other favored groups. A change in public attitudes occurred, beginning in the earlier part of this century, which allowed politicians to abandon their roles as agents whose primary task was to protect private property rights and to defend the rights of freedom of exchange and freedom of contract."[29] Instead, they became more brazen in their attempts to revoke individual rights for political gain, and the nationalization of the old-age-insurance industry was permitted to take place.

Thus, what is necessary for truly effective reform is yet another change in the constitutional setting. The value of limited government was understood by writers such as Thomas Jefferson and James Madison, as well as many of their contemporaries. Economic liberties must once again be appreciated and accorded the same respect that civil liberties seem to be given. This may not be as difficult a task as it might appear at first. As mentioned above, the tremendous costs imposed on individuals in all segments of the population by the old age insurance monopoly will provide them with incentives to investigate and eventually advocate the privatization alternative.

A number of very distinguished authors have misunderstood or ignored this basic point, and some have even declared Social Security to be the most successful government program ever. That may be true, hut it in no way means that citizens would not be far better off without it. Furthermore, it is often claimed that the existing system is successful because "it has majority approval." But as Friedrich Hayek has noted, representative democracy under majority rule, although it is our only protection against tyranny, does not produce what the majority wants. Rather it produces what each of the interest groups making up the majority must concede to the others to get their support for what it wants itself.[30] Government policy is largely determined by a series of deals with special interests, and Social Security is no exception. In fact, Hayek further noted, majority rule is a meaningful phrase only if used to describe agreement on general rules of law, not legislation, because the amount of information necessary to make truly informed decisions about legislation (i.e., the effects of the Social Security system) is prohibitive. By contrast, individuals do have a conception of the general direction they would like their government to go in, and the protection of rights to life, liberty, and property is one direction that has wide acceptance. The immediate problem facing the political economist and other concerned citizens is to bring to the attention of the citizenry the Pact that these rights have been revoked by the Social Security system and other governmental interventions and should be reinstated immediately.

Finally, recent events have hinted at prospects for effective reform, for Congress recently voted to place itself and a large part of the federal bureaucracy under the umbrella (web?) of the Social Security system. On this matter, the authors of Cato's Letters said of politicians;

> [W]hen they make no laws but what they themselves and their posterity insist he subject to; when they can give no money, hut what they must pay their share of; when they can do no mischief, but what must fall upon their own heads in common with their countrymen; their principals may expect then good laws, little mischief, and much frugality.[31]

I am generally proud of the fact that I do not consider myself to be an economic forecaster, but I would like to offer a political forecast. Soon after the 1984 elections, Congress will either attach an amendment to a strip-mining hill that will exclude members of Congress from Social Security, start up a "supplemental" retirement program for themselves (perhaps by altering the campaign finance laws), or seriously consider privatization. In any event, the taxpayer will benefit; for if either of the former two options is chosen, Congress itself will help to expose the Social Security system for the fraud that it is.

# NOTES

1. Ferrara, Peter J. (1980), *Social Security: The Inherent Contradiction*. Washington, D.C.: Cato Institute, 1980.

2. See, for example, Feldstein, Martin (1974), "Social Security, Induced Retirement, and Aggregate Capital Accumulation," *Journal of Political Economy* 82(5): 905–926; and idem (1977), "Social Security and Private Savings: International Evidence in an Extended Life-Cycle Model," in M. Feldstein and R. Inman, (eds.), *The Economics of Public Services*. New York: Halstead Press.

3. It has been estimated that the rate of return provided by the Social Security system is approximately 10 to 15% of the return to private-sector alternatives. See Ferrara, chaps. 4 and 9.

4. See, for example, Pechman, Joseph A., Henry J. Aaron, and Michael K. Taussig (1968), *Social Security: Perspectives for Reform.* Washington, D.C.: Brookings Institution; and Munnell, Alicia H. (1977), *The Future of Social Security.* Washington, D.C.: Brookings Institution.

5. The constitutionalist perspective is most commonly linked with Hayek, Friedrich A. (1979), *Law, Legislation, and Liberty*, vol. 3, *The Political Order of a Free People.* Chicago, IL: University of Chicago Press; and Buchanan, James M. (1977), *Freedom in Constitutional Contract.* College Station, TX: Texas A&M University Press. For a discussion of the transformation of ideas regarding the appropriate role of government in the economy, see Siegan, Bernard (1980), *Economic Liberties and the Constitution.* Chicago, IL: University of Chicago Press.

6. Buchanan, James M. (1983), "Notes on Politics as Process," paper presented at the 1983 meeting of the Public Choice Society, Savannah, GA, March 25.

7. This is not to imply that government is necessarily the only institution that can perform these tasks. Many have argued that private courts, for example, would be superior to the present system.

8. For a more general discussion of this phenomenon, see Jensen, Michael C., and William H. Meckling (1978), "Can the Corporation Survive?," *Financial Analysts Journal* January/February: 31–37.

9. Ferrara, 275.

10. See Manne, Henry (1965), "Mergers and the Market for Corporate Control," *Journal of Political Economy* 73(2): 110–120.

11. See Mises, Ludwig von (1969), *Bureaucracy*, 2nd edn. Westport, CT.: Arlington House Publishers; Tullock, Gordon (1965), *The Politics of Bureaucracy.* Washington, D.C.: Public Affairs Press; and Niskanen, William (1971), *Bureaucracy and Representative Government.* Chicago, IL: Aldine-Atherton Press.

12. See Brozen, Yale (1973), "Advertising, Competition, and the Consumer," Intercollegiate Review 8(Summer): 235–242.

13. See Benham, Lee (1972), "The Effect of Advertising on the Price of Eyeglasses," *Journal of Law and Economics* 15(October): 337–352; and Brozen, Yale (1982), *Concentration, Mergers, and Public Policy.* New York: Macmillan.

14. Wagner, Richard E. (1976), "Advertising and the Public Economy: Some Preliminary Ruminations," in David Tuerck, ed., *The Political Economy of Advertising.* Washington, D.C.: American Enterprise Institute, 81–100.

15. U.S. Department of Health, Education, and Welfare (1976), *Your Social Security*. Washington, D.C., June, as cited in Ferrara, 66.

16. Ibid.

17. Shore, Warren (1975), *Social Security: The Fraud in Your Future*. New York: Macmillan, 21.

18. Darby, Michael, and Edi Karni (1973), "Free Competition and the Optimal Amount of Fraud," *Journal of Law and Economics* 16(April): 67–88.

19. Wagner, 97.

20. As a similar phenomenon, a group of women are currently suing their insurance company for charging them higher health-insurance rates than men with similar medical histories because of the fact that women live, on average, about 10 years longer than men. If this practice is ruled illegal, insurance companies will be apt to offer less medical insurance to women in the future.

21. Demsetz, Harold (1969), "Information and Efficiency: Another Viewpoint," *Journal of Law and Economics* 12(April): 1–22.

22. Hayek, Friedrich A. (1945), "The Use of Knowledge in Society," *American Economic Review* 35(September): 519–530.

23. For an elaboration of this view, see Tideman, T. Nicolaus (1983), "Toward a Restructuring of Normative Economics," Working Paper, Department of Economics, Virginia Polytechnic Institute.

24. Shepsle, Kenneth (1978), "The Private Use of Public Interest," mimeographed, Center for the Study of American Business, Washington University-St. Louis.

25. Ferrara, 253.

26. A current example of this time-worn tradition is the crusade to revitalize Herbert Hoover's Reconstruction Finance Corporation (RFC). I recently discussed a paper of mine on that subject at the U.S. Chamber of Commerce in Washington, D.C. Judging from the Chamber's magazine and television shows, one gets the impression that it is a bastion of free-market capitalism. However, at that meeting I found that many, though not all, of the Chamber's board members, along with several former bureaucrats in attendance, were staunch advocates of more centralized economic planning "if only done correctly." Several people there offered detailed scenarios of how they, as central planners, would decide which industries should survive through government subsidization and which should not.

27. This, in fact, is the primary reason for most redistributive programs of the government. See Tullock, Gordon (1983), *Economics of Income Redistribution*. Boston, MA: Kluwer-Nijhoff.

28. Ferrara chap. 6.

29. This change in the constitutional setting has also led to many of our general economic problems caused by the government's monetary and fiscal policies. See Buchanan, James M., and Richard Wagner (1977), *Democracy in Deficit: The Political Legacy of Lord Keynes*. New York: Academic Press.

30. Hayek, *Law, Legislation, and Liberty*, vol. 3: 11.

31. *Cato's Letters*, letter 62, January 20, 1721: 128, as cited in, Hayek, *Law, Legislation, and Liberty*, vol. 3: 9.

# Chapter 21
# The Futility of Bureaucracy

During a recent debate with Harry Jaffa on the topic of my book, *The Real Lincoln*, Jaffa invoked the Lincoln mythology to declare that September 11 "proves" more than ever that we need a strong federal government.

I argued that just the opposite is true: September 11 was a spectacular failure of the FBI, CIA, INS, FAA, Department of Defense, and indeed the entire federal government to perform what it says is its most basic function, protecting American citizens against foreign aggressors. Indeed, the federal government still stands in the way of genuine airline safety by forbidding airline pilots, most of whom have military experience, from arming themselves to protect the passengers and crew.

More important, such failures are *inherent*, and regardless of how many new bureaucracies may be formed, things will not improve. Government failure is the normal course of events.

The government's proposals to "abolish" the INS and replace it with two new bureaucracies, and its "consolidation" of eight "national security" agencies into one mammoth "Department of Homeland Security" are classic examples of rearranging the chairs on the deck of the *Titanic*.

Government bureaucracies always fail to live up to their promises because they are not market institutions. As such, there is no possible way of ascertaining how efficiently the bureaucracy is run since there are no profit-and-loss statements in the government sector, only "budgets."

The amount of a bureaucracy's budget has nothing to do with how well it pleases consumers, since there are no consumers in the sense that there are consumers in a private-sector marketplace. Instead, budgetary amounts are determined by arbitrary bureaucratic rules and by politics.

Spending decisions within a bureaucracy are economically arbitrary as well, as Mises explains in his classic 1944 book *Bureaucracy*. There are no profits or losses and thus no feedback between the producer and the consumer. This becomes especially obvious in the rare occasion when a bureaucracy must cut its spending. There is no way to evaluate the relative contribution of any capital or labor input, or the merit of any output. It is all guesswork.

Because there is no rational economic calculation taking place, politics rushes in to fill the vacuum. In politics, failure is success. The worse any government bureaucracy performs, as a rule, the *more* money it gets. The budgets of *all* of the federal "national security" agencies have skyrocketed in the past six months precisely because of their spectacular failures.

The NASA budget rose after it exploded a space shuttle; the worse the government schools become, the more money they get; the war on drugs is a more abysmal failure each year, which guarantees that we spend more and more money on it; the list is endless. This is exactly the opposite of what occurs in the free market, where success in pleasing consumers is rewarded financially and failure punished.

All government bureaucracies have powerful incentives to grow, regardless of whether or not such growth actually serves the public. Every bureaucrat is inherently an empire builder, because that is how he advances in his career. The route to promotion in managing a bigger and better-paying bureaucracy is to prove that one can "manage" a large number of people.

And since there are no profits or shareholders in government, bureaucrats "profit" personally by spending taxpayers' dollars lavishly on perquisites – a large staff, travel, office space, etc. Thus, there are built-in incentives to maximize the number of subordinate bureaucrats, regardless of what this may mean for public service. Cost *maximization* characterizes all government bureaucracies, as opposed to cost *minimization* in private, competitive markets. Not to mention the notoriously shoddy quality of all government "services."

Since consumer welfare cannot guide decision making in government, decisions are based on mountains of Byzantine rules and regulations and red tape. As Mises wrote in *Human Action*, "Whenever the operation of a system is not directed by the profit motive, it must be directed by bureaucratic rules." This, of course, is fundamentally in conflict with running an efficient, profitable enterprise. This Iron Law of Bureaucracy means that no government bureaucracy could possibly be operated in an efficient manner.

In his 1966 book, *Inside Bureaucracy*, Anthony Downs made a number of generalized observations about government bureaucracy that help illustrate its inherent futility. Here's a small sample:

• No one can fully control the behavior of a large bureaucracy. The larger a bureaucracy becomes, the poorer is the coordination among its actions. So much for the alleged "efficiency" of a consolidated, gigantic "homeland security" bureaucracy.

• Any attempt to control one large bureaucracy tends to generate another one. (Case in point: The INS is being "abolished" and replaced with two new bureaucracies.)

• The greater the effort made by top-level bureaucrats to control their subordinates, the greater the efforts made by the subordinates to evade control.

• All bureaucrats develop strong loyalty to the organization, as opposed to serving consumers, since that is the source of their job security and promotion. Hence, all the news by White House, FBI, and CIA "cover-ups" of their mistakes and failures in recent months.

• As a bureaucracy grows, the level of talent initially rises and then declines. Washington is a city of peons.

• As bureaucracies grow older, their top officials shift their focus from performing "social functions" to ensuring the institution's budgetary growth. This means dealing ruthlessly with "whistle blowers."

• Each bureaucrat tends to distort the information he passes upward in the hierarchy, exaggerating those data that are favorable to him, and ignoring those that are critical. He also tends to tell his superiors only what he thinks they want to hear, which is not necessarily consistent with reality. And we think we can rely on these people to protect us from terrorists.

• Each bureaucrat will comply with those directives from his superiors that serve his own self-interests, and will subvert those that don't.

• In any large bureaucracy a significant amount of what goes on is completely unrelated to the bureau's goals.

• As any bureaucracy grows, the proportion of wasted activity rises steadily. But it's only taxpayers' money.

• The larger a bureaucracy, the more resistant it will be to any change. Of course; there are no market pressures.

• Every bureaucrat is a vigorous propagandist for the expansion of his organization. Governments at all levels spend billions of dollars annually attempting to fool the public into believing that their failures are really successes.

There are bureaucracies in the private sector, of course, but the inefficiencies of corporate bureaucracy are disciplined by consumer and stock market pressures, the market for corporate control, the competitive labor market for management, and free-market competition in general. No such discipline exists in government, where bureaucratic failure is perversely rewarded.

In sum, the incessant promises by Washington politicians to "reign in," "rationalize," or "coordinate" the bureaucracy should not be taken seriously by anyone.

# Chapter 22
# Government and Market:
# A Critique of Professor James Buchanan's
# "What Should Economists" Do?

## 1. Introduction

Political science may be defined as the systematic thorough and rational analysis of politics. In order to approach this field in a scientific manner, the analyst must avail himself of the relevant empirical insights as well as normative considerations, since political science straddles, or is composed of, or touches upon, endeavors such as economics, ethics, sociology, history, etc., in addition to politics itself.

To the extent that political science is interdisciplinary, economics is its first cousin. A sub field of the dismal science, public choice, has perhaps made the greatest strides, from within economics, to bridge the gap in the direction of political science. The public choice school of economic thought is dedicated to the notion that political choices and decision making may be profitably studied using the tools of economic analysis. If there is a father of public choice, it is James Buchanan.[1] His Nobel Prize in economics[2] was awarded to him, in large part, because of his path breaking work in the analysis of political institutions from an economic perspective.

Such a research agenda is sometimes characterized as "social science imperialism," the attempt of one field within this broad calling to take over the "turf" of another, or as "economic imperialism," the endeavor to establish a beachhead of dismal science on to what had been traditionally counted as the territory of a different discipline. Public choice is an attempt, par excellance, on the part of economists to seize the intellectual property of political scientists.[3] It is one of the main purposes of the present paper to assess whether or not, and if so to what extent, have economists of the public choice school succeeded in wresting away realms traditionally the preserve of political scientists.

## 2. A Contradiction

What was the thesis of Buchanan and Tullock (BT) in their 1971 book, *Calculus of Consent* (CC)? They put forth the view that government is really just another sort of market; that the political marketplace and the political marketplace are just two sides of the same coin; that dollar votes and ballot box votes follow the same rules (e.g., downward sloping demand curves); that, at the very least, there is a strong analogy between the two.

But Buchanan (1979, pp. 30, 31) contradicts this thesis. Here, he maintains that there are two ways of viewing human economic organization. The first, a means-ends perspective, sees the "wealth of nations" as the goal, and economic allocation as a problem to be solved. In this conception, the market, as a mechanism, is appropriately compared with government, "as an alternative mechanism for accomplishing similar tasks."

However, continues Buchanan, "The second ... is wholly different, although subtly so, and it is this second conception that I am trying to stress in this paper. And what is this second view of human economic organization?" It specifically rejects the idea of macro level goals, such as maximizing the "wealth of nations," or the challenges of overall economic allocation. Rather, it takes on a more individualistic or micro stance. "It is, instead, the institutional embodiment of the voluntary exchange processes that are entered into by individuals in their several capacities." It is not that there are no purposes in this second concept. There are. It is just that these are held by private individuals, with no thought as to how this impacts the entire society. Here, Buchanan (p. 31) observe(s) men attempting to accomplish their own purposes, whatever these may be. Buchanan can only have it both ways, that is, can remain true to CC, if he accepts the first of these two visions. If, and to the degree he embraces the second, as he says he does in this later work, then he must, upon pain of contradiction, renounce the thesis of CC.


## 3. Public Goods

His further comments in this context would appear to buttress the claim that he had abandoned the CC thesis. For next lie discusses the "local swamp (which) requires draining to eliminate or reduce mosquito breeding" (p. 32). One would expect the Buchanan of CC to wax eloquent about externalities, free riders, and the need for government to make good this "market failure." Instead, we are treated to an outright rejection of this typical view: "Defined in the orthodox, narrow way, the 'market' fails; bilateral behavior of buyers and sellers does not remove the nuisance.... This is, however, surely an overly restricted conception of market behavior."

How then will the market work? How can people, without the aid of the state[4] work together to solve the problems of the swamp?

Here he continues in a vein perfectly consistent with that of a libertarian: "Individual citizens will be led, because of the same propensity, to search voluntarily for more inclusive trading or exchange relationships." Were he to continue in this vein, one can almost bear Buchanan maintaining at this point, Rothbard-like,[5] that the entire swamp, and much of the surrounding area, will be owned by one corporation; then, the negative externalities of the mosquitoes will he internalized by this land company. Unless they solve this swamp problem, the surrounding land values will not increase; they will not be able to sell fishing, boating, swimming, housing rights. That prospective golf course will remain on the drawing boards forever.

In the event, Buchanan says none of this, unfortunately. But he does do the next best thing: he discusses the internalization of externalities, albeit in a completely different context. He states (p. 32):

> How is the 'free rider' problem to be handled? This specter of the free rider, found in many shapes and forms in the literature of modern public finance theory, must be carefully examined. In the first place, there has been some confusion between total and marginal effects here. If a pretty woman strolls through the hotel lobby, many tired convention delegates may get some external benefits, but, presumably, she finds it to her own advantage to stroll, and few delegates would pay her to stroll more than she already does.

Not so good. Had Buchanan remained perfectly true to the free market vision, had he more closely tied the strolling woman case to that of the mosquito-laden swamp, he would have speculated about the possibility that there was too little strolling compared to the optimal amount.[6] Then, this would have led him, as if by "an invisible hand" to enquire as to the identity of the person with a financial interest in seeing to it that the incidence of strolling increased. Obviously, this would be the hotel owner, the analog to the land arid water company of the previous example.

## 4. Market Failure

Unhappily, this author then completely drops the ball. He resorts to the same tired old traditional "market failure" analysis he just finished excoriating (pp. 32, 33):

> There may be cases where the expected benefits from draining are not sufficiently high to warrant the emergence of some voluntary cooperative arrangement. And, in addition, the known or predicted presence of free riders may inhibit the cooperation of individuals who would otherwise. In such situations, voluntary cooperation may never produce an 'efficient' outcome for the individual members of the group. Hence, the 'market,' even in its most extended sense, maybe said to 'fail.'

All he is saying, here, is that even with a full private property free enterprise system, there may still he some swamps which remain undrained. This might well be true. But Buchanan has no warrant for claiming that if this occurred, it would be a "failure." On which stone tablets is it written that all undrained swamps are an affront to the Almighty? Who says that the optimal number of mosquito infested swamps is zero? The neoclassical economists live and die by empirical considerations, but what evidence could he adduced in behalf of this claim? On the contrary, if the market "fails" in this manner, it is prima facie evidence that for those few swamps which remain in the pristine form, it is a success to leave them exactly as they were.[7] The "market failure-ists" never put forth their own independent criterion of the optimal number of undrained swamps. They rely on the claim that there are externalities to assume, a fortiori, that the optimal level will not be reached through voluntary economic action. Consider the possibility of swamp ownership by a group such as Ducks Unlimited, or the Sierra Club, or some such other environmental group. Suppose they owned a large holding with a swamp located in the middle of it, such that the mosquitoes never strayed onto the property of other rural people. That is, this "harm"[8] never reaches out to those who view it negatively. Why isn't this a case of economically rational swamping?

## 5. Voluntarism?

However, Buchanan does redeem himself at least partially. He poses the challenge, "What recourse is left to the individual in this ease (of market failure)?" Arid his answer (p. 33):

> It is surely that of transferring, again voluntarily, at least at some ultimate constitutional level, activities of the swamp-clearing sort to the community as a collective unit, with decisions delegated to specifically designated rules for making choices, and these decisions coercively enforced once they are made.

This is all well and good, if interpreted sympathetically enough. The constitutional state would he directly analogous to the "big land company" that would own both the swamp and the surrounding effected area. Of course it would be legitimate for it to enforce its decisions "coercively," because they would be no more coercive than would be those of the business firm in demanding its right to evict trespassers. The government would be like a private club, where everyone had agreed to pay dues, to be bound by the rules created by the majority, subject perhaps to a bill of rights agreed upon at the outset, etc. But all this soon comes unglued when we realize that Buchanan is not talking about some ideal situation, some model he has concocted entirely from his imagination. Rather, he is offering this as an analysis of real world governments such as that of the United States. And here, Spooner's (1966)[9] insights render nonsensical all such claims. There simply is no such agreement, signed by all citizens at any given time, in all of U.S. history. The closest we come to this model is when a scant few men signed the Declaration of Independence. Buchanan's is an attempt to analyze not merely theoretical governments, but extant ones. He may have succeeded in the former case, in coming up with some very interesting fairy tales, but with regard to the latter his effort must be judged a dismal failure.

As it happens, Buchanan comes very close to admitting his whole scheme is self-contradictory; that the voluntary elements of the free enterprise system cannot be reconciled with the essentially coercive elements of the state. He states (p. 34):

> Insofar as individuals meet one another in a relationship of superior-inferior, leader to follower, principal to agent, the predominant characteristic in their behavior is 'political,'... Economics is the study of the whole system of exchange relationships. Politics is the study of the whole system of coercive or potentially coercive relationships.

But it is not true that hierarchy is per se exploitative. The orchestra conductor leads the musicians, not the other way around; the · employer, within limits, controls the behavior of the ·employee; it is the principal, not the agent, who exerts the commands. But all of this occurs in the market, where all relationships are reciprocal and voluntary. How, then, to explain how someone can "boss" someone else around, and yet not coerce him? The answer is simple. As long as the "inferior" person has agreed to be bound by the dictates of the "superior" (usually but not always because of monetary payments), the relationship is a legitimate, voluntary one. Take away this essential prior agreement, and a legitimate hierarchical one is rendered coercive.

## 6. Visions

It is just barely possible that we have been too hard on Buchanan. Maybe his model is merely an imaginary one, in which ease we have no serious objections; perhaps he does not really mean to apply it to the real world. Evidence for the former hypothesis abounds. He tells us (p. 144):

> In my vision of social order, individual person are the basic component units, and 'government' is simply that complex of institutions through which individuals make collective decisions, and through which they carry out collective as opposed to private activities... In my vision or my model, individual persons are the ultimate decision makers.

The word "vision" clearly, is compatible with the idea that Buchanan is dealing with a theoretical construct, not the real world. But then he takes it all back. He asserts (p. 144): "if we want to discuss governmental decision processes we must analyze the behavior of individuals as they participate in these processes." Now it is just barely possible that people could take part in political processes in a purely theoretical manner; then, the fact that there is no evidence that they have agreed to be bound by the constitution would not count against Buchanan. So far, we have been arguing not that if the constitution is like a private contract, but w actually was a private contract, that we have no serious reservations with the Public Choice Model of constitutional economies. This is because if the state really is akin to the market, then any force excited by it on "unwilling" participants is really justified, for these persons agreed beforehand to be bound by the view of the majority.[10]

## 7. Tyranny of the Majority

Buchanan (1979: 150) criticizes Arrow (1951) not for the latter's analysis, with which he agrees in any case, but for the latter's wishes about that analysis. Specifically, Arrow proved that given simple majority voting, no unique and consistent social ordering of the social welfare function would emerge. Arrow was unhappy with this result, yearning for stability, while in Buchanan's view. "If we had a majority voting rule that would, in fact, produce internally consistent choices in the Arrow sense, we should, indeed, have a tyranny of the majority."

But this is highly problematic. BT have all along been asserting their constitutional thesis, namely, that the populace has agreed to be bound by the dictates of the majority. How can Buchanan, then, turn around and castigate any determination of the majority at all as "tyrannical"? That is, even if a majority of Nazis, for example, were to vote to eliminate all Jews, this would still not be tyrannical, at least according to the thesis put forth by BT. This is because the Jews, initially, made a decision to be bound by the will of the majority. If they feared animosity emanating toward them from the Nazis, they never should have constitutionally agreed to be bound by majority decision.[11] Since they have, by stipulation, they should calmly accept their fate, and not denigrate their fellow citizens with such a harsh and unjustified a characterization as "tyrannical."

## 8. Unanimity

Buchanan (1979: 153) states:

> If we reject the notion that there must exist a public or general interest apart from that of the participants, we are necessarily led to the conclusion that only upon unanimous consent of all parties can we be absolutely sure that the total welfare of the group is improved.

In this, he is totally correct. First of all there is no general or public interest over and above that of the citizenry. There are only separate people. All groups, nations, collectives, etc. are merely gatherings of unique individuals. Even a marriage, perhaps the closest collective of all, is still composed of two nonidentical people. There is no third party in the marriage, over and above the two of them. "Two's company, three's a crowd."

The only problem is that BT talk about a near or "relative" or "conceptual" unanimity.[12] In their view, this can also justify state activity. Put this as highly problematic. Suppose that the near unanimity consists of 98% of the populace. But this still leaves the other 2% which can be victimized by them. Now it might pay for the 2% to agree to be bound by political voting of the 98%; perhaps this will be better for their, under certain circumstances, than a situation where the state is nonexistent. Maybe the 98% could more heavily, or efficiently, brutalize the 2%

under anarchy[13] than under archy.[14] But that is for them (e.g., the minority) to say. There is no warrant for maintaining that the 2% must have agreed with this assessment. Perhaps, in some eases (e.g., Nazi Germany, for the Jews) they may prefer to go it alone, unprotected by the niceties of the political process.

## 9. Bureaucracy

Buchanan (1979: 162) states: "The administrative hierarchy of a modern corporate giant differs less from the federal bureaucracy than from the freely contracting tradesmen envisaged by Adam Smith."

Now this is undoubtedly true-but only superficially. For example, it is surely the case that the employees of Big Government and Big Business are housed in similar office buildings; that the memos they pass along to each other are parallel in many specifics; that there are as many levels in the chain of command in the one case as in the other. Moreover, it cannot be denied that in this same regard both of these are as far apart as it is possible to imagine from the small firm with one or two employees. The latter has no chain of command worthy of that name at all, The boss usually initiates, but typically depends on trusted workers to contribute; there are no memos; they work in a basement or in a garage or in a small shop or office. Not for them the trappings of Bigness.

But Buchanan's point is just like saying that a big man and a seal are more alike (since they weigh about as much) than is a big man and a small baby. It is akin to asserting that Pope Paul H's kinship with his replica in Madame Taussaud's Wax Museum is greater than that which exists between him and someone else, say Professor Buchanan. It amounts to concentrating on superficial similarities, and ignoring important, but underlying differences. Big Business and Big Government may look alike to an ignorant outside observer (or even to an insider, a participant), but they are very different as pertains to the voluntariness of each institution. Business no matter how Big, cannot compel customers to make purchases; they must attain consent. Government, no matter how Small, may legally do so.

They also differ as far as survivability is concerned. Business, no matter how Big, must satisfy customers; if it fails to do so, it are forced into bankruptcy. Government, in contrast, particularly the bureaucracy,[15] boasts of no such automatic feedback mechanism. If you don't like how they run things at the Post Office, or at the Motor Vehicle Registry, you cannot take your "business" else-where. If many people boycott these institutions, and they lose money hand over fist, there is still no tendency toward dissolution. Instead, the government merely hands over additional funds mulcted from the long suffering taxpayer.

307

## 10. Value Free Policy Prescriptions

Buchanan (1979: 180) holds the following view:

> In a sense, public-choice analysts can take on a normative role in advocating some matching of policy proposals with the institutional realities of modern politics. We can talk meaningfully about the 'best' rules, or the 'nth best' arrangements, often quite independently of the ultimate policy targets. In other words, we can talk normatively about 'process' or 'procedure,' while staying clear of normative discussions of 'end-states.'

This sounds altogether too much like the "value free" chemist being asked by the Nazis about the most efficient way to attain their goals. Yes, to be sure, the words offered by the scientist under such a condition would be indistinguishable from those uttered in an entirely different context. But context is all. Sentences indicating that water is composed of two parts oxygen and one part hydrogen, or the poison gas can best be produced in such and such a way, or that the most efficient oven will be composed of this metal not that, are non normative sentences. But uttering them, an act may or may not be value free. Contrary to Buchanan, the usual presumption is that speech acts are normative exercises. Why would the speaker have spoken them did he not prefer a world which included these statements to one which did not? And is this preference not to be considered a value? And is the attainment of a value not to be considered nonnative?

## 11. A Contradiction?

Buchanan (1979: 181) holds the following view, which we shall call A:

> We should care, and we should think about, what the fiscal constitution for political democracy should look like, what sort of institutions should be most efficient in the working of democratic policies.

Let us contrast this with another statement, call it B, which reads as follows (Buchanan, 1979: 186):

> I found myself less interested in the old question, How should tax shares be allocated? And at the same time more interested in the new question, How are tax shares allocated in a democracy?

While it might be too harsh to claim that A and B are explicit contradictions of each other, one must acknowledge that they, at the very least, lead the reader in rather different directions. According to B, we should eschew old normative questions. But A is a nonnative issue. Now let us bring into the analysis opinion C (Buchanan, 1979: 188):

> Individuals do not pay 'prices' for partitionable units of (public) goods, They pay 'taxes' which are coercively imposed through a political

process and this coercion is, in turn, made necessary by the free rider motivation inherent in general collective action. Few persons will voluntarily pay taxes if they expect to receive the benefits from generally available public goods.

One problem with C is that it is logically incompatible with BT's oft-made claim to the effect that the polity is a voluntary one at the outset. If we all agree to be part of the government (e.g., citizen how can it be "coercive" to compel us to pay our fair share of taxes, as determined democratically? After all, in joining up, we have agreed to be bound by the will of the majority, and the vote was, presumably, in favor of leveling taxes. Another difficulty is that coercion is by no means "made necessary" by the free rider motivation. It is not at all logically "necessary" that the government force people to contribute to programs it is pleased to think provide for the betterment of non-contributors, "One man's meat is another man's poison"[16] There is not a single solitary act, from defense to mosquito eradication, which benefits all people. Pacifists, and members of the fifth column of the beleaguered country, are harmed by its attempt to defend itself. They would actually prefer that the nation not be militarily secure. Members of Earth First!, who believe that there are altogether too many human beings inhabiting the planet, and that they are "excessive protoplasm" which should be destroyed would actually welcome disease bearing mosquito infestation: But suppose, just for the sake of argument, that all people had the same evaluations of all of these goods and services; that there were no pacifists, internal enemies, nor misanthropes. Would it then be "necessary" for the government to force people to contribute for these "good" ends? Not a bit of it! For we would still have to weigh the good to the clone as a result of compulsion against the bad inherent in using this fiduciary device. Also problematic is the fact that C and B are somewhat incompatible. B claimed an interest in positive economics. A is nothing if not normative. While we are on the subject of internal contradictions in the public choice philosophy, let us consider (Buchanan, 1979: 189–190):

> In ordinary markets, the presumption that all persons choose rationally does little to distort empirical reality because the rationality of only a few participants who can affect results at the appropriate margins of adjustment guarantees the equivalence of outcomes as between what we might call the full rationality and the partial rationality models. The situation in 'public markets' is not at all analogous. Solutions do not emerge as the outcome of the mutual interactions of many participants who make private and independent decisions. The result reflects the choice of the median voter, or his representative, who may or may not be fully rational in the sense that informs traditional price theory. The presumption of fully informed rationality here is much more severely restrictive than in any other market setting.

Where is the contradiction? The constitutional argument of BT, the claim that there are really two kinds of "markets," the political and the economic, the view that the polity is really a contract between all citizens, is predicated on the vision that there is a strong analogy between the political and economic realms. And yet in this quote Buchanan concedes that the situation between the two "is not at all analogous." In so doing, however, he strives valiantly to maintain that this analogy is valid. He does so by calling the political realm a "public market" and by referring to politics as an "other market setting." But this is clearly not the case, as even Buchanan (partially) admits. The point is, we can infer rationality in the market because there is a weeding out process which occurs every minute. Those who act rationally in ferreting out future consumer desires, and in ministering to them in an expeditious manner, earn profits; those who fail in this regard, and instead produce Edsels, suffer losses. But people who acquire profits, other things equal, tend to make more and more decisions and have greater and greater control over resources than those who bear losses. And the same goes for consumers and investors. Those who make wise choices prosper; those who do not see their wealth reduced. Over time, such a process ensures that market activity at least tends toward rationality.

In the political sphere, no such occurrence takes place. Those who vote for the eventual winner do not receive additional ballots for the next election. Those who vote for the loser do not suffer any diminution in their treasure. Nor can this sort of analysis be applied to any aspect of politics: The analogous "weeding out" process is completely missing. As a result, there is no case for supposing a move toward rationality, ceteris paribus.

## 12. Conclusion

We began this paper by posing the question of whether economists of the public choice stripe have succeeded in claiming for their own (in behalf of the entire profession) areas of study traditionally under the sway of political scientists. That is, do the tools of traditional economic analysis succeed in explaining, characterizing, pigeon holing, or in any other way accounting for intellectual realms · which lie squarely in the province of political science, or even in territory lying somewhere in between these two disciplines? Clearly, given the foregoing, I find no warrant for any such claim, at least in this case. While the lines of demarcation between the various social sciences cannot be impenetrable unshakeable inviolable barriers, while forays from one onto the territory of another are thus in principle acceptable,[17] success in this regard cannot be claimed in the present case.

## NOTES

1. Gordon Tullock deserves, also, to be mentioned in this context, since he co-authored with James Buchanan several of the tomes which have set up the foundations of public choice. As well, Tullock has contributed mightily to this field on his own and with others besides Buchanan. See for example Tullock (1980a,b, 1985, 1967).

2. In justice, this Nobel Prize should have been given to both Buchanan and Tullock.

3. In the interests of full disclosure, I am an economist, not a political scientist. My Ph.D. is in the former field not the latter. True confession: my natural predilection is to support forays of this sort.

4. Nowadays, the government is the least likely source of the solution to the mosquito challenge. It is not part of the problem, not the solution. For under the aegis of the Environmental Protection Agency, swamp draining, or interfering with practically any body of water, or "wetlands," will likely be prohibited outright. And if not prohibited, then postponed, and made far more expensive than before.

5. See on this Rothbard (1962, 1973, 1982, 1990). See also Hummel (1990), Hoppe (1993), Block (1983, 1990).

6. E.g., "market failure." Not to be sure, of the external diseconomy mosquito type, but of the mirror image failure to promote an external economy of the stroller sort.

7. This would merely show that in the view of the economic actors who stand ready to lose money by making poor decisions, the benefits of clearing of the marginal swamp are more than offset by the costs. Or, that the costs of internalizing the externalities, whether through restrictive covenants, or single ownership, are lower than the benefits of these activities.

8. Remember, one man's meat is sometimes another man's poison.

9. See also Rothbard (1973, 1982) and Hoppe (1993).

10. Some people might take from this line of thought that it is always illegitimate to impose one's will on people who have not agreed to be bound by it, beforehand. This is only roughly correct, and it may be worthwhile to explore why such a line of reasoning is not entirely valid.

So we ask, what is the case · for supposing that it is legitimate to use force even against people who have not agreed to be bound by it? Let us return to the Hobbesian state of nature for this exercise. According to the libertarian perspective, Public Choice's main competitor within the broadly based free enterprise camp, each individual has a right to be free from aggression in his person, and in his legitimately held property. This in turn, is based on either original homesteading, or trades based on such title. Therefore, if someone attempts to inflict damage on a person or his property, he has a right to defend himself and what is his through use of violence if need be. This means that it is legitimate to use force against a would be aggressor, even if this latter person has not agreed to be bound by anything at all, as would be true in a state of nature.

11. Not that they could have done anything about it, given that for Buchanan, their signatures on the dotted line is not needed.

12. For the view that we all accept government "implicitly," and thus no explicit unanimity is needed to justify it, see Buchanan (1971: 254).

13. The overwhelming majority of brutality and mass murder occurs within or between governments (Conquest, 1986, 1990); thus it might appear that anarchy has had a bad press, since the opposite view is perhaps more prevalent.

14. For critiques of anarchy, see Buchanan (1977), Nozick (1974). For defenses, see Spooner (1966), Hoppe (1993), Barnett, (1977), Childs (1977); Evers (1977); Rothbard (1977); Sanders (1977).

15. Governments come and go, according to elections. Here, there is at least an analog between the dollar vote and the ballot box variety, however weak is the latter in comparison to the former (it takes four years to be consummated; only a "package deal" of candidate A vs. B is offered – the voter cannot pick and choose as he wishes). But in the case of bureaucracy, not even a Buchanan can seriously maintain that there is a process where consumer or citizen dissatisfaction automatically translates into termination.

16. On this see Buchanan (1969), Buchanan and Thirlby (1981), Mises (1966), Rothbard (1962, 1973, 1977, 1989).

17. And highly so, since intellectual pursuits are all but impossible when frozen in concrete.

## REFERENCES

Arrow, Kenneth (1951), *Social Choice and Individual Values*. New York: John Wiley and Sons.

Barnett, Randy (1977), "Whither Anarchy? Has Robert Nozick Justified the State?," *The Journal of Libertarian Studies* 1(1): 15–21.

Becker, Gary S. (1976), *The Economic Approach to Human Behavior*. Chicago, IL: University of Chicago Press.

Becker, Gary (1964), *Human Capital*. New York: The National Bureau of Economic Research.

Becker, Gary S., and Kevin M. Murphy (1988), "A Theory of Rational Addiction," *Journal of Political Economy* 96(August): 675–700.

Becker, Gary (1957), *The Economics of Discrimination*. Chicago, IL: The University of Chicago Press, 1957.

Block, Walter (1990), "Resource Misallocation, Externalities and Environmentalism in the U.S. and Canada," *Proceedings of the 24th Pacific Northwest Regional Economic Conference*, 91–94.

Block, Walter (1983), "Public Goods and Externalities: The Case of Roads," *The Journal of Libertarian Studies: An Interdisciplinary Review* VII(1): 1–34.

Buchanan, James M. (1979), "Public Choice and Public Finance," in *What Should Economists Do?* Indianapolis, IN: Liberty Press.

Buchanan, James M. (1969), *Cost and Choice: An Inquiry into Economic Theory*. Chicago, IL: Markham.

Buchanan, James M. (1977), "A Contracterian Perspective on Anarchy," *Freedom in Constitutional Contract*. College Station, TX: Texas A & M University Press.

Buchanan, James M., and Gordon Tullock (1962/1971), *The Calculus of Consent: Logical Foundations of Constitutional Democracy*. Ann Arbor, MI: University of Michigan Press.

Childs, Roy A., Jr. (1977), "The Invisible Hand Strikes Back," *The Journal of Libertarian Studies* 1(1): 23–34.

Conquest, Robert (1990), *The Great Terror Edmonton*. Alberta: Edmonton University Press.

Conquest, Robert (1986), *The Harvest of Sorrow*. New York: Oxford University Press.

Evers, Williamson M. (1977), "Toward a Reformulation of the Law of Contracts," *The Journal of Libertarian Studies* 1(1): 3–13.

Hoppe, Hans-Hermann (1993), "Fallacies of the Public Goods Theory and the Production of Security," in *The Economics and Ethics of Private Property: Studies in Political Economy and Philosophy*. Boston, MA: Kluwer.

Hummel, Jeffrey Rogers (1990), "National Goods versus Public Goods: Defense, Disarmament, and Free Riders," *Review of Austrian Economics* 4: 88–122.

Mises, Ludwig von (1949, 1963, 1966), *Human Action*. Chicago, IL: Regnery.

Nozick, Robert (1974), *Anarchy, State and Utopia*. New York: Basic Books.

Radnitzky, Gerard, and Peter Bemholz (eds.) (1987), *Economic Imperialism*. New York: Paragon

Rothbard, Murray N. (1990b), "Law, Property Rights, and Air Pollution," *Economics and the Environment: A Reconciliation*, Walter Block, ed. Vancouver: The Fraser Institute.

Rothbard, Murray N. (1977), "Robert Nozick and the Immaculate Conception of the State," *The Journal of Libertarian Studies* 1(1): 45–57.

Rothbard, Murray N. (1937a), *For a New Liberty*. New York: Macmillan.

Rothbard, Murray N. (1989), "The Hermeneutical Invasion of Philosophy and Economics," *Review of Austrian Economics* 3(1): 45–60.

Rothbard, Murray N. (1962), *Man, Economy and State*. Los Angeles, CA: Nash.

Rothbard, Murray N. (1973b), "Value Implications of Economic Theory," *American Economist* 17(Spring): 35–39.

Rothbard, Murray N. (1982), *The Ethics of Liberty*. Atlantic Highlands, NJ: Humanities Press.

Rothbard, Murray N. (1977), "Toward a Reconstruction of Utility and Welfare Economics," San Francisco, CA: Center for Libertarian Studies, Occasional Paper 3.

Sanders, John T. (1977), "The Free Market Model versus Model versus Government: A Reply to Nozick," *The Journal of Libertarian Studies* 1(Winter): 35–44.

Spooner, Lysander (1870/1966), *No Treason*. Larkspur, CO.

Tullock, Gordon (1980a), "Rent-Seeking as a Negative Sum Game," in J. M. Buchanan, R. D. Tollison, and G. Tullock (eds.), *Toward a Theory of the Rent-Seeking Society*. College Station, TX: Texas A&M University Press.

Tullock, Gordon (1985), "Adam Smith and the Prisoner's Dilemma," *Quarterly Journal of Economics* 100: 1073–1081.

Tullock, Gordon (1967), "The Welfare Cost of Tariffs, Monopolies and Theft," *Western Economic Journal* 5(June): 224–232

Tullock, Gordon (1980b), "Efficient Rent Seeking," in J. M. Buchanan, R. D. Tollison and G. Tullock (eds.), *Towards a Theory of the Rent Seeking Society*. College Station, TX: Texas A&M University Press, 51–70.

Tullock, Gordon (1974), *The Social Dilemma: Economics of War and Revolution*. Blacksburg, VA: Center for the Study of Public Choice.

# Chapter 23
# Economic Competition and
# Political Competition: An Empirical Note

## 1. Introduction

The separation of ownership from control in government renders politicians and bureaucrats only partly subservient to the demands of consumer/taxpayers. At the national level of government competition via the electoral process leaves politicians and bureaucrats considerable latitude because of the rational ignorance effect (Tullock, 1967). Beginning with Tiebout (1956), it has been argued that at the local level of government competition among jurisdictions restricts a bureaucrat's ability to pursue policies which do not reflect the desires of taxpayers and to shirk the monitoring of public service provision. Recent theoretical work by Wagner (1974) and Epple and Zelenitz (1981) has shown that jurisdictional competition is indeed expected to establish constraints on the choices made by local governments and to induce cost effectiveness in the provision of local public services. Epple and Zelenitz found that such constraints are expected to exist, but are not sufficient to prevent local governments from exercising some monopoly power.

This note provides some empirical evidence which supports these theoretical findings. In the next section a reduced form public expenditure model is estimated which includes several different indices of political competition as independent variables, in order to test the null hypothesis that the correlation between jurisdictional competition and public spending is zero. The final section includes a summary and the conclusion.

## 2. Political Competition and Local Public Expenditures:
### Some Empirical Evidence

To test the null hypothesis that the correlation between jurisdictional competition and public spending is zero, two concentration ratios were constructed for a sample of sixty-five of the largest county government areas in the U.S. Similar to the four-firm concentration ratio of industrial organization theory, the two ratios used are: (1) the percentage of total government spending in a county government area by the four largest jurisdictions, where jurisdiction size is measured in terms of the amount of expenditure. County government areas include municipalities, townships, special districts, and county governments. (2) The percentage of "own tax revenues" taken in by the four largest jurisdictions. A reduced-form public expenditure model similar to those developed by Bergstrom and Goodman (1973) and by Borcherding and

Deacon (1972) was estimated, adding the concentration ratios as independent variables. The Bergstrom-Goodman and Borcherding-Deacon models attempted to assess the technology of local public service provision via the median voter model. The demand equation posits a log-linear relationship between output ($Q$), the median voter's income ($I$) and tax price ($t$) such that

$$Q = AI^{\alpha}t^{\beta} \tag{1}$$

where $t$ = median voters' share (T) of the cost per person per unit of service, $[C(Q)/QN]$.

The cost schedule of providing $Q$ follows from the specification of the service technology where facilities ($X$) are produced by a Cobb-Douglass technology with labor (L) and capital (K) such that

$$X = L^{\theta}K^{\delta}. \tag{2}$$

Public services per resident are provided through a constant elasticity congestion technology, $Q$, where

$$Q = X/N^{\epsilon}. \tag{3}$$

The parameter $\epsilon$ is the congestion elasticity and measures the percentage increase in $X$ needed to hold $Q$ constant for a percentage rise in $N$. For pure public goods, $\epsilon = O$; for private goods, $\epsilon = 1$.

With fixed factor prices the minimal costs of producing $X$ are given by

$$C(X) = cX_{\eta} \tag{4}$$

where $c$ = function of factor prices and the parameter $\theta$ and $\delta$ where $\eta = 1/(\theta + \delta)$.

Substituting $X = QN^{\epsilon}$ into C(X) defines C(Q). The tax price can now be defined, which, when substituted into the demand equation along with $Q = X / N^{\epsilon}$ gives a demand equation for facilities. Finally, the cost of facilities defines

$$X = [C(X)/c]^{1/\eta} \tag{5}$$

which is equated to the demand for facilities equation to give a reduced-form expenditure equation of the form

$$C = \hat{A}I^{\hat{\alpha}}(Tc)^{\hat{\beta}}N^{\hat{\epsilon}} \tag{6}$$

which can be estimated using OLS. The major explanatory variables in the empirical work done by Borcherding and Deacon and subsequent researchers are thus population, median income, and public wages as a proxy for factor prices. The parameter estimates $\hat{\alpha}$, $\tilde{\beta}$, and $\tilde{\epsilon}$ are obtained by estimating equation (6) in log-linear form. In keeping with the work of these previous authors, a number of other explanatory variables are added to reduce the probability of misspecification errors. Other variables which are expected to have an effect on public expenditures are per capita intergovernmental revenues, percent black population, and percent urban population. The latter two variables attempt to capture the diversity of demands for local public goods. In addition, the above-mentioned concentration ratios were added as independent variables and are the focus of this test. Data for the variables defined in Table 1 were obtained from the U.S. Department of Commerce, Bureau of the Census, *Census of Governments*, and the *Census of Population*. The reduced-form expenditure model was estimated first with per capita general expenditures as the independent variable and then for per capita expenditures on the other expenditure categories listed in Table 1. The county government areas chosen were all those with a population of over 300,000 in 1975. Adequate data were available for sixty-five such counties. The OLS estimates of the public expenditure model are presented in Tables 2–4. Eight of the concentration ratio coefficients were found to be statistically significant at the .10 level or better. Six of these coefficients were positive, as expected, and two were negative. Both of the negative coefficients were for the tax concentration ratio, one for general expenditures, and the other for sanitation expenditures. The model was also estimated for education expenditures. The coefficients for the concentration ratios were negative but insignificant and are not reported in Tables 2–4 since the existence of independent school districts within many of the county governmental areas would confound the effect of the concentration ratios. Thus the results are mixed but do tend to support the contention that a reduction in the degree of interjurisdictional competition tends to increase the cost of providing local public services. One reason that a negative coefficient might be observed for the tax concentration ratio but not for the expenditure concentration ratio is as follows. If it is true that more concentrated local governmental areas exhibit higher service costs and consequently, higher tax burdens, then one would expect the higher tax prices to be met with a reduction in the quantity of public goods demanded and consequently, a reduction in per capita expenditures. A high expenditure concentration ratio which leads to production inefficiencies may not lead to reduced citizen demands for local public goods since intergovernmental revenues are used to finance much of these expenditures. Production inefficiencies will only be met with reduced public goods demand if they are accompanied by tax increases.

In summary, the evidence presented here does suggest a positive correlation between concentration and the cost of providing local public services.

Table 1. Definition of variables in the public expenditure model

| Variable | Description |
|---|---|
| IGR | Per capita intergovernmental revenue |
| POP | Population |
| PBLK | Percent black population |
| PCI | Median per capita income |
| PWGE | Average monthly public wage |
| PURBN | Percent urban population |
| CE | Expenditure concentration ratio |
| CT | Tax concentration ratio |
| E | Per capita general expenditures |
| EPOL | Expenditures on police |
| EFRE | Expenditures on fire protection |
| EHWY | Expenditures on highways |
| ESAN | Expenditures on non-sewage sanitation |
| EWLF | Expenditures on welfare |
| EHOSP | Expenditures on hospitals |
| EADM | Administrative expenditures on general control and financial administration |

Table 2. Estimates of the public expenditure model for general expenditures and for police and fire protection

| Variables | $E_{CE}$ | $E_{CT}$ | $EPOL_{CE}$ | $EPOL_{CT}$ | $EFRE_{CE}$ | $EFRE_{CT}$ |
|---|---|---|---|---|---|---|
| Constant | −5.314* | −5.03* | −12.726** | −12.725** | −14.560** | −15.020** |
| | (−2.580) | (−2.469) | (−4.521) | (−4.530) | (3.729) | (−3.787) |
| IGR | .684 | .686 | .694 | .698 | .781** | .795** |
| | (.389) | (.388) | .548) | (.537) | (7.10) | (7.227) |
| POP | −.113 | −.119) | −5.587** | −4.505** | −.142 | −.153 |
| | (−.068) | (−.072) | (−4.711) | (−3.796) | (−1.214) | (−1.308) |
| PBLK | −1.927 | −1.626 | .139 | .145 | .113 | .121 |
| | (−.628) | (−.528) | (.063) | (0.66) | (.071) | .132) |
| PCI | .883** | .835** | 1.053** | 1.034** | .962*** | .973*** |
| | (3.258) | (3.060) | (2.793) | (2.712) | (1.839) | (1.832) |
| PWCE | .355 | .353 | 4.256** | 3.086** | 5.076** | 1.639** |
| | (1.409) | (1.395) | (12.125) | (8.742) | (10.423) | (3.330) |
| PURBN | −.149 | −1.406** | .730 | .766 | 1.392* | 1.407* |
| | (.432) | (−4.052) | (1.521) | (1.583) | (2.090) | (2.088) |
| CE | 1.309** | | .147 | | .664* | |
| | (7.933) | | (.639) | | (2.019) | |
| CT | | −1.541** | | 1.426** | | .571*** |
| | | (−9.692) | | (6.395) | | (1.836) |
| $\bar{R}^2$ | .750 | .750 | .666 | .664 | .597 | .590 |
| F | 28.489 | 28.458 | 19.235 | 19.086 | 14.518 | 14.161 |

\* Significant at .05 level.
\*\* Significant at .01 level.
\*\*\* Significant at .10 level.

*Table 3.* Estimates of the public expenditure model for highways, sanitation, and welfare

| Variables | EHWY$_{CE}$ | EHWY$_{CT}$ | ESAN$_{CE}$ | ESAN$_{CT}$ | EWLF$_{CE}$ | EWLF$_{CT}$ |
|---|---|---|---|---|---|---|
| Constant | −3.504 | −3.777 | −7.972 | −7.826 | −43.029** | −41.167* |
|  | (−1.123) | (−1.191) | (−1.469) | (−1.431) | (−3.283) | (−2.509) |
| IGR | .755 | .765 | .650** | .651** | 1.385** | 1.374 |
|  | (.661) | (.673) | (4.276) | (4.283) | (3.764) | (1.069) |
| POP | −1.145 | −1.053 | .152 | .148 | −.486 | −.501 |
|  | (1.070) | (−.993) | (.938) | (.238) | (−1.240) | (1.295) |
| PBLK | −2.950 | −3.650*** | .267 | .274 | −6.944** | −3.292** |
|  | (−1.484) | (−1.836) | (.234) | (.238) | (−32.910) | (15.903) |
| PCI | 1.107** | 1.107** | 1.036 | 1.001 | 1.758 | 1.455 |
|  | (2.648) | (2.611) | (1.425) | (1.367) | 1.001) | (.832) |
| PWGE | −.135 | −1.02* | −.468 | −.470 | 4.450** | 4.345** |
|  | (−.347) | (−2.595) | (−.691) | (−.694) | (2.720) | (2.685) |
| PURBN | −1.058*** | −1.037*** | −.360 | −.301 | −.304 | .139 |
|  | (−1.917) | (−1.924) | (−.389) | (−.324) | −.136) | (.063) |
| CE | .445*** |  | 2.178** |  | −.646 |  |
|  | (1.745) |  | (4.916) |  | (−.604) |  |
| CT |  | .363 |  | −1.709** |  | −1.334 |
|  |  | (1.464) |  | (−11.243) |  | (−1.305) |
| R² | .572 | .566 | .320 | .320 | 3.52 | .367 |
| F | 13.238 | 12.913 | 5.301 | 5.300 | 5.965 | 6.294 |

\*    Significant at .05 level.
\*\*   Significant at .01 level.
\*\*\*  Significant at .10 level.

Table 4. Estimate of the public expenditure model for hospitals and administrative expenditure

| Variables | EHOSP$_{CE}$ | EHOSP$_{CT}$ | EADAM$_{CE}$ | EADM$_{CT}$ |
|---|---|---|---|---|
| Constant | −42.589* | −41.270* | −5.878* | −5.745* |
|  | (−2.608) | (−2.515) | (−2.494) | (−2.417) |
| IGR | 1.803** | 1.784** | 1.218 | 1.274 |
|  | (3.937) | (3.912) | (.805) | (.839) |
| POP | .368 | .372 | 2.004 | −2.101 |
|  | (.753) | (.765) | (1.415) | (−1.480) |
| PBLK | .605* | .618* | 4.785*** | 5.102*** |
|  | (2.300) | (2.368) | (1.818) | (1.923) |
| PCI | 1.753 | 1.604 | −.204 | −.209 |
|  | (.801) | (.730) | (−.646) | (.657) |
| PWGE | −1.440 | −1.546 | .891** | .876** |
|  | (−.707) | (−.760) | (3.031) | (2.979) |
| PURBN | 5.337*** | 5.525*** | 1.179** | 1.181** |
|  | (1.917) | (1.980) | (2.933) | (2.923) |
| CE | −.966 |  | −.167 |  |
|  | −.725) |  | (.869) |  |
| CT |  | −1.188 |  | −.153 |
|  |  | (−.926) |  | (−.823) |
| R$^2$ | .335 | .339 | .345 | .344 |
| F | 5.600 | 5.678 | 5.810 | 5.791 |

\*     Significant at .05 level.
\*\*    Significant at .01 level.
\*\*\*   Significant at .10 level.


## 3. Summary and Conclusions

This paper has examined the proposition that more concentrated or consolidated metropolitan areas will produce public goods less efficiently than if there were a greater degree of interjurisdictional competition. The empirical evidence garnered in Section 3 suggests that interjurisdictional competition does tend to reduce the cost of providing local public services and, consequently, local government expenditure levels.

# REFERENCES

Bergstrom, T., and R. Goodman (1973), "Private Demand for Public Goods," *American Economic Review* June: 286–296.

Borcherding, T., and R. Deacon (1972), "The Demand for Services of Non-federal Governments," *American Economic Review* December: 891–901.

Epple, D., and A. Zelenitz (1981), "The Implications of Competition among Jurisdictions: Does Tiebout Need Politics?" *Journal of Political Economy* December: 1197–1217.

Tiebout, C. (1956), "A Pure Theory of Local Expenditures," *Journal of Political Economy* December: 416–424.

Tullock, G. (1967), *Toward a Mathematics of Politics.* Ann Arbor, MI: University of Michigan Press.

Wagner, R. E. (1974), "Supply-side Aspects of the Theory of Local Government," Working Paper, Center for the Study of Public Choice, VPI & SU, Blacksburg, VA.

# Chapter 24
# An Empirical Assessment of
# the Factor-Supplier Pressure Group Hypothesis

## 1. Introduction

The intertemporal growth in government spending has been the focus of much analytic effort on the part of economists. While there has been some debate over the extent to which government spending as a percentage of net national product has been increasing over time in the U.S.A., there is little doubt that the increased size of government has had a tremendous effect on the allocation of resources and distribution of wealth.[1]

Among the most prominent economic explanations of the growth of government spending are "Wagner's law"[2] and Baumol's (1967) "unbalanced growth hypothesis." "Wagner's law" maintains that the public sector tends to expand as economic progress or the growth of national income takes place. The statement of this law, based originally on Wagner's own causal observations, has spawned a great amount of empirical research aimed primarily at estimating income elasticities of demand for governmental services in democratic countries.[3] Many authors have concluded that these elasticities are positive and in some cases may be greater than unity. This approach to the study of governmental growth is unsatisfactory, however, for a number of reasons. First, Wagner and Weber (1977) have found that "Wagner's law" is not really a law but an empirical observation that holds true in some instances but not in others. Second, this literature is based on what might be termed a perfectly competitive theory of government whereby governments respond perfectly to citizen preferences in much the same way a firm in a perfectly competitive industry would cater to consumer preferences. However, the recent theoretical and empirical literature on the economics of bureaucracy[4] reveals that the separation of ownership from control in government renders governments only partly subservient to citizen (owner) preferences. After a very careful survey and extension of the empirical literature on public sector growth, Borcherding (1977) has concluded that the increased demand for governmental services explains no more than one-half to two-thirds of the growth of government spending in the U.S.A.

Next, the Baumol hypothesis states that it is less possible to reduce labor inputs in the service industries than in nonservice industries, and that government has an exceptionally high proportion of service activities. Consequently, since it is more difficult to increase productivity in the service industries than in more capital intensive industries, one would expect a gradual increase in the relative price of services as economic growth takes place. Resources will therefore shift to the service sector.

In order for this hypothesis to be true, it would be necessary that expenditures on labor inputs into the provision of government services grow faster than on non-labor inputs. This is not likely to be true. Orzechowski (1974) has found that the federal government sector is capital-, not labor-intensive, relative to both all industry and the service sector. In fact, he found that capital expenditure per employee is ten times larger in the federal sector than in the service sector. Thus although the federal sector appears to have an inherent productivity advantage over the private sector, productivity growth is less in the former.

In light of these reasons for dissatisfaction with "Wagner's law" and Baumol's hypothesis as explanations for the growth of government spending, a number of other explanations, deduced from public choice theory, have been advanced and are surveyed by Borcherding (1977) and Peltzman (1980). In the remainder of this paper we shall investigate one particularly appealing argument developed by Gordon Tullock (1974) known as the "factor-supplier pressure group hypothesis." According to this hypothesis much of the increase in government spending can be explained by the fact that factor suppliers (public employees) are permitted to vote and to exercise political influence in many ways. An expansion of the public sector increases payments to factor suppliers and at the same time pulls more people into the market who combine their political power with the original participants to produce even further increases in government spending. Buchanan (1977) puts this hypothesis into perspective in the following statement:

> Why is there an obvious conflict of interest present when bureaucrats are allowed to vote in elections organized by the jurisdiction that employs them? Bureaucrats are no different from other persons and, like others, they will rationally vote to further their own interests as producers when given the opportunity. Clearly, their interests lie in an expanding governmental sector, and especially in one that expands the number of its employees. Salaries can be increased much more readily in an expanding agency than in a declining or stagnant one. Promotions are more rapid in an organization that is increasing in size than in one that is remaining stable or declining in size. From this it follows directly that bureaucrats will vote for those politicians and parties that call for overall governmental expansion rather than for their opposites.

## 2. Previous Tests of the Factor-Supplier Pressure Group Hypothesis

There have been at least two previous attempts to test this hypothesis. The first test was performed by Craswell (1975), who investigated the relation between changes in the number of beneficiaries and employees for two public programs – aid to families with dependent children (AFDC) and higher education – and changes in per capita state government expenditure levels over four-year periods from 1952–72. Craswell presented estimates of both the simple correlation coefficients between the growth in beneficiaries or employees and the growth in expenditure levels and of a simple regression for each hypothesis. In the regression equation the dependent variable, change in per capita expenditure, was regressed on the change in number of beneficiaries or employees in the two programs. Craswell's results do appear to provide some support for the factor-supplier pressure group hypothesis but his model is mis-specified as it omits other relevant explanatory variables. Greene and Munley (1979) have attempted to remedy this problem by studying the same two programs and adding other independent variables to the public expenditure model.[5] Their results were mixed, finding some support for the hypothesis in some periods and none in others. They conclude that their findings provide little support for the hypothesis.[6]

Although these past tests provide little support, if any, for the factor-supplier pressure group hypothesis, there appears to be substantial room for further testing in light of the following observation made by Tullock (1977). As a general rule, civil servants live near where they are employed, whether by state or local or federal government. Thus they are always able to apply political pressure for expansion of their market share. The producers of capital goods, on the other hand, are most often not located in the local government which purchases their product. For example, police officers are spread throughout the country and are employed by all local governments but the cars that they drive are produced in only a few places. Given these circumstances, one would expect less direct voter pressure on local governments to expand capital purchases than to hire more civil servants. Furthermore, one would expect the federal sector to be relatively more capital intensive than the local government sector. We do observe this difference as Orzechowski has pointed out. Cummings and Ruhter (1980) also provide empirical evidence in support of this proposition. Considering these observations, it seems more appropriate to begin testing the factor-supplier pressure group hypothesis at the *local* level of government than at the state (or federal) level as Craswell and Munley and Greene have done.

The rise in local public expenditure levels has certainly been a much discussed topic in this era of Proposition 13. The data in Table 1 show the increase in local public expenditures during the 1962–77 period as well as average monthly wages and employment levels for several selected functions.

Table 1. Changes in local public expenditures, average monthly public wages, and public employment levels, 1962-1977 (monetary values in constant 1972 dollars)

| Service | % Change in aver. monthly wage | % Change in public employment | % Change in local public expenditures |
|---|---|---|---|
| All functions | 33% | 76% | 170% |
| Police protection | 48 | 71 | 111 |
| Fire protection | 51 | 23 | 116 |
| General control | 35 | 130 | 67 |
| Education | 30 | 80 | 132 |
| Hospitals | 51 | 81 | 174 |
| Parks and recreation | 31 | 97 | 142 |
| Public welfare | 35 | 127 | 151 |
| Sanitation | 33 | 16 | 91 |
| Highways | 31 | 4 | 35 |
| Financial administration | 33 | 237 | 126 |
| Housing and urban renewal | 32 | 142 | 54 |

Source: Calculated from U.S. Bureau of the Census, Census of Governments, various volumes.

All dollar amounts are in constant 1972 dollars. These data are only meant to illustrate the sharp rise in the amount of real resources going to the local public sector during this period as well as the accompanying increase in public employment and salaries. The 170% increase in real local public expenditures exceeds the 135% increase for the federal sector during this time period, while the 33% increase in real wages in the local public sector is almost double the 18% increase in the nonagricultural private sector. As an additional piece of information, nonwage supplements increased, in real terms, by 174% in the local public sector and 146% in private industry during this time according to the National Income and Produce Accounts of the United States.

Since past research on productivity growth in the local public sector (Hatry and Fisk, 1971) indicates that it probably lags behind that of the private nonagricultural sector, these data may provide at least casual empirical support for the proposition that public employee groups have been successful at increasing the size of the public sector as well as their factor payments.[7] 1980 Census Bureau data were not available at the time of this writing, but preliminary reports by the Advisory Commission on Intergovernmental relations estimate that per capita state and local spending are actually expected to be lower in 1980 than in 1978. Penner (1980) suggests that this might be explained by a number of events inducting the "taxpayer revolt" which has led 16 states to legislate limits on taxing and spending as of January 1, 1980, the decline in local public school enrollments, and an apparent slowdown of the growth of federal grants to state and local governments. This does not invalidate the factor-supplier pressure group hypothesis since pressure group activity is only one of many variables that affect expenditures and one might anticipate that expenditure growth would shrink less rapidly in a large employment area than a small employment area. In the next section some further tests of the factor-supplier pressure group hypothesis will be conducted in the context of the growth of local public expenditures.

## 3. Further Tests of the Factor-Supplier Pressure Group Hypothesis

To further test the factor-supplier pressure group hypothesis the following two models in equations (1) and (2) were estimated for a sample of county government areas in the U.S.A., each of which had a population of 250,000 or more in 1970.[8] The models are similar to those developed by Bahl and Saunders (1965) and Oates (1975) in previous studies of the determinants of changes in local public expenditures. The major difference between the work of these previous authors and equations (1) and (2) is the addition of the "change in public employment variable," $\Delta$EMPL, as an independent variable.

$$\Delta E_i = \alpha + \beta_1 \Delta POP_i + \beta_2 \Delta DENS_i + \beta_3 \Delta PCI_i + \\ + \beta_4 \Delta IGR_i + \beta_5 \Delta PSE_i + \beta_6 \Delta EMPL_i + e_i \quad (1)$$

$$\Delta E_i = \alpha + b_1 \Delta POP_i + b_2 \Delta DENS_i + b_3 \Delta PCI_i + \\ + b_4 \Delta IGR_i + b_5 \Delta EMPL_i + e_i \quad (2)$$

where $\Delta E_i$ = intertemporal change in real per capita expenditures in the $i$th county area for the $j$th service category

$\alpha$ = constant term

$\Delta POP_i$ = change in population in the $i$th county

$\Delta DENS_i$ = change in population density, defined as population per square mile, in the $i$th county

$\Delta PCI_i$ = change in per capita real income in the $i$th county

$\Delta IGR_i$ = change in real per capita intergovernmental revenues in the $i$th county

$\Delta PSE_i$ = change in public school enrollment in the $i$th county

$\Delta EMPL_i$ = change in the number of public employees in the $i$th county

$e_i$ = random error term

These equations were estimated for two different time periods, 1957–67 and 1967–77. Changes in per capita expenditures, per capita income, and per capita inter-governmental revenues were all computed in constant 1967 dollars to extract the effects of inflation. Equation (I), which includes changes in public school enrollment as an independent variable, was estimated for general expenditures and as well as for expenditures on education since education comprises a major component of local budgets. Equation (2) was used for the remaining service categories, which include general control, police protection, fire protection, sanitation, hospitals, and highways.

An increase in population is expected to increase the demand for government services and, consequently, the rate of growth of public spending, although the coefficient for the variable could be negative as the dependent variable is the change in *per capita* expenditures. Increased population density is expected to increase the demand for services such as fire protection, police protection and sanitation. Population density also has an effect on the cost of providing various services so that the expected sign of its coefficient is indeterminate. Assuming governmental services to be normal goods, one would expect increased income to increase expenditure levels. The expected sign of the intergovernmental revenue variable is indeterminate since some types of aid are substitutes for local revenues while others such as matching grants tend to stimulate local spending. The focus of the tests is on the coefficients of the employment variable. A positive and significant coefficient would add support for the factor-supplier pressure group hypothesis. The OLS estimates of equations (1) and (2) for the expenditure categories for which data were available are shown in Tables 2 and 3. For the 1967–77 time period, the coefficients for the employment variable were all positive as expected, but only the coefficient for the general control function was found to be statistically significant. One explanation for why general control employees (i.e., lawyers) seem to have been quite successful at generating increased general control expenditures is that lawyers have a comparative advantage in political activities. Therefore since the expected returns to investing in political activity (trying to influence the size of their budget share) are greater to them than to some other groups, one would expect them to expend more effort and resources into such activity. One would also expect the most highly unionized service employees, firemen, policemen, and teachers, to have a greater impact on budgetary expansion than less well organized groups. The higher coefficients for the employment variable for these functions seem to bear this out, although the statistical insignificance renders this statement a rather loose speculation.

For the 1957–67 period, adequate data were available only for the five functions listed in Table 3 and for general expenditures. A low F-statistic rendered the estimates for the general expenditure category statistically insignificant, so that particular category was omitted from Table 3. All of the coefficients for the employment variable were positive except for the case of highways, where it was negative but insignificant. The employment coefficient for the sanitation function was found to be positive and highly significant at the 0.001 level.

In essence, the above results do provide some support for the factor-supplier pressure group hypothesis, especially for the general control and sanitation functions. The predominance of positive coefficients for the employment variable leads me to believe that the espoused effects of public employees may be stronger than the tests of statistical significance would indicate. Also, it is likely that available public employment statistics underestimate true employment levels. One reason for this is that they don't include those "employed" by local governments through contracts who are, for all practical purposes, public employees. Furthermore, as Bennett and Johnson (1980) point out, government officials often disguise the actual number of full time employees by granting them part-time status on days in which census data are collected. I suspect that more accurate public employment data would strengthen support for the factor-supplier pressure group hypothesis. In addition, since there exists no general theory of how local public spending levels change over time, more accurate results might be obtained once such a model is developed.

Table 2. Estimated coefficients of the expenditure model: General expenditures and selected functions, 1967-77 (t-statistics in parentheses)

| Variable | General expenditures | Education | General control | Police | Fire protection | Sanitation | Hospitals | Highways |
|---|---|---|---|---|---|---|---|---|
| ΔPOP | 2272.73[b] (3.409) | -232.56[b] (-3.360) | 10.64 (0.415) | 1086.95 (0.439) | 416.67[a] (3.759) | -714.28[a] (-40.02) | -240.38[a] (-51.98) | -714.28[a] (-54.90) |
| ΔDENS | 214.14[a] (4.219) | 62.50 (1.381) | 1470.58[a] (77.932) | 62.50 (0.125) | -1.93 (0.355) | 526.31[a] (89.05) | -55.87[a] (15.59) | -217.39[a] (-15.43) |
| ΔPCI | -8.06 (-0.089) | 71.43 (1.326) | 95.24[a] (8.76) | -163.93 (0.540) | -3.48[b] (-3.00) | -434.78[b] (17.83) | -63.29[a] (-42.11) | -55.55[a] (-5.00) |
| ΔIGR | 42.73 (0.555) | 5.88 (0.025) | 10.10 (0.002) | -833.33[a] (-10.080) | 76.92 (0.058) | 4.76 (0.002) | -970.87[a] (-5.388) | 6.25 (0.006) |
| ΔPSE | 11.36 (1.262) | -163.93[a] (-4.098) | | | | | | |
| ΔEMPL | 14.53 (0.238) | 6.83 (0.180) | 96.15[a] (42.21) | 45.45 (0.955) | 14.29 (0.181) | 1.428 (0.059) | 1.04 (0.081) | 8.55 (0.880) |
| Constant | 31.84[c] (2.780) | 27.21[b] (3.480) | 3.172[a] (5.295) | 9.77[a] (5.234) | 4.61[a] (5.179) | 5.77[a] (5.799) | 47.59[a] (3.550) | 0.58 (0.087) |
| $R^2$ | 0.226 | 0.319 | 0.146 | 0.163 | 0.360 | 0.456 | 0.430 | 0.284 |

[a] Significant at 0.001 level.
[b] Significant at 0.01 level.
[c] Significant at 0.05 level.
Sample size = 66.

Table 3. Estimated coefficients of the expenditure model: Selected functions, 1957-67 ($t$-statistics in parentheses)

| Variable | Education | Sanitation | Police protection | Fire protection | Highways |
|---|---|---|---|---|---|
| ΔPOP | 2.48 (0.925) | 161.29 (0.003) | 144.93 (0.478) | −6.99 (−0.004) | 9090.91[c] (1.545) |
| ΔDENS | −115.61 (0.520) | 57.14 (0.086) | 2857.14[a] (117.14) | −126.58 (−1.001) | 250.00[a] (68.871) |
| ΔPCI | −4.89 (−0.836) | 4.292 (0.043) | 14.71 (0.559) | −10.31[a] (−10.010) | −.60[b] (2.951) |
| ΔIGR | 1.36[a] (5.434) | 63.29[c] (2.092) | 34.72[a] (4.409) | 1.35 (0.042) | 5.68 (1.046) |
| ΔEMPL | 4.07 (0.388) | 65.79[a] (5.827) | 75.77 (0.978) | 4.24 (0.142) | −16.59 (−1.329) |
| Constant | 76.45[a] (7.399) | 2.44[a] (4.604) | 4.27[a] (4.028) | 3.44[a] (6.552) | 16.23[b] (3.067) |
| $R^2$ | 0.385 | 0.480 | 0.269 | 0.436 | 0.454 |

[a] Significant at 0.001 level.
[b] Significant at 0.01 level.
[c] Significant at 0.05 level.
Sample size = 46.

## 4. Summary and Conclusions

The main purpose of this paper has been to empirically assess Tullock's factor-supplier pressure group hypothesis. Theory predicted that public employees would be most able to use their political power to expand public spending levels at the local level of government. Therefore, in contrast to the two previous attempts to test this hypothesis, the empirical tests focused on the growth of *local* public spending. The test results lead to the conclusion that the political power of public employee groups is an important determinant of the growth of local public spending, although the extent of their influence is as yet unknown. General control personnel and sanitation workers were found to be exceptionally successful at influencing budgetary growth. In terms of the former group these results lead me to suspect that the results of Bennett and Johnson's (1980) research on federal government growth apply to the local public sector as well. That is, while there may be debate over how much local public spending has increased as a percentage of net national product, its composition has changed in that proportionally more resources are being used for the purposes of administrative rule-making. As is the case with federal governmental regulation, increased regulation of the local public economy is sure to have substantial allocative and distributive effects which form an agenda for future research.

# NOTES

1. Bennett and Johnson (1980) point out that although statistics on the recent growth of government may not be too startling, they underestimate the overall impact of governmental growth. The reason for this, according to Bennett and Johnson, is that "... a massive shift has occurred toward policy making and administrative levels." In other words, 100 regulation writing bureaucrats at the Department of Energy will have a far greater impact on resource allocation than will 100 air force mechanics or postal clerks.

2. See Wagner and Weber (1977) for a review of the origins of this "law."

3. Bird (1971), Ganti and Kolluri (1979).

4. For a discussion of much of this literature along with many references, see Buchanan and Brennan (1980).

5. The additional independent variables used by Munley and Greene are income growth, population change, change in population density, percent of total expenditures in the previous period that were debt financed, change in per capita federal grants, and change in public school enrollment.

6. It is interesting to note that Munley and Greene found some support for the hypothesis in the case of higher education but not AFDC. Tullock's hypothesis is, after all, concerned with public employee groups, not beneficiaries, although using beneficiaries seems to be a straightforward extension. It may be instances that the hypothesis was supported for the case of higher education because the public employees involved have lower costs of organizing lobbying support – they do belong to unions in many instances. In contrast, AFDC recipients are often a geographically dispersed group, which increases the cost of collective action.

7. Buchanan and Tullock (1977) report that pay of state and local employees as a percent of pay of nongovernment employees rose from 101% in 1952 to 110% in 1972.

8. Data were obtained from U.S. Department of Commerce, Bureau of the Census, *Census of Governments*, various volumes, the *Statistical Abstract of the U.S.* and the County-City *Data Book*.

# REFERENCES

Bahl, R., and R. Saunders (1965), "Determinants of Changes in State and Local Government Expenditures," *National Tax Journal* 18(March): 50–57.

Baumol, W. J. (1967), "Macroeconomics of Unbalanced Growth: The Anatomy of Urban Crisis," *American Economic Review* 57(June): 415–426.

Bennett, J., and Johnson, M. (1980), *The political economy of federal government growth: 1959–1978.* College Station, TX: Center for Education and Research in Free Enterprise.

Bird, R. M. (1971), "Wagner's 'Law' of Expanding State Activity," *Public Finance* 26(January): 1–26.

Borcherding, T. (1977), "The Sources of Growth of Public Expenditures in the U.S., 1902–1970," in T. Borcherding (ed.), *Budgets and Bureaucrats: The Sources of Government Growth.* Durham, NC: Duke University Press, 45–70.

Buchanan, J. M. (1977), "Why Does Government Grow?" in *Budgets and Bureaucrats: The Sources of Government Growth.* Durham, NC: Duke University Press, 3–18.

Buchanan, J. M., and G. Brennan (1980), *The Power to Tax: Analytical Foundations of a Fiscal constitution.* Cambridge: Cambridge University Press.

Buchanan, J. M., and G. Tullock (1977), "The Expanding Public Sector: Wagner Squared," *Public Choice* 31(Fall): 147–151.

Craswell, R. (1975), "Self-generating Growth in Public Programs," *Public Choice* 21(Spring): 91–97.

Cummings, F., and W. Ruhter (1980), "Some Tests of the Factor-Supplier Pressure Group Hypothesis," *Public Choice* 35: 257–266.

Ganti, S., and B. Kolluri (1979), "Wagner's Law of Public Expenditures: Some Efficient Results for the United States," *Public Finance* 2: 225–233.

Greene, K., and V. Munley (1979), "Generating Growth in Public Expenditures: The Role of Employee and Constituent Demand," *Public Finance Quarterly* 7(January): 92–109.

Hatry, H., and D. Fisk (1971), *Improving Productivity and Productivity Measurement in Local Governments.* Washington, D.C.: The Urban Institute.

Oates, W. (1975), "Automatic Increases in Tax Revenues – The Effect on the Size of the Public Budget," in W. Oates (ed.), *Financing the New Federalism.* Baltimore, MD: Johns Hopkins University Press, 139–160.

Orzechowski, W. (1974), "Labor Intensity, Productivity, and the Growth of the Federal Sector," *Public Choice* 19(Fall): 123–126.

Peltzman, S. (1980), "The Growth of Government," *Journal of Law and Economics* 23(2): 209–287.

Penner, R. G. (1980), "Why Local Spending Is Finally Slowing," *New York Times* 7 December, Sect. D, 2.

Tullock, G. (1974), "Dynamic Hypothesis on Bureaucracy," *Public Choice* 19(Spring): 127–31.

Tullock, G. (1977), "What Is to Be Done?" in *Budgets and Bureaucrats: The Sources of Government Growth.* Durham, NC: Duke University Press, 275–288.

Wagner, R. E., and W. Weber (1977), "Wagner's Law, Fiscal Institutions, and the Growth of Government," *National Tax Journal* 30(March): 59–68.

www.ingramcontent.com/pod-product-compliance
Lightning Source LLC
Chambersburg PA
CBHW060322200326
41519CB00011BA/1808